T2-CSE-074

GROWING OLD
IN
AMERICA

GROWING OLD
IN
AMERICA

Edited by

Beth B. Hess

Transaction Books
New Brunswick, N.J.

Library of Congress Catalog Number: 76-1778.
ISBN: 0-87855-140-9 (cloth); 0-87855-604-4 (paper).
Printed in the United States of America.

Library of Congress Cataloging in Publication Data
Main entry under title:

Growing old in America.

    Includes bibliographies and index.
    1. Aged—United States—Addresses, essays, lectures.
2. Aging—Addresses, essays, lectures. 3. Gerontology—Ad-
dresses, essays, lectures. I. Hess, Beth B., 1928-
HQ1064.U5G75   301.43'5'0973   76-1778
ISBN 0-87855-140-9
ISBN 0-87855-604-4 pbk.

Contents

To Dick, Larry, and Em
For Yetta, Albert, and Eva

Acknowledgments

My own involvement in social gerontology began a decade ago as a graduate student at Rutgers—the State University. In the wave of interest in aging that followed the White House Conference of 1960, the Russell Sage Foundation sponsored a major research project under the direction of Matilda White Riley, then Professor of Sociology at Rutgers. Over a five-year period we produced three volumes on *Aging and Society* (*see* Part V) and a number of monographs, journal articles, and working papers.

Since then, Professor Riley and her associates, now scattered across the Northeast, have managed to meet periodically at the Russell Sage Foundation, Rutgers, and Bowdoin to continue our work on the Sociology of Age Stratification, with the support of the Social Science Research Council Committee on Work and Personality in the Middle Years.

While the generous funding of Russell Sage and the S.S.R.C. have made it possible for us to pursue this investigation, the productiveness of our efforts is the result of Matilda Riley's own genius and driving force. Our thanks are also long overdue to Jack Riley, Anne Foner, Marilyn Johnson, and Joan Waring—the aging "team."

We are grateful to Irving Louis Horowitz for inviting us to edit this addition to the distinguished series of Transaction Readers. Making sociology come alive to undergraduates and nonsociologists is one of the most difficult, but certainly most needed tasks at hand, and none has pursued it more diligently than he.

Introduction

Growing old is an inevitable and irreversible biological process, yet the objective statuses and subjective experiences of aging individuals are the products of social processes. The meaning of aging emerges from the interaction of the organism with its environment (including other persons), in specific social systems, within a culture at a given historical moment, Thus, the sociological study of aging covers all levels of analysis from the state of the organism to abstract cultural norms; we cannot understand aging and the condition of old people without some awareness of the multitude of variables impinging upon the individual. Since a variable is something that varies, we must take note of historical changes affecting the organism (for example, life expectancy, health status, and availability of medical care); the social settings (family and employment factors); the age structure of the society as a whole and its economic system; and the cultural level beliefs and norms that define appropriate behavior and relationships within and among age groups. The opening essay attempts to survey these changes in order to "locate" the current cohorts of old people. The second set of essays in this volume is designed to place the examination of today's aged in America within a cross-cultural and cross-temporal perspective, while the four chapters in Part III concern another time dimension, that of the transition to old age and its role adjustments in this society at this historical moment. Thus the stage is set for the fourth and most extensive part of this book, "Varieties of the Aging Experience," a look at the many milieus in which old people strive to generate supportive systems and bring their lives to a successful conclusion. The final set of chapters illustrates a few of the many ways in which sociological information may be utilized—to press for change in particular societal institutions, and to develop the field of sociology itself.

C. Wright Mills described the sociological imagination as dealing with the intersection of biography and history, the interplay of individuals with the institutions of their society as these develop through time. Human behavior is analyzed as adaptation to the changing conditions of existence. Clearly, the sociological perspective is uniquely suited to the study of aging; or, conversely, to study aging and society is to do sociology. Furthermore, the selections in this volume illustrate the many ways in which sociology is done: through survey data, cross-cultural comparison, case histories, participant observation, interview, structural analysis, historical records, personal reports—whatever source of information broadens and deepens our understanding of how and when personal problems become public issues.

As many authors in this volume remark, the study of aging and old people is not a common or popular one for any discipline or age group in our society. Like Peter Pan, we do not wish to grow old and prefer not to think about it. In not doing so, however, we affect our own chances for successful aging, as well as add to the pall of benign neglect that has fallen on those already old. We hope that this volume, and the introduction of social gerontology into the general curriculum, will lift this veil of indifference, so that students become involved with the fate of their elders, which will be, after all, their own destiny.

GROWING OLD
IN
AMERICA

Overview

1

America's Aged: Who, What, When, and Where?

Beth B. Hess

The White House Conference on Aging of January 1960 is a convenient benchmark of our societal concern with the aged. Congress had been stirred in the late 1950s to establish a Subcommittee on the Aged and Aging, but had failed to act on a number of bills designed to provide health insurance, medical care, and nursing-home construction to meet the most crucial needs of old people. If a social situation becomes a social problem only when recognized as such by members of a society, then we can say that by 1960 the condition of America's aged could no longer be accommodated in the taken-for-granted world of citizens and lawmakers. Obviously, the old did not suddenly appear, impoverished and stricken with chronic illness. What had happened by 1960 was the convergence of secular trends in demography, our economy, family system, and societal goals that (a) rendered "problematic" the ability of large numbers of old people to command sufficient resources—power, property, prestige—to ensure a dignified old age, and (b) created a climate of opinion in which the alleviation of these problems could be defined as a public responsibility.*

Let us look closely at these long-term trends, and their consequences for the aged.**

Population Trends

While, as we shall see later, their own health and incomes are problems *for* the elderly, what makes the aged a concern *of* society is best described demographically: the population 65 and over has increased relatively and absolutely over the century, often at rates far higher than those for the population as a whole. In 1900, persons 65 + comprised but 4.1 percent of the total; today, they make up about 10 percent, comparable to the proportion of blacks in society. Projections for the remainder of this century, however, suggest that this percentage will remain relatively stable; that is, depending upon fertility rates, old people will make up between 9 and 11 percent of our population through the year 2000. If there is an unexpected increase in the birthrate, then the proportion of old people would decrease somewhat; if, however, the current low birthrates persist, then the proportion of old people would be closer to the higher figure.***

*One decade later, the 1971 White House Conference on Aging was, predictably, more concerned with program implementation, training of professionals, funding, and other "nuts and bolts" topics.

**Data for this discussion are from volume I of *Aging and Society: An Inventory of Research Findings*, (New York: Russell Sage Foundation, 1968), by Matilda White Riley, Anne Foner, and Associates; and, for material after 1968, U.S. Department of Commerce, Bureau of the Census, Current Population Reports Special Studies, Series P-23, no. 43, "Some Demographic Aspects of Aging in the United States," February 1973; and U.S. Department of Commerce, Bureau of the Census, *Statistical Abstracts of the United States*, 1974.

***Since the proportion in any age group depends upon the age distribution of the rest of the society, one reason why the percentage of old people levels off through 2000 is that they are the survivors of very small birth cohorts during the Depression. They are followed by the very large baby-boom cohort of 1945-57, which moves through our age structure like a melon swallowed by a snake, so that when *they* reach old age after 2010, the proportion of old people will be very high. However, they will, in turn, be followed by the very small cohort of our current zero-population growth years.

The sex composition of the elderly population has changed dramatically since 1930, when the proportions of older men and women were almost equal, as they had been since the turn of the century. From 1930 on, however, while gains in life expectancy are recorded for both sexes, those for women have been greater. The percentages of women in the older age groups are 3 to 4 percent higher than those of older men in the population, and this differential is projected into the measurable future. In 1970, there were 72.1 males for every 100 females 65 + (77.6 in the age group 65-74, and 63.7 for those 75 and over). In 1980 the figure is estimated as 69.1, and by 1990, a mere 67.5. Clearly, whatever forces affect mortality for men will continue; it remains to be seen whether those favoring women will persist (there is much guesswork today that the trends toward sex equality will lead to more smoking, drinking, and tension-producing occupational statuses for women, thus increasing their vulnerability to accidents and to cardiovascular and neoplasmic deaths, which account for higher male mortality rates).

However, life expectancy *has* increased for all: in 1900, a white male had an average life expectancy at birth of 48.2 years, and a white female had 51.1—only a three-year differential; but by 1969, the comparable figures are 67.9 and 75.1—a full seven years. Nonwhite expectancies have risen from 32.5 for males and 35 for females in 1900 to 60.7 for men and 68.4 for women in 1969—an increase of almost 100 percent, but with the same sex difference as it is for whites. Most of these gains are related to lowered risk of death at birth, and enhanced chances of surviving childhood as infectious diseases have been brought under control. That is, most of the increased life expectancy comes at the earliest years, although some gains have been made at the older age levels. It seems unlikely, then, that we shall see any remarkable increases in life expectancy, unless there is a breakthrough in control of mortality at the older ages. Indeed, most of the gains seem to have been made by the 1950s, so that death rates at older ages have not improved much in the last two decades.

What all these statistics mean is that old people make up a sizable segment of our population, that most of these will be women, and that most of us can count on living to at least 65. In sociological terms, what we have here is the emergence of a new life stage, a period of joint survival for the married pair or of extended widowhood, which was not a common experience for members of preceding generations. Now that living to and through one's sixth decade is a general expectation, the problem becomes how to integrate this expectation into our life plans, how to learn the appropriate norms and behaviors, and how to develop supportive social structures, where so few exist today.

Health Factors

Growing old is, physiologically, to experience progressive declines in body function, and, psychologically, gradually to lose sensory and cognitive capacities, but the rate and order and timing of such processes vary from individual to individual. We do not yet know the "grand secret" of aging: whether an internal clock runs down at a genetically set moment provided other accidents have not occurred; whether some crucial substance gradually deteriorates; or whether an accumulation of decrements, insults, and injuries to the various body parts overwhelms the capacities of resistance.

This is all very depressing to read about; mastery and control are important to us; to lose these in relation to our own bodies must be profoundly distressing. It is difficult to accept graciously these signs of deterioration in ourselves, and we often shrink from those who already carry such stigmata. Our attitudes toward the old are thus compounded of fear and anxiety; old people are memento mori, reminders of death in a culture that is steadfastly turned to the here and now, and that accords little value to nearness to eternity.

Such attitudes have a lot to do with how we view our own aging and how we treat old people; but the major health considerations of the aged are very immediate, indeed. Having survived to old age, which by definition involved better than average stamina and luck, one experiences the inevitable losses in hearing and sight, in short-term memory, and in sheer physical mobility; all of which can be adjusted to by adaptations in life-style, use of prosthetic devices, and lowered expectations of self. It is, rather, the high probability of chronic disease that haunts the aged: the need for extended care, the high medical costs, the knowledge that debilitation is progressive. Old people simply require more medical attention than younger people because there is more "going wrong" with their minds and bodies.

All this is "natural." What is not natural, not the way things have to be, is the fact that, up until only a few years ago, medical expenses could wipe out a lifetime of savings for old people, could deplete nest eggs, and could drag patients and their children into debt (provided even that decent care facilities could be found for those requiring nursing services). For those who manage to avoid serious chronic illness, there are still the mundane medical needs: eyeglasses, hearing aids, setting of bones broken from falls in bathrooms and on stairs, diet supplements, and so on.

It was primarily the realization of this problem that led to congressional action in the 1950s. Some form of health insurance for the aged was a necessity whose time had come, yet the inevitable was resisted well into the 1960s by, of all groups, the medical and hospital establishments.* Pressure from the sizable voting bloc of old people, and from their adult children, finally persuaded the legislators to enact Medicare for all old people, and, later, Medicaid programs for the impoverished of any age. Nonetheless, Medicare does not fully cover medical costs for old people; some initial expense is borne by patients; home nursing services are limited; only 80 percent of some physician and hospital bills are paid for; the allowance for outpatient treatment for mental illness is $250; ordinary checkups, glasses, hearing aids, and false teeth are apparently not "medical"; and prescription drugs were originally excluded. Nor can these benefits be seen as the opening wedge for more extensive services: the recession of 1974-75 has produced such budget-cutting, antiinflationary suggestions as reduction of the food stamp program and the raising of both premiums and minimums that older patients must pay before Medicare takes over.

Thus, personal health and medical expenses remain major preoccupations of the aged. One's health status is associated with a number of measures of activity and morale among the

*Richard Harris, A Sacred Trust (New York: The New American Library, 1966). The book's jacket announces this, all too accurately, as, "The story of America's most powerful lobby—organized medicine —and its forty-five year, multimillion dollar fight against public health legislation."

aged, as one might expect, but most important is the individual's own assessment of his or her health. Regardless of actual medical condition, those who rate their health status favorably are likely to express greater satisfaction, less depression, and higher morale than those who rate their health unfavorably. And, in general, old people function remarkably well considering their proneness to chronic illness as well as the normal decrements in the health of aging itself. All but a small minority are able to carry on their major activities and maintain independent residences, despite the fact that over three-fourths suffer from at least one long-term deteriorating condition. Many, if not most, older people have learned to live with their disabilities, have adapted to the inevitable aches and pains in such a manner as to enhance their abilities to find satisfactions in what they can do.

Economic Variables

Modern industrial societies require increasingly higher levels of expertise with each successive cohort of labor-market entrants. Job allocation becomes based more upon achievement criteria—talent, education, personality variables—and sheer luck than upon ascribed characteristics such as parental influence, social status at birth, and transmission through descent lines. As the nature of work roles keeps pace with expanding technology, recently learned skills tend to be more marketable than old ones. Furthermore, over the twentieth century, the proportion of unskilled labor steadily declines as the range of managerial and service occupations expands. Small businesses, self-owned enterprises, and family land-holdings all become absorbed into larger and presumably more efficient economic units—agribusiness, chain stores, national and international corporations, and mass production facilities.

What these trends mean is that many of the skills and jobs of older workers are rendered obsolete, and in any case cannot be directly handed on to sons and daughters (assuming even that the latter would even want the small farm or stationery store, for example). As wage earners rather than as self-employed persons, most workers of any age group are dependent upon retirement pensions, Social Security benefits, and personal savings to live on in old age. However, to the extent that these are pegged to preretirement earnings, those with relatively unskilled employment or who were blanketed into Social Security only within the last two decades, obviously have limited pension bases and/or savings. It was not until 1975, furthermore, that workers could carry accumulated pension credits from one employment to another; prior to this, one lost any vested pension rights if fired or when changing employer; and if the company went out of business, so did one's pension claims. The new law further protects the retired worker by placing controls over the use of pension funds by the unions and corporations holding them, many funds having been dissipated by poor investment practices or downright embezzlement.

Those fortunate enough to retire with pension claims intact, or with full Social Security benefits, now find themselves receiving fixed monthly checks in a double-digit inflationary period. In 1972, the median income of families with heads aged 65 and over was a bit over 50 percent of the median for all families in the U.S. (a median is the point at which half of all units fall above and half below a midpoint). Reflected here is the fact that only one-fourth of family heads 65 + are in the full-time labor force, a proportion expected to decline to one-fifth by 1980 as mandatory retirement becomes institutionalized throughout the economy, making way for the very large pool of young job entrants born between 1946 and 1957. Indeed, it is likely that the age of involuntary retirement will be lowered in response to this population pressure and that of a recessionary economy.* Many older workers, however, are protected by the seniority clause in union contracts, as well as by federal and state laws forbidding discrimination on the basis of age. The long-term trend, however, is in the direction of ever-lowered ages of retirement, so that what was once the experience of a very few will now become the common condition of elderly men and women: a period of retirement from the material rewards and social networks of work. In a positive way, this can also be thought of as a period

*As illustrated in the case of New York City in 1974; as a budget-cutting measure when several thousand employees were to be laid off, one seriously considered proposal was to lower the age of mandatory retirement to 63, extruding older workers who could retire on pension, while preserving jobs for younger workers with families to support.

for rest and leisure, freedom from scheduling, with time to pursue hobbies and avocations.

While the depressed incomes of the aged must be measured against lessened financial responsibilities—few have dependent children and many have mortgage-free homes —a large number of persons 65+ fell below what the Bureau of the Census judged to be a "low income level"* in 1971. About 14 percent of aged family heads and 42 percent of aged "unrelated" individuals were in this category—ranging from 11.4 percent for white, male family heads to 68.4 percent for black, female unrelated individuals!

In 1973, about 8.5 million men received Old Age, Survivors, Disability, and Health Insurance (Social Security) benefits averaging $182.55 per month, and over 6.7 million women received average payments of almost $146 per month. An additional 1.8 million individuals were recipients of Old Age Assistance (public welfare) of $76 monthly. It is estimated that about thirty million persons, retirees and their dependents, are involved in private pension plans, but these arrangements are so diverse and the monthly payments so disparate that it is difficult to generalize about them. There are, then, four major sources of retirement income: personal savings, private pensions, Social Security, and public welfare. The last three of these tend to be fixed over long periods, while the cost of goods and services tend to rise over time; the burden of inflation is not evenly distributed across age groups.

In sum, the economics of aging are rather grim. Employment opportunities, pension benefits, and income levels in general all present difficulties in maintaining an adequate standard of living and sense of security in the face of other types of decline.

Family System Changes

In brief, ours is a society in which individuals have wide discretion in choice of mate, where newlyweds are expected to set up residence apart from other kin, to have primary obligations to one another (conjugality) rather than to blood relatives (consanguinality), and to depend upon achievement

* This is $1,931 for an unrelated individual, and $3,424 for a two-person family with head 65+.

rather than ascription for placement in stratification hierarchies. To these ends, we encourage both physical and psychological independence of the generations. Sentiment replaces duty in governing relations between parents and their adult children. Social and geographic mobility (both encouraged in modern industrial economies) attenuate family ties; the married pair turns in upon itself, a privatized, semiisolated unit functionally specialized for primary socialization of infants, emotional support, and nomos building (the social construction of meaning and reality). Thus, even though most old people report seeing and doing something for their adult offspring during the year—and a good four-fifths live within an hour's distance from one of their children—the ideal subscribed to by both generations is one of "closeness at a distance," of basically independent existences.

A concomitant set of trends has to do with the timing of family events (see chapter 6). Throughout the century, age at first marriage has steadily declined for both men and women (although there has been a sustained upturn since 1970). Furthermore, since 1957 the number and spacing of children has been regulated in such a manner as to compress the childbearing phase of family formation. Typically, today, all offspring have been born by the time the mother is 30; they enter school full time at age five and remain there for the next twelve years; and at age 18 are legal adults, many having left home to join the labor force or to go to college. In effect, child rearing involves a much smaller proportion of the parental life span than ever before in our society. This trend, when complemented by the increases in life expentancy already noted, has produced a new stage in the family life course: the "empty-nest" period in which parents can expect an additional two decades of survival without primary parental obligations. At the very ages at which, in 1900, one if not both parents would have died, leaving dependent children at home, this new stage has been tacked on, covering the years of transition to old age (see Part III).

As for the living arrangements of the aged, this obviously varies by age and by sex. Since more surviving males had married women younger than themselves, it is not surprising that almost three-fourths of men 65+ in 1971 were living as heads of families; that is, their wives (and possibly adult children) were alive and living with them. Only 42.5 percent of women 65 + were living as heads of families or wives of the head (the effect, of course, of their having been married to men older than they and hence more likely to have died). Of the rest, seven percent of the men and 15 percent of the women live as "other relatives" presumably with their grown children; and almost 15 percent of the men and over 36 percent of the women live on their own as "primary individuals." A small fraction, less than two percent of either sex, live with another single individual; and, what is generally not well known, only 3.6 percent of the men and 4.6 percent of the women live in any type of long-term care institution—old-age home, hospital, nursing home, and the like. In general, the younger the old person (65-74, for example) the more likely he or she is to be living with a spouse or independently; at 75 and over, these proportions decline, while the percentages in institutions and living with own children tend to rise.

Clearly, most old people do manage to maintain independent residence, and we know from attitude surveys that this is also their preference. The proportions living with their children have declined since 1960, as those living alone have risen commensurately. That more women than men are found in both these categories reflects, as already noted, the high probability of their being widows, especially after age 75. In 1971, only 17 percent of men 65 + were widowed as compared with over 54 percent of women 65 +. Even at ages 75 and over, fewer than 30 percent of men are widowed, while over 70 percent of the women are. Some of this differential is due to the higher probability of remarriage, at all ages, for men than for women. In general, this difference is expected to continue, if not increase; since 1961, the percentage of widowed men declined slightly, while that for women has gone up.

When considering the family status of old people we must also bear in mind that marital status and income are closely related. For example, in 1970 the median income for male heads of families 65 + was $5,011, while that of unrelated individuals was $2,250 for men and $1,188 for women. That over one-third of old women live alone (double the rate for old men at all age levels) on what must be in many cases bare survival incomes, suggests a compounding of poverty and loneliness more acute for women than for men in our society (though most social science research, and works of fiction, have concentrated on the plight of old men).

Nonetheless, for both men and women, the ability to maintain residential independence is seriously undermined through low income, failing health, probable loss of spouse and friends, and, frequently, physical and social deterioration of the "old" neighborhood.

Residential Patterns

One last secular trend requires brief mention: the large-scale population movements in this century off the farms, into the cities, and out again into the suburbs. In all this flow, the elderly are apt to be left behind, especially in the small towns and villages. In general, concentrations of old people are less a result of their own mobility than of that of younger age groups. For example, in 1970-71, almost one-fourth of those aged 20-24 had moved within the same county, and over 16 percent to another county, as compared with 5.4 percent and 2.9 percent, respectively, for those 65-74. The more affluent elderly do appear to have moved in large numbers to Florida, Arizona, and other clement climates, but Census data for 1971 show clearly that the bulk of old people have simply stayed behind in those states and areas from which large numbers of young people have migrated.

When taken in conjunction with the tendency for newly-weds to live apart from parents, and the likelihood of geographical and social mobility for younger cohorts, the overall effect of these residential trends is to increase the isolation of the older generation(s). On the other hand, being with others who share a common past and current fate can reduce feelings of separation. These considerations will be explored further in Part IV.

Within-group Variations

Although we have done so for ease of presentation, it is in many ways inaccurate to present statistics on the aged as if those 65 and older were a homogenous group. Quite apart from the issue of subjective definitions (for example, "You're as old as you feel"), there are many objective distinctions between the aged at the younger and the older ranges, between men and women, and between white and nonwhite. Most obviously, all the conditions that make old age a problem—poor health, low income, lack of employment, death of spouse and friends— are intensified for most nonwhites (see chapters 16 and 21), and simply get worse with increasing age for all old people.

Neugarten* has suggested distinguishing between the "young-old" and the "old-old," since the two groups differ substantially along all the dimensions we have been discussing. When data from both age groups are combined, the condition of the young-old appears more disadvantaged than it is in actuality, while that of the old-old is less so. In terms of capacities, needs, and resources, we may be moving toward a two-tiered old age, especially if retirement from work and from child rearing continue to occur at earlier ages than in the past for large numbers of men and women. A first period of "empty-nest" joint survival in relatively good health and financial condition will be followed by a period of what we typically think of today as "old age," that is, declining social, psychological, physical, and financial resources.

An interesting prospect, resulting from the general increases in life expectancy and proportional rate of growth of the population seventy-five and over, is the increasing likelihood of four-generation families. By the turn of the century a large number of young adults will have not only surviving parents but grandparents also, and their offspring will know their great-grandparents as well. Clearly, a more complex set of kinship relationships will be experienced by family members, especially those in the two "middle" generations who must simultaneously juggle both parent and child roles vis-á-vis other adults. A second major determinant of aging experience, implicit in all the foregoing, is socioeconomic status. To have enjoyed adequate nutrition and medical care throughout life is no guarantee against the physical decrements of age, but surely must confer some benefits in terms of lowered morbidity and mortality. And while money does not bring happiness, it can be a hedge against misery, the daily

*See, for example, "Age Groups in American Society and the Rise of the Young-Old," Annals of the American Academy of Social and Political Science 415 (September 1974) : 187ff.

worry about sheer survival that afflicts so many old people. But even these advantages are subject to erosion in a deteriorating economy, as was witnessed in a front-page article in the *Wall Street Journal* of 30 December 1974, "Fearful Future: Sagging Economy Jars Security and Serenity of Leisure Life." Nonetheless, whatever the troubles in paradise, persons with higher incomes seem also to have more *inner* resources than do those with lower incomes.

Cultural Variables

Underlying all the particular trends noted above are several basic aspects of cultural and social change in the United States throughout the century, along with other trends that have appeared only recently. One of the long-term phenomena is the very rate of change itself, accelerating at an ever-increasing tempo, so that the experience of one generation becomes irrelevant or incomprehensible to the succeeding one. The reality of people who grew up in the Depression and even during the Second World War is not the same as that known to the cohorts born in postwar affluence and tempered by Vietnam and Watergate. Possibly, the rate of change is such that we should measure sociological generations by decades rather than by reproductive generations.* The disjunction between social and biological aging suggests that generation or cohort gaps will increase, with the eldest most cut off from mainstream values and behaviors. However, this prospect assumes that older persons are not capable of change or not receptive to innovation, which is highly debatable. If attitudes are not as fixed as many psychologists have assumed, and if socialization is a two-way process with elders learning from their juniors (especially during the latters' adolescence), these "gaps" need not become abysses. On the other hand, given factors tending toward social-structural isolation of at least the oldest generation, the major task of old age may become that of remaining in contact with the rest of society, just as the societal goal must become that of facilitating such

*The concept of "social generations" is one of the enduring insights of Karl Mannheim, first addressed in the essay, "The Problem of Generations," 1928, in K. Mannheim, *Essays on Sociology of Knowledge* (London: Routledge and Kegan Paul, 1952).

contacts. As will be evident throughout the essays in this volume, all age groups have something to learn from their predecessors' lives. And if these other age groups do make the effort, they are frequently better able to comprehend and appreciate not only their predecessor's experiences and feelings, but also their own.

At the moment, however, the condition of the elderly is profoundly affected by the dominant value system of our society, call it "instrumental activism" or the "work ethic." In a society in which productivity is still a sign of grace, few of the aged are employed. The irony here is that while the ideology is beginning to lose its hold on some of the young, it remains a guiding belief system for those least likely to realize it. Men who have defined themselves in terms of their jobs find it difficult to fashion an acceptable self-image out of nonwork, and women who have defined themselves in terms of mother-hood and marriage are, literally and figuratively, "at a loss" when husbands die and grown children leave home.*

In a society where money determines procuring essential goods and services, the aged have very little financial capability. The alternative of appealing for aid to one's children or of becoming a public welfare recipient are equally abhorrent to people nurtured on the ideals of independence, individualism, and self-sufficiency. To the extent that aged parents have been successful in transmitting these values to their offspring, they are loath to invoke latent obligations, via the rule of reciprocity, on their own behalf (although this is often an unstated premise).

In a society that celebrates youth and beauty, the aged are an affront to our sensibilities. While there are many sources of this tendency toward the denial of death,** and

*Often to the point of losing contact with reality and embracing the sick role; see Pauline Bart, "Mother Portnoy's Complaint," Transaction/Society 8, no. 1/2 (November-December 1970).

**It frequently takes someone from a different society to point out such deeply ingrained denials; the most telling statement on our attitudes toward death coming from Evelyn Waugh (The Loved One) and Jessica Mitford (The American Way of Death). Perhaps the ultimate denial is cryonics; see Clifton D. Bryant and William E. Snizek, "The Iceman Commeth," Transaction/Society 11, no. 1 (November-December 1973).

hence aging, in our culture (see Part III), the extreme emphasis on physical attractiveness probably flows from the shift in the system of mate selection. When family-based criteria are replaced by relatively free choice, the ideology of romantic love that rationalizes such selection makes beauty a marketable commodity, indeed the primary one for women. How else may we judge our value in the marriage market? And how to hold on to a mate who is bound to us only by ties of affection? And, finally, how to be certain that we are still sexually attractive except through heroic efforts to keep physical deterioration at bay? In 1973, toiletries and toilet goods were the single largest category of TV advertising expenditures (net time and program costs), accounting for roughly 17 percent of the total; third place went to proprietary medicines, many of which are designed to disguise the effects of aging (see ch. 7).

The shift from a gerontocentric (elder-dominated) to a pedocentric (child-centered) family system may be an unintended outcome of those changes in public health that assure the survival of most neonates, so that parents can invest emotional capital in each child, and also of those advances in contraceptive technology that enhance the probability that children born are children planned for. Children who are consciously desired and likely to live to adulthood are quite likely to become the center of their parents' attention and concern. An additional factor here is a latent function of the whole Industrial Revolution, which separated work place from family, so that once women and children were removed from the factory, the division of labor within the family became a division in space as well:the household became the exclusive sphere of the wife-mother, the world of work became that of the husband-father. Confined to the home, one suspects that Parkinson's Law comes into operation, and household tasks expand to fill the time allotted to them: homemaking and child care are upgraded and this professionalization of motherhood and household management, of course, keeps a consumer--goods economy rolling. When the care and training of infants becomes a sacred task, comparable to work for men, contemporary mothers become exceedingly self-conscious about it, hence their all-but-obsessive concern over every act of their offspring (what other group of parents has been so dependent upon what the child-care experts—usually men—are advising this year?). Needless to say, the popularization of Freudian psychology in America has done little to reduce parents' anxieties. Thus, the child-centered family and the youth-centered marriage market lead inevitably to a relative down-grading of later life stages, just as the independence of the nuclear family had the unanticipated effect of leaving elders to fend for themselves. Added to this mix are the mobility aspirations of immigrant parents for their children, and the tendency of many parents to sacrifice for the next generation while minimizing their own needs; that one's children have "made it" is reward enough.

Ultimately, as Rosow so eloquently states at the outset of Part II, what makes old age a problem in modern societies is the erosion of resources, that control over scarce goods and services that enhanced the position of the elderly in other times and places: knowledge, property, control over mate selection, ascribed positions, family firms, and other means of entrée into the economic order. Today, knowledge and skills are quickly replaced, sons and daughters make their own way through the marriage market and the economic system. There is little that can be directly handed on and thus little that can be withheld to command respect and care in old age (see chapter 20). The ties that bind generations are based on earned respect, through expressions of affection and emotional support; but even here, we are aware since Freud of deeper currents of envy and hostility flowing between parents and children.*

We have learned from the ecologists that there is no such thing in nature as a "free lunch"** and so, too, in the social order, where costs may also be latent, unintended, and unanticipated. William Goode*** has pointed this out in his

*Even in traditional societies; see Robert A. LeVine, "Intergen-erational Tensions and Extended Family Structures in Africa," in *Marriage and the Family*, eds. Meyer Barash and Alice Scourby (New York: Random House, 1970).

**See *The Closing Circle*, by Barry Commoner (New York: Alfred A. Knopf, 1971).

***William J. Goode, *World Revolution and Family Patterns* (Glencoe, Ill.: The Free Press, 1963).

analysis of worldwide family trends: one of the costs of conjugality, privacy, free mate choice, and economic independence of generations—all the "liberating" currents of contemporary family life—is precisely the loss of resources and increasing isolation of the aged. But recognizing that the current status of the aged is the result of so many forces beyond our control does not excuse the indifference with which their problems have been treated or, rather, not treated. Yet this analysis also suggests that, as it is with human problems generated by social change throughout history, the challenge of adapting to new conditions of existence may, in time, produce the requisite norms and supportive structures. Today's aged are in the process of working out solutions that will enhance the lives of future cohorts; it remains for the other age groups to provide the goods and services needed to make such adaptation possible. We, too, shall be growing old in America.

Aging through Time and Space

Introduction

It is fitting that this collection opens with Irving Rosow's "And Then We Were Old." This is the first major essay on aging to appear in *Transaction/Society*, and is adapted from one of the first and most influential contributions to social gerontology in the 1960s. Rosow's title suggests many things about growing old and about the state of knowledge of old people at the time he wrote. "There is a hint of bewilderment, surprise, as if old age had secretly sneaked up on us." Given the age-denying attitudes and behaviors endemic in our culture, perhaps this is how it does happen to many. Not only are individuals unprepared for old age, but also as a society we were certainly not prepared in 1960 for the discovery of the aged as a social problem.

A comparison of Rosow's data, from a decade ago, with that in the preceding essay, taken from the most recent Census and Current Population Reports, demonstrates that we have yet to face the fundamental issue raised by Rosow of "reworking . . . our national aspirations and values."

David Gutmann takes a very different tack in his cross-cultural study. Gutmann is concerned with universal psychological processes affecting the personalities of men at different ages. He finds striking parallels across cultures, including those far removed from the Western tradition that produced the psychoanalytic and ego development theories with which he works. These similarities lead Gutmann to conclude that deeper forces are at work than sociologists have taken into account in their cognitive-cultural mode of explanation. The active mastery of young men, he claims, stems from their ability to maintain ego defenses, while the diffuse sensuality (especially orality) of old men represents a loss of capacity for retaining ego boundaries. This regression to infantile behaviors is a prelude to death, and not the liberation from repression that several contemporary philosophers have hailed as the next stage in human freedom.

Sociologists are frequently uncomfortable with material that confirms biological and psychological determinants of behavior, but we would be very foolish to deny such sources of motivation altogether, and most especially when considering the aged. If Gutmann's thesis is correct, then we should ponder the ways in which specific societies encourage or discourage the maintenance of ego boundaries, or how, by recognizing such inevitable outcomes, members can learn to accommodate to them.

One of the most persistent myths, among sociologists of the family as well as the general public, concerns what William Goode has called "the family of nostalgia": an idealized vision of several generations living together happily, often in the same home, as typical of preindustrial America. Not only is there no evidence that multigenerational households were common in our society at any time, there is even less evidence to support that assumption that family bonds were so warm and close that aged relatives were willingly cared for by loving juniors. As has already been noted in this volume, the status of the aged rests primarily upon their control of resources desired by younger members of the family; elders have ruled as much by awe and fear as by respect; and intergenerational tensions are a univeral aspect of family life. Many societies deal with intrafamily strains by rigidly prescribing the relationships among kin, expectations that are shared, supported, and sanctioned by others in the community (see ch. 20 for a current example in Appalachia). In other words, the assumption that families used to care for their own and did so unquestioningly, in contrast to the presumed indifference of families today, ought not to be taken for granted, but treated as a variable itself to be explained. We must examine under what circumstances families do or do not fulfill such obligations, rather than take such relationships as the normative case, against which nonsupportive behavior is defined as "deviant."

The first step toward an accurate portrayal of family life in the past is to examine the actual records of the time: birth, marriage, and death certificates, property transfers, public expenditures, and whatever else was worth recording in the town and village halls of yesterday. Perusal of these archives has lead to many revisions in family sociology over the last decade, as duly noted by Michael Zimmerman, a graduate student at Rutgers-the State University, in the introduction to his chapter, "The Aged Poor in Preindustrial New York City." Zimmerman and those whom he cites as pioneering this type of study have been most ingenious in ferreting out their data, often buried in a 200-year accumulation of vital statistics; and in almost every case, the findings have contradicted some commonly held belief about the "family of nostalgia." In the Zimmerman essay, the status of indigent aged in the largest urban center of preindustrial America provides an empirical base for revising our picture of the historical family in this country.

Robert C. Coles has written (one is tempted to say "transcribed from life") the stories of those whom our society has shunted to the side: the poor, the nonwhite, children of the slums and backwaters, and in this particularly moving essay, the aged. To listen to Domingo and Delores García, in their own words, and through the unobtrusive descriptions of the narrator, is to capture the existential essence of growing old: of bearing and raising children, some of whom die in infancy, others in adulthood, and still others who grow up and away from their parents; of the struggles and sorrows and joys of daily life; of the solace of faith and the caring for one another that marks their old age as it did their younger, busier years. Without a single word of professional jargon (Coles is a psychoanalyst and frequent contributor to the social sciences), or even editorial comment, an important message is conveyed: to grow old is to have the opportunity to grow in spirit. What

Coles has produced here is an exquisite example (the technical term *case history* jars) of Erikson's eighth and last task of ego development,* that of achieving integrity. To look back and see one's life as a flowing, integrated whole, and to perceive an underlying meaning to it all, is to resist the despair that so easily overtakes those who cannot find in their past the connective tissues of devotion and forgiveness, or the inner strength of faith.

Moving easily between the cultural and psychological levels of explanation, Coles neatly bridges the gap between the two, exemplified in the first two chapters of this section.

In the concluding chapter of Part II, Harley Browning puts it all together, tracing, across time and space, the interplay between biology and society. The circular interdependence of all levels of social life are neatly illustrated.

Improvements in nutrition, distribution of resources, medicine, and health care result in increased life expectancy, and this biological phenomenon, in turn, has unanticipated latent consequences for the timing of what we think of as purely personal events. Our choices at the individual level— age of marriage, spacing of children, educational attainment, career choice, work history—are all conditioned by broader secular trends operating throughout the society. Here, indeed, biography meets history, and the future of the social order will be determined by the sum of these choices at the personal level.

*Coles himself has written a biography of Erikson that is also a superb exposition of ego theory; *Erik Erikson: The Growth of His Work* (New York: Atlantic Monthly Press, 1970).

2

And Then We Were Old[*]

Irving Rosow

*Did primitive man treat his aged
better than modern man?*

The old are with us, but not of us.

More than 17,000,000 persons over sixty-five live in America today, making up almost nine percent of the population; but this is not why they are a problem. They increase ever more rapidly—one million every three years; nor is this why they are a problem.

They trouble us precisely because we are such an affluent society. They have become a standing embarrassment, a mute reproach to social conscience. Our productivity makes the sheer cost of meeting such social problems of secondary importance; we can view them against larger national goals and the kind of society we want to become. The price of social

*This work originally appeared in *Transaction/Society* 2, no. 2 (January-February 1965): 20-26. This chapter was adapted from the author's more extensive and theoretically sophisticated treatment of this theme: "Old Age: One Moral Dilemma of an Affluent Society," *The Gerontologist* 2, no. 4 (December 1962): 182-91. The interested reader will find the original essay well worth careful study.

change is not a critical economic issue—it is basically a moral concern and a value choice.

The old lack money and they lack medical care.

But even if these needs were met, their problem would still not be solved. We must not confuse provision for material needs with a general solution. Although many specific needs are involved, the old in America suffer primarily from lack of function and status. And this will not be changed until the younger groups themselves change, so that the old can have self-respect and honor among us. But before younger people can change, many of our institutions and values must first alter—so we are caught in a major dilemma.

How do other cultures handle their aged? What conditions support the social position of old people—their prestige, status, or power? What fosters their social integration?

Leo Simmons has studied this problem among almost a hundred primitive societies represented in the Yale cross-cultural files. Others, such as Conrad Arensberg and Solon Kimball, provide supplemental data on more recent nonindustrial cultures as well. Taken together, they cover all stages of preindustrial development, from the simplest food-gathering groups to advanced agricultural economies with complex systems of private property.

These studies show that the welfare of the aged varies according to seven factors that involve the resources that old people command, the functions they perform, and the state of social organization. Their position in their society is relatively stronger if:

They own or control property on which younger people are dependent. In this way they maintain their own independence while simultaneously governing the opportunities of the young. In rural Ireland, for instance, a son may not succeed to his inheritance before his fifties, and he may be deferential to his parents almost into their senility.

Their experience gives them a vital command or monopoly of strategic knowledge of the culture, including the full range of occupational skills and techniques, as well as healing, religion, ritual, warfare, lore, and the arts. As the principal bearers and interpreters of cultures in which there is little change and no science, the old have a strategic function in transmitting this knowledge to younger people.

They are links to the past and to the gods in tradition-oriented societies. In classical China, for example, old age was honorific and revered on religious as well as other grounds; and when the old died they were worshipped as ancestors.

The extended family is central to the social structure. A clan can and will act much more effectively to meet crises and dependency of its members than a small family. Mutual obligations between blood relatives—specifically including the aged—are institutionalized as formal rights, not generous benefactions.

The population clusters in relatively small, stable communities in which the governing values are sacred rather than secular; community structure is fairly clear-cut, with formal age grading and definite roles linked to different ages; almost all contacts between group members are face-to-face and personal; and an individual relates to the same group of people in many different contexts instead of many diverse groups—one at home, a second at work, and a third in church, for example.

The final two factors are rather surprising. They show that the relative welfare of the old person in his group improves to the extent that:

The productivity of the economy is low and approaches the ragged edge of starvation. The greater the poverty and the struggle to survive, the *relatively* better off old people are by the standards of their group. With low marginal productivity and a primitive division of labor, labor may be cheap, but the contribution of each additional pair of hands to the small gross product is valued.

To be sure, in such primitive economies extremely dependent old people are not sentimentally cared for indefinitely. Their fates are determined by the balance between what they put in and take out of the system. But, so long as an old person's productivity exceeds his consumption, including the time and effort required for his care, the culture retains and makes a place for him. However, when the balance shifts and his dependency threatens the group, then he tends to be expelled. Although the particular form of this fate may vary, swift death is common. The Masai of Africa unceremoniously throw the old dependent outside the village *bwoma* and forget about him, while the Polar Eskimos rather sorrowfully "put him out on the ice"—in both cases to die. But when his needs impose a severe strain on the group's resources, his *social* death precedes the physical.

Finally, there is high mutual dependence within a group. The great interdependence among members promotes mutual aid in meeting survival problems. Here the aged are benefactors as well as beneficiaries of reciprocity.

A range of studies indicates that even in America, old people are relatively better off and accepted when they own family farm land, live in small communities, are members of racial or ethnic minorities with extended kinship obligations, or belong to unskilled, working-class groups where interdependence and mutual aid are standard conditions of survival. These findings argue well for the generality of the seven principles.

However, social change is systematically weakening these principles, regardless of local variations.

Property ownership

This has spread broadly through the population during the past generation. But it has been attended by an important separation between capital ownership and management in which control is *not* particularly centered in the hands of older people. Further, the growth of the economy has created many new jobs, but mainly for younger people. At the same time, changes in higher education have opened the gates of the universities to many more of the younger generation.

These developments have increased young people's opportunities and reduced their dependence. While an old property owner may be financially independent, he no longer has significant control over the life chances of the young; and they have less need to defer to him.

Strategic knowledge

Old people's skills, experience, and knowledge are no longer critical factors in our culture and seldom make them authorities. The speed and pervasiveness of social change now transform the world within a generation, so that the experience of the old becomes largely irrelevant to the young. The lifetime of a seventy-five-year-old person spans man's leap from the horse and buggy to the hydrogen bomb and space travel. Occupational and other skills are now taught through formal education rather than informally. The young and middle-aged learn attitudes and life-styles largely from age mates and the mass media. Nor have the old solved the problems of the world successfully enough to inspire respect and confidence. Therefore, they are considered neither strategic agents of instruction nor founts of wisdom.

Religious links

Our society has never venerated the aged as peculiarly sacred links to ancestors, gods, or the past. The old are not protected by religious tradition.

Kinship and extended family

Kinship and family ties have been weakened in this century by occupational demands and frequent moving. Shifting job markets require flexibility of movement at the same time that urban homes have shrunk in size. The smaller isolated family has become the norm, and responsibility to one's spouse and children now takes clear priority over obligations to parents. Although children still do help aged parents, especially in the working classes, the major responsibility for old people has shifted to the government and other organizations.

Community life

Urbanization and residential mobility have also seriously weakened local community ties. Changing neighborhoods, turnover of residents, and urban impersonality have undermined those stable neighborhood structures that used to accommodate older people.

Productivity

Clearly, by any conceivable index, our productivity is tremendously high and growing. Because of automation, there is widespread displacement and no general labor scarcity outside of selected occupations. Since old people do not appreciably command skills in those occupations where labor is short, they are in little demand on the labor market. Except under special conditions, such as boom or war, they are not important to the work force.

Mutual dependence

Our economic growth and the drastic rise in living standards have undermined our mutual dependence. Greater income and opportunity have extended the range of personal choice and the freedom of action. Many goals can now be achieved with comparatively little reliance on other individuals, but this independence has been bought at the expense of solidarity and reciprocity. Except for the civil-rights movement, it is a far cry indeed from the collective action of industrial unionization in the thirties.

Therefore, those factors that reinforce the position of old people in less advanced societies undermine the aged in America. We are too wealthy as a nation and too prosperous as individuals to *need* the old person. He can do little for us that we cannot do ourselves.

Younger groups have the power. And they tie help for the aged to need—and to political weight—rather than to right. By contrast a number of foreign nations, notably the Scandinavian and Low Countries, but including England, France, Germany, and Israel, have various programs for older people that are far more comprehensive, taken for granted, and self-regulating than ours.

The High Cost of Aging

Some features of American life are positively *inimical* to old people. We are youth-oriented, so that children and young persons have a prior claim on our resources. We view this as an investment in the future rather than in the past, and it reflects pragmatism if not equity.

Also, though it has traditionally been difficult for men over forty to get employment, occupational obsolescence is occurring at steadily younger ages. Moreover, technological development affects not only the manual and less skilled workers, but is also now reaching relentlessly into higher professional and managerial ranks and into the most advanced, complex levels of science.

In many fields, the fund of human knowledge doubles in about ten years, and as new ideas and techniques are introduced, experience counts for less and less. Consequently, the electronics engineer will eventually step aside for the solid-state physicist. Because of reluctance and the decline in learning ability as people grow old, we cannot expect easy retraining in new skills during middle age or later. Actually, advances in knowledge will result in a shorter work life and a younger retirement age in the future. By the end of the century the twenty-five hour week and retirement at fifty may well be commonplace—and these are conservative estimates.

While older workers can still make some contribution, their productive capacity and quality are generally lower at sixty-five than at thirty or forty. They may be kept productive if they are placed in carefully selected jobs, but it is another question whether they can be kept working at competitive costs. Beyond sheer obsolescence lie two other obstacles to their continued employment:

Less productive older workers involve higher direct and indirect costs. Therefore, employers are asked to subsidize the aged either by absorbing higher expenses or by lowering profit margins. In either case, we expect them to assume the costs, and in our economy, their lack of enthusiasm for this is scarcely surprising.

The second obstacle to continued employment is the "efficiency" norm of large-scale enterprises. Routine personnel procedures in recruitment, hiring, and job placement aim to eliminate inefficient individual processing. But the optimum assignment of old workers requires custom job-tailoring and personal attention. In other words, sheer bureaucratic pride in "running a taut ship" itself militates against individual treatment.

Thus changes in technology, the occupational system, urbanization, residential mobility, and the family have all been harmful to old people. The aged have been shorn of their major functions and supports; they have lower social status and no incentive to accept old age as rewarding. Consequently, to avert the stigma of age, they systematically deny that they are declining or getting old. To admit to being old is the final surrender.

How can they preserve the illusion of youth, of keeping age at bay? In general only by maintaining those factors that integrate an old person into society. But can their middle-age patterns be continued into old age?

Property and power

We have seen earlier that old people cannot easily retain the bases of power, and that property may give them independence, but little control over or deference from others.

Group memberships

People are integrated into society not only by the resources they command and the functions they perform, but also through their social networks. Here the picture for the old is equally clear. Data on their associations show that participation in clubs and organizations declines steadily with age as low income, widowhood, and illness increase. Their informal relationships similarly diminish as neighborhoods change, families separate when children marry and pursue jobs, relatives and friends move away or die. More of their time is spent at funerals than ever before. In other words, old people progressively lose their group supports as networks of relatives, friends, and neighbors wither away through time.

What possible substitutes exist for these deteriorating social ties? One is the formation of new friendships with younger people nearby. However, younger age groups tend to be indifferent to or reject the old. This is trenchantly expressed in Joyce Cary's novel, *To Be a Pilgrim:*

> Love is a delusion to the old, for who can love an old man? He is a nuisance; he has no place in the world. The old are surrounded by treachery, for no one tells them truth. Either it is thought necessary to deceive them, for their own good, or nobody can take the trouble to give explanation or understanding to those who will carry both so soon into a grave. They must not complain of what is inevitable; they must not think evil. It is unjust to blame the rock for its hardness, the stream for its inconstancy and its flight, the young for the strength and the jewel brightness of their passage. An old man's loneliness is nobody's fault. He is like an old-fashioned hat that seems absurd and incomprehensible to the young, who never admired and wore such a hat.

It is consistent with this that research shows small chance of success for the development of friendships between old and young. Younger people have negative stereotypes about the old; and their attitudes do not change as a result of contact, exposure to, or experience with them. For example, my own studies of local friendship patterns show that in a large apartment building with old and young residents, less than four percent of friendships in the building were between the age groups. There is an effective social barrier between older and younger people that proximity does not destroy. The aged, incidentally, are the only group for which this is true. Contact and exposure do break down invidious stereotypes about other groups; but not about old people. This is not only because age is devalued, but also because different age groups seldom are peers sharing a common role, similar life experiences, and a common fate.

Major social roles

People are also defined and located in society according to their major role attributes, such as marital status, work, income, and health. To the extent that an older person can maintain his middle-age characteristics in this respect, his later years pose few serious problems. But if these change, old age becomes strained, problematic, and demoralized. Older people are relatively well off and socially integrated if they are (a) married and living with spouse; (b) still at work; (c) have no major loss of income; and (d) are in good health. But they are apt to be in serious difficulty if they are widowed, retired, have suffered a large drop in income, and are in poor health.

What chances have they of showing up favorably on these four factors?

Marital status

As expected, the aged show more marital disruption than any other age group. Of those over sixty-five, only about forty-five percent are still married and living with spouses. One-fourth of the men and more than one-half of the women are widowed.

But even these overall figures conceal the sharp rise in marital dissolution with increasing age. Each ten-year period after sixty-five finds an additional twenty percent widowed. For example, 15 percent of the men 65-69 are widowed compared to 58 percent of those over 85. For women, widowhood increases from 41 percent of those 65-69 to 83 percent of those 85 or older. Widowhood affects more women than men and probably has a more telling impact on them. This will probably continue because women are generally younger than their husbands, they have lower mortality rates at every age, and their life expectancy rises ever faster. For example, in 1920, there were about equal number of men and women over sixty-five; by 1940; there were almost eleven women for every ten men; by 1950, there were fully twelve women for every ten men. The surplus of older women will presumably increase— and so will the strains of widowhood.

Work

The proportion of people over sixty-five in the labor force has declined steadily for the past sixty years. Two-thirds of the men were working in 1900 compared to scarcely one-third today, only about half of them full time.

More important, of those men still working, almost one-half are *self-employed*, but precisely in those sectors of the economy where the independent operator is steadily giving way. The family farmer and small businessman are losing out to corporations; and professionals are increasingly entering business or government as salaried employees. Thus, the economy itself is steadily undermining the possibilities for self-employment.

What about the remaining older workers, those on wages? Except for a minority protected by effective seniority and flexible retirement provisions, they are very vulnerable. On the free labor market, older workers are in the traditionally marginal position of Negroes—the last hired and first fired. Apart from illness and a few atypical industries, one overriding factor governs whether older people work; when labor is scarce, old people have jobs; when labor is abundant, they do not. It is as stark as that. And in an era of automation, labor shortages promise to be ephemeral and localized.

Income

So long as older people continue to work, their income holds up reasonably well. Indeed, if their health is good, they may even be better off than earlier because their homes are usually paid off, their children independent, and their own needs more modest. But for the two-thirds who are retired, income is chopped to approximately *half* of their former earnings. Furthermore, despite steady increases in Social Security benefits from the early fifties, retirees have not received a pro rata share of our growing productivity. Between 1940 and 1960, all workers' *real* income after taxes rose by fifty-one percent while real Social Security benefits increased by only seventeen percent, or one-third as much.

For the aged as a whole, income figures are appalling, and one cannot conceive how many of them manage to keep body and soul together at today's prices. It is perhaps a tribute to human resilience and adaptability. According to the Social Security Administration, among persons over sixty-five in 1960, about one-fourth of the women had no income at all, almost three-fourths had less than $1,000 per year, and fewer than one in ten had as much as $2,000 annually. The situation of men was not quite so bad, but it was bad enough. More than one-fourth had less than $1,000, one-third between $1,000 and $1,999, and about 40 percent had $2,000 or more per year. Fewer than one person in four had an income approaching $40 per week. Try to imagine an old couple or even a single person subsisting on less than this at recent price levels!

Health

Modern medicine has reduced infectious diseases so that the aged suffer mostly from chronic illness. Older people generally expect more aches, pains, and creaks in their daily lives, and they accept this as normal so long as they are still able to get around and function independently. For the most part, they do manage. Only about fifteen percent have serious loss of mobility or capacity to function.

The foregoing losses do not affect persons over sixty-five uniformly. A major dividing line occurs at seventy-five. Significantly more people over seventy-five are widowed, retired, have low incomes, and are in very poor health.

Staying in the Race

We suggested earlier that old people are still fairly well integrated in society if their earlier social characteristics remain unchanged—if they are married and living with spouse, are still working, have adequate income, and tolerable health. But, what are the purely statistical chances that a person over sixty-five will show up favorably in *all four* respects? For the moment, we can arbitrarily take $2,000 per year as a minimum adequate income. Then, if we combine the individual probabilities of a favorable rating on each of the four separate role factors—marital status, work, income, and health—we find these results: the chances of a man over sixty-five having a favorable rating on *all* four items is only about seven percent, and of a woman, less than one percent. This means that, on the average, only about seven men in a hundred and fewer than one woman in a hundred have a *good* chance of preserving the major bases of their social integration. The odds are somewhat better for those 65-69 and are drastically worse in each successive older group as illness, retirement, and widowhood exact their toll. Thus, the chances of retaining roles and, therefore, social integration are poor for the age group as a whole and steadily deteriorate with increasing age.

If the forces that protect the position of the aged are weak, could the old at least safeguard their material interests through organized political action? Do they have the potential power to wrest a larger, more equitable share of what our society has to offer? Obviously, politicians think that potential political strength is there, among old people and their families, and they are bidding for votes.

The basic problems are whether old people can relinquish their younger self-images, accept the negative implications of age, and mobilize politically to redress their deprivations. Can they admit that they have low status and act publicly on this basis? Or will pride, apathy, or wishful thinking prove stronger than their collective interests? Can the usual determinates of voting behavior and political action—social class, occupation, ethnicity, religion, region, and rural-urban residence—be overcome to weld together diverse groups on the basis of age? Can ingrained political alignments be uprooted and mobilized into an effective new political force?

Possibly, if two conditions can be met—if political goals center on immediate material benefit, and if the aged are also organized in stable *nonpolitical* groups, each having a common identity *not* related to age. Thereby action around collective interests could be encouraged by other group supports.

The overall picture is fairly bleak. It indicates that our values and institutions undermine the position of the aged. Our society makes little meaningful place for them, and current trends are further shrinking even that little room. The historical changes, particularly technological and economic, that victimize the aged cannot easily be reversed. And sheer hortatory pleas are unavailing. These are cold, bitter facts; but they are the realities.

Beyond Security

There are no simple answers to the question, "What is the solution to the problems of the aged?", for the question itself has different levels; it can refer to symptoms or to causes. Some limited, practical measures are possible—even though they only ameliorate symptoms. After all, if we try to make terminal-cancer patients as comfortable as possible, we can do at least as much for the aged.

We might consider two alternatives. First, we can provide adequately for old people's material welfare and security. This means assuring them of all the medical care they need without quibbling about their eligibility or whether it will cost two billion or three billion dollars and without burying the patient, the doctor, or the hospital in paperwork. This is possible. It also means assuring all older people of a genuinely adequate income and decent standard of living, again without quibble or cavil. This would require major revision of the entire Social Security program and its income provisions. But this, too, is possible. One often wonders how pressing old people's problems would be if their income were simply doubled or tripled and they had the freedom of action that they are now denied. In the long run, how willingly and generously we approach such material needs may be as significant as what we do.

Second, we must consider how best to insulate old people from the social insults of age; specifically how to ease their loss of status and the indifference of younger people. Isolation and other problems grow as the aged lose their roles and their contacts, but these demoralizing pressures might slacken if the aged had ready access to other old people of similar background. Similarity of life experience and a common fate are a firm basis of communication, mutual understanding, and group formation. We are not advocating the formal segregation of the aged; but insofar as potential friends are found in the immediate environment, this might insulate them from the rebuffs of society, increase the prospect of new social ties, and partially revitalize their lives. Environments that integrate old people into local groups warrant careful study, and some research on this is being completed.

But we must not concentrate only on symptoms—particularly if we are successful in treating them. There is little doubt that some important concessions will be made, whether willingly or grudgingly, to the material needs of the aged, especially medical care and income. These must not be neglected; but we may still be barely scratching the surface of the problem.

More fundamental answers must be sought to the status issue. Basic solutions will be almost impossible unless our material values shift and our institutions change. We will have to place a higher value on our human resources, on social rights, on truth and beauty, not because they are practical but for their own sake. This is necessary before a life of genuine dignity and respect will be possible for older people—or for the young.

Actually, the crucial people are *not* the aged, but the *younger* groups. It is *we* who determine the status and position of the old. The problem is that of alienation—not only the alienation of old from young, but also of the young from each other, and of man from man. No real way out of this dilemma exists without a basic reworking of our national aspirations and values. Anything less than this will see us treating only symptoms, nibbling at the tattered edges of our social problems without penetrating to their hearts.

3

The Hunger of Old Men[*]

David Gutmann

Young men in Kansas City are more like young Navajo men than they are like old men in Kansas City. Old Druze tribesmen from the hills of Galilee are very like old Maya Indians from Mexico; the resemblances between the two are stronger than any similarities between young and old Maya or young and old Druze men. Middle-aged men from Kansas City have much in common with middle-aged Druze, Maya, and Navajo men and little in common with younger and older Kansas City men.

Obviously, these statements cannot be true. Shared environment, genetic heritage, culture, and level of civilization will always tie men more closely together than could age alone. But aging releases powerful psychic forces, particularly those that affect the perception of reality and the management of vital concerns, or so cross-cultural research using personal interviews and projective tests indicates. Further, this research indicates that insofar as they concern basic stances

*This work originally appeared in *Transaction/Society* 9, no. 1/2 (November-December 1971): 55-66.

toward the conception and mastery of reality, the statements in the first paragraph are true after all.

The first research took place in Kansas City. There we found that men, as they age, move through successive, distinct modes of creating, defining, and managing experience. Younger men, 35 through 49, had an active-productive orientation; they thought that life would not be lived unless they lived it. Older men, aged 50 through 64, were found to have a more passive-receptive orientation; they lived more by the motto, "If you want to get along, you've got to go along." Finally, the oldest men, 65 and over, were apt to deal with problems projectively, through distortions of reality, rather than instrumentally.

The Kansas City study was repeated in several preliterate societies: Navajo, lowland and highland Maya of Mexico, and the Druze of Israel. Though data analysis has not yet been completed, thus far the results from the various studies support the American findings: In all cases, age was a better predictor of mastery orientation than was culture. Like the younger men in Kansas City, the younger Druze, Maya, and Navajo were mainly concerned with controlling the sources of security for themselves and their dependents. These young men see the power for good and evil as lodged within themselves: their task as they define it is to control their own destructive potential and to maximize their good, productive powers. In every society studied, older men also agree that power can be put to good or bad use; but it is now in other hands, and their task is to manage power in its external manifestations. As they see it, their task is to make themselves acceptable to the good powers (the gods, the priests, village notables, or their grown-up sons) who will then intervene in their behalf against the bad powers (evil spirits, witches, envious neighbors, and so forth) who threaten them. The definition of what is good and bad power varies by culture; but constant *across* cultures is the older man's need to please the good agents on whose power he now relies, and to recruit them to his service. Finally, the oldest men, when they could not get what they needed through compliance and accommodation of this sort, turned to magical tactics, confounding wish and reality, somehow turning *the way things ought to be* into *the way things are*, managing deprivation and threat through defensive denial.

In sum, across a wide variety of cultures, young men rely on and relish their own instrumentality and the products of their energy. Moreover, they see themselves as a source of strength for others. Older men come to rely on winning favor of the more powerful, while the oldest men, especially in times of trouble, live on dreams. These age stages have less to do with actual behaviors than they have to do with modes of perceiving reality and relating to it. In short, we have been describing transcultural age changes in the masculine ego. The question arises as to whether these changes are limited to the ego, to the psychosocial aspects of the personality, or whether they are more inclusive, extending to the psychosexual realm as well.

Psychoanalytic theory asserts an intrinsic association between the passive-dependent ego orientation and the oral needs of the personality. For instance, Otto Fenichel has stated that the association between dependence and oral eroticism is an essential one, grounded in human biology:

The biological basis of all attitudes of dependence is the fact that man is a mammal, and that the human infant is born more helpless than other mammals and requires feeding and care by adults. Every human being has a dim recollection that there were once powerful or, as it must seem to him, omnipotent beings whose help, comfort, and protection he must depend on in time of need. Later, the ego learns to use active means of mastering the world. But a passive-oral attitude as a residue of infancy is potentially present. Often enough, the adult person gets into situations in which he is again as helpless as he was as a child; sometimes forces of nature are responsible, but more often social forces created by man. He then longs for just such omnipotent protection and comfort as were at his disposal in childhood. He regresses to orality. There are many social institutions that make use of this biologically predetermined longing. They promise the longed-for help if certain conditions are fulfilled. The conditions vary greatly in different cultures. But the formula, "If you obey, you will be protected," is one that all gods have in common with all earthly authorities. It is true that there are great differences between an almighty god, or a modern employer and a mother who feeds her baby; but nevertheless, it is the similarity among them that explains the psychological effectiveness of authority.

Given the passive-dependent ego orientations that we had observed in old men from a variety of cultures, we proposed that their concerns with external gifts of affection and support, with powerful external providers, and with magical defense against threat would be matched by a heightened interest in the production, preparation, and, most of all, the pleasurable consumption of food and drink. Furthermore, the relationship between the psychosexual and the psychosocial vectors of personality is presumed to be intrinsic and unchanging and we would expect to find the predicted relationship in many cultures: *In any society*, a high degree of manifest orality should predict, for that individual, the character and behavior traits considered passive, receptive, and dependent by local standards.

If this relationship is found to be distributed across cultures, then the observed similarities in ego process within age groups and across cultures are neither accidental nor superficial, but mark pervasive reorientation of the masculine personality at its deepest levels. Furthermore, it is unlikely that such standard and pervasive changes are caused outside the organism itself; thus, the case for a developmental explanation of the observed age differences is strengthened. Finally, if the predicted relationship is found to remain constant across several cultures, then psychoanalytic theory is shown to be a useful tool for personality-culture studies.

Psychoanalysis was nurtured in the sophisticated, urban civilization of Western Europe and the United States; the Druze and the Navajo, major subjects of this report on increased orality in late life, are distinctly non-Western in their cultural values and social forms. Furthermore, the Arizona Navajos and Galilean Druze tribesmen differ strikingly from one another as well. Both groups are composed of traditional agriculturists, but there are few other similarities. The Navajo are migratory herdsmen living in small bands based on kinship and scattered across the high desert plateaus of northeastern Arizona. Their world is dynamic. What for us are normal or neutral events are for the Navajo charged with personal, often magical, significance. The Navajo character mingles suspicion and humor, toughness and vulnerability, pragmatism and superstition, apathy and a delight in movement. The Druze are sedentary farmers and live in organized villages. They speak Arabic and their values and social forms are similar to those of the agriculturists of the Levant, but they practice a secret, closed religion that has ordinarily attracted the enmity of the Muslims and Maronite Christians among whom they have lived. Druzes have ordinarily been a minority population and they have survived eight centuries of persecution through the cultivation of industry, fierceness in battle, and political sophistication. Druzes are almost rigidly self-consistent in character: They are pious, stubborn, and rational rather than emotional, reserved, hospitable, and formal. Among both the Navajo and the Druze, old men have a fairly secure and valued status.

For our research, leading and respected members of the Navajo and Druze communities helped us recruit subjects. They asked for the help of all men of reasonable reputation and without important physical or mental disabilities aged thirty-five through ninety-five. Since socioecological variables such as community size, remoteness, proximity to roads, and the like could have psychological effects on feelings of dependence or independence, subjects were chosen from strategic points along the Druze and Navajo versions of the folk-urban continuum. This was to prove an important and revealing addition to our research.

In the end we collected three Druze and three Navajo subsamples. Each regional cohort was roughly comparable across cultures in age composition, residence patterns, and location on the folk-urban continuum. For the Navajos, the remote-traditional subsample included 39 Navajo speakers, aged 35 through 95, living in isolation around Navajo Mountain and the Rainbow Plateau. The 33 Druze equivalents were found in isolated, exclusively Druze, extremely conservative mountain villages of the Galilee: Kissera, Ain-El-Assad, and Beit Jahn. For the intermediate, or outlying-traditional sample, 21 Navajo speakers living on the western, traditional side of the reservation, far from major settlements but close to main roads were chosen. Twenty-four equivalent Druze were found in Hurfeish, a traditional village cut by a main road leading to a neighboring Israeli *kibbutz*. The urban Navajo sample was composed of 29 traditional Navajos living in or around Tuba City, Arizona, the administrative center of the reservation. Twenty-one comparable Druze were found in Daliat-Il-Carmil and Osfiych, villages on Mount Carmel, near the Israeli seaport of Haifa.

The research method employed is explained separately elsewhere in this chapter, but briefly put, the subjects were interviewed through interpreters, asked about their memories, their problems and ways of dealing with them, and their dreams. They were also asked to comment on a series of T.A.T. cards—drawings showing familiar and unfamiliar scenes and designed to evoke revealing projective responses. All references to food and drink, growing or gathering food, oral taboos, and the like were coded and weighted in one of five categories. These categories described a continuum from the most distant or externalizing forms of orality management to the closest, most present, and personal expressions of orality.

Younger Men Score

Our prediction was that the younger men would score most highly at the externalizing end of the continuum and that older men would score highly on more personal variables, with the oldest scoring highest at the opposite end of the continuum.

Specifically, we thought younger men, aged thirty-five through forty-nine, would rely on externalized or past projections, expressing their own oral needs as if they were those of others, or a part of their own infantile past. If younger men admitted to present oral concerns, we predicted that the expression would center on present production of food and not present pleasure in it. We predicted that older men, aged fifty through sixty-four, would show a more even balance between the closer and more distant elements of the array. Of the measures of externalizing, we expected the more personal past-projection score (P.P.S.) to be higher than the more distant externalized-projection score (E.P.S.). On the more proximal end of the continuum, we expected the middle-aged men would score higher on the more directly receptive present-syntonic or oral-pleasure score (P.S.S.) than on the more active measure of the present-production score (P.R. P.S.). Finally, for the oldest group, sixty-five and over, it was our expectation that the dominance of the variables on the present, receptive, and personal side of the array would be complete. Present-syntonic scores would be highest, externalized-projection scores lowest; present-production would supersede past projection as a medium for maintaining some distance from full oral receptivity.

Table 1 maps the mean scores for each of the dependent orality variables by age and culture. The results appear to be consistent with our predictions. For both cultures, and especially for the Navajo, externalized projection, a measure of projective references to the hunger of others, is clearly favored by men in the 35-49 age group. By contrast, present-syntonic score, the measure of receptivity, and pleasure in food, accounts for little more than ten percent of the total orality scores of the younger Navajos and Druzes. The only present and personal score favored by the younger men, notably the younger Druze, is that measuring references to the subject's present production of food and to the dependence of others on him for sustenance. In effect, the orality profile of the younger men, particularly that of the younger Druze, can be decoded as, *"Other people are hungry and dependent; it is my job to feed them."*

In the profile of the middle-aged group, we can see the swing predicted toward a balance between external and internal expressions of orality. For both the Navajo and Druze, the externalized-projection score has dropped and the present-syntonic score has risen to the same degree. For both cultures, the men of this age group are clearly becoming more open and perhaps more vulnerable to their oral-receptive needs. But there is also buffering against full orality in their continuing expressions of externalized projection and present production. It appears that these older men still wish to keep their distance from direct expressions of oral need. The Druze in particular seem to keep this distance. The score for direct pleasure is second highest of the Navajo scores for this age group, while it is second lowest for the Druze, exceeding only the oral-rejection or sour-grapes score (O.R.S.). It would appear that the middle group of Navajos either take present pleasure in their food and drink or they externalize and project their oral needs.

Table 1

The Management of Orality: All Druze and Navajo Subjects Compared,
by Culture and by Age

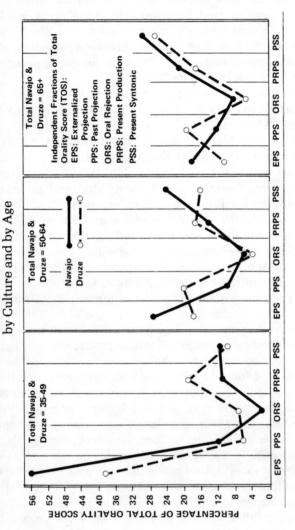

Thus, the middle-aged Druze is more flexible, acknowledging oral interests as part of the self, but at the same time keeping his distance by projecting orality into the past or by expressing it in terms of present involvement in the production of food.

The score profile of the oldest subjects is the reverse of that shown by the youngest men. The present-syntonic score, a measure of open acknowledgment of oral receptivity, is higher than any other score. The externalization of oral needs is at its lowest, the E.P.S. being the second lowest Druze score and the third lowest Navajo score. Thus, in both cultures it appears that the oldest men no longer bother to buffer their orality or deflect oral expressions into less personal, more active modes than the frank, *"I like to eat,"* represented by the present-syntonic score. The oldest men have come increasingly to define both their pleasures and their pains in terms of food and drink and they are therefore likely to be dependent on the good favor of those who can succor them. If the younger man's implicit statement is, *"Others are hungry and it is my job to feed them,"* the older man's response in this implicit cross-generational dialogue reads, *"I need food for pleasure and security and I depend on others to supply it."*

This transcultural age increase in directly oral concerns matches both the Kansas City findings and the expectations suggested by psychoanalytic theory. It points to a universal reactivation of oral drives in older men. Young men, it seems, are bothered by oral-dependent yearnings and repress them or manage them through fantasy, but in later life there appears to be a return of the repressed and orality is restored to consciousness.

This is, of course, a very general statement of the findings. In fact, it will be noted that the differences between cultures noted in the discussion of the responses of the middle-aged subjects persist among the old. On the externalizing end of the scale, Navajos continue to favor externalized projection over past projection; the Druze reverse these priorities and accentuate the power of past projection. Even at this age level it is their second highest score. Again, it appears that the Navajos manage orality in either/or terms: Either someone else is hungry or they are. The more flexible Druze move, *within* the general externalizing stance, from the more distant E.P.S. to the more personal P.P.S., from, *"He is hungry,"* to,

"As a child, I was hungry." This suggests that the Druze have a greater capacity for self-differentiation and that this better articulated sense of self is a source of support in later life. They can revise their own history instead of projectively distorting the present reality. These inferences from the orality profile differences are consistent with our field impressions of the Druze and the Navajo.

Statistical analysis of the results confirms these impressions of the meaning of the score profiles at each age level, and in particular confirms our impression of covariance between the externalized-projection score and the present-syntonic score, the two extremes of our array of styles of oral expression. In the case of E.P.S., while the independent variables for age, region, and culture all contributed to variance in E.P.S., the age effect is independent of the regional and cultural effect. In the P.S.S. measure, age and region both had significant effects on the scores, but these effects proved to be independent. Finally, support for our finding that age increase in P.S.S. is an independent effect tied to a decrease by age in E.P.S. is found in a negative correlation between these variables significant at the .01 level.

Other scores showed less consistency. Overall, the past-projection score did not have the age career predicted for it. It does rise to some degree as the Druze grow older, but no consistent Navajo pattern was discerned. This appears to reflect cultural differences. The Navajos do not have an armory of coping styles. They cannot express their oral needs while keeping distance from them by projecting them on the screen of their distant childhood. The Druze are expert in this and their P.P.S. goes up with age and with decline in E.P.S.

As for the present-production score and the oral-rejection score, no significant age effects were found either within or across cultures. The oral-rejection scores of the urban Navajo and Druze were relatively high: a reflection of the temptations of the big city and a preoccupation with its forbidden pleasures, liquor and drugs. Remote, traditional Druze have a significantly high present-production score, but this may mean only that remote, sedentary agriculture can more readily make use of the abilities of older men than migratory sheep raising in comparable isolation in Arizona.

Persistence Across Cultures

When comparing two very different peoples, the surprises do not come in the differences between them; what is surprising are the interregional differences that persist across both cultures. For instance, while E.P.S. declines by age, it also declines by proximity to urban life. By the same token, while P.S.S. goes up with age across regions, it is always lowest among the remote Druze and Navajo traditionals. While there is no significant age effect for past-projection scores, these scores rise by proximity to the city, more so for the Druze than the Navajo, but the change is statistically significant for both groups.

That is to say, the urbanites of either culture score significantly lower on externalization, significantly higher on past projection, and significantly higher on directly expressed oral pleasure than do men of their group and their age who live farther out in the hills. Urban men seem more conscious of their own oral-receptive needs, both in the past and present, and seem less inclined to hide them from themselves through externalization than do more isolated men. Urban men are like old men. They are less buffered against the direct experience of oral need.

Comparison of Table 1 with Table 2 shows a striking fit between the orality profiles of younger men and of remote-traditional men, between the profiles of middle-aged men and intermediate-traditional men, and between old men and urban men. Remote-traditional life calls forth a self-structure, at least for expression of oral need, which is closest to that of the youngest men, regardless of region. Thus, not only does the psychic structure of the young Druze resemble that of the young Navajo, but it also resembles those of Druze and Navajo men of any age who live in the most isolated areas. Similarly, the urban milieu seems to sponsor a structure that, in terms of orality, is closest to that of the oldest men, regardless of culture or region.

The transcultural similarities in age and regional profiles make sense if we assume that instrumentality as a personal variable declines both with age and with distance from the remote-traditional sector. Full commitment to personal instrumentality requires the suppression of sensuality and receptivity: whatever his social background, the man who must do

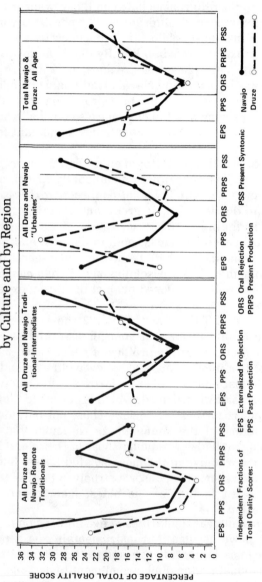

Table 2

The Management of Orality: All Druze and Navajo Subjects Compared, by Culture and by Region

PERCENTAGE OF TOTAL ORALITY SCORE

All Druze and Navajo Remote Traditionals

All Druze and Navajo Traditional-Intermediates

All Druze and Navajo "Urbanites"

Total Navajo & Druze: All Ages

Navajo
Druze

Independent Fractions of Total Orality Scores:

EPS Externalized Projection
PPS Past Projection
PRPS Present Production
ORS Oral Rejection
PSS Present Syntonic

stoop labor in the tropic sun, fight a battle, or track prey for days across the ice floes cannot afford to be overly conscious of his fatigue, his fear, or his wish for comfort. Either he forges his body into a weapon or a tool or he and his dependents die. The socializers of children in remote-traditional enclaves constantly hammer this message home by words and by example. Thus, in terms of our profiles, externalized-projection scores are high for this sort of man and expressions of pleasure in eating and drinking are rare. That is, they are rare for the youngest men regardless of region and for the most remote and traditional regardless of age. The remote-traditional sectors both demand and promote individual instrumentality. Life is difficult in the hills. A man must rely on himself for sustenance, and on the sons he has trained. But in the cities, even in such modest urban scenes as Tuba City, Arizona, and the far outskirts of Haifa, industry and instrumentality are relatively separate from personal security. In the cities, men depend for sustenance on organized systems of production and distribution not so directly responsive to and dependent on individual industry. In the city, able-bodied men can go hungry because of economic forces outside their control. On the other hand, a disabled man can get help from a variety of formal and informal social agencies if he is in the city. There, men of whatever age and physical state are always "aging," that is to say, dependent and receptive. And if we assume that full instrumentality requires the repression of sensuality, then it is not surprising to find that limited instrumentality in the cities leaves the city man more receptive to his oral promptings than his lonely, rural counterpart. The psychic meaning of instrumentality is discussed below. At the moment, it is enough to note that despite the pervasiveness of cultures, both age and *psychosocial ecology*—that is, the point on the folk-urban continuum—account for more of the variance in orality scores than does culture.

Theories of Aging

Considerably more analysis is required before a rigorous, consistent demonstration of the power of the psychosocial ecology on dealing with orality, and, by implication, on perceptions of reality, can be given. However, the orality of old men has been marked by others in the past and explication of this phenomenon is somewhat easier, particularly given our original research design. Leo Simmons was particularly struck by its manifestation. The first chapter of his study, *The Role of the Aged in Primitive Society* (New Haven, Conn.: Yale University Press, 1945), is called, "Assurance of Food." Simmons argues, as we do, that food has a special as well as universal importance for the aging. He illustrates this thesis with examples from more than thirty preliterate cultures, widely differing on every measure. He notes that across this diverse cultural range older men have typically used their prestige to ensure the choicest foods for themselves, by making them taboo for younger men. But where I see in these developments the tracings of universal psychological laws that for the most part operate outside human awareness, Simmons explains them as direct consequences of human awareness, in this case the awareness of mortality. As Simmons puts it: "A dominant interest in old age is to live long, perhaps as long as possible. Therefore, food becomes a matter of increasing concern. Its provision in suitable form, on regular schedule, and in proper amounts depends more and more upon the efforts of those who are in a position to provide or withhold it. And, as life goes on, the problem of supplying and feeding the aged eventually reaches a stage at which they require the choicest morsels and the tenderest care."

In brief, Simmons's is a cognitive explanation; he assumes that old men value eating because they recognize the connection between nutrition and longevity; fear of death stimulates a reasonable interest in the health-giving qualities of food. He makes the rather extreme assumption that older men across his wide range of cultures all symbolize food in the same way or have the same rational understanding of nutrition. In my own research, only the highland Maya said anything that could be taken as supporting this position. The old men from the other groups mentioned food just as much but without making this particular connection.

Simmons implicitly denies the psychoanalytic explanations explored in our studies, asserting, in effect, that older men's rationality would dictate their strong oral interests without any contribution from irrational or unconscious sources. In terms of this study, Simmons would not agree with our prediction that high syntonic-orality scores are related to a passive or magical ego position. The data analysis bearing on this point has not been completed, but an independent study (made with an associate) of our Navajo subjects' dreams provides some confirmation of this hypothesis. The ego mastery position—active, passive, magical—represented through the form and content of the dreams was estimated. My associate Alan Krohn selected a sample of dreams in which the mastery position of the dreamer was an important element. Active dreams were set outdoors; regardless of content, the dreamer played a central and organizing role in the action. In passive dreams, the dreamer was either absent or on the periphery, others were the main actors and the dreamer was either inert or at the mercy of some arbitrary force. In magical dreams, the passive characteristics persisted; though the dream events were highly improbable, the dreamer took them as portents of specific events of his waking life. Our prediction, that a significant association would be found between mastery position and syntonic orality, was confirmed to a significant degree: of 25 subjects who reported active mastery dreams, 17 had syntonic-oral scores below the median, while of 27 subjects reporting passive or magical mastery dreams, 19 had syntonic-oral scores above the median.

Mastery

Along similar lines, the T.A.T. protocols for the Navajos are being examined for indications of mastery tendencies. The hypothesis is that subjects with lower syntonic-oral scores would tell a majority of active mastery stories to the T.A.T. cards, while those whose T.A.T. protocols revealed a preponderance of passive and magical mastery stories would have syntonic-orality scores above the median. This examination has so far covered only the responses of the remote-traditional Navajos. Of 18 men with syntonic-orality scores below the median, 12 told T.A.T. stories of active mastery; of 20 whose T.A.T. stories concentrated on passive or magical elements, 14 had syntonic-orality scores above the median. By the same token, the externalized-projection score, which presumably registers the counterdependent, counteroral position, shows a significant positive correlation with T.A.T. stories of active mastery content. In sum, the management of orality appears to be coordinated with the basic ego stances that differentiate individuals, and not with the drive for survival that all presumably have in common.

Simmons contends that the hunger of old men represents a rational preoccupation with death, but if this were the case, total orality scores should increase with age. In point of fact, they remain relatively constant. What changes reliably and predictably with age is the *manner* in which oral concern is expressed. Age does not change the sheer amount of oral interest, but rather the management of this interest and its expression. Younger men, though far from death, do not lack oral interest, they merely keep oral concerns out of direct consciousness by externalizing and projecting them. Their orality is waiting in the wings against the time when they can turn over the responsibility for provision to others and relax into the consumer's role. Nor is the self-acknowledged orality of old men created by the threat of death. Though this orality can be assimilated to the old man's need to deny mortality, the bases of his present oral dispositions were formed much earlier. He thought of them then as an unconscious threat; now he sees them as a conscious resource.

Our older subjects may value food in the rational sense, but there is no doubt that they love it. They love it, not because if preserves life, but because, as a pleasure, a comfort, it helps them deny death. A dream, reported by a sixty-five-year-old highland Maya, but typical for this age cohort in other cultures, represents a fusion of oral-erotic themes with defensive magical denial. In his interview, Don Cyrilo had told us that his death was near and his dream report alternates between images of threat and images of oral comfort: "I dream that they are cutting meat and that they give me the meat as a gift. . . ."

"I run from something. I escape through a crack in the wall. A man tries to catch me, and I can't run. Then, suddenly, I fly away. A woman calls me but I don't want to go to her. I am offered food. They offer me grains of corn. I put it in a pocket and eat it." Here we see, without much camouflage, the threat of death: the man who implacably pursues; the woman who calls. But the threat of death is countered by oral versions of denial. Pursued by death, Don Cyrilo magically flies away; he is offered gifts of meat and grain. The same recruitment of oral comforts to the service of denial came out in Don Cyrilo's discussion of his drinking: it makes him forget his troubles, and it gives him the wings that he dreams of. After two days of drinking, he feels no pain: "I don't feel alive. It's just like flying."

A comparison of our data on the highland Maya and the Navajo reveals a similar point. The older men, far more than the younger, use some form of sensual intake as a remedy against discontent. Younger men are likely to forget their troubles by getting to work, by making something happen, but older men look to received supplies, especially food, for their comfort. Just why oral pleasures should increase feelings of security is not clear. Impressions gained from individual interviews and unbuttressed by statistical analysis suggest that an important function of denial at the end of life is to reconstruct the climate of the beginning, of early childhood. The initial life experiences in any culture center on feeding, and this fact may determine the universal enlistment of oral pleasures in later life attempts at denial. The following statement made by a tough old Navajo medicine man (eighty-three years old; now deceased) at the end of a three-hour interview illustrates the relationship: "Every time I eat the white man's bread—white bread—I eat plenty, but I don't know what happens to it. It doesn't stay down here. What I need is corn meal mush, dumplings. I'm expecting my daughter —she comes around once in a while and sometimes she makes the corn meal. . . . When I was a baby about a year old I found that they were putting that in my mouth, this corn meal mush. That's what I'm raised on, but I'm still hungry for it."

This notion that the hunger of old men has irrational sources is also supported by some unexpected findings concerning other forms of sensuality, those not related in any rational sense to nutrition or longevity. Especially striking is the way aging men in different cultures come more and more to think of the eyes as registers of the beauty of the world rather than as more prosaic gatherers of information.

An Eye for the Sensual
This trend toward visual sensuality is illustrated with vividness in the age distribution of story themes elicited by one of the standard T.A.T. cards, used in its original form at all sites. The card shows a lightly clad, athletic man climbing a

rope. A tally was made of all stories in which the hero is either looking or being looked at. The distribution of such stories by age indicates that younger men tend more often than older men to propose that the hero is looked at rather than looking. Younger Americans in particular see the climber as the center of some audience's admiring attention: "He's showing off his strength. . . the audience gets a thrill out of looking at him." According to these younger men, the rope climber produces visual bonuses for a receptive audience, but he uses his own eyesight in the service of this assertive production. Older Americans are more likely to see the climber as looking to the audience for response and direction. It is up to the audience to decide whether he is doing a good job and to tell him so. The shift from confident assertion to cautious dependence is clear. Similarly, the younger Maya and Navajo usually suggest that the rope climber is checking progress toward some goal. But for older Indians, the looking is in itself the goal of the climbing. There is nothing instrumental about it. The hero has climbed up not to find out how far he has to go or to make a signal, but to see something beautiful or to get a better view. In the same vein, a few older men in Kansas City, and no younger men, thought of the climber as a sexual voyeur.

This same age trend toward heightened pleasure in visual activity comes out to another card, one of the set devised for use with American Indian subjects. It shows a male figure in a breechcloth standing on a cliff looking out over a (possibly) barren landscape. Again, younger Indians, particularly younger Navajo, offered an instrumental, competitive, productive, mobile interpretation: He is looking for lost sheep, at the crop, at grazing lands; he is looking for the enemy; he is seeking a route through wild country. But for the older Maya and Navajo, the looking is eroticized, it is pleasurable in itself. Although the landscape shown on the T.A.T. card is virtually featureless, these older subjects say the hero has come to some high point to look at beautiful scenery.

In psychoanalytic theory, oral and visual pleasure drives are intrinsically linked and it may not be accidental that both should move to psychic prominence in later life. Fenichel, for example, explicitly links scoptophilia with oral eroticism: "The eye may represent pregenital erogenous zones symbolically. As a sense organ it may express oral incorporative and oral sadistic longings in particular . . . ." And later: "Such 'oral' use of the eyes represents the regression of visual perceptions to the incorporation aims that were once connected with early perception in general." In other words, psychoanalytic theorists would predict from the older man's evident orality his ocular receptivity. From their perspective, the visual activity comes under the dominance of the oral-incorporative modality; the old man eats his world through his eyes.

The Pleasure Principle

The trend toward visual sensuality, then, may be considered as only one indicator of an intrinsic psychosexual development of later life, the regression of eroticism toward its oral origins. But it is also possible that the increase in oral and visual pleasures are two equally dependent events brought about by an independent assertion of the pleasure principle in later life. Paradoxically, this possibility rests on psychoanalytic theories of the course of libidinal development in early life. These theories profess that in infants, all bodily functions are exercised for the erotic pleasures they afford. Later growth and maturation require that the erotic goals of the individual organs must be suppressed and that erotic strivings must be relegated to a single organic system, the genital, in order that the utilitarian demands of life can be met.

Sandor Ferenczi has written, "If there were no such separation of pleasure activities, the eye would be absorbed in erotic looking, the mouth would be exclusively employed as an oral-erotic instrument, instead of being employed in necessary self-preservative activities. . . ." What is being described here, this rearrangement of organic functions, is part of the libidinal preconditions for the organism's development toward active mastery. The growing individual can no longer depend on the instrumentality of others, and thus must amplify and coordinate the instrumental potential of his own body parts. They must cease to be independent pleasure receptors and must take up their collaborative, productive functions.

Old Hippies

This presumably universal process is varied in its effects by sex, culture, and place on the folk-urban continuum. Thus, women generally rely on the instrumentality of men; by the same token they are more diffusely sensual in their erotic makeup. Urbanized men also rely on instrumentalities and resources outside of themselves; and, as we have seen, do not repress and compartmentalize their sensuality to the same degree as isolated men of the same culture. Some aspects of the famous generation gap can be understood in these terms as well. The hippie, if you will, has renounced instrumentality to amplify and even make a politics out of sensuality and receptiveness, a style usually reserved for the aged. Like the old men I have known in various parts of the world, the hippie is diffusely sensual: *oral*—drugs, wine, and macrobiotic foods; *aural*—loud rock music; *visual*—light shows, movies, posters, and hallucination; *tactile*—group-grope, bare feet, and water-beds. And the hippie's main ego defenses are, like those of the aged, based on projection of his own aggressivity onto others, that is, the pigs, the system, the establishment; on denial of existential limitations and on magical fatalism—astrology, Tarot, the I-Ching. And again as it is with the aged, these regressive defenses are based on low ego boundaries, on a facile capacity for confounding fantasy and actuality, to legislate *"the way things ought to be"* into *"the way things are."* Thus, the generational conflict is between the "aged" hippie and the "young" father who, "square" that he is, is addicted to his instrumentality and to the material goods that he can provide and possess by virtue of his achievement.

Such people—alienated youths, urban men, women in general—have had less opportunity or less incentive to limit their various capacities for pleasure and in later life may experience a less vehement turn toward sensual receptivity. But in the case of men trained to the productive life, there may be a return of the repressed such that the individual moves from productivity to receptivity and becomes, as in childhood, dependent on the active mastery and instrumentality of others. Consequently, the early life developments outlined are re-versed, the capactiy for erotic pleasure is no longer limited to the genitals: the eye can once again be absorbed in erotic looking, the mouth once again devoted to oral-erotic pleasures. The libido can ebb back to its original reservoirs of mouth, eyes, skin, and sphincter; it can be fractioned according to its original, archaic, anarchistic goals.

Accordingly, I no longer consider the later-life swing to orality as the pivotal development of aging, the source of secondary developments of the ego. Rather, it now appears that the shift to orality is just one phase, within one zone of a more general movement in later life toward diffuse erotic sensitivity. Not the mouth alone is affected; the reawakened sensitivity is diffused over all the organs of sense and incorporation. The younger man's capacity to experience intense (but brief) orgasm is replaced in later life by a capacity for milder, polymorphous pleasure of the sort now advocated for all ages by Herbert Marcuse and Norman O. Brown, who argue that the escape of sensuality from its genital bonds represents liberation and life enhancement. But their optimism does not seem to be warranted, at least not for the periods of middle and later life. Our findings suggest the opposite, that openness to pregenital yearnings is associated with bodily weakness and morbidity. Thus, we find that Navajo subjects in good health (according to U.S. Public Health Service records) are likely to have significantly higher externalized-projection scores than subjects in the same age range suffering from severe or fatal illness. By the same token, as shown in Table 3, severly ill Navajo subjects are much more likely to have syntonic-orality scores above the median than are men of the same age group in relatively good health. We do not yet know if the entry of oral yearnings into consciousness precedes the onset of illness, or follows it. The important point is that the high externalization, low syntonic-orality profile is significantly associated with physical health; and that the reverse pattern is significantly associated with illness.

Thus, the regression of the libido toward its earliest sources seems to come about when older men lack the volition and the energy to maintain the ego defenses and the ego boundaries upon which active mastery is based. The resulting loss of ego integration leads inevitably to the older man's disengagement from the arenas that require and sponsor his focused instrumentalism. He becomes dependent on the instrumentality of those "parental" figures—his wife, his

Table 3
The Seriously Ill Have Higher Syntonic-Orality
Scores (S.O.S.) than the Healthy

	Age Group	Healthy	Moderate Chronic Illness	Potentially Terminal Illness
SOS equal to or less than median	35-54	10 ⎫	8 ⎫	2 ⎫
	55-69	12 ⎬ 24	10 ⎬ 25	3 ⎬ 8
	70+	2 ⎭	7 ⎭	3 ⎭
SOS equal to or above median	35-54	2 ⎫	4 ⎫	8 ⎫
	55-69	3 ⎬ 11	8 ⎬ 19	10 ⎬ 26
	70+	6 ⎭	7 ⎭	8 ⎭

grown sons, the village local authorities, the gods—to whom he has conceded the responsibility for his care. The older man's surrender of instrumentality in turn accelerates the processes of ego erosion and libidinal diffusion that, rather than being life enhancing, may well be the psychic precursors of physical death.

Doing Research on the Hunger of Old Men, or How to Use Thematic Apperception Tests [T.A.T.s] and "Naturalistic" Interviews to Get Orality Scores

Our information on the Navajo and Druze tribesmen was gathered through intensive, open-ended, "naturalistic" interviews followed by administration of specially designed Thematic Apperception Tests (T.A.T.s). In an attempt to blunt the effect of suspicion of our work by the Navajo and Druze subjects, they were first invited to question the interviewer's motives and his plans for using the information gathered. Once some initial rapport was reached, the subjects were interviewed at length through local interpreters. They were asked about their most serious concerns in their past and present lives, their childhood memories, the sources of their contentment, the causes of any discontent, and their remedies against it, and about their dreams. These topics were not covered in any particular order; the informants' subjective priorities shaped the interviews. Upon completion of the interviews, the subjects were asked to discuss a set of T.A.T. cards, a series of simple drawings showing both familiar local scenes and unfamiliar images. These pictures, though relatively neutral in content, are designed to provoke projective interpretations from the subjects. One card, for instance, shows a lightly clad athlete climbing a rope. The subjects are asked what the card shows. Typically, responses to the card are divided between those who see the climber as performing for an audience and those who see him as climbing up to get a better look at something. Clearly, these responses represent quite different attitudes. Further material for inference is provided by statements of the purpose of the climbing: "to show off," "to thrill the audience," "to see something beautiful," "to get a better view."

In order to check the hypothesis that oral interests increase in later life, all mentions of eating, cooking, food sale, food purchase, and food production were noted and assigned weights that reflected the intensity of the oral need presumably expressed through them. Mentions of food production or preparation were given lower scores than mentions of eating or drinking. Mentions of food consumption by others were scored lower than mentions of food consumption by the respondent himself. Each expression of oral interest was also mapped by various coordinates: for instance, by time location, depending on whether the reference was to the present, to the respondent's youth, to his childhood, or to the historical past of the tribe. We also distinguished between reference to food and drink in the interview proper, and reference made in projective portions of the discussion, the T.A.T. descriptions, or dream reports. Finally, we distinguished between positive (oral-syntonic) and negative (oral-rejecting) reference; a lower score was also given in those cases where foodstuffs or food-related activities were described as disagreeable, poisonous or harmful, or taboo.

The sum of these weighted references constituted the respondent's total orality score (T.O.S.). This measure could not be used directly because a high score might represent an especially long interview rather than an oral need, per se. Dividing the raw score by the number of respondent words yielded a highly imprecise figure useful only for intersubject comparisons. Accordingly, our final comparisons—between generations, between regions, and between cultures—employ a series of standardized scores expressed as a percentage of the total orality score. Each of these scores, which are discussed below, represents an independent data base and is derived from a major coding distinction.

The externalized-projection score (E.P.S.) represents the percentage of the respondent's total orality score contributed by T.A.T. and dream references to food production, preparation, consumption, and deprivation. Examples are: "This is a picture of a very hungry boy," or, "In my dream a man asks me for food." These projective references to cooking, hunger, and eating presumably originate in the respondent's own needs; they do not originate in the deliberately ambiguous T.A.T. cards; nor in the dream figures produced by the respondent's own fantasy. Thus, in such mental activity the respondent is taken to be expressing his own oral concerns. He is saying, *"He [and not myself] is the hungry one."* This score, then, represents the respondent's tendency to manage his orality through externalization, projection, or depersonalization.

The past-projection score (P.P.S.) reflects the percentage of the T.O.S. contributed by the respondent's positive memories of food consumption during his childhood. Here is a Navajo example: "When I was a boy, there was more green grass and good grazing. Berries and piñon nuts for eating grew all over the ground. Now we have to get our food from the trading post." Such recall of the past is selection. The subject cannot relate his entire history, but he can choose out of the pool of memory those images that have relevance to his present psychic state. The assumption is that the respondent is projecting a present oral need on the screen of his own remote past. *"As a child [but not now], I was hungry, receptive."* We assume that this score, like that for externalized projection, is a tapping of some tendency toward externalization and projection of oral needs. In contrast to the externalized-projection score, however, the past-projection score presents oral needs as part of a superseded self rather than as a part of the present self.

The oral-rejection score (O.R.S.) represents the proportion of the T.O.S. contributed by negative mentions of eating and drinking, cooking and production of food wherever they arose, in the interview, the T.A.T. stories, or the dream reports. References to the bad effects of strong drink are included in this score. Here are two examples, Navajo and Druze, respectively: "I tell these young men not to drink, not to get in a fight and go to jail"; "I like to hunt pig, but you know that we Druze are not permitted to eat pig." This score is regarded as a measure of oral ambivalence: oral topics are discussed, but eating and drinking are seen as leading to trouble, not pleasure. In sum, it is a sour-grapes measure.

The present-production score (P.R.P.S.) reflects the percentage of the T.O.S. that is contributed by references to food production, preparation, or trading in the respondent's present life. Here is a Druze comment included in this score: "I am pleased to work in my apple orchard." Navajo: "We raise sheep and sell the mutton." This score taps tendencies toward autonomy and needing to have others dependent on the subject for food and drink. The subject is concerned with oral supply, but not in a directly receptive way. He wants to be in charge of producing the supplies that he needs. Presumably then, he can best enjoy consumption if he is consuming the products of his own skill and labor, and if he can demonstrate that others are dependent on him for the consumption. Thus, like the oral-rejection score, the present-production score may pick up ambivalent attitudes toward consumption; while the respondent is not rejecting his orality, he is giving an active and instrumental cast to his discussion of his present receptive needs.

The present-syntonic score (P.S.S.) comprises the portion of the T.O.S. stemming from references to eating and drinking and their pleasures in the subject's present life. References to food and drink as a remedy for discontent are included here. A Navajo example: "My relatives bring me the food. Sometimes they bring me that great big roast rib." Druze: "I feel better about these problems when I drink good coffee." There is no hedging or rationalization in this score. The pleasures of consumption are an unquestioned resource, one of the good things of life.

It can be seen that these scores, in the order presented, represent a continuum with the most distant or externalizing forms of orality management at one end and the closest, most present and personal forms at the other. This order corresponds to the hypothesized sequence of age change through the orality variables. The prediction was that younger men, regardless of culture or regions within the culture, would maintain distance from their orality, while older men would manifest it in direct and personal ways.

4

Old-Age Poverty in Preindustrial New York City*

Michael Zimmerman

In the space of a century there has been a marked increase in both the overall number of persons considered to be elderly and in the percentage of elderly relative to other age groups in American society. The number of persons over 65 years of age, for example, rose from three million in 1900 to nearly twenty million in 1970. Compared with the total population, the percentage of the 65-and-over group has more than doubled during this period, from 4.1 percent in 1900 to 9.9 percent in 1970. Indeed, the co-occurrence of a declining birthrate and an increasingly lower mortality rate has resulted in the historically unique phenomenon of an "aging society."

Accompanying these demographic changes has been the increased recognition of and attention to the particular needs and problems of the elderly. The burgeoning body of literature in social gerontology and related areas is but one indicator of this growing concern. Yet, there is nothing new about old age, and every society has had to respond in some fashion to the problems of adjustment to aging. The early poor laws of many states in America, for instance, clearly defined the family as

*Reprinted by permission of the author.

81

the unit with primary responsibility for the maintenance of the aged. However, the inability or failure of families to provide for their aged members has always been backstopped by some broader social assumption of responsibility in America. It would be instructive, therefore, to compare the present system of maintenance of the aged with the system of maintenance in an earlier period of American society.

Prior Work on the Family and the Aged

Theoretical Work

Little research has been done on the care and treatment of the aged in pretwentieth-century America. Two reasons can be offered for this. First, the demographic changes discussed earlier are relatively recent, and social scientists have understandably devoted their energies to the analysis of this contemporary "social problem" before turning their attention to the past for a comparative and developmental perspective.

Second, the general acceptance of an ideal image of the preindustrial family on the part of sociologists and historians has limited empirical investigation of the actual position of the aged in relation to the family system of the past. Much of sociological theory has assumed that the elderly in preindustrial periods were invariably cared for by members of their extended family, and thus the maintenance of the aged was not a social problem. Furthermore, this image of the preindustrial family has often been correlated with certain assumptions concerning economic activity and social life. Given the predominance of small independent businesses, for example, it has been asserted that the status and position of the aged was, on the whole, better than it is in modern society. The aged, as the story goes, continued to participate in the "most important social structures and interests," even if in a reduced or ancillary capacity.

Conversely, these same sociological theorists have asserted that the elderly have lost their social function as a result of the disintegrating effects of industrialization upon the extended family. The major consequence of this loss of social function, it is alleged, has been the isolation of the elderly from kinship, occupational, and community ties. Consequently, this depiction of the maintenance of the elderly within the pre-industrial extended family explains, in part, why many sociological treatises on the aged dwell on the theme of "reintegration."

Empirical Research

The preceding scenario with regard to the situation and care of the elderly in preindustrial periods has been question-ed by a number of scholars concerned with preindustrial family life. As Ethel Shanas, et al., note,

> What information is available does not, in general, support the theories that suggest that old people in the family have been isolated as a result of industrialization. Evidence for preindustrial periods suggests that three-generational households were rare in both the United States and in Great Britain and that a large number of old people lived alone in towns and villages alike.

Additional supporting evidence of this claim can be gathered from Eugene Freidmann's analysis of early census records of New York. His examination of the 1703 Census of New York City demonstrated that "at least 40 percent of the aged were not living in three-generational households. . . ." Moreover, his analysis of the New York State Census of 1865 "indicated that only 2.8 percent of the families contained three genera-tions—and this would include households whose oldest mem-ber was less than 60 or 65." Professor Freidmann concluded by stating.

> we lack evidence that the three-generation or the extended-kinship family was ever a prevailing if even a common family form in this country. And, although evidence is inadequate, we do not know whether a majority of the aged were ever cared for in this manner in our country's history. Certainly, the amount of mobility which has characterized American life—not just with the onset of industrialization and urbani-zation but from early in our history with the opportunity for sons to break from the parental household and establish their own households on the frontier—would act to deter the development of a three-generation family system.

The Definition of Old Age in Preindustrial New York City

If a significant proportion of the aged population in early nineteenth-century New York City did not live with their extended family, then how did they manage? Did they have suffcent savings to support themselves during this stage of life that is generally characterized by incapacities and infirmities? And, what of the aged with chronic illnesses—who cared for them?

An answer to each of the above questions is dependent upon how New Yorkers in earlier periods defined old age and how they responded to the problems of adjustment to aging. Today, a person is typically defined as *old* when he or she reaches sixty-five years of age, the usual age of mandatory retirement. Even if a person is not forced to retire, perhaps because of self-employment or nonemployment, the eligibility for the various social support mechanisms available after sixty-five helps to foster the definition of old age.

In the early nineteenth century, on the other hand, there were none of the present-day support mechanisms such as Social Security, pensions, and savings banks. People could rely only upon personal savings in periods of prolonged unemployment due to disabilities or infirmities. As it is the case today, accumulated savings were undoubtedly insufficient for a substantial number of the elderly. Therefore, in the absence of the modern support mechanisms, more persons continued to work as long as it was physically possible. If infirmities no longer allowed a worker to perform his trade, the solution was to find employment of a less strenuous nature (if his aged condition at all permitted it). That such was the case is evident by a number of 1826 petitions to the Common Council of the City of New York for the position of Inspector of Wood. The petition of John Van Orden is worth quoting at length:

> The petition of the subscriber respectfully shewith, that your petitioner is informed of an additional Inspector of Wood is considered to be necessary for the public convenience of the present 15th Inspection District, and begs leave to present to your honorable body this application . . . .
> Your petitioner begs leave to state to your Honorable body that in the War which gave liberty to his native country, he

was a soldier in her service, that for many years he was one of the Cartmen of this city, that he is now too far advanced in life to perform hard bodily labour, has a family to support, and is poor: and therefore most Respectfully solicits your Honourable body to favor him with the appointment of inspector of wood, the duties of which he is well acquainted with, having performed them during the long illness of the late Inspector of the said district.

It was, then, general infirmities and an inability to work that were the defining characteristics of the aged in early nineteenth-century New York City.

This functional definition of old age was supplemented by differing chronological definitions. The Association for the Relief of Respectable, Aged, and Indigent Females, for instance, offered assistance only to women who were at least 60 years of age. In addition, 50 years of age was regarded by some as the minimal limit defining old age, especially for men. Evidence of this comes from the 1824 *Report on the Settlement and Relief of the Poor*, compiled by the then secretary of state of New York, John Yates. In this report, Yates suggested that "no male person in health, with the use of all his facilities, and being between the ages of 18 and 50 years, shall be placed upon the pauper list, or be maintained at the public expense." Thus, while infirmities and an inability to work were, without a doubt, the crucial criteria of old age, the institutions and organizations devoted to the care of the elderly may have also influenced this general labeling process.

Aging and Poverty in Early New York: Introductory Comments
As already implied, the incapacitation of old age in conjunction with the absence of a comprehensive system of income maintenance had another important consequence for the elderly: to be considered aged in this period most likely meant a certain degree of indigence. Knowing that this was the case, where might an elderly person turn for assistance? Friends and relations were probably the ones the aged turned to first. Yet, the circumstances of one's nearest and dearest

were often little better than one's own, and this alternative was an impossibility for many needy aged.

This failure of the family to provide for the elderly, as noted earlier, has always been backstopped by a broader social assumption of responsibility in America. Throughout the early history of New York, this backstop was the system of poor relief—a combination of philanthropic organizations and municipal assistance. This societal response to the structural poverty of the elderly reveals much about their maintenance in preindustrial New York, and their relationship to the family system. It can be hypothesized that if the aged in preindustrial periods were predominantly cared for by members of their extended family, then one would expect to find few records of elderly persons who received assistance from the network of welfare institutions in early nineteenth-century New York City. As will be demonstrated, such was not the case. In fact, the aged, throughout this period, were a significant segment of the poor and dependent population of the city.

For reasons that will be discussed, the municipal government was unable to bear the burden of the city's increasing pauper class alone. The benevolence of private citizens was needed to help with the overload. With respect to the care of the aged, there was only one philanthropic society in this period that was solely concerned with the relief of the aged, and only a portion of the aged—respectable and indigent females—at that.

Since this benevolent society was but one of more than one hundred such groups of the period, the conclusion might be drawn that the problems of the aged poor were considered to be relatively insignificant in comparison to those of other needy groups. However, a closer examination of the historical records indicates otherwise. As W. K. Jordan points out about early philanthropy in England, "the aged poor are mentioned and are included in almost every fund established to secure some measure of help for the poor." This was also true of early philanthropy in New York, and informs one of the somewhat hidden nature of the subject. Given this fact, the history of the aged poor can best be approached through an examination of the network of welfare institutions and organizations in early New York.

New York City, 1820-1840: An Overview

The existence of such an extensive network of philanthropic organizations in these decades is indicative of both the increasing number of well-to-do and the increasing number of poor in New York. On the one hand, after years of trailing behind the commercial development of other Eastern seaport cities, New Yorkers were finally witnessing the rapid expansion of the city's export and import trade. Industry, especially the clothing industry, was also very much on the increase at this time. This economic growth, in turn, was the pull, while a variety of unsettling conditions were the push, which brought an increasingly heavy stream of immigrants from Europe. The city's population jumped from 123,706 in 1820 to 312,710 in 1840. By the end of the period of this study, the dominance of New York as a commercial center over its chief competitors was assured, and the city had sustained a rate of growth that was unmatched by any other contemporary city.

On the other hand, there were the typical urban problems that accompany rapid economic and population growth. For the first time, New Yorkers had to cope with the problems of public health, the proliferation of slum areas, and the unemployment brought about by financial panic and depression. Added to these urban problems were the more divinely inspired threats of the inclemency of winter and the frequent visits of disease. For example, the middle of this period was marked by the first and perhaps most severe visit of cholera in the history of the city. And the years at both the beginning of the 1820s and the end of the 1830s were ones of economic depression. Each of these problems and concerns directly and indirectly helped to create what contemporaries saw as an alarming problem of poverty.

Philanthropy in New York

As already mentioned, the benevolence of New Yorkers in this period was substantial. By the 1820s, societies and organizations of every description had been formed to meet the needs of the city's poor. On the whole, each of these philanthropic groups was organized to meet the needs of a particular problem, such as the shortage of fuel during the winter, or to assist the indigence of a specific group. There was as yet no central relief agency that coordinated the numerous and diverse charitable efforts of the citizens of New York.

In addition, it is important to note that not all of these organizations were founded to alleviate the temporal needs of the poor. According to what one historian has called the "harsh moralism" of the times, spiritual relief and assurance of salvation were as important (at least to the members of the particular organizations) as the comforts of the body.

The A.R.R.A.I.F.

Meanwhile, the distress of the aged did not go unnoticed. On 7 February 1814, after ten months of preliminary efforts in soliciting subscriptions and donations, a group of women founded the Association for the Relief of Respectable, Aged, and Indigent Females (A.R.R.A.I.F.). This was the only philanthropic society during this period that was organized specifically for the care of any segment of the aged poor.

Citing the existence of organizations established to aid dependent groups of almost every description, these women clearly saw themselves as responding to an unmet need. In addition, this manifest interest in assisting aged females may have been accompanied by underlying interests. Many of the members, for example, were approaching old age themselves. As the officers stated in their fifteenth annual address to the members, "the revolution of a few short years may find us the subject of a benevolence similar to that which we are now privileged to excercise toward the pensioners of this Society." This statement in combination with the not infrequent mention of the death of an officer of the society gives the impression that the benevolent activities of the association were, for many of these women, a form of self-preparation for and socialization into old age.

It is also of some significance that many of the early officers of the association had husbands who were active in other benevolent activities. As Carroll Rosenberg, a historian of early philanthropy in New York, notes, "Mrs. Anson Phelps, whose husband had long been a manager of the New York City Tract Society, was a manager of the ARRAIF, as were Mrs. William Vermilye, Mrs. Charles Minturn, (and) Mrs. Theodore Dwight, all wives of prominent male supporters of New York's city mission." There is no mention of these or other husbands actively assisting in the establishment or operation of the association. Nevertheless, the women probably benefited, if only in an informal and indirect manner, from the organizational experience of their husbands.

The organizational format adopted by these women was a common one of the period. It consisted of a first and second directress, a treasurer and secretary, and twelve managers, all of whom were selected by a majority of the members of the society at the annual meetings. The officers of the society formed a visiting committee, "from which a Subcommittee shall be chosen in rotation, whose duty it shall be to visit any indigent female that may apply for relief, not under the age of sixty years, unless strongly recommended by necessitous circumstances, in which the committee shall have discretionary powers."

As the name of the society implies, the subjects of their charitable efforts were to be aged females, over the age of sixty, who were of indigent circumstances, and yet of respectable standing. But what did these women mean by "respectable"? This word seemed to connote a variety of things. It definitely meant that the intemperant were excluded as possible candidates for relief. In fact, a number of aged pensioners were later disassociated from the assistance of the society because of intemperance. It also meant that any female receiving relief had to be "of approved moral character," and it was the duty of the visiting committee, on the basis of interviews with the applicant and neighbors, to ensure the moral standing of all potential pensioners.

But the word *respectable* seemed to stand for much more. It indicated, for these women, a definite connection between the possession of wealth and the moral character of a person. In their own words,

> of all the afflicted family of mankind, these persons seem to be the most interesting objects of bounty, who, having once lived well, and enjoyed the comforts and conveniences of life, are reduced in the course of events which no human foresight could control, to want and misery. *Their sufferings are greater than those of others, because they are contrasted sufferings;* and their feelings are more acute than those of others, because they are more refined.

This is perhaps as close to a straightforward definition of *respectable* as one finds from a reading of the society's annual reports. While it is true that respectable was not simply synonymous with well-to-do, it nevertheless seemed to signify at least a certain degree of material comfort. As such, the continual repetition and reiteration of this word in relation to the society's potential and actual recipients reveals the importance of a degree of prior social standing in determining the ability of an aged and indigent female to receive assistance from this association of women.

It is difficult to know all the factors that caused the indigence of this particular group of aged females. However, the "case histories" of many of the pensioners are related in the annual reports of the association, and a general impression can be gathered as to their circumstances. As might be suspected, their poverty was the result of the death or absence of a relation who had been their sole possible means of support. A son or daughter, for example, may have moved to another city before the infirmities of the pensioner existed. Given the absence of a system of rapid and reliable communication, when hard times came, there was nowhere to turn but to the benevolence of others.

Until 1838, when the society erected an aged asylum, only "outdoor" relief was given to its pensioners. The extent and form of assistance was dependent upon the circumstances and needs of the recipient, and although the majority of pensioners required permanent assistance, there were each year a number of aged females who received only temporary aid. In general, three forms of assistance were dispensed: a monthly cash stipend—the size of which depended on the resources of the association—fuel during inclement periods, and clothing. In addition, the more uncommon needs of some of its pensioners were also met, such as travel expenses to relatives, and the purchase and installment of stoves.

Consistent with the temperament of the period, the women of the association were not only concerned with the material well-being of their pensioners, but their spiritual health as well. Avowedly nonsectarian in religious affiliation, the women nevertheless thought it necessary to write into their constitution that the visiting committee "shall, according to the best of their abilities, and as opportunities may offer, endeavor to impress on the subjects of their benefactions the necessity and importance of religion." Further, when planning the construction of the aged asylum, they did not forget to include an adjoining chapel so, in their words, "no extremity of weather, or ordinary indisposition, will deprive your pensioners of the inestimable privilege of a stated and regular attendance upon the means of grace." Without a doubt, the women of the association found it easier to deal in this area of relief than in the more mundane matters of temporal assistance.

As the demand for the assistance of the association grew, so did its efforts. In 1823, for example, an auxiliary society was formed, the specific objective of which was to provide clothing to the aged pensioners of the parent organization. The association, however, had to compete with the other philanthropic societies in the city for donations and subscriptions, and there was never a year in which the association was free of financial difficulties. These financial concerns, in turn, prompted the members to adopt a number of resolutions that further limited the ability of needy women to receive aid.

In 1814, the founding year of the society, there were 150 aged females on its list of permanent pensioners. The society attempted to sustain roughly this number for the next three years, only to find that they were barely able to balance their budget. A grant of $300 from the municipal government in 1815 only delayed the inevitable. The very next year the officers, at their fourth annual meeting, proposed a resolution to limit the number of pensioners to 125. Noting the great increase in applications for relief, the members reluctantly voted and passed the resolution. Yet another revision of the rules governing applicants came the following year. This time the subject was aged female immigrants. Again, out of financial necessity, the members were forced to eliminate aid to these poor by adopting a three-year residency requirement for all applicants.

Despite these financial troubles, the women of the association were able to continue their relief of a portion of the city's aged poor. In the decades of the 1820s and 1830s, the society established itself as one of New York's permanent philanthropic organizations. Then, in 1838, the association opened the city's first old-age home. This was a turning point not only for the association, but for the care of the indigent aged as well.

Prior to the establishment of the home, the aged pensioners of the society had to provide their own shelter. The society could only assist in the payment of rent. In addition, because of the lack of centralized facilities, the association did not provide medical services. The occurrence of severe disease or mental derangement in one of the pensioners was more than this system of outdoor relief could handle. Thus, these aged women with extreme disabilities were usually removed to the public almshouse, where medical care and supervision was available. All this, the women anticipated, would change with the erection of the aged asylum.

Immigrant Aid Societies, Trade Associations, and Savings Banks

As important as the association was with regard to the history of the maintenance of the aged, it assisted only a small segment of the aged poor. The question now becomes: Where did the other categories of the indigent elderly go for help? Again, we are faced with the somewhat hidden nature of the subject; for, as noted earlier, the aged poor were mentioned and included in almost every fund established to secure some measure of relief for the poor.

The numerous immigrant aid societies of the period may have offered some assistance to the aged of their respective countries. For example, in 1821 The French Benevolent Society supported over one hundred persons who were either aged and infirmed or destitute widows with small children. But, an immigrant aid society was, in general, no wealthier than their native countrymen; for the Irish and the Germans, the two largest immigrant groups in these decades, the support of a charitable organization of any meaningful size was impossible.

There were, in addition, many occupation societies and trade organizations that devoted a portion of their energies to charitable purposes. Throughout the early history of the Marine Society of the City of New York, assistance was given to the widows of deceased members, some of whom were most likely aged. The General Society of Mechanics and Tradesmen and the Firemen's Exempt Society of the City of New York also had pension funds for widows and disabled members. By and large, however, it is doubtful that the majority of these organizations had the funds to support any significant portion of their members in cases other than temporary sickness.

This problem of the lack of provision for the time in life when one is no longer able to work was, nevertheless, receiving some attention. As a solution to the problem, some suggested the establishment of a savings bank. This innovative idea was first seriously proposed and acted on by the Society for the Prevention of Pauperism in its "Report on the Subject of Pauperism," the first comprehensive survey of the problem of poverty by a private group in New York City. Their interest in the establishment of a savings bank did not stem directly from a concern for the indigent aged. However, after the society opened the first savings bank in New York in 1819, others, with a specific eye to old age, followed their example.

Citing the success of the savings bank established by the society, the American Seamen's Friend Society founded a similar institution for all connected with seafaring life in 1829. Before this date, it was the custom of seamen either to hold their earnings themselves or give their savings to the landlord of the boardinghouse where they would stay while in port.

Both of these practices were subject to numerous perils. A night of drunkness, for instance, could make a sailor easy prey for a thief or an extortionist. As an article in the *Sailor's Magazine and Naval Journal* pointed out, "a fund laid up in the savings bank would be a good reliance in old age or sickness. The almshouse, and Hospital are, at best, poor retreats; and a man's own money is a better fund, in time of need, than the good-will of his friends." Nonetheless, there were a number of problems with the actual operation of savings institutions that were yet to be worked out. If, for example, a sailor lost his savings book, he had no recourse or claim to his money. This, in addition to the novelty of the idea, did not appeal to most sailors. Like the notion of retirement, the widespread use of savings banks was still a thing of the future.

The Municipal System of Relief

If an aged and indigent person did not receive assistance from one of the many philanthropic societies, where could he or she turn? The system of relief administered by the municipal government was the only place left.

Since 1736, when the first almshouse was constructed, the city's government had operated a system of indoor and outdoor relief. As the city's population, and in particular its poor population, expanded, the public relief system did also. As one historian remarks, "from the close of the Revolution to after 1825, social-welfare costs constituted the greatest single municipal expenditure year after year, amounting usually to about one-fourth to one-fifth of the city's total budget." Indeed, between 1 April 1821 and 1 April 1822 alone, a total of 3,762 paupers were in or admitted into the public almshouse, with 1,445 of these persons remaining in the house on the latter date. During the same year, the expenditures on the outdoor relief, which always supported more persons than the almshouse, came to $7,738.38.

From early on, the aged poor had been a portion of the paupers receiving public relief. Because the records of outdoor-relief recipients no longer exist, it is impossible to know how many aged benefited in this way. Most likely, there was a good number of indigent elderly who received the donations of food, clothing, firewood, and perhaps even cash, annually. On the other hand, much information can be gathered from the existing records as to the number and care of the aged in the almshouse.

The almshouse during the 1820s and 1830s was located in Bellevue, an area that at the time of its construction in 1816 was still fairly remote from the heart of the city. Actually, it was not just one institution, but an entire complex of institutions. Raymond Mohl, a historian of early social welfare in New York, described it as follows:

Spread over several acres, an eleven-foot wall enclosed the establishment on three sides, while the fourth side opened onto the East River. In addition to the large stone almshouse—the largest structure in the city—the complex of buildings consisted of a workhouse, a penitentiary, two hospitals, and a number of smaller structures, including bakery, icehouse, greenhouse, soap factory, stables, fire station, chapel, and superintendent's residence.

Complementing this large number of buildings was an equally large number of staff members. However, according to an 1800 ordinance outlining the government of the almshouse, the main responsibility for its management lay with five unpaid commissioners and one salaried superintendent. The commissioners were vested with policymaking powers, while it was the task of the superintendent to implement their decisions and to supervise the internal management of the house. Further, the superintendent was instructed to separate the different descriptions of poor into classes: the men from the women, the sick from the healthy, and the virtuous from the depraved. This ordinance, with minor exceptions, was reaffirmed in 1834 when a law was enacted officially creating an Alms House Department.

The virtuous poor—the sick and disabled, the insane, and the aged—were considered to be the primary objects of the poorhouse. As the 1800 ordinance referred to earlier stated: "The design of the institution is to provide for the comfortable maintenance of such paupers as are unable to gain subsistence by labor, and have either legal settlement in the city, or no legal provision for their support." That this theoretical aim was met in practice is confirmed by the commissioners' reports and reviews of the conditions in the institution. Not a single one of these general reports neglects to mention the great number of paupers "bowing under a load of Years and the Infirmities of Old Age."

Much more, however, can be said than simply that there were aged poor in the poorhouse. Two separate reviews of the health of the paupers by the superintendent in the early 1820s show that the aged were quite a large proportion of the almshouse population. One of these reports, dated 26 May 1823, lists 216 elderly men and women, or 16 percent of the total population of 1,376. The proportion of aged becomes even more significant if one takes into account the fact that 525 of the total of 1,376 were children. Thus, considering only the adults, 27 percent (111) of the 405 men and 24 percent (105) of the 446 women were classified by the superintendent as suffering from old age.

The majority of these aged paupers were certainly not the little ladies of respectable standing discussed earlier. In fact, for them the poorhouse was probably a place of horror, much as nursing homes are regarded by some of today's elderly. At least this was the attitude of the officers to the ARRAIF toward the almshouse. A characteristic statement to this effect can be found in their third annual report: "We feel grateful that, through the indulgence of Divine Providence, our efforts have, in some degree, been successful, and have preserved many who once lived respectfully from becoming residents in the ALMS HOUSE."

A demographic analysis of the almshouse admissions records reveals additional information about the poorhouse population in general and the aged subgroup in particular. These records, which were kept on a daily basis, contain the following information for each individual: sex, age, occupation, race, and nativity. Monthly samples—January 1 to February 1 and June 1 to July 1—were taken from the admissions records from the years 1827, 1830, 1835, and 1840. These monthly samples were then compared on the basis of the above demographic characteristics in order to reveal trends in the composition of the poorhouse population during the early nineteenth century. Last, a more intensive analysis was made of the January 1835 sample. By controlling for seasonal fluctuations in the number of persons admitted—winter always brought with it a rise in temporary indigence—it is possible to regard the background characteristics of the persons admitted in January of 1835 as fairly representative of the entire period under study.

The average age of the admissions in January of 1835 (N = 403) was 30 years. This was basically true of both the women, who comprised 40 percent (160) of the 403, and the men, who comprised 60 percent (243) of the 403. This summary measure, however, conceals the fact that almost one-fourth of the total admissions were under the age of 15 (26 percent of the female population and 18 percent of the male population). Furthermore, in light of the superintendent's report discussed earlier, it is of some surprise that the persons who were 51 years of age and over comprised only 11 percent (43) of the admissions. An explanation of these seemingly contradictory figures will be offered later.

An examination of the nativity and occupation of the admissions is important for several reasons. Business and harbor activities were often slowed as a result of the inclemency of winter, financial depression, and the like. As is the case today, these economic fluctuations affected some businesses, and some occupations with certain businesses, more adversely than others. Given the additional fact that some immigrant groups arrived penniless, and then entered at the bottom of the stratification system, one would hypothesize that it was these foreigners who were most affected by economic fluctuations. In turn, one would expect to find that it was these foreigners who were most heavily dependent upon the municipal welfare system.

During the first half of the nineteenth century, especially after 1920, the largest number of immigrants arriving at the port of New York came from Ireland, and the second largest group came from Germany. Because of linguistic and cultural differences, both groups, but especially the Irish, had difficulty in assimilating into American society. The Irish of this period were better off in terms of occupational skills than the massive migration of Irish peasants in the late 1840s. Nevertheless, they, as a group, took jobs at the bottom of the stratification system, as common laborers and the like. These Irish, indeed, were the ones most severely affected by seasonal and economic fluctuations. As the sample of the records indicate, they were approximately 30 percent (122) of the admissions, the largest foreign or native group in the poorhouse. The next largest group were native New Yorkers, 26 percent (102) of the admissions.

More interesting is the fact that 50 percent (51) of the native New York group were children—most likely illegimate, unwanted, or orphaned and thus abandoned—while 78 percent of the Irish group were between the ages of 15 and 50. Even taking into account that 39 percent (47) of the Irish group were women, the majority of whom were widows, this still leaves 48 percent (57) of the Irish who were men of prime employable age. And, as noted earlier, not all of these Irish men were without a trade or some salable skill. Of the 57 Irish men between the ages of 15 and 50, 37 percent (21) were skilled, 44 percent (25) were unskilled, and the remainder were farmers.

As previously mentioned, the elderly—for present purposes defined as persons who were 51 years of age and over—

comprised only 11 percent (43) of the total admissions. On the basis of previous information, one would expect to find both a higher percentage of men and a higher percentage of Irish in this age group. Both expectations are, in fact, substantiated by a closer examination of this group.

There were twice as many aged men than aged women admitted into the poorhouse in the sampled month (29 men, 14 women). This sex ratio held true for all ethnic groups. Why this might be the case can be partially explained by the special status of widows and the fact that there were a number of philanthropic organizations devoted to the assistance of aged women and widows. Further, the largest percentage of these aged men and women came from Ireland (42 percent or 18 of the 43). This is consistent with the overall breakdown of admissions and to be expected, since the Irish were the least able to provide for the nonproductive members of their family.

It will be recalled that the superintendent's report categorized 25 percent (216 of 851) of the adult population in the poorhouse (on or about the day of the report) as suffering from old age. However, even when only the adult population of the admissions in the sample is considered, only 13 percent (43 of 319) might be classified as aged. The discrepancy between the two sources of information indicates that once many of these aged persons entered the almshouse, they stayed until their death. Thus, one would expect that the number of elderly entering at any one time would be less than their actual number in the poorhouse. If this was the case, it may be that the almshouse served, as one of its many functions, as an old-age home for at least a segment of the city's elderly.

Regardless of the length of stay, the caretakers of the almshouse still had to provide for the care of their many aged inmates. The reports of the commissioners contain conflicting statements as to the general treatment of the elderly. On one hand, a report stated, in glowing terms, that the elderly received the best of care. The aged, it notes in the report, spend much of their time reading the Bible. The superintendent checked on them regularly, and "with unfeigned gratitude and respect," he inquired into any unmet need or want, which if expressed was immediately looked after.

Another report, ten years later, reveals what is probably a more accurate picture. "What must be the suffering of the aged poor," reads the report,

> when they discover that they are in the power of those whom they know feel the task that they execute is one of imposition and not of duty and pleasure. And can it be doubted that the very object of humanity which was intended for the benefit of the poor and aged citizens, who once contributed to the support of the city, but who are now unfortunately the recipients of its bounty, is entirely frustrated by the improper employment of such attendants upon the sick? And is it not of great consequence that none should assist except their recommendations be good? If there be any class of citizens who have claims to our compassion and attention, it is the aged and respectable poor. By an inattention to their wants poverty is made a crime; for the idle, the dissolute and vagrant receive the same protection and comfort.

As both of the above reports demonstrate, public officials felt it their duty to provide for the benevolent care of the aged poor. Given the conditions within the institution—overcrowding, the nonprofessionalization of nurses, the difficulty of adequately separating the many classes of paupers—the best care of the elderly could not be assured. This does not imply, however, that their treatment was cruel, or, for that matter, worse than the general lot of paupers in the poorhouse. On the whole, then, it seems that every effort was made to meet the indigence of the aged in a kind manner.

Conclusion

These separate pieces of information, taken as a whole, offer sufficient evidence to support the claims that a substantial proportion of the aged and infirm of New York City were not cared for by their families. Public officials and private citizens recognized the existence of this "social problem"; that is, the fact that many aged persons, for whatever reasons, were in need of assistance. The municipal government responded, as has been seen, by explicitly including the aged as one of the worthy recipients of institutional relief in the city's poorhouse. For their part, private citizens established a number of philanthropic organizations that were either wholly or partially concerned with the welfare of the aged. Thus, it would seem that contemporary sociological assumptions as to the family and the maintenance of the elderly in preindustrial America are in need of revision.

It would be, of course, a mistake to simply replace one set of historically false generalizations with another equally undocumented set of generalizations. In an introductory essay such as this, it is more than enough to set forth the problem and to open the field of the social history of the aged for comparative and developmental research. We need to know, for example, if the New Yorker's response to old-age poverty was typical of nineteenth-century urban America. Additionally, was the care and maintenance of the elderly significantly different in nineteenth-century rural America as compared with nineteenth-century urban America? What, if any, regional differences were there? And, most important, how can a developmental perspective help us to understand the problems of the aged today and the utility of current policies and programs? These are just some of the questions to be answered; questions in which this essay will hopefully stimulate an interest.

References

I Primary Sources

  A *New York City Records*

The New York City Municipal Archives and Record Center contains an invaluable collection of manuscripts for students who are interested in the social-welfare history of New York City. Among the several subcollections in the Center, *The Almshouse Admissions Records* and *The Filed Papers of the City Clerk of New York* are the most important. *The Filed Papers of the City Clerk*, for example, contain the original petitions of the various individuals and organizations cited throughout the essay.

A complete set of the printed minutes, proceedings, and documents of the Common Council of the City of New York and its numerous administrative bodies can be found at the New York Municipal Reference and Research Center. Included in this repository are the Board of Aldermen and Board of Assistant Aldermen *Documents*, which after 12 May 1834 were issued separately; *The Minutes of the Common Council of the City of New York, 1784-1831* (21 vols., 1917); and *The New York State Laws*. The annual reports of the superintendent of the almshouse, printed in the Aldermen *Documents*, are a particularly revealing source of information with regard to the general conditions in the almshouse and the general characteristics of its population.

Of great importance to the history of American social welfare is *A Report on the Settlement and Relief of the Poor*, compiled by John Yates, then the secretary of state of New York. As the first comprehensive review of the New York State welfare system, this report is a cogent statement of the difficulties in the operation of the welfare system, given the eligibility requirements at that time. The report, however, is much more than a review of conditions; it is a major social policy statement that revamped the welfare structure in early nineteenth-century New York. A recent reprint of the Yates Report can be found in a volume of historical essays entitled *The Almshouse Experience* (New York: Arno Press, 1971).

B Associations and Societies

The annual reports of the various associations and societies mentioned in this essay are an interesting and often the only record left by these organizations. Though these reports are to a certain extent self-serving proclamations of the benevolence of these associations, they contain a wealth of information concerning their activities and the recipients of their efforts. In addition, there are numerous statements that if read with an analytical and interpretative eye tell much about contemporary attitudes toward poverty and contemporary distinctions between different categories of the poor. In this respect, the indigent aged were always regarded as belonging to the deserving and virtuous poor and specifically set off from the depraved and undeserving poor.

For a variety of reasons, particular attention was paid to trade and occupational societies. It was of importance to document contemporary attitudes toward work and old age, for example, the absence of any notion of retirement in the modern sense of the term. Nevertheless, secondary sources indicated that some provision for illness and old age was made on the part of trade and occupational societies. Thus, it was necessary to gain at least some impression of the extent of assistance offered by these voluntary associations.

Among the most important reports discussed in this essay are:

American Seamen's Friend Society, *Sailor's Magazine and Naval Journal, 1829-1831*. Copies can be found at Alexander Library, Rutgers University, New Brunswick, New Jersey.

Association for the Relief of Respectable, Aged, and Indigent Females, *Annual Reports 1-30* (New York, 1814-1844). These reports are located at the New York Public Library (hereafter N.Y.P.L.).

Fireman's Exempt Benevolent Fund of the City of New York, *By-Laws, Minutes, and Reports* (1835-1840), NYPL.

General Society of Mechanics and Tradesmen, *Charter and By-Laws* (New York, 1822), NYPL.

Marine Society of the City of New York, *A Memoir of the Society. . . Read at its 107th Annual Dinner* (1925).

New York Association for Improving the Condition of the Poor, *Annual Reports 1-10* (1843-1853). Arno Press has recently issued a reprint of these first ten annual reports.

New York City Mission and Tract Society, *Annual Reports 2-10* (1829-1837), NYPL Annex.

Society for the Prevention of Pauperism in New York City, *Annual Reports 1,2,4-6* (1818-1823), NYPL.

II Secondary Sources

A *The Aged and the Family*

The only works that address themselves directly to the care of the elderly in early America in any sort of empirical manner are Eugene Friedmann's "The Impact of Aging on the Social Structure," in *The Handbook of Social Gerontology*, edited by Clark Tibbitts (Chicago, 1960), and Ethel McClure's *More Than a Roof: The Development of Minnesota Poor Farms and Homes for the Aged* (St. Paul, 1968). For other works related to the aged in preindustrial societies, see Leo W. Simmons, "Aging in Preindustrial Societies," in *The Handbook of Social Gerontology*, edited by Clark Tibbitts (Chicago, 1960), and George Rosen's *Madness in Society*, especially chapter eight on "The Psychopathology of Aging: Cross-Cultural and Historical Approaches" (New York, 1968).

Social historians of the family in preindustrial times have generally not been concerned with the aged and their relationship to the family structure. However, the works of Peter Laslett, *The World We Lost* (London, 1969), and *Household and Family in Past Time* (London, 1972), do offer some insight into the size and composition of preindustrial families and thus in an indirect manner the situation of some segments of the aged. Also see Philip J. Greven, Jr., *Four Generations: Population, Land, and Family in Colonial Andover, Massachusetts* (Ithaca, New York, 1970).

The literature in the areas of social gerontology and the sociology of the aged is vast. For the purposes of this essay, this body of material can be roughly divided into two categories: those works that make the assumption that the elderly in preindustrial societies were typically cared for by members of their extended families and were thus integrated into the most important structures of society, and those works that recognize that in many preindustrial societies there were a significant number of elderly who, for whatever reasons, were dependent upon the goodwill of society. Furthermore, it seems to me that the current debate in social gerontology over disengagement and engagement theories to some extent revolves around the premise that the majority of the aged in some vaguely defined earlier period of modern society were "integrated" in a systematic sense.

Examples of the first type of interpretation can be found in Talcott Parsons, *Essays in Sociological Theory* (New York, 1954), and Erdman Palmore, "Sociological Aspects of Aging," in *Behavior and Adaptation in Later Life,* edited by Ewald W. Busse and Eric Pfeiffer (Boston, 1969). For the second type of interpretation, see Ethel Shanas, et al., *Old People in Three Industrial Societies* (New York, 1968). On the current debate in social gerontology, over engagement and disengagement theories, see Elaine Cumming and William Henry, *Growing Old: The Process of Disengagement* (New York, 1961); Irving Rosow, *The Social Integration of the Aged* (New York, 1967); and G.L. Maddox, "Disengagement Theory: A Critical Evaluation," in *The Gerontologist* 4: 80-83.

B Philanthropy and Social Welfare

By far the most authoritative work on the English background of modern philanthropy is W. K. Jordan's *Philanthropy in England, 1480-1660* (London, 1959). For the history of American philanthropy, see both of Robert Bremner's books: *American Philanthropy* (Chicago, 1960), and *From the Depths* (New York, 1956). The best source concerning philanthropy and philanthropic organizations in the early nineteenth-century New York City is Raymond Mohl's *Poverty in New York, 1783-1825* (New York, 1971). See also Carroll Rosenberg, *Religion and the Rise of the American City* (Ithaca, New York, 1971); David M. Schneider, *The History of Public Welfare in New York, 1609-1866* (Chicago, 1938); Martha Branscombe, *The Courts and the Poor Laws in New York State, 1784-1929* (Chicago, 1943); the Rev. J. F. Richmond, *New York and Its Institutions, 1609-1873* (New York, 1903); and Roy Lubove, "The New York Association For Improving The Condition of the Poor: The Formative Years," in *New York Historical Society Quarterly* 43 (1959): 307-327.

C New York City History

On the commercial and industrial development of the city, see Robert G. Albion, *The Rise of New York Port, 1815-1860* (New York,

1929); Robert Ernst, *Immigrant Life in New York City, 1825-1863* (Port Washington, New York, 1949); and Carroll Rosenberg, *Religion and the Rise of the American City* (Ithaca, New York, 1971). For population growth during the first half of the nineteenth century, see David T. Gilchrist, ed., *The Growth of Seaport Cities, 1790-1825* (Charlottesville, Virginia, 1967), and Kate H. Claghorn, "The Foreign Immigrant in New York City," in *The United States Industrial Commission Reports* (Washington, D.C., 1901). Many of the above sources are excellent social histories of the period as well.

General discussion of the urban problems of early nineteenth-century New York City can be found in Raymond Mohl's *Poverty in New York, 1783-1825* (New York, 1971), and Carroll Rosenberg's *Religion and the Rise of the American City* (Ithaca, New York, 1971). On the cholera epidemic of 1832, see Charles Rosenberg, *The Cholera Years* (Chicago, 1962). For the history of the two major depressions of the period, see Samuel Rezneck's two articles: "The Depression of 1819-1822, A Social History," in *The American Historical Review* 39 (1933): 28-47, and "The Social History of an American Depression, 1837-1843," in *The American Historical Review* 40 (1934-1935): 662-87. On social stratification in New York City during the first half of the nineteenth century, see Robert Ernst, *Immigrant Life in New York City, 1825-1863*, referred to above, and Douglas T. Miller's article, "Immigration and Social Stratification in Pre-Civil War New York," in *New York History* 49 (1968): 157-68.

5

Una Anciana *

Robert C. Coles

The man I shall call Domingo García is eighty-three years old.
Once, he was measured as exactly six feet tall, but that was
half a century ago. He is sure that he has lost an inch or two.
Sometimes, when his wife, Dolores, grows impatient with his
slouch and tells him to straighten up, he goes her suggestion
one better and tilts himself backward. "Now are you happy?"
he seems to be asking her, and she smiles indulgently. His wife
is also eighty-three. She always defers to her husband. She
will not speak until he has his say. As the two of them
approach a closed door, she makes a quick motion toward it,
opens it, and stands holding it, and sometimes, if he is
distracted by a conversation and is slow to move through, one
of her hands reaches for his elbow while the other points. "Go
now," is the unstated message, "so that I can follow."

They were born within a mile and within two months of
one another, in Cordova, New Mexico, in the northcentral part
of the state. They are old Americans by virtue not only of age

*This work originally appeared in The New Yorker, "Profiles," 5
November 1973; reprinted by permission of The New Yorker
Magazine, Inc., © 1973.

but of ancestry. For many generations, their ancestors have lived in territory that is now part of the United States. Before the Declaration of Independence was written, there were people not far away from Cordova named García and living, as they do, off the land. Domingo and Dolores García are not, however, model citizens of their country. They have never voted, and no doubt the men who framed the Declaration of Independence would not be happy to see the boredom or indifference that these New Mexicans demonstrate when the subject of politics comes up. They don't even make an effort to keep abreast of the news, though they do have a television set in their small adobe house. When Walter Cronkite or John Chancellor appears, neither of the Garcías listens very hard. For that matter, no programs engage their undivided attention, and at first one is inclined to think them partly deaf. But the explanation is taste, not the effects of age. Mrs. García does like to watch some afternoon serials, but without the sound. She takes an interest in how the people dress and what the furniture in the homes looks like. The actors and actresses are company of sorts when Mr. García is outside tending their crops or looking after their horses and cows. Language is not a problem; both Garcías prefer to speak Spanish, but they can make themselves understood quite well in English. They have had to, as Mrs. García explains in English and with no effort to conceal her long-standing sense of resignation: "You bend with the wind. And Anglo people are a strong wind. They want their own way; they can be like a tornado, out to pass over everyone as they go somewhere. I don't mean to talk out of turn. There are Anglos who don't fit my words. But we are outsiders in a land that is ours. We are part of an Anglo country, and that will not change. I had to teach the facts of life to my four sons, and, doing so, I learned my own lesson well."

She stops and looks at their pictures, on top of the television set. That is one function of the set, which was given to her and her husband by their oldest son. Like his father, he is named Domingo, but, unlike his father, he attended—though he did not finish—high school, in Española, on good days a ride of twenty minutes or so by car. Now he lives in Los Alamos.

"I am a mother. You will forgive me if I am proud; sometimes I know I have been boastful, and I tell the confessor my sin. Domingo was a smart child. He walked quickly. He talked very well from the start. He did good work in school. We would take a walk, and he would point something out to me; often. I had never noticed it before. Before he'd entered school, he told me he wanted to become a priest. I asked him why. He said because he'd like to know all the secrets of God. It was my fault, of course. He would ask me questions— those endless whys all children ask, I later learned, after I had my second and third and fourth sons—and I would be puzzled, and not know what to answer. So I would say the same thing my mother used to say to us: 'That is one of God's secrets.' She died when she was ninety, and well before that my little Domingo had asked her when she would die. He had spoken out of turn, and I lowered my head in shame—as I was taught to do when I was a girl, as I brought up my children to do, as, thank God, my grandchildren now do. But my mother smiled, and said, 'That is one of God's secrets.' After that, I think, I started to copy her words with my boy Domingo—though memory becomes moldy after a while and falls into pieces."

"I am taking you through side streets. I am sorry. Maybe we never know our own confusion; maybe it takes another to help us see what we have come to. I wanted to tell you about Domingo's teachers. They were Anglos. Today, some of our own people teach in the schools, but not many. Domingo was called brilliant by his teachers. They called me in. They said he was the only child in his class who was bright and who belonged, really belonged, in school. They made me listen to their trials. I was young then, and obedient. I listened. Maybe now I would ask them please to excuse me, but I have to go home—the bread I have to make, you know, before supper. But my husband says no, even this very year we would still stay and nod our heads. Can you dare turn away from your child's teachers, just to satisfy your own anger? Our Spanish-speaking young people, our college students, say yes; but they live far away, under different conditions, not these here."

"The teachers never mentioned college to me. They weren't that hopeful about Domingo. I don't think they even thought about a person like us going to college. He just might be worthy of high school, I was told. They had never before said that about one of our children, I was told. He is an exceptional boy, I was told. How did it come about, I was asked. Well, of course, I smiled and said I didn't know. They asked about Domingo's father: Was he smarter than the others? I said no, none of us are 'smart'—just trying to get by from day to day, and it's a struggle. That was a bad time— 1930 and the years right after it. Weeks would go by and we would see no money. (We still see little.) And I had already lost four little children; the last two were born in good health, but they died of pneumonia—one at age two, one at age three. You can put yourself in my shoes, I hope. Then, if you will just carry yourself back in time and imagine how hard it was for us, and how little we knew, you will see that I had no way of answering those teachers. On the way home, I asked myself, Is young Domingo 'smart'? Is his father 'smart'? I was afraid to ask his father that evening. He was so tired, so fearful we'd lose even the land under us. He said he'd die and kill us, the child and me, before we went to a city and became lost. When I heard him speaking like that, I forgot the teachers and their questions. I served him my bread, and he felt better. Reassured—that is the word."

She stops and serves bread. She pours coffee. It is best black, she says in a matter-of-fact way; the visitor will not be judged for his weak stomach or poor taste. She again apologizes for her failure to tell a brief, pointed, coherent story. Perhaps she should be asked a question or two right now, she says. Her mother was "sunny," was "very sunny," until the end, but she worries about "clouds" over her own thinking. The two Domingos in her life scoff at the idea, though. After the coffee, she wants to go on. She likens herself to a weathered old tree within sight outside the house. It is autumn, and the tree is bare. She likens the coffee to a God-given miracle: suddenly one feels as if spring had come, one is budding and ready to go through another round of things. But she is definitely short of breath, coffee or no coffee, and needs no one to point it out. "Tomorrow, then."

In the morning, Dolores García is usually far stronger, and quicker to speak out, than later in the day. "Every day is like a lifetime," she says, and immediately disavows owner-ship of the thought. Her husband has said that for years, and, to be honest, she has upon occasion taken issue with him. Some days start out bad, and only in the afternoon does she feel in reasonably good spirits. But she does get up at five

every morning, and most often she is at her best when the first
light appears. Her visitor arrives at around nine o'clock. By
then, he is convinced, she has done enough to feel a little tired
and somewhat nostalgic. "Each day for me is a gift. My
mother taught us to take nothing for granted. We would
complain, or beg, as children do before they fall asleep, and
she would remind us that if we were *really* lucky we would
have a gift presented to us in the morning: a whole new day to
spend and try to do something with. I suppose we should ask
for more than that, but it's too late for me to do so. I prefer to
sit here on my chair with my eyes on the mountains. I prefer to
think about how the animals are doing; many of them have put
themselves to sleep until spring. God has given them senses,
and they use them. Things are not so clear for us. So
many pushes and pulls, so many voices—I know what Babel
means. I go in town shopping, and there is so much
argument—everyone has an opinion on something. The only
time some people lower their heads these days is on Sunday
morning, for an hour, and even then they are turning around
and paying attention to others. What is she wearing? How is
he doing with his business? Do we any longer care what the
Lord wants us to know and do?"

"I am sorry. I am like a sheep who disobeys and has to be
given a prod. I don't lose my thoughts when they're crossing
my mind; it's when they have to come out as words that I find
trouble. We should be careful with our thoughts, as we are
with our water. When I'm up and making breakfast, I watch
for changes in the light. Long before the sun appears, it has
forewarned us. Nearer and nearer it comes, but not so
gradually that you don't notice. It's like one electric light
going on after another. First there is dark. Then the dark lifts
ever so little. Still, it might be a full moon and midnight. Then
the night is cut up. It becomes a sliver of what it was, and
Domingo will sometimes stop for a minute and say, 'Dolores,
she is gone, but do not worry. She will be back.' He has
memories like mine: his mother lived to be eighty-seven, and all
her life she spoke like mine. 'Domingo, be glad,' she would tell
him. Why should he be glad? His mother knew: 'God has
chosen you for a trial here, so acquit yourself well every day,
and never mind about yesterday or tomorrow.' We both forget
her words, though. As the sun comes out of hiding and there is

no longer any question that the dark will go away, we thank dear God for his generosity, but we think back sometimes. We can't seem to help ourselves. We hold on and try to keep in mind the chores that await us, but we are tempted, and soon we will be slipping. There is a pole in our fire station. Once the men are on it, there is no stopping. We land with a crash, like them, on those sad moments. We feel sorry for ourselves. We wish life had treated us more kindly. I wonder what would happen to us if we did not have a job to do. We might never come back to this year of 1973. We would be the captives of bad memories. But no worry—we are part of this world here. The sun gets stronger and burns our consciences; the animals make themselves known; on a rainy day the noise of the water coming down the side of the house calls to me—why am I not moving, too?"

She actually does move rather quickly—so quickly that she seems almost ashamed when someone takes notice of her quickness, even if silently. When in her seat, she folds her arms, then unfolds them and puts her hands on her lap, her left hand over her right hand. Intermittently, she breaks her position to reach her coffee cup and her bread. "Domingo and I have been having this same breakfast for over fifty years. We are soon to be married fifty-five years, God willing. We were married a month after the Great War ended—it was a week before Christmas, 1918. The priest said he hoped our children would always have enough food and never fight in a war. I haven't had a great variety of food to give my family, but they have not minded. I used to serve the children eggs in the morning, but Domingo and I have stayed with hot bread and coffee. My fingers would die if they didn't have the dough to work over. I will never give up my old oven for a new one. It has been here forty years and is an old friend. I would stop baking bread if she gave out. My sons once offered to buy me an electric range—they called it—and I broke down. It was a terrible thing to do. The boys felt bad. My husband said I should be more considerate. I meant no harm, though. I didn't deliberately say to myself, Dolores García, you have been hurt, so now go and cry. The tears came, and I was helpless before them. Later, my husband said they all agreed I was in the right: the stove has been so good to us, and there is nothing wrong—the bread is as tasty as ever, I believe. It is a sickness,

you know—being always dissatisfied with what you have, and
eager for a change."

She stops there and looks lovingly around the room. She
says she is attached to every piece of furniture. Her husband
made it all: a round table, eight chairs, with four more in their
bedroom, the beds there, the bureau there. She begins to tell
how good Domingo is at carving wood. "That is what I would
like to say about Domingo: he plants, builds, and harvests; he
tries to keep us alive and comfortable with his hands. We sit on
what he has made, eat what he has grown, sleep on what he
has put together. We have never had a spring on our bed, but,
I have to admit, we bought our mattress. Buying—that is the
sickness. I have gone to the city and watched people. They are
hungry, but nothing satisfies their hunger. They come to stores
like flies to flypaper: they are caught. I often wonder who is
better off. The fly dies. The people have to pay to get out of the
store, but soon they are back again, the same look in their
eyes. I don't ask people to live on farms and make chairs and
tables, but when I see them buying things they don't need, or
even want—except to make a purchase, to get something—
then I say there is a sickness. I talked to the priest about this.
He said yes, he knows. But then he shrugged. I knew what he
was thinking: the Devil is everywhere, and not until Judgment
Day will we be free of him. I watch my son Domingo and his son
Domingo. They both have plans: next year, we buy this; the
year after, that. Such plans are sad to hear. I try to tell them,
but they do not listen. Those are the moments when I feel old—
the only time I do. I turn to the priest. He says I am sinning—
my pride makes me think I can disagree with the way the whole
country works. I reply, 'No, Father, just what I hear my own
son and grandson saying.' Hasn't a mother got the right to tell
her own flesh and blood that they are becoming slaves—that is
it, slaves of habits and desires that have nothing to do with
living a good life?"

She sighs, and stops talking. She breaks her bread up into
small pieces and eats them one by one. She stirs her coffee
with a stick her husband made expressly for the purpose; it is
about six inches long, smoothed out and painted green. He
jokes with her: one day she will decide to add milk to her
coffee, because her stomach will demand it, and she will
comply; then she will really need that stick. But she has never

used milk. Eventually, she puts the stick down and resumes talking. "I am not a priest. I read the Bible, go to church, make my confession, and know I will soon need to come back to tell more. But a good life is a life that is obedient to God's rules, and a life that is your own, not someone else's. God, and God alone, owns us; it is not right that others own us. There are many kinds of slavery. My children would come home from school and tell me that they were glad they were not colored, because colored people once were slaves. 'Watch out,' I'd say. Their father would agree—you can become a slave without even knowing it. You can be white and have money but not own your soul. I remember years ago I took the children to town; they were young and they wanted to see Santa Claus. He would come once, and only once—and it turned out we had missed him. Next year, I told the boys. They pouted. They besought me. They wanted me to take them somewhere, anywhere, as long as they could catch sight of Santa Claus. I held my ground. They would not stop. I said 'No is no.' They said, 'Please.' Finally, I had to go after them. I talked as if I were giving a sermon in church. Maybe I ought not to have spent so much of their time and mine, but I had to tell them, once and for all, that we have our land, and we feed ourselves and live the best lives we know how to, and we must never feel empty and worthless because of a Santa Claus, or because a salesman has beckoned us and we have said, 'No, I haven't the money.' "

"Later, I wondered whether I'd done the right thing. I told my husband that Santa Claus is different. Children love him, and why not try very hard to take them to see him? He thought for a while. When he thinks, he takes up his pipe and uses it more than he usually does. With each puff, I say to myself. There goes one of his thoughts—and I wonder when he'll share them with me. Soon he does, though. It never fails; he puts his pipe down, and then I know I'm to get ready and pay attention. I sit down, and soon I hear. He always starts with, 'My wife, let me tell you what I think.' Soon I know what he thinks, because he's not one to hide behind pretty phrases. As for Santa Claus, Domingo told me what he thought of him: very little. I will never forget his words. He said that Santa Claus has been captured by the storekeepers. He said that they have him locked up, and he will never be free until we

stop turning Christmas into a carnival, a time when people
become drunk on their greed and take to the stores in order to
indulge themselves. Of course, the priest lectures us in the
same way. And I know we all can be greedy. I eat too much of
my bread—more than I need. I shouldn't. Sometimes I punish
myself: the oven is empty for a day or two—once, for a week,
after a holiday. That time, Domingo couldn't stand it any
longer. 'I am starving,' he told me—even though I made him
cereal and eggs instead. But bread for him is life, and I never
stopped so long again. I had made a mistake. A nun said to me,
'Punishment for a sin can be a sin.' If you are proud of yourself for doing penance, you are defeated before you start.''

She stops to open the window and summon her husband.
Maybe he should say exactly what he told his boys a long time
ago about Santa Claus. But no, it is hopeless—he will not come
in until he has finished his work. He is like a clock—so many
minutes to do one thing, then another. The cows know the
difference between him and anyone else. He is quick. They get
fast relief. When one of her sons tries to help, or she does, or a
grandchild, it is no good. The animals are restless, make a lot
of noise, and Domingo pleads: Leave him his few jobs; then,
when he goes, sell the animals. As for Santa Claus, forgotten
for a moment, the gist of Domingo's speech is given by his wife:
"My children, a saint is in chains, locked up somewhere, while
all these stores have their impostors. Will you contribute to a
saint's suffering? Santa Claus was meant to bring good news:
the Lord's birthday is in the morning, so let us all celebrate by
showing each other how much love we feel. Instead, we say, I
want, I want, I want. We say, More, more, more. We say, Get
this, then the next thing, and then the next. We lose our heads.
We lose our souls. And somewhere that saint must be in hiding
—maybe in jail, for all we know. If not, he is suffering. I tell
you this not to make you feel bad. It is no one's fault. We are all
to blame. Only, let us stop. If we stop, others will not, I know.
But that will be their sorrow, not ours to share with them.''

She is not ready to guarantee every word as his. He is a
man of few words, and she readily admits that she tends to
carry on. Then, as if to confess what is not a sin, and so is not
meant for a priest, yet bothers her, she goes further and
admits to talking out loud when no one is around. She is sure
her husband doesn't do so, and she envies him his quiet self-

assurance, his somewhat impassive temperament. "He is
silent not because he has nothing to say. He is silent because
he understands the world, and because he knows enough to
say to himself, What will words and more words do to make
the world any better? I have wished for years that I could be
like him, but God makes each of us different. When our son
Domingo went to school, they began teaching him English. We
had learned English ourselves, enough to speak. But we didn't
speak it—only Spanish. When Domingo started learning
English, we decided to speak it more and more at home. The
same with the other boys. Often, I would rehearse my English
by myself. I would learn words and expressions from the priest
and from the mayor of the town. He was a cousin, and was
always doing business with Anglos. I learned to talk to myself
in English—to my husband in Spanish but to myself in English.
Once, my husband overheard me, and he thought I was
delirious. He asked if I had a fever. I said no, none at all. He
said I sounded as if I did. I said I was learning to speak English.
He said he could speak English, but not to himself. Then he
laughed, and said, 'Dolores, you have spoken Spanish to
yourself, too. I have heard you.' Since then, I have been more
careful, and I don't believe my husband knows that I still have
the habit. I do not talk to teach myself English, though. I talk
because my mind fills up with words and then they spill out.
Sometimes I talk with someone I imagine nearby. Sometimes I
talk to myself. Sometimes it is in Spanish, sometimes in
English."

After all the talk of talk, she has nothing more to say. She
has to clean the house. She has to start a soup. She always has
soup. As one pot begins to empty, she starts another going. It
contains bones and vegetables. Soup—that is all it is called.
Then she has to sew. There are clothes to mend, clothes to
make. Her eyes aren't what they used to be, but with glasses
she can see well enough. And, finally, the radio. She prefers
the radio to television. She listens to music. She listens to the
weather forecast and either nods or scoffs. Her sons hear the
forecasts and actually believe what they hear. She knows
better. She decides early in the morning what the weather will
be like, and only wants to know how good those weathermen
are, with their instruments and their reports from God knows
what cities far off. She feels sorry for them: they have a lot to

learn. She hopes that one day they will go outside and look at
the sky rather than take their readings. It is one more bit of
foolishness we have to live with now. "Years ago, there were
not these weather reports all the time. We would go out and
size up the morning. We could tell. We felt the moisture before
it turned to rain. If we had any questions, we prayed, and then
more often than not we found an answer. I don't believe it
was God's either. The priest long ago warned us not to ask Him
for favors, and not to expect His answers for the small favors
we want. He is up there; we are down here. Once we are born,
it is up to us. We pray to show our faith. If we have faith, we
can do what is necessary. Not everything was good in the old
days: we used to ask God's help all the time and be
disappointed. My mother would pray that her bread might
come out good. I would pray for rain. I think we have stopped
that, Domingo and I."

Now it is time to rest. Several times each day, she and her
husband do so. It is up to her to call him, and she does it in
such a way that he knows why. In a matter-of-fact way, she
speaks his name, and slowly he comes in. It is ten o'clock when
they rest first. They lie down for five or ten minutes only, but
that does miracles for them. They get up refreshed not only in
body but in mind and, evidently, soul. "I pray. I thank God for
the time He has given me here, and ask Him to take me when
He is ready, and I will tell Him I will have no regrets. I think of
all I have seen in this long life—the people, the changes. Even
up here, in this small village, the world makes its presence felt.
I remember when the skies had no planes in them, houses no
wires sticking up trying to catch television programs. I never
wanted a refrigerator. I never needed one. But I have one. It is
mostly empty. I have one weakness—ice cream. I make it, just as I
make butter. I used to make small amounts, and Domingo and I
would finish what was there. Now I can make and store up
butter and ice cream and give presents of them to my sons and
their children. No wonder they bought us the refrigerator! As I
lie on our bed and stare at the ceiling, I think how wonderful it
is—eighty-three, and still able to make ice cream. We need a
long rest afterward, but between the two of us we can do
a good job. The man at the store has offered to sell any extra
ice cream we have; he says he can get a good price. I laugh. I
tell him he's going to turn me into a thief. It would be dishonest

to sell food you make in your home for profit at a store. That's
the way I feel. My husband gets angry: "What do you mean,
"dishonest"?' he will say. I answer back: My idea of what is
dishonest is not his. So we cannot go on about this. It is in my
heart where the feeling is, not in my head. 'Oh, you are a
woman!' he answers, and he starts laughing. Later, he will tell
me that he was picking weeds, or taking care of our flowers,
and he thought to himself, She is right, because to make food is
part of our life as a family, and to start selling—that is to say
that we have nothing that is ours. It is what he always comes
back to: Better to have less money and feel we own ourselves
than more and feel at the mercy of so many strangers."

The two Garcías show a burst of energy after they get up.
As they have rested, said their prayers, reminisced, they have
also given thought to what they will do next, and so when they
are ready they set out decisively. They know that they have
limited time, know that soon they will have to interrupt their
working rhythm for lunch and another rest afterward. "I am a
new person several times a day," she points out, then adds,
right away, "But I can suddenly get quite tired." She feels
"weakness" and "a loss of breath" come on—her way of
describing the effects of a cardiovascular difficulty common to
people in their eighties. Yet she sees no doctor—hasn't seen
one in decades. "There are no doctors near here. I would have
to go to Española. I would if there was a need. I have pains all
over. It is arthritis, I know. One can't expect joints to hold up
forever. I do not believe in aspirin. I do not believe in
medicines. I have to pant like our dog when I move too fast for
too long. I have to stop and catch up. It is the lungs and the
heart, I know. My son wants me to go get a checkup. My ankles
swell at the end of a day, but the next morning they are down
again. The body has its seasons. I am in the last one; winter is
never without pain and breakdowns. I don't want to spend my
last years waiting on myself and worrying about myself. I have
already lived over twice as long as our Saviour. How greedy
ought one to be for life? God has His purposes. I wake up and
feel those aches and I notice how wrinkled my skin is, and I
wonder what I'm doing still alive. I believe it is wrong to ask a
question like that. One lives; one dies. To ask questions with no
good answers to them is to waste time that belongs to others. I
am here to care for my husband, to care for this house, to be

here when my sons and my grandchildren come. The young have to see what is ahead. They have to know that there is youth and middle age and old age. My grandson Domingo asked me a while ago what it is like to be one hundred. He is ten. I told him to be one hundred is to live ten of his lifetimes. He seemed puzzled, so I knew I had been thoughtless. I put my arms around him. I put my hand beside his and we compared skins. I said it is good to be young and it is good to be old. He didn't need any more explanations. He said that when you're young you have a lot of years before you but when you're old you have your children and your grandchildren and you love them and you're proud of them. I put my arms around him again and hugged him tight, and in a second he was out there with his father and his grandfather looking at the cows."

She doesn't spend much time with the cows, but the chickens are hers to feed and look after. She cleans up their fenced-in enclosure, and delights in their eggs. She and her husband have one hard-boiled egg each for lunch every day. She gives her sons eggs regularly; a nephew and a niece also get some. She feeds the chickens leftovers and, in addition, some of her fresh bread. She is convinced that they lay better eggs because of her bread. One day, for the sake of a visitor, she borrowed a store-bought egg and compared it with one of hers: each was dropped in hot water for poaching, and hers did indeed stay much more nearly intact and prove to be tastier. "Animals today are turned into machines," she remarked after the experiment. She shook her head. She tried not to be gloomy, but she was worried. "No one my age has the right to demand that the world stand still. So much was wrong in the past that is better now. I didn't want this refrigerator, but it is good to have, now that I'm used to it. My grandchildren have had narrow misses with death, but doctors have saved them. I still mourn the children I lost. Even if I'd been rich back then, I might have lost them. Now there are medicines to kill the bad germs. But to see chickens or cows being kept in one place and stuffed with food that isn't really food—chemicals, Domingo says they are fed—so they will grow fat all of a sudden and have their eggs or become fit for slaughter: that is unnatural. I ask myself, Did God form the beasts of the field and the fowls of the air so that they should be treated this way by man? I asked the priest once, and he scratched his head and said he would have to think about it. The next time I saw him, I looked at him hard and he remembered my question. 'Mrs. García, you don't make it easy for me,' he said. I smiled, and said I didn't want to cause any trouble but I couldn't help thinking about some of these things. He answered, 'I don't know what to day.' Then I decided I'd best not trouble him any more. He once told me that a priest knows only what Christ promised us; he He will bring about His promises—that's not for man to know. I thought afterward I ought to confess to him my boldness—the sin of pride. Who am I to decide they have no right to run those chicken farms? But, God forgive me, I still believe it is wrong. I still believe animals ought not to be turned into machines."

She arranges the eggs she brings in very carefully; she takes them out of her basket and puts them in a bowl. Some are brown, some white. She likes to fix them up like flowers, have them give a freckled appearance from afar. As she uses some, she rearranges those left. She handles them not only with care but with affection. Sometimes, as she talks and does her work with the eggs, she will hold a warm one in her hand. "I feel comforted by a fresh egg. It is sad to feel it get colder, but that is life. My granddaughter loves to help me collect eggs. The other day, she asked me if the eggs inside a woman are the same kind as those that come out of a chicken. I was taken aback. I told her I didn't think so. Then I wondered what else to say. My husband said later there isn't anything more to say. I felt I'd failed the little girl, though. I had changed the subject on her before she knew what had happened. A few minutes later, I could tell that her mind was back with the eggs and she wanted to ask me more questions. But I wouldn't let her. I didn't tell her no—at least, not directly. I just kept up my line of chatter. The poor girl, she was overcome by her grandmother's words—and by her own shyness. This time, I didn't go to the priest later and ask him what I should have said. I have never talked to him about such matters. When one is young, they are too personal, and, besides, what is there to ask, and what is there to say? Also, a priest is entitled to respect: he is not living a worldly life, and there is much he doesn't know. I think our new priest is like a youth, even if he is fifty; I mean, he has never tasted of life. That is what a priest is about, of course; his passions go up toward the altar,

and then to Heaven. So I sat and thought about how to talk
with my granddaughter the next time. I hope I can do her some
justice. Time will tell. One never knows what to say except
when the moment is at hand."

She stops abruptly, as if this were one conversation she
didn't want to pursue. Anyway, she has been dusting and
sweeping the floor as she talked, and now she is finished. Next
come the plants, a dozen or so of them; they need to be
watered, and moved in or out of the sun. She hovers over them
for a minute, doing nothing, simply looking. She dusts them,
too. She prunes one. "I've been waiting for a week or so to
do this. I though to myself, That plant won't like it, losing so
much. I dread cutting my toenails and fingernails. I am shaky
with scissors. But I go after the plants with a surer touch. They
are so helpless, yet they are so good to look at. They seem to
live forever. Parts die, but new parts grow. I have had them so
long—I don't remember the number of years. I know each
one's needs, and I try to take care of them at the same time
each day. Maybe it is unnecessary nonsense, the amount of
attention I give. I know that is what Domingo would say. Only
once did he put his belief into words, and then I reminded him
that he has his habits, too. No one can keep him from starting
in one corner of his garden and working his way to the other,
and with such care. I asked him years ago why not change
around every once in a while and begin on the farthest side,
and go faster. 'I couldn't do it,' he said, and I told him I
understood. Habits are not crutches; habits are roads we have
paved for ourselves. When we are old, and if we have done a
good job, the roads last and make the remaining time useful:
we get where we want to go, and without the delays we used to
have when we were young. How many plants died on me when
I was first learning! How often I forgot to water them, or
watered them too much because I wanted to do right! Or I
would expose them to the sun and forget that, like us, they
need the shade, too. I was treating them as if they needed a
dose of this, a trial of that. But they have been removed from
God's forests, from nature, and they need consideration.
When we were young, my husband also used to forget chores;
he'd be busy doing one thing and he'd overlook another. But
slowly we built up our habits, and now I guess we are
protected from another kind of forgetfulness. The head tires

easily when you are our age, and without the habits of the years you can find yourself at a loss to answer the question: What next?"

She turns to lunch. She stirs the soup. She warms up the bread. She reaches for the eggs. She sets a simple, careful table, a large spoon and a knife for her, her husband, and their guest. Each gets a napkin from a set given her half a century ago by her mother and used on Sundays, holidays, special occasions. She is apologetic. "I fear we often look at these napkins but don't use them. No wonder they survive so well! They remind us to behave ourselves, because it is no ordinary day, and so we eat more carefully and don't have to use them. They are usually in the same condition when I put them away as when I took them out. My grandmother made them, gave them to my mother, and now I have them. My three daughters died as infants; I will give the napkins to my eldest son's wife. I tried to do so when they were married, but she said no. I insisted, and only got more refusals. If she had been my daughter, she would have accepted. But I was not hurt. It takes time to move over from one family and be part of another. She would accept the napkins now, but they would become frightened if I suddenly offered them. 'Is she sick? Does she know something we don't know? How have we neglected her, that she offers us what she loves to put on her own table?' So I will have them until the end, when all possessions obtain new masters."

She has to go outside. It is cold and windy but sunny. There is some fresh milk there in a pail—from cows that, she hastens to add, present no danger of sickness to a visitor who up until that moment has taken for granted the word *pasteurized* that appears on every milk bottle or carton. And she has herself and her husband as proof—a touch of reassurance that she obviously enjoys being able to offer. "My sons' wives sometimes hesitate, too. I can see on their faces what they think. They deny it, but I know: Is it safe to drink milk right from the cow? They are from the city, and they have no way of understanding that many cows are quite healthy and their owners know when they are sick. Anyway, Domingo and I survived without store milk, and we are not young, and not so sick we can't work or eat—or drink milk."

She wraps herself in a sweater she has made and, upon
opening the door, quickly turns back for a moment: "Oh, the
wind," But she persists, and is gone. When she is back, she
resumes where she has left off. "The wind can be a friend or
an enemy. A severe wind reminds us of our failures—something we forgot to fasten down. A gentle wind is company. I
have to admit I can spend a long time listening to the wind go
through trees, watching it sweep across the grass. Domingo
will come in and say, 'Oh, Dolores, come out and watch the
wind go through the grass.' I hurry out. I often wonder if the
ground feels it—like hair being combed and brushed. I walk
with our dog, and he gets scents from far off, carried by the
wind. I tell him not to be tricked. Better to let things quiet
down, then take another scent. He is over ten and should not
run long distances. He doesn't know his own limits. But who
does, exactly? It takes a lifetime to get used to your body, and
by the time you do, then it is almost time to say goodbye and go
elsewhere. I often wonder whether the wind carries our souls
skyward. It is another of my foolish ideas, and I put it to the
priest long ago—not this one but the one who came before him.
He was annoyed with me. 'Mrs. García,' he said, 'you have an
active imagination.' I apologized. He reminded me that God's
ways are not ours. I wanted to tell him that the wind comes
mysteriously from above and might be one of many good,
strong arms our Lord has. But I knew that to keep quiet was
best. He was a very stern priest, and outspoken. He would not
have hesitated to talk to me severely and warn me publicly that
I would pay for that kind of talk in Hell. Once, he cuffed my
husband because Domingo told him he'd heard that much of
our weekly collection was being sent to Africa or Asia, to
places far off, and meanwhile so many people hereabouts
were without work and were going hungry."

"It was in the bad years—in the nineteen-thirties. We
were poor, but at least we had our land. Others had nothing.
And the priest was fat. He was waited on, and he dined on the
best; we were told that by the woman who cooked for him.
Mind you, she did not serve him. He had to have someone
special to do that. And he paid them a pittance. They had
children they were supporting—and, alas, husbands, too. In a
good mood, he would promise them an eternity in Heaven. On

bad days, he would threaten them with Purgatory and no escape—so, of course, they would leave his kitchen in tears, clutching their rosary beads all the way home. My husband heard of this and was enraged. He said terrible things. I pleaded with him to stop. We were so poor, and the bank threatened to take away our small farm. Some people had thought of marching on the bank. The bank officials heard of the plan and never made a move against us. By then, I had lost four children. I will not repeat what Domingo said about the priest, or the Church. The worse his language, the harder I prayed. I knelt by my bed and prayed one evening after he had carried on a full hour, it seemed; it must really have been a few minutes, I now know, but I thought he would never stop. Then a heavy wind came, later that evening, and I was sure God was approaching us to exact his punishment. And why not, after Domingo's outburst? Domingo was tidying up outside. He had calmed down. I had heard him say a Hail Mary, but I pretended to be lost in my own work. He didn't want me to know that he had taken back the words he had spoken; he is proud. I decided to pray for him, but I was sure something bad would happen. Nothing did, though; the wind came, then left. A week afterward, I told Domingo of my fears. He laughed, and said we are too intelligent, both of us, even without education to be superstitious. I agreed. But a month later he came in one day for lunch and he told me he had to confess something to me. I said, 'Not to me, to the priest.' No, he had very little to tell that priest—only the briefest of admissions once a month. I said nothing. He said that he'd been afraid, too, that evening after he lost his temper. When the wind came, and he was outside, and the horses started whinnying and the dog ran back and forth, he did not know what to do or why the animals were upset, so he had got down on his knees and asked God's forgiveness. He'd even asked Him to take us both, with the house—through a tornado, perhaps. But soon it became very still, and I think both of us must have been holding our breath, without knowing we were doing so together—like so much else we do. I fear that when he goes I will, or when I go he will. But I have no right to such thoughts; it is not up to me or to Domingo but to our Lord and Saviour. We are sinners, though, and we can't help being selfish. There will be no future for either of us alone. I only hope we are not tested by being separated for too long by death."

When her husband comes in, without being called, she says that it is now noon. They go by the sun. They have a clock in their bedroom, but they rarely use it. They forget to wind it, except when their son Domingo is coming and they want to show him that they like his present. "Domingo gave us the clock, and I treasure it," she says. "I look at it and think of him. We have only two sons. It is nice to be reminded of them. I don't mean to sound as if I pitied myself. Our son Domingo works at Los Alamos. He says it is maintenance he does; he looks after all those scientists. They leave their laboratories in a mess, and someone has to pick up after them or everything would stop one day. He gets a good wage, and jobs are few around here, so he is lucky to be there. He could have stayed with us, worked on the land. But all we have is our animals and the crops—no money. I put up many jars for the winter, but jars of food are not enough to attract young people, and I see their view. There are a hundred like Domingo who would like his job. Before they brought in the laboratories at Los Alamos, there was nothing anywhere near here. Domingo would be in Albuquerque, I believe, if it hadn't been for Los Alamos. My younger son is down there. I've never even been to Santa Fe. He drives up here on weekends. His life is different, in the city. I don't ask him much; I wouldn't understand. His wife longs to come back here. He does, too. But how can they? No work. Domingo was interviewed several times for his job. He took a test, I believe. He did well. The teachers who predicted good for him—they were right. It's too bad he didn't finish high school; the war came—the one against Japan and Hitler."

"Then came the next war. My second son, Francisco, went to Korea. He was there for many months. I remember well the Saturday morning that I got news of him. I remember the day he came home. I was sitting in this very chair. I had to mend some of my husband's clothes. I was almost through, and my mind, as it does, was already preparing for the next step in the day—a visit outside to pick some tomatoes. Suddenly, the door opened, with no warning. Who could it be? The front door, hardly ever used, rather than the side one, right here. My boy Domingo—he lived with us then, and worked as a handyman in the school where they had always thought so well of him. He had his suit on. 'Domingo,' I said, 'why the suit?' He did not answer. For a second, I wondered how he had slipped in and put it on without my knowing. We will do anything not to see what is right before us. I believe I might have wondered and wondered about such petty questions, but after Domingo came his father, also with a suit on. I got up and shouted, 'It is not Sunday!' I said it over and over again. 'It is not, it is not!' Then I started crying. They never told me. I never asked. I just knew. My husband asked me if I wanted to change my dress. I said no. I am a plain woman, and my son was a plain man—no pretenses. He did not die in his Sunday clothes. They turned around, and I followed them. We walked down that road, two miles. I saw nothing. I heard nothing. I was alone, even though they were with me, one on each side. Once, I must have looked near collapse. I felt their hands and was surprised to see them standing there. Then I dropped my beads. I picked them up, but I didn't say the Rosary. I just kept holding on to the beads. They had brought the body to the basement of the school building, a United States flag around it. Later, after the funeral, they wanted to give me that flag. I said no, it could stay at the school. Let children see what war means. That is something they should learn—as much as how to read and write and count."

She has gone beyond her sense of what is correct for her to say. Who is she to talk about wars? They come about through events she has no knowledge of. She has a place in God's scheme of things, and best to stay in it. But something makes her restless, however she tries to put aside her doubts and misgivings. She stands up, walks toward her plants and examines them, one by one. They are all right. She goes back to her chair. Then she is up offering coffee, serving a delicious chocolate marble cake she has made—with the help of a packaged mix, a concession to her daughter-in-laws's urging. Once again seated, she interrupts a conversation about "the new road"—the road in front of her house, which now, for the first time, is paved—to put into words what she can't stop thinking about. "There was another time. Two years ago, before that road was fixed up to be so strong it can ignore the weather, I had walked down to talk with my neighbor. She had suffered badly from pneumonia but was on the mend. As I came

toward the house, I saw them again. You know, this time I
thought my mind had left me. I wiped my eyes, but they
wouldn't go away. I called to them, but they didn't answer, so I
was sure they were not there. It was late afternoon, a time when
shadows begin to appear and one can be fooled anyway. So I
wiped my eyes again, and when they remained I looked
around, hoping to see them in back of me, too. Then I would
know: my eyes, my head—something for a doctor to heal, or a
warning from God that it won't be long. Well, soon they
were upon me; it was only when I *felt* them that I believed they
were there and I was there. I remember thinking that perhaps
I'd fallen asleep at my neighbor's, or maybe I'd taken a
nap at my own house and now was waking up. In a second, one
can have such thoughts. In another second, one can know
everything without hearing a word. It was my third son. I said,
'How did it happen?' My husband couldn't talk. I held on to him
and wanted him to tell me, but he was speechless. My son
Domingo tried to tell me, but he couldn't finish his story. He
had used the word *car*, and that was enough for me. Later,
they tried to give me the details, and I begged them to stop.
Those suits on a day in the middle of the week! There have
been days since when I have wanted to burn those suits or tear
them to shreds. There have been days when I have lost all
faith. I dared not go to confession—I could not let a priest hear
what was in my mind. I cringed before God, knowing He hears
everything, even what is not spoken but crosses the mind—a
rabbit of an idea, suddenly upon you, quickly chased away,
but back again in an unsuspecting moment, when all is quiet.''

With that, she stops talking and looks out of the window.
What ought a visitor to do—sit still and wait or find an excuse
to leave immediately? Suddenly, she makes the question
rhetorical. She is talking again, a bit more softly and slowly
and reflectively, but with no apparent distress. And she seems
to want to talk. "The mountains, our mountains—I look at them
when I need an anchor. They are here. They never leave us.
Birds come, stay awhile, leave. The moon is here, then gone.
Even the sun hides from us for days on end. Leaves don't last,
or flowers. We have had a number of dogs, and I remember
them in my prayers. But those mountains are here. They are
nearer God than we are. Sometimes I imagine Him up there, on
top of one or another mountain, standing over us, getting an

idea how we're doing. It is wrong to think like that, I know. But a poor old woman like me can be allowed her foolishness. Who is without a foolish hope? Who doesn't make up dreams to fit his wishes? Sometimes I walk up toward the mountains. I can't go as far now as before. I don't tell my husband I'm going; he would worry that I'd lose my breath completely and no one would be around. But I go slowly, and, as I say, I have to be content with approaching those hills."

"The other day, I walked toward them, and there was a meeting on the side of the road. I stopped and listened. I never went any farther. They were our young, and some people from the city. Chicanos—they spoke of Chicanos. We are Chicanos —nothing else will do, they said. I came home and told my husband. Yes, he said, we are Chicanos. We are so many things, he said. Mexican-American, Mexicano, they'd call my boys at school, those Anglo teachers. I would say nothing. They thought then it was their right to call us what they pleased. Spanish—we are Spanish. Many of us may have some Indian blood, too. But I will tell you: I am a woman and a mother, and Domingo is a man and a father, and both of us belong to this country and no other, and we owe allegiance to the State of New Mexico. Should we give ourselves one name or another, or should we get each day's job done? I can't believe Christ wants us to be Anglo against Chicano, or Chicano against Anglo. But the world is full of bitterness, and when will there be an end to it, when, I wondered while I walked home. It is a bad thing to say, but I was glad to come upon that meeting; it took my mind off myself and my memories. I saw that others want to know why there is so much injustice in the world. For a few days after my son was killed in the accident, I wondered again whether God cared. I know He is there, watching over us, but I would wake up in the night and my forehead would be wet and I would be shaking. I had dreamed that God had fallen asleep and so we all were going to suffer: the Devil would win his fight. I thought of those days, now gone, while I listened to the young people shouting 'Chicano!' They mentioned all the bad, nothing good. Domingo says that is how it goes when people have been hurt, and I nodded, because I remembered how I once felt."

One morning, in the midst of a conversation, she scolds herself for talking too much. She falls silent. She glances up at a picture of Christ at the Last Supper. Her face loses its tension. She slumps a bit, but not under the weight of pain, or even age. She feels relaxed. There are a few dishes to wash. There is a curtain that needs mending. There is not only bread to make but also pies. Her grandchildren love her pies, and she loves seeing the pies eaten. "Children eat so fast," she says with a sigh of envy. She begins talking again. She resumes her activity. She says she has to pick at her food now. "When one is over eighty, the body needs less," she observes—but immediately afterward she looks a little shy, a little apprehensive. "I have no business talking like a doctor. Once, the priest told me I talk like him. I told him, 'I have raised children; it is necessary at times to give them sermons and hear their confessions.' He smiled. If I had another life, I would learn to be a nurse. In my day, few of our people could aim so high—not a woman like me, anyway. It is different today. My sons say their children will finish high school, and my Domingo in Los Alamos says his Domingo does so well in school he may go on to a college. I laugh with my husband—a Domingo García in a college? Maybe the boy will be a doctor. Who knows? He likes to take care of his dog. He has a gentle side to him. He is popular with the girls, so I don't think he's headed for the priesthood. He tells me he'd like to be a scientist, like the men his father looks after in the laboratories. I worry that he would make those bombs, though. I wouldn't want that on his conscience. My son told me they do other things there in the laboratories, not just make bombs. I said, 'Thank God!' "

"Of course, all that is for the future. I do not know if I will be around to see my grandchildren have children of their own. One cannot take anything for granted. The priest laughed at Domingo and me last Sunday, and said, 'You two will outlast me. You will be coming here when you are both over one hundred.' I said, 'Thank you, Father, but that is a long way off, to be a hundred, and much can happen.' 'Have faith,' he said, and he is right. One must."

She pauses for a few seconds, as if to think about her own admonition. Then she is back on her train of thought. "Sometimes, after church, Domingo and I walk through the cemetery. It is a lovely place, small and familiar. We pay our respects to our parents, to our aunts and uncles, to our children. A family is a river; some of it has passed on and more

is to come, and nothing is still, because we all move along, day
by day, toward our destination. We both feel joy in our hearts
when we kneel on the grass before the stones and say a
prayer. At the edge of the cemetery, near the gate, is a statue
of the Virgin Mary, larger than all the other stones. She is
kneeling, and on her shoulder is the Cross. She is carrying it—
the burden of her Son's death. She is sad, but she has not given
up. We know that she has never lost faith. It is a lesson to keep
in mind. We always leave a little sad at the sight of our Lord's
mother under such a heavy obligation. But my husband never
fails to hold my arm, and each Sunday his words are the same:
'Dolores, the Virgin will be an example to us this week.' It is as
if each Sunday he were taking his vows—and me, too, because
I say back to him, 'Yes, Domingo, she will be an example to us.'
Now, mind you, an hour later one of us, or both of us, will have
stumbled. I become cranky. Domingo has a temper. I hush him
and he explodes. He is inconsiderate and I sulk. That is the
way with two people who have lived together so long: the good
and the bad are always there, and they have become part of
one life, lived together.''

She hears his footsteps coming and quickens her activity a
bit. She will not be rushed, but he needs his coffee, and she
needs hers. Often, she doesn't so much need coffee as need to
drink it because he is drinking it. An outsider may observe how
they take coffee: he lifts his up, she follows; he puts his down,
and soon hers is also on the table. Always they get through at
the same time. This particular morning, Domingo is more
expansive and concerned than usual—a foal has just been
born. "Well, enough. I must go check on the mother and her
infant," he says. Near the door, he turns around to say
goodbye. "These days, one never knows when the end will
come," he says. "I know our time is soon up. But when I look at
that mother horse and her child in the barn, or at my children
and their children, I feel lucky to have been permitted for a
while to be part of all this life here on earth." His hand is on
the door, and he seems a little embarrassed that he has spoken
so. But he has to go on. "I am talking like my wife now. After
all these years, she sometimes falls into my silences and I
carry on as she does. She is not just an old woman, you know.
She wears old age like a bunch of fresh-cut flowers. She is old,
advanced in years, *vieja*, but in Spanish we have another word

for her—a word that tells you that she has grown with all those years. I think that is something one ought to hope for and pray for and work for all during life: to grow, to become not only older but a bigger person. She is old, all right, *vieja*, but I will dare say this in front of her: she is *una anciana*. With that, I declare my respect and have to hurry back to the barn."

6

The Timing of Our Lives*

Harley L. Browning

The social consequences of the biologically complete life

Only quite recently in his history has man been able to exercise any important and lasting influence on the control of his mortality. In Western Europe mortality declines have been documented for periods ranging up to several hundred years, but this accomplishment recently has been overshadowed by the spectacular drops in mortality in many developing countries. They are now accomplishing in a few decades what the European countries took many generations to achieve. In Mexico, to cite one remarkable example, male life expectancy at birth has nearly doubled within the span of a single generation (1930-65). During this period, the life expectancy of Mexican men rose from thirty-two to sixty-two years.

Man's great leap forward in mortality control, which now permits so large a proportion of those born in advanced societies to pass through virtually all important stages in the life cycle, must surely be counted among his most impressive

*This work originally appeared in Transaction/Society 6, no. 11 (October 1969): 22-27.

accomplishments. Yet, there has been no systematic effort to follow out all the ramifications of this relatively new condition. If a Mexican boy born in 1965 can expect to live twice as long as his father born in 1930, can he not also expect to pass through a life cycle markedly different in quality and content from that of his father?

One would think that a man who had little chance of living beyond thirty-five would want to cram all the important stages of his life into a brief period. Conversely, one might expect that if given twice the time in which to live out his life cycle, an individual might plan and space out the major events in his life, such as education, marriage, birth of his children, beginning of his work career, and so on—to gain the optimal advantage of all this additional time. But, in reality, little intelligent use is being made of the extension of life expectancy in terms of the spacing of key events in the life cycle.

Here, for purposes of exploring the possibilities opened up by recent advances in mortality contol, I want first to document the astonishing increase in life expectancy of recent times. From there we can examine some of the implications that can be drawn from it and consider the potential consequences of increased longevity in altering the timing of events in the life cycle. Finally, I shall comment on the feasibility of planning changes in the life cycle to better utilize the advantages of reduced mortality rates. Since my purpose is to set forth a perspective for the linking of life expectancy and life cycle, I have not attempted systematically to provide data for all of my generalizations. Therefore, my conclusions must be taken as exploratory and tentative.

In the investigation of the relationship of changes in life expectancy to changes in life cycle, it is worthwhile to consider two groupings of countries—the developed countries, where life expectancy has been increasing over a considerable period of time, and the developing countries, with their recent and very rapid increases.

For the developing countries, an important question for which we have little evidence as yet is how much people are aware at all social levels of the dramatic change in life expectancy. Perhaps it is not generally "perceived" because the change has not had time to manifest itself in the lifetime of many persons. The fact that in Mexico there is now so great a generational difference in life expectancy that the son may expect to live almost twice as long as his father surely will have considerable impact upon the family and other institutions. But we can only know these changes for certain as the son passes through his life span, well into the next century, a time when all of us will be dead.

Mexico is a striking case but by no means an isolated one. A number of other developing countries will achieve much the same record within a fifty-year period or less. Thus, for a substantial part of the world's population, the mortality experience of succeeding generations will differ markedly and to an extent unparalleled in any other historical period.

There are striking extremes between conditions in primitive and preindustrial countries with unusually high death rates and the situation that many countries in Western Europe and Anglo-America either have already reached or are closely approaching. For instance, India between 1901 and 1911 represented the conditions of extremely high mortality under which mankind has lived during most of his time on this earth. A male child born in this period and locale had a life expectancy of slightly less than twenty-three years. Today such conditions are extremely rare. At the other extreme, a boy born in the United States in 1950, for example, could expect to live almost to age seventy-four.

As is well known, the greatest improvement in mortality control has come about through the reduction of deaths in infancy and early childhood. In India around 1901, nearly one-half of those born were lost by age five. By contrast, under the conditions prevailing in the United States in 1950, 98.5 percent of male children were still living five years after birth.

For the purposes of relating life expectancy to life cycle, however, it is not the losses in the early years that are of the most importance. Death at any time, including the first few years of life, is of course a "waste," but the loss of "investment" at these ages for both parents and society is not nearly so great as for those persons who die at just about the time they are ready to assume adult responsibilities. This is when such significant events in the life cycle as higher education, work career, marriage, and family take place. For this reason, the focus of this chapter is upon the fifty-year span from age 15 to 65. By age 15 the boy is in the process of becoming a man and is preparing himself either for college or entry into the labor force. Fifty years later, at age 65, the man is either retired or, if not, his productivity is beginning to decline noticeably in most cases.

But what are the consequences of these changes that have recently permitted a substantial part of the world's population for the first time to live what Jean Fourastie has called "a biologically complete life." What can be the meaning of death in a society where nearly everyone lives out his allotted three-score and ten years? Is death beyond the age of sixty-five or seventy really a "tragic" occurrence? The specter of early and unexpected death manifested itself symbolically in countless ways in societies with high mortality. Of France in the twelfth century, Fourastie writes, "In traditional times, death was at the center of life, just as the cemetery was at the center of the village."

Not everyone believes that the great increase in life expectancy is entirely favorable in its consequences. Some argue that perhaps advanced societies now allow too high a proportion of those born into them to pass through to advanced ages. "Natural selection" no longer works effectively to eliminate the weak and the infirm. In other words, these people maintain that one consequence of improved mortality is that the biological "quality" of the population declines.

While we can grant that a number of individuals now survive to old age who are incapable of making any contribution to their society, the real question is how numerically important a group they are. My impression is that their numbers have generally been exaggerated by some eugenicists. The cost of maintaining these relatively few individuals is far outweighed by the many benefits deriving from high survivorship. In any event, the strong ethical supports for the preservation of life under virtually all conditions are not likely to be dramatically altered within the next generation or so.

Whatever the problems occasioned by the great rise in natural increase, no one would want to give up the very real gains that derive from the control of mortality man now possesses. One of the most interesting features is the biological continuity of the nuclear family (parents and children) during the period when childbearing and child rearing take place. In most societies the crucial period, for men at least, is between

25 and 55. But only a little more than a third of the males born under very backward conditions survive from age 15 to 55. By contrast, almost 94 percent in Europe and Anglo-America reach this age. The fact that until relatively recently it was highly probable that one or both parents would die before their children reached maturity had a profound effect upon family institutions. In "functional" terms, the survival of the society depended upon early marriages and early and frequent conceptions within those marriages. Andrew Collver has shown this very effectively in his comparative study of the family cycle in India and the United States:

> In the United States, the married couple, assured of a long span of life together, can take on long-term responsibilities for starting a new household, rearing children, and setting aside some provisions for their old age. In India, by contrast, the existence of the nuclear family is too precarious for it to be entrusted entirely with these important functions. The joint household alone has a good prospect for continuity.

Not all societies with high mortality are also characterized by the importance of joint households. But all societies of the past in one way or another had to provide for children who were orphaned before they reached maturity. One largely uncelebrated consequence of greatly reduced mortality in Western countries, for example, has been the virtual disappearance of orphanages. In the United States, the number of complete orphans declined from 750,000 in 1920 to 66,000 in 1953. In this way a favorite theme of novelists a century or so ago has largely disappeared. Were Dickens writing today he would have to shift his attention from orphans to the children of divorced or separated parents. The psychological and economic consequences of whether homes are broken by divorce or separation rather than by the death of one or both parents obviously may be quite different.

I need not elaborate the obvious advantages of increased life expectancy both for the individual and his society in terms of advanced education and professional career. Under present conditions it is now possible for an individual realistically to plan his entire education and work life with little fear of dying before he can carry out his plans. In this respect, the developed countries have a considerable advantage over developing countries, for the former do not suffer many losses on their investments in the training and education of their youth. But under conditions that are still typical of a large number of countries, a third of those who have reached the age of fifteen never reach age forty-five, the peak productive period of an educated person's life. In such countries, primary education for everyone may be desirable but a part of the investment will be lost for the substantial number who will die during their most productive period.

Another consequence, perhaps overlooked, of the improvement of life expectancy in advanced countries is the fact that while even the rich and powerful were likely to die at early ages in older societies, now everyone, including the poor, can expect to pass through most of the life span. Considerable attention in America is now concentrated on conditions of social inequality, and clearly very large differences exist for characteristics such as education, occupation, and income. But in a society where about eighty-five of every one hundred persons can expect to reach their sixty-fifth birthday, extreme differences in longevity among the social strata do not exist. This is not to say that mortality differentials do not exist; they do, but not nearly to the degree found for other major socioeconomic variables. For the poor, unfortunately, increased longevity may be at best a mixed blessing. Too frequently it can only mean a prolongation of ill health, joblessness, and dependency.

What is still not well appreciated are the consequences of the prolongation of life for the spacing of key events in the life cycle. Obviously, wholesale transformation of the life cycle is impossible because most of the events of importance are to one degree or another associated with age. Retirement cannot precede first job. Nevertheless, the timing of such events or stages as education, beginning of work career, marriage, and birth of first and last child is subject to changes that can have marked repercussions on both the individual and the society.

One of the difficulties of dealing with the life cycle is that it is rarely seen in its entirety. Specialists on child development concentrate only on the early years, while the period of adolescence has its own "youth culture" specialists, and so on.

But another important reason why changes in the life cycle itself have not received much attention is the lack of data. Ideally, life histories are required so that the timing of each event can be specified, but until quite recently the technical problems in gathering and especially in processing detailed life histories on a large scale were so great as to make the task unfeasible. Now, however, with the help of computers, many of these problems can be overcome.

Let us examine one particular instance—age at first marriage in the United States—in which one might expect increased life expectancy to have some effect either actual or potential on the life cycle. The data are reasonably good, at least for the last seventy years, and age at first marriage is an event subject to a fair amount of variation in its timing. More interesting, age at first marriage can greatly affect the subsequent course of a person's life and is indicative of changes in social structure.

In the time period of concern to us, 1890-1960, the generational life expectancy in the United States at age 20 increased 13 years for males and 11 years for females. This is not so great an increase as is now occurring in developing countries but it is still an impressive gain. With an appreciable extension in his life expectancy, a person might reasonably be expected to alter the spacing of key events in his life cycle in order to take advantage of the greater "space" available. In particular, we might expect him to marry at a somewhat later age. But exactly the opposite has happened! Between 1890 and 1960 the median age at first marriage for males declined about four years, a very significant change. For females, the decline was only two years, but their age at first marriage in 1890 (22) already was quite low.

Is this not strange? During the period of an important extension in life expectancy, a substantial decline in age at first marriage has occurred. Unquestionably, many factors go into an adequate explanation of this phenomenon. One of the reasons why age at first marriage was high around the turn of the century was the numbers of foreign born, most of them from Europe where marriage at a later age was characteristic, even among the lower strata. Immigrants who arrived as single men had some difficulty finding wives and this delayed their first marriage. In addition, around the turn of the century, middle-class men were not expected to marry until they had completed their education, established themselves in their careers, and accumulated sufficient assets to finance the marriage and a proper style of living.

The greatest drop in age at first marriage occurred between 1940 and 1960, especially for females. During this period a great many changes took place in society that worked to facilitate early marriages. "Going steady" throughout a good part of adolescence became accepted practice. Parents adopted more permissive attitudes toward early marriage and often helped young couples to get started. The reduced threat of military conscription after 1946 for married men with children was also a big factor along with a period of general prosperity and easy credit that enabled newlyweds to have a house, furnishings, and car, all with a minimal down payment. And not only is marriage easier to get into, but it is now easier to get out of as well; divorce no longer carries the stigma once attached to it.

Of course, many early marriages are not wholly voluntary and in a substantial number of cases the couple either would never have married or they would have married at a later age. David Goldberg has estimated, on the basis of a Detroit survey, that as high as twenty-five percent of white, first births are conceived outside of marriage, with a fifth of these being illegitimate. He states:

> We have been accustomed to thinking of the sequence marriage, conception, and birth. It is apparent that for a very substantial part of the population the current sequence is conception followed by birth, with marriage intervening, following birth or not occurring at all. This may represent a fundamental change in marriage and fertility patterns, but historical patterns are lacking. An increase in illegitimate conceptions may be largely responsible for the decline in marriage age in the postwar period.

Unfortunately, there is no way to determine if the proportion of illegitimate conceptions has risen substantially since 1890.

The causes of early first marriage are not so important for the purposes of this chapter as their consequences for subsequent events of the life cycle. For one thing, age at first marriage is closely related to the stability of the marriage. The high dissolution of teenage marriages by divorce or other means is notorious. One may or may not consider this as "wastage" but there is no question about the costs of these unsuccessful unions to the couples involved, to their children, and often to society in the form of greater welfare expenditures.

Not only has age at first marriage trended downward, especially since World War II, but family formation patterns have also changed. For the woman, the interval between first marriage and birth of her first child has diminished somewhat and the intervals between subsequent births also have been reduced. As a result, most women complete their childbearing period by the time they reach age thirty.

Marriage, Work, and Babies

The effects of these changes on the family cycle are as yet not very well understood. But the lowering of age at first marriage among men encompasses within the brief span of the early twenties many of the most important events of the life cycle—advanced education, marriage, first stages of work career, and family formation. This is particularly true for the college educated. Since at least four of every ten college-age males will have some college training, this is an important segment of the population. Each important stage of the life cycle requires commitment and involvement of the individual. If he crowds them together, he reduces both the time he can devote to each of them and his chances for success in any or all of them.

From our discussion of increased life expectancy and the timing of one particular aspect of the life cycle, age at first marriage, we might conclude that there is little relationship between the two. Man has been able to push back the threat of death both in developing and developed societies but he has not seen fit to make much use of this increased longevity. Must this be? Would not the "quality" of the populations in both developing and developed countries be improved by a wider spacing of key events in the life cycle? I believe a good argument can be made that it would.

First, take the situation in the developing countries. What would be the consequences of raising the age at marriage several years and of widening the interval between births? The demographic consequences would be very important, for, independent of any reduction of completed family size, these changes would substantially reduce fertility rates. Raising age at marriage would delay births as a short-run effect and in the long run it would lengthen the span of a generation. At a time when there is much concern to slow down the rate of population growth in most developing countries, this would be particularly effective when coupled with a concomitant reduction in completed family size.

A second effect of the raising of age at marriage and widening the spacing of births would be to allow these societies to better gear themselves to the requirements of a modernized and highly trained population. A later age at marriage for women could permit more of them to enter the labor force. This in itself would probably result in lowered fertility. In most developing societies, the role and position of the woman outside of the home must be encouraged and strengthened.

Accommodating the Sex Drive

The case of the developed countries, particularly the United States, is somewhat different. I see very few advantages either for the individual, the couple, or the society in the recent practice of squeezing the terminal stages of education, early work career, and marriage and family formation into the period of the early twenties. There simply is not time enough to do justice to all of these events. The negative effects are often felt most by the women. If a woman is married by age 20, completes her childbearing before 30, and sees her children leave home before she reaches 50, she is left with a long thirty years to fill in some manner. We know that many women have difficulty finding meaningful activities to occupy themselves. True, the shortening of generations will permit people the opportunity of watching their great-grandchildren grow up, but does this compensate for the earlier disadvantages of this arrangement? From the standpoint of the society, there are few if any advantages.

If an argument can be made that little intelligent use is being made of the extension of life expectancy in terms of timing key events in the life cycle, what can be done about it? In any direct way, probably very little. "Licensing" people to do certain things at certain ages is, to my mind, appropriate only in totalitarian societies. So far as I am aware, contemporary totalitarian societies have made relatively little effort to actively regulate the timing of events in the life cycle. The Chinese, for example, have only "suggested" that males defer marriage until age thirty. But if the state is not to force people to do things at specified ages, at least it might educate them as to the advantages of proper spacing and also make them aware of handicaps generated by early marriage and, particularly, early family formation. Both in developing and developed countries there probably is very little direct awareness of how spacing will affect one's life chances and how something might be done about it.

Obviously, if marriage is delayed, then something must be done to accommodate the sex drive. Fifty years ago the resolution of this problem was for men to frequent prostitutes while women had fainting spells, but neither alternative is likely to gain favor with today's generation. Perhaps Margaret Mead has once again come to our rescue with her proposal that two kinds of marriages be sanctioned, those with and those without children. Under her "individual" marriage young people could enter into and leave unions relatively freely as long as they did not have children. This, of course, would require effective contraception. Such a union would provide sexual satisfaction, companionship, and assuming the women is employed, two contributors to household expenses. This arrangement would not markedly interfere with the careers of either sex. Marriages with the purpose of having children would be made more difficult to enter into, but presumably many couples would pass from the individual into the family marriage. This suggestion, of course, will affront the conventional morality, but so do most features of social change.

References

Eisenstadt, S. N. *From Generation to Generation*. Glencoe, Illinois: Free Press, 1956. Sets forth the normative approach to the life cycle and its key events.

Glick, Paul. *American Families*. New York: Wiley, 1957. Represents the demographic approach to the family life cycle.

Hadden, Jeffrey K., and Borgatta, Marie L., eds. *Marriage and the Family: A Comprehensive Reader*. Itasca, Illinois: F.E. Peacock, 1969. Has a number of good articles on the family life cycle.

Transitions

Introduction

The meaning given to being a certain age is clearly dependent upon cultural and societal variables, such as average life span, criteria of mate choice, and norms regulating entry and departure from valued statuses. Aging, by definition, is a process, and one that may be said to begin at birth; it becomes a negatively loaded term when associated with loss, and this will vary across cultures and across time. At what moment do individuals begin to lose those qualities and things that have been positively evaluated in that society? If beauty, then with the first wrinkle; if status, honor, or economic position, then with the realization that one has gone as far as one can go, and that younger claimants are right behind. On the one hand, it can be argued that the anxieties of these transition years will make authentic old age even more difficult to bear; but on the other hand, it may well be that after the first agonies, a resolution and acceptance occurs, easing the ultimate passage to old age. An excellent case in point is the Marchallin, heroine of Richard Strauss's *Der Rosenkavalier* (itself an extended essay on time, in words and music). She is a noblewoman in the Austria of Maria Theresa

145

and mourns her "lost" youth and approaching old age, yet the libretto describes her as in her early thirties! But at the court in Vienna, in 1745, where women were favored for their youth and fresh beauty, where epidemics decimated the populace without regard for rank, and where life expectancy was not much more than four decades, thirty-two could indeed seem "old." By the end of the opera, she has, however, come to accept her "losses" with the grace of a wise and noble woman.

Inge Powell Bell's analysis of the aging crisis for contemporary American women is not all that distant from the Marchallin's lament. In any society where women are valued as sexual objects rather than for their own talents and accomplishments, the first signs of beauty loss are traumatic, threatening to one's value as a human being. While Bell's concerns center on sex stratification, her comments are equally relevant to the study of age stratification, and the differential timing and impact of the transition to old age for men and women. The "crisis" of aging is tied to the other statuses we occupy, or do not occupy, in other hierarchies.

Is there a mid-life "crisis" or transition period for men, a point at which the future seems shorter than the past, when options have been foreclosed, and one must come to terms with limitations? Orville Brim looks at the most recent work in developmental psychology and concludes that there is ample evidence of personality change in the middle years in response to a number of changes in the body and in the social world of the aging male. Brim has been a notable proponent of theories of continuing personality change and development, which goes very much against the grain of our belief in consistent, fixed personality traits. The influence of Freud has been so pervasive in our society,* and our absorption with childhood so complete, that most Americans are convinced that everything that happens in infancy determines everything that happens in adulthood, and that once the child's personality is formed, these traits remain basic motivators of behavior. Brim suggests that this belief in consistency is necessary because

* My own feeling is that Freud's success in America is due to the compatibility of psychoanalysis with the Puritan ethic—innerlooking, guilt ridden, emphasizing the individual's responsibility for his/her own state of grace. Success or failure is a private outcome, whether in business or in love.

we have entrusted the fate of the society to middle-aged males and *must* perceive them as stable individuals. However, the psychological literature clearly demonstrates that we cannot predict adult behavior from knowledge of childhood personality; therefore, there are events that occur beyond childhood which can shape personality, and reshape it. We have already discussed Erikson's concept of personality change even in old age; and in chapter 3, Gutmann (who is cited by Brim) detailed the nature of some of these ego processes. Brim discusses seven "causes," from changes in the state of the organism, to changes in social structure, which might lead to a kind of stocktaking and subsequent reorganization of the self. While it may distress some to be confronted with the concept of personality plasticity, there is also something liberating in the realization that growth and change are lifelong processes, through the middle years and on to the very end.

The Neugarten data to which Brim refers comes from one of the few sustained researches on aging. Neugarten and her associates have spent decades examining the social-psychological processes and correlates of aging. That there are clear stages of cognitive development in children is well documented by Piaget, Kohlberg, and others. The question Neugarten and others have asked is "are their similar shifts in cognitive style, in orientation to the world and others, and in self-perception among mature adults?" In chapter 9 Neugarten summarizes some of her findings, permitting us to distinguish what might be called *normal* trajectories of the aging self, or at least typical responses to the strains of role transition in adulthood.

Clearly, the first three chapters of this section bring into question any easy assumptions that adult personalities are simple reflections of childhood experience, or that the middle years are a placid plateau of sameness. To the contrary, roles are being assumed and relinquished, one's children become adults, and one's parents become old-old—and these transition points lead to rearrangements of interpersonal relationships and changes in intrapersonal self-perception.

Death is also a transition. Glaser and Strauss* have written of "Death as a Status Passage," much as one would of

---

*Glaser, Barney G., and Strauss, Anselm L., *A Time for Dying* (Chicago: Aldine, 1968).

puberty rites, widowhood, marriage, or retirement. Status passages are important societal events, frequently surrounded by ritual and myth that support the individual through the period of change while reaffirming the integrity and cohesion of the group. Although in our culture, we find elaborate ceremonies to assure the departed a proper passage to the next world, we are curiously indifferent to the status passages of those left behind. In the chapter from Donald Hendin's *Death as a Fact of Life*, he discusses the question of grief and bereavement in contemporary America. There are many subcultural variations on this theme—but these are for the most part localized in time and in the social networks involved. As the Lopata study (chapter 11) will later indicate, widowhood is not a fully institutionalized status in our society, and much "grief work" is ad hoc.

Issues of when life ends, euthanasia, "death with dignity," the role of the physician, and the dying process—all treated in Hendin's book, though not in this brief excerpt— have become urgent today, partly because of the higher probability of individuals living to advanced ages, and partly because of the techniques developed in the medical field that prolong life, such as the transplanting of organs, installing pacemakers, utilizing kidney machines, and using any of the variety of "heroic" measures to inhibit death among the very old. What rights does a patient have to request cessation of medical effort? Can we select the time and place of our demise? To whom is a physician responsible—his patient, his peers, a professional code; and how much should he tell the patient's family, or, indeed, the patient? These are now topics of fierce debate in ethics, medicine, and the social sciences. In a sense, death has become an issue of public concern and debate because it no longer takes place in private; people who die in hospitals rather than at home draw attention to questions regarding medical practice, the ethics of prolonging life, and the "right to die with dignity." Furthermore, when aged relatives do not die in our homes, we have little socialization to grief; and when it is no longer likely that one of our parents will die before we reach adulthood, bereavement is not a typical experience of a young American. In other words, death *in* the household is *not* a fact of life for most young people; it occurs at a remove in time and space, and is that much less real. Although answers are complex and will take some time to formulate, at least the questions are now being raised, with no little effect on our choices in old age.

7

The Double Standard*

Inge Powell Bell

There is a reason why women are coy about their age. For most purposes, society pictures them as "old" ten or fifteen years sooner than men. Nobody in this culture, man or woman, wants to grow old; age is not honored among us. Yet women must endure the specter of aging much sooner than men, and this cultural definition of aging gives men a decided psychological, sexual, and economic advantage over women.

It is surely a truism of our culture that, except for a few kinky souls, the inevitable physical symptoms of aging make women sexually unattractive much earlier than men. The multimillion dollar cosmetics advertising industry is dedicated to creating a fear of aging in women, so that it may sell them its emollients of sheep's fat, turtle sweat, and synthetic chemicals that claim, falsely, to stem the terrible tide. "Did you panic when you looked into the mirror this morning and noticed that those laugh lines are turning into crow's feet?" "Don't let your eyes speak your age!" "What a facelift can do for your morale!"

*This work originally appeared in *Transaction/Society* 8, no. 1/2 (November-December 1970): 75-80.

A man's wrinkles will not define him as sexually undesirable until he reaches his late fifties. For him, sexual value is defined much more in terms of personality, intelligence, and earning power than by physical appearance. Women, however, must rest their case largely on their bodies. Their ability to attain status in other than physical ways and to translate that status into sexual attractiveness is severely limited by the culture. Indeed, what status women have is based almost entirely on their sexuality. The young girl of eighteen or twenty-five may well believe that her position in society is equal to, or even higher than that of men. As she approaches middle age, however, she begins to notice a change in the way people treat her. Reflected in the growing indifference of others toward her looks, toward her sexuality, she can see and measure the decline of her worth, her status in the world. In Simone de Beauvoir's words,

> she has gambled much more heavily than man on the sexual values she possesses; to hold her husband and to assure herself of his protection, and to keep most of her jobs, it is necessary for her to be attractive, to please; she is allowed no hold on the world save through the mediation of some man. What is to become of her when she no longer has any hold on him: This is what she anxiously asks herself while she helplessly looks on the degeneration of this fleshly object which she identifies with herself.

The middle-aged woman who thicky masks her face with makeup, who submits to surgical face- and breast-lifting, who dyes her hair and corsets her body is as much a victim of socially instilled self-hatred as the black person who straightens his hair and applies bleaching creams to his skin.

The most dramatic institutionalization of different age definitions for men and women is the cultural rules governing the age at which one can marry. It is perfectly acceptable for men to marry women as much as 15 or 20 years younger than they are, but it is generally unacceptable for them to marry women more than four or five years older. These cultural rules show up very plainly in the marriage statistics gathered by the Department of Health, Education, and Welfare. At the time of first marriage, the age differential is relatively small; the groom is on the average 2.2 years older than his bride. When widowers remarry, however, the gap is 8.3 years; and when divorced men do, the gap is 4.5 years.

These age differentials put the woman at a disadvantage in several ways. First, whatever may be the truth about age and sexual performance, our culture defines the young as sexually more vigorous and desirable. Thus, the customary age differential means that the man gets the more desirable partner; the woman must settle for the less desirable.

More important, the divorced or widowed woman is severely handicapped when it comes to finding another marital partner. Let us take, for example, a couple who divorce when both are in their thirties. What is the difference in the supply of future marriage partners for the man and for the woman? The man can choose among all women his own age or younger. This includes all those women below twenty-five, many more of whom are as yet unmarried. **The woman**, by contrast, is limited by custom to men her **own age or older**. She has access only to age brackets in which most **people** are married. She is thus reduced to the supply of men who come back on the marriage market as a result of divorce or widowerhood or to those few who have not yet married. It is easy to see which of the two will have an easier time finding companionship or a marriage partner. It is also easy to surmise that the awareness of this difference makes divorce a much more painful option for women than for men and thus puts many women at a continuous disadvantage within a strained marriage.

Statistics bear out our supposition that women have a more difficult time remarrying than men (see table). It has been estimated that, while three-quarters of divorced men remarry, only two-thirds of divorced women ever do. In a study of widows and widowers done in 1948, Paul Glick found that half the men who had been widowed from five to fourteen years, two-thirds of the men had remarried, but only one-third of the women had.

Only a small proportion of these discrepancies is due to the shorter life expectancy of men and thus their relative scarcity in the upper-age brackets. For example, in the age brackets 45-64, there are a little over three times as many widowed and divorced women without mates as there are single widowed and divorced men. Yet in the total population the ratio of women to men in that age bracket is only 1.05 to 1. In the over-65 age bracket there are over three-and-a-half times as many divorced and widowed women still alone; yet in the population as a whole, the ratio of women to men in this age bracket is only 1.2 to 1.

Still, the difference in life expectancy between the two sexes does work to a woman's disadvantage in another way. The gentleman in the ad below is making explicit an expectation that is made implicitly by most men:

RECENTLY DIVORCED, 53, affectionate, virile, tall, good-looking, yearns for the one utterly feminine, attractive, loving woman in her 30s, 40s with whom he can share a beautiful new life.

At age 50, this gentleman had a life expectancy of 23 years. (It is a little less now). If he finds a woman of 35, her life expectancy will be 41.27. In other words, he is affectionately offering her a statistical chance of 18 years of widowhood. And she will be widowed at an age when men of her own age will be looking for women in their thirties and forties. At best, he may live to a ripe old age. When he is 75 she will be 57.

Now let us consider the case of a much larger group: women who have husbands. As middle age approaches, many of these married women find that they, too, are vulnerable to the difficulties posed by the different definitions of age in men and women. For them, however devoutly they may wish it as they tidy their homes, take care of their teen-aged children or play bridge, sexual adventure is usually out of the question. This is not just because of the more restrictive mores that bind them to fidelity; their age has already disqualified them for anything else. Not so for the husband. If he is a successful man, his virility will be seen as still intact, if not actually enhanced, and the affair becomes very much the question. Indeed, if he is engaged in a middle-class occupation, he is almost inevitably surrounded by attractive, young females, many of whom—the receptionist, the cocktail waitress at the downtown bar, the airplane hostess—have been deliberately selected to flatter his ego and arouse his fancy. In addition, many of the women hired to fulfill more ordinary functions— the secretaries, typists, and the like—find the older man desirable by virtue of his success and wealth. Thus, the middle-aged wife, unless she is one of the statistically few whose husband is truly happy and faithful, is put into competition with the cards stacked against her. And even if her husband does not leave her for a younger woman or begin having affairs, she will probably experience anxiety and a sense of diminished self-esteem.

The mass media glamorize and legitimate the older man-younger woman relationship. Successful actors continue to play romantic leads well into their fifties and sometimes sixties (for example, Cary Grant). Frequently they are cast opposite actresses at least half their age, and the story line rarely even acknowledges the difference. They are simply an "average" romantic couple. The question of whether the twenty-year-old heroine is out of her mind to marry the greying fifty-five-year-old hero is not even raised.

How many men and women in different age groups remarry?
(Number of marriages per 1,000)

Widowed	Women	Men
45-64	16.2	70.1
65 and over	2.0	17.4
Divorced		
25-44	179.0	306.6
45-64	45.2	89.5
65 and over	9.7	26.5

The Prestige Loss

Occupation is man's major role; unemployment or failure in his occupational life is the worst disaster that can befall him. The question, "What do you do?" is seldom answered, "Well, I'm married and a father. . . ." But because men draw their self-esteem and establish their connections to others very largely through their jobs, retirement is a time of psychic difficulty and discomfort for most men. The woman faces a similar role loss much earlier. Her primary role in life is that of mother: her secondary role is that of homemaker, and her tertiary that of sexual partner. We have already seen that the role of sexual partner, and sexually desirable object, is impaired for many women as middle age approaches. Now we must contemplate the additional fact that the woman's primary role—that of mother—also disappears during middle age.

Indeed, with decreasing family size and increasingly common patterns of early marriage, women are losing their mother role much earlier than formerly. In 1890 the average woman took care of children until her mid-fifties. Today most women see their children leave home when they are in their late forties. Whereas in 1890 the average woman lived 30 years after her last child had entered school and 12 years after her last child married, today, with longer life expectancy, the average woman lives 40 years after her last child enters school and 25 years after her last child marries. Thus, women lose their major role long before the retirement age arrives for men.

Loss of sexual attractiveness and the maternal role comes at a time when the husband is likely to be at the peak of his career and deeply involved in satisfying job activities. Bernice Neugarten, in describing how people become aware of middle age, says:

> Women, but not men, tend to define their age status in terms of timing of events within the family world, and even unmarried career women often discuss middle age in terms of the family they might have had. . . .
> Men, on the other hand, perceive the onset of middle age by cues presented outside the family context, often from the deferential behavior accorded them in the work setting. One man described the first time a younger associate helped open a door for him; another, being called by his official title by a newcomer in the company; another, the first time he was ceremoniously asked for advice by a younger man.

Little research has been done on the prestige accorded men and women in different age brackets. The few studies available point to older women as the lowest prestige group in society. In a projective test asking middle-aged persons to make up a story about a picture that showed a young couple and a middle-aged couple in conversation, Neugarten found that the older woman was seen as more uncomfortable in her role than any of the others and was the only figure who was as often described in negative as in positive terms. Mary

Laurence found that respondents tended to rate women as having more undesirable personality traits than men through all age ranges, but the age group rated most severely was women over forty.

A study of characters in American magazine fiction from 1890 to 1955 found a decline in the number of older women appearing as characters. By 1955 there were none at all. The middle-aged woman almost never sees herself and her problems depicted in print or on the screen. When they are, she sees mostly negative stereotypes. Her dilemma is very similar to that of the black ghetto child who finds in the "Dick and Jane" first reader a world that is irrelevant at best, invidious at worst. To have oneself and one's experiences verified in the mythology and art of one's culture is a fundamental psychological need at every stage of the life cycle.

Women's own attitudes toward aging are shown in the interesting finding that, in the listings of the Directory of the American Psychological Association, women are ten times as likely to omit their age as men. Thus, even professional women, who presumably have roles that extend undamaged into middle age, are much more likely than men to feel that their advancing age is a serious impairment.

On the question of whether middle-aged women are actually unhappier or more maladjusted than middle-aged men, the evidence is conflicting and inconclusive. A few studies by various researchers found little or no difference between middle-aged and old men and women on such factors as personality change, engagement with life, and reported satisfaction with life. One study found older women more satisfied than older men.

One problem with these efforts, though, is that some of them lump together the middle-aged group with persons past retirement age. Some of the findings may therefore be due to the fact that the retirement age is far more stressful and acute for men than for women. Women have never invested much in careers and have been adjusting to role loss for many years. In old age an additional factor works in favor of women. Women are closer to relatives and thus more sheltered from complete isolation.

The studies present another problem in that the respondents themselves judged how happy or satisfied they were. The trouble with this is that subordinated groups learn to expect less and therefore to be satisfied with less. A middle-aged woman whose husband has had several affairs may report that her marriage has been satisfying because society has taught her to expect infidelity from her husband. A man whose wife had behaved in similar fashion would be less likely to regard his marriage as satisfying. Indeed, social conditioning would probably dictate a more painful crisis for the cuckolded husband. Moreover, measuring the satisfaction levels of people who are already so thoroughly "socialized" does not take into account the wife's feelings the first time she saw her own mother experience such treatment from her father and realized that a similar fate was in store for herself. It does not measure the emotional cost of adjusting to the expectation of abuse. In fact, if we were to confine our evidence to degrees of self-reported satisfaction, we might conclude that a great variety of social inequities create no emotional hardships for the subjugated. However, Pauline Bart shows that middle age is much more stressful for women than for men and this finding corroborates the work of Judd Marmor, who has reported that middle-aged women manifest psychiatric disorders three to four times as frequently as middle-aged men.

The Economic Loss

Discrimination against older women in employment is important because of the large number of people affected. The number of older women in the labor force has been growing rapidly in recent decades. In 1965, 50.3 percent of women in the age range of 45 to 54 and 41.4 percent of those 55 to 64 were employed. These percentages had risen sharply from 1940, when they were 24.5 percent and 18 percent, respectively. In 1960, 40 percent of the total female work force was over 45 years old.

Discrimination against older workers of both sexes in industry is well documented. A 1965 Department of Labor survey concluded that half the job openings in the private economy are closed to applicants over fifty-five years of age, and one-fourth are closed to applicants over forty-five. Women are particularly disadvantaged by this discrimination because as a result of their typical work and child-rearing cycle, many women come back on the labor market after a long period of absence (and are perhaps entering the market for the first time) during precisely these years. There is very little evidence on the question of whether older women are relatively more disadvantaged than older men. Edwin Lewis states that age is a greater detriment to women than to men, but cites no evidence. A Department of Labor publication on age discrimination in employment claims that men are slightly favored, but the evidence is very incomplete. The study found that, compared to the percentage of unemployed older men and women, women were hired in somewhat greater numbers. But unemployment rates are based on self-reporting and are notoriously influenced by the optimism of a given group about the prospects of finding employment. Older women, many of whom are married, are less likely to report themselves as seeking work if they are pessimistic about the possibilities of getting any. The study also surveyed the employment practices of 540 firms and found that, although differences were slight, men were disadvantaged in a larger number of occupational categories. But in clerical work, in which twenty-four percent of women over forty-five are engaged, discrimination against women was decidedly greater.

The problem of discrimination against older men and women is complicated by the fact that a study would have to take into account whether discrimination was practiced because of expected lack of physical strength, long training or internship programs, or physical attractiveness. The former two considerations figure much more frequently in the case of men and certainly have more legitimacy as grounds for discriminating than the factor of physical attractiveness, which usually arises solely because the woman is seen as a sex object before she is seen as a productive worker. As long as this is the employer's orientation, it will probably do little good to cite him the studies proving that middle-aged women office workers are superior to young women in work attendance, performance, and ability to get along agreeably with others. It would also be necessary to see how much relative discrimination there is within occupational categories. There is little discrimination in certain low-paid, undesirable jobs because the supply of workers in these categories is short. Women tend to be predominantly clustered in precisely these job categories.

A check of one Sunday's Los Angeles *Times* want ads yielded a count of 1,067 jobs advertised for women and 2,272 advertised for men. For both sexes, specific upper-age limits or the term *young* were attached to less than one percent of the job listings, and there was almost no difference between men and women. However, 97 (or nine percent) of the female ads used the term *girl* or *gal*, while only two of the 2,272 male ads used the term *boy*.

To check out my hunch that *girl* is an indirect way of communicating an age limitation, in a state where discrimination by age is supposedly illegal, I called five employment agencies in southern California and asked interviewers who handle secretarial and clerical placement what he or she thought the term *girl* meant from the employer's side and how it would be interpreted by the average job seeker. Four of the five employment interviewers stated that the term definitely carries an age connotation for employer and job seeker alike. They defined the age implied variously as: "under 30"; "under 35—if we were looking in the 35-45 category we would use the term *mature*; over 45 we don't say anything"; "It means a youngster. I certainly don't think a 45-year-old would go in if she saw that ad"; "It does mean age, which is why we always use the term *women* in our company's ads (although we may use the term *girl* on a specific listing)." The last person would not state a specific age because she was obviously worried about being caught in violation of the law, to which she frequently alluded. Only one of the five replied in the negative, saying "to me *girl* is just another word for *woman*. You can hardly use the term *woman* in the wording of an ad." Everyone I questioned agreed that the term *girl Friday* (a tiny proportion of our cases) carries no age connotation. Several, however, mentioned that the terms *trainee, recent high-school grad,* and *high-school grad* were used to communicate an age limitation.

Along with the term *girl*, a number of ads use physical descriptions—almost entirely lacking in men's ads. "Attractive gal for receptionist job" is typical. More specific are the following excerpts from the columns in the Los Angeles *Times*:

"Exciting young atty seeks a sharp gal who wants a challenge"; "Young, dynamic contractor who is brilliant but disorganized needs girl he can depend on completely"; and one headlined "Lawyer's Pet," which goes on to say, "Looking for a future: want challenge, 'variety,' $$$? Young attorney who handles all phases of 'law' will train you to become his 'right hand.' " Few women over thirty would consider themselves qualified to apply for these jobs.

The use of the term *girl* and the reaction of one employment-agency interviewer who considered this as the only proper way to connote *woman* in a want ad underscores the extent to which women's jobs are still considered young girls' jobs, that is, the relatively unimportant work that a girl does before she gets married. One employment-agency interviewer stated that his agency frequently had requests for a certain age level because companies want to keep the age range in a certain department homogeneous for the sake of congeniality. It is significant that he mentioned only the "twenties" or "thirties" as examples of such desirable age ranges.

One is tempted to make a comparison between the term *girl* and the insulting racist use of *boy* for all blacks, regardless of age. In both cases, the term indicates that the species under discussion is not considered capable of full adulthood. In both cases, blacks and women are acceptable and even likable when very old, as "uncle" and "grandmother," but somehow both are anachronistic as mature adults.

Given the scarcity and conflicting nature of the data, it is impossible to say with certainty that older women suffer more from discrimination than older men. The question certainly merits further and more systematic exploration.

Caste and Class

The division of this chapter into sexual, prestige, and economic loss was taken from John Dollard's analysis of the sexual, prestige, and economic gains of whites at the expense of blacks in his classic study, *Caste and Class in a Southern Town*. The choice was not an accident; spokesmen of women's liberation have often drawn heavily on the analogy between the problems of blacks and of women. Yet equally often one hears objections to the analogy. Blacks are, as a group, isolated in the lowest economic strata and physically ghettoed into the worst parts of town, while women, being inextricably connected to men through familial ties, do not share a drastic, common disability. It has also been suggested that to compare the plight of women with that of blacks is to belittle the importance of the need for black liberation. Most of these critics care as little for black liberation as for the liberation of women and need not be taken seriously.

Yet the intellectual objections to the analogy should be discussed. The argument actually rests on the assumption that middle-class status cushions all of life's shocks and that middle-class women are always comfortably imbedded in middle-class primary groups. It assumes further that the woes of lower-class women are all essentially class connected rather than specifically sex connected. The loneliness of widowhood, the anguish of a woman losing her husband to a younger woman, the perplexity of the woman whose children have left home and who finds herself unwanted on the labor market—these are real hurts, and they go deep, even in the middle class. Further, the notion of the individual as being deeply rooted in his primary groups certainly reflects a partial and outmoded view in a highly individualistic society where the nuclear family, usually the only long-lasting primary group, has become extremely unstable. In our society, men and women are expected to get through life essentially alone. This is true even of the woman who is able to maintain good family ties throughout her life. It is even truer for those who suffer the more common fate of having these ties weakened by discord or severed by death or separation. For the lower-class woman, of course, these difficulties are harsher and more unrelieved, but in every class the woman must bear them alone.

The differential definition of age in men and women represents a palpable advantage to men at the expense of women. It multiplies the options for emotional satisfaction on his side while it diminishes them on hers. It raises his prestige and self-esteem at the expense of hers. All men in our society benefit to some degree from this custom, while not a single woman who lives into middle age escapes bearing some of the cost. If we are ever to restructure this society into one of true equality for both sexes, this is one of the crucial points at which we must begin.

8

Male Mid-Life Crisis: A Comparative Analysis[*]

Orville G. Brim, Jr.

To have many middle-aged men in society is practically a modern phenomenon. In earlier times, ninety percent of the species were dead by age forty. Prehistoric man lived less than three decades. The life span of an ancient Greek or Roman was about four decades. Today more than a tenth of the population in this nation are males between the ages of forty and sixty, numbering nearly twenty-five million. These norm bearers and decision makers, bill payers and power brokers have been the subjects of commentary and serious study for only a short time. In 1932 Walter B. Pitkin wrote *Life Begins at Forty*, and in the mid-thirties Charlotte Buhler, Else Frenkel-Brunswick, and Erik Erikson had started their studies of personality changes during the middle years. But until a decade or so ago, most studies of adults were not developmental in perspective; most of the information we had about adults came from cross-sectional studies, as a by-product of other research

*Invited address to Division 20, at the 82d Annual Convention of the American Psychological Association, New Orleans, September 1974. Reprinted by permission of the author and the editors of *The Counseling Psychologist*.

interests. With few exceptions, the dominant view was that
nothing of significance takes place in the male personality
during the mid-life period. People felt life ended at forty and
there was nothing to do but wait around for retirement and
death.

This is still the prevailing view, it seems. Robert Sears
reports that in teaching his course at Stanford on human
development through the life cycle, it comes as a surprise to
many students to recognize that their parents may be having
their own growth and adaptation crises. It is reminiscent of the
story about Stalin's young son, before the revolution, who said
to his mother, "Father should get out and do something; all he
does is walk in the park with Lenin." Why this attribution of
constancy of personality should occur for mid-life males, in the
face of the experiences and evidence noted later, is a puzzle
worth working on. We know that one attributes more trait
consistency over time to others than to one's self, that lives
seem more coherent from the outside than from the inside, but
this should apply equally at all ages and to women as well as to
men, if it is a fundamental cognitive process in attribution.
Could it be that society is heavily invested in this particular
age-sex category; and must therefore count on conformity and
stability? Is it motivated also by matters not quite so
pragmatic; namely, that these men are fathers, and children,
of all ages, desire a stable father figure? Are middle-aged men
rewarded for stoicism, and punished for expressions of
uncertainty and suffering?

The body of scholarly work here under consideration
challenges the premises that nothing happens to men in
mid-life, and that middle-aged males need no help or attention.
And, there is fiction (Leggett; Bissell; Stern); popular work
(LeShan); self-help books (Hills; the O'Neills; Bergler;
Vorspan); and mass-media treatments—for example, True
Story magazine carries a lead article entitled "I Am the Wife
of a Man in a Mid-Life Crisis," and the next season in
television will see the launching, I am told, of a series on males
at mid-life called "A Second Chance."

Because the concept of male mid-life crisis implies
personality change, this work is germane. Here, too, there is
fiction—the genre of work dealing with personality change,
the stories and great legends of metamorphosis, for example,

Dr. Jekyll and Mr. Hyde, Here Comes Mr. Jordan, and *Seconds.* The popular and self-help literature is really vast on this topic, what Martin Lieberman describes in a recent review (of Schutz's *Here Comes Everybody*), as a plethora of technologies, a smorgasbord of methods to change human beings. And there are notable, serious, scholarly works, say Jerome Frank's *Persuasion and Healing* and John Mann's *Changing Human Behavior.* . . .

Some Definitions

As Neugarten reports (1965): "The evidence shows and most agree that the individual as he moves through the adult years becomes transformed in appearance, social or life patterns, interests, relationships, and also with regard to inner qualities, for example, mode of experiencing and expressing emotions and motivations and preoccupations." There are hundreds of investigations that substantiate personality change in adulthood, in reactions to situations, in attitudes, in reference groups, in self-descriptive items, in sources of gratification, in dyadic relationships, in the objective descriptions by friends, and on psychological tests. The data come from self-reports, longitudinal studies, observational materials, individual protocols, personal descriptions attesting to the fact that "everybody is working on something," and, significantly, the inability to predict adult personality from childhood, or even adolescence. Change, not continuity, seems the natural state of the organism.

The classic criticism of this view of adult personality change is, of course, that of the psychoanalyst. (Jung and Erikson are major exceptions: both postulated changes, for example, Jung commenting on the increase in introversion in middle and later life and the reorganization of value systems that characterizes adult change, and Erikson postulating a mid-life developmental task of stagnation vs generativity.) But for most, the psychoanalytic view is in opposition: That the sense of identity is essentially established in adolescence and that it produces consistency in behavior thereafter; that the character structure becomes fixed in early adulthood and the essential nature or personality remains unchanged (Neugarten 1973). Previously I noted some other causes of the view that adult male personality does not change, namely, the mistaken attribution of continuity, the anxiety from perceiving the primary male figure in society as in uncertain change, and the normative pressure for stoicism. For these reasons, the burden seems to have been on behavioral scientists to demonstrate change, rather than what seems more difficult, to demonstrate continuity.

Behavioral change is the ultimate criterion, but it cannot be measured except inferentially because it expresses itself variably over different situations. Therefore one needs various observers, in different situations over time, to capture the change either as manifest in changes in their responses or their ratings. Thus, it is difficult to demonstrate personality change except by this kind of summary of evidence from a variety of times and places.

Even the best of research is criticized as showing only phenotypic changes, leaving the genotypic personality underneath these surface manifestations still the same. The answer can be made as a threefold challenge to the psychoanalytic view:

(1) that it is impossible for psychoanalysts to be convincing as Neugarten (1965) says, in moving from phenotypic behavior at time one to an accurate conceptualization of the genotypic trait that underlies it, and then to a conceptualization and measurement of the different phenotypical behavior appropriate at time two;

(2) even if one says that traits like "ego strength" change little over time in contrast to other personality traits (for example, interpersonal relationships or attitudes or self-esteem or social roles), one might be prepared to yield to the clinician the territory of "ego strength" and its durability, and move on to work with what is left, which, in my view, is effectively almost all of the adult personality;

(3) if one takes the position that it is the natural state of the male adult to be stable in personality, we must ask how much of the stability depends on an unchanging environment? In primitive slow-changing environments there is likely to be continuity in personality, but in the United States, where both work and family situations are in rapid alterations, life-span personality change may be increasing —coming to public attention compared to four decades ago—and continuity of personality increasingly difficult to demonstrate.

The male mid-life crisis is one of many concepts that are candidates for inclusion in theories of life-span human development; and in this brief essay I shall appraise whether this concept of crisis is suitable as a building block for more general theories of life-span development. Theorists of mid-life male changes have focused on different components of the person.

Lowenthal and her colleagues are concerned with the individual's goal domain, past, present, and future; with his/ her values; with aspects of psychological functioning such as morale and anxiety; with behavior-trait changes and modes of adaptation. Levinson and his colleagues use the concept of "life structure." It is meant to integrate traditional social-structural perspectives with personality-structure concepts. From the sociological perspective, one can think of life structure as containing a uniquely personal, social system, with one's own set of unique statuses and roles, residences, the physical space one spends time in, his leisure, his travel, and the like. From the psychological viewpoint, one can think of it as consisting primarily of role behavior and related motives, attitudes, and beliefs, both conscious and unconscious. Life structure can be viewed as separate from social organization, when one compares his specific unique arrangements with that of the larger order and contrasts his position with what he might become, wishes to be, or was. And it can be viewed as separate from personality, when one says, "his life doesn't fit his personality." The studies of Neugarten over a twenty-year period have examined the life-span developmental process with reference to many personality characteristics—values, preferences, attitudes toward death, definitions of and expectations for age grades, perspectives on time, to name a few.

These scholars and most others mentioned here use the term *transition*, and some use the term *crisis*. The transition concept clearly implies a change that moves the person from one position or stage to another. Hence, implicit in the word *transition* is the concept of stages or stable periods in personality. Lowenthal, et al. use the concept of transition in connection with changes in statuses and roles, for example, marraige or retirement; Levinson, et al. also use the term *transition* in connection with changes in stages of life structure, for example, "getting into the adult world," "becoming one's own man." Even so, the definition of transition for Levinson is difficult to pin down. Sometimes he says it is making something out of that which is new, but most often it is both death and rebirth, the best of the old along with the best of the new; in this way he speaks in allegory rather than using a precise definition. Neugarten thinks of stages—whether social or psychological—less formally, but this usage clearly would be acceptable.

As for the concept of "personality crisis," in mid-life and at other times, it implies a rapid or substantial change in personality—and it is probably both rapid *and* substantial rather than either one alone—that is dislocating with respect to one's sense of identity in that his usual reference groups, his role models, his principles, his values, his dyadic relationships evolve so that the whole framework of his earlier life is in question. At the extreme are the fundamental and familiar religious conversions, and currently the dramatic mind-changing consequences of certain behavior-modification programs.

We can also say that there are crises without transitions or personality changes, but this requires a different definition of crisis, namely, one of intense suffering, such as a temporary physical ailment, or extreme fear for an event that does not take place, neither of which need yield any significant durable change in personality.

Theorists agree that there can be transitions in personality without crisis. For instance, Clausen reports that in the Berkeley growth study lowered aspirations and downward mobility are made with a smooth transition for a substantial number of the subjects. He goes on to add that those in transition often are not aware of it, that there are individual differences in how much and how often persons reflect on these matters—some subjects having undergone substantial change but thinking about it only when interviewed, while others seem to have mused about it almost every day.

But for some unknown number of men, a mid-life crisis resulting from personality change is a notable experience. An elusive concept to pin down, it reminds me of the story of the

Southern mountain man who, when asked if he believed in baptism, said, "Believe in it, I've seen it." Elliott Jaques refers us to this theme in the *Divine Comedy*. "This masterpiece of all time was begun by Danté following his banishment from Florence at the age of 37. In the opening stanzas he created his setting in words of great power and tremendous psychological depth. He begins: 'In the middle of the journey of our life, I came to myself within a dark wood, savage and harsh and dense, the thought of which renews my fear. So bitter is it that death is hardly more.' "

Causes and Content

The causes set forth for personality changes, transitions, or crises during the male mid-life period by the several theorists can be summarized in these concepts: (1) endocrine changes, (2) aspiration-achievement gap, (3) resurgence of "The Dream," (4) stagnation vs growth ("generativity"), (5) confrontation with death, (6) relationships within the family, and (7) social status and role changes. I have not tried to order these theoretically, a point I consider shortly, but they are arrayed from the biological to the social structural.

1 Endocrine Changes

From about age thirty on there is a gradual decline in testosterone and cortisol, and from thirty through the remainder of life there is a gradual decline in secretion of androgens for the male. There are other steroids identified, many of which are produced in large amounts and with greater age trends than the foregoing, but they are not as yet linked theoretically to physiological processes. There is much to be examined on this psychobiology frontier—in this unknown area of hormonal changes during the male mid-life period. To what extent the changes themselves contribute to individual self-reappraisals or vulnerability to stress we simply do not know at this time.

2 Aspirations and Achievements

Work still takes the largest single percentage of one's waking hours and constitutes for most a fundamental influence on the development and change in the sense of self through the life cycle. The search for self-esteem—to be valued by others who matter, and to be valued by one's self; to feel in control of the world, one's life course, time, and self in its values and behavior; to believe one is distinctive, unique even, that one counts for something special in the common pilgrimage of man; to sense personal growth and development so that one is something more than as of a week ago—the pursuit of these and other elements in the summary sense of self-esteem pervades the work of most people.

The aspirations in life that men set for themselves are primarily expressed through the institution of work. Over the course of the working life, from entry to the mid-life period, it is likely that although aspirations may be adjusted downward on occasion, one usually believes there is enough time left for the desired level of achievement to be reached in future years. But during the mid-life most American males must adjust their career aspirations of earlier years downward to fit current reality. A man may be told that he has risen as high as he can go in his place of work; that his present position must be accepted by him as the achievement level for his lifetime. In one of our best-known studies, Chinoy reports that automobile workers, comparing their career dreams with what they have actually accomplished, solved the problem of discrepancies by considering their work to be temporary and by maintaining their hopes of becoming an entrepreneur or farmer. Eventually, though, "the worker faces a day of reckoning when he is called upon to admit that he is 'trapped,' that his American dream of being his own boss is not to be fulfilled."

This causative factor has been in the explanatory theories of many commentators on the mid-life period: for example, William James, Buhler, Kuhlen, Butler, Slotkin, make use of the aspiration-achievement gap and its reconciliation as the source and content of personality change. While many men may make this adaptation, in small steps, in a gradual alteration of one's self-image, so that a transition to a new sense of self is accomplished without a crisis, for others depression emerges as one realizes he can no longer count on seemingly limitless years ahead.*

*We note that moving toward old age there is cross-cultural evidence showing a decline in expressions of competition and risk (Gutmann), and a concern in the older age period not with reducing the aspiration-achievement gap but simply in holding on to what one has achieved, in protecting what one has from others, usually younger insurgent groups.

3 Resurgence of "The Dream"

Levinson and his colleagues most clearly set forth the view that maturation requires one to go through a period of suppression of certain aspects of the self in order to develop and commit to a given life structure, involving an occupation and a family, and that during middle age the suppressed aspects of the self push toward the surface and demand that the man reappraise who he is and what he has been doing. They use the concept of "The Dream" as a youthful aspiration, as an early image of the future self that never dies.

It seems to me that the major component of "The Dream" for males involves their work. It makes a sharp contrast, though, to the aspiration-achievement problem just described, because the middle-aged malaise may arise even though one achieves what he set out to do. The man may feel that he has attempted too little, not stretched himself, not seized opportunities. He may feel it is meaningless and ask, is this what I really wanted? Was it worth all I had to give up? Do I want to go on doing these things for the years I have left? What of those parts of myself that I had to neglect—to suppress—to sacrifice? There is a pervading sense of great sadness in these mid-life men of unfulfilled dreams, and it is the resolution of this crisis that is crucial to Levinson's theory. The man must give up the early-adulthood life structure, allowing resurgence and expression of "The Dream," and work through the mid-life transition to the restructuring for middle adulthood.

4 Stagnation vs Growth

Erikson, in his work on stages of psychosocial development, sets one adult task as the resolution of the issue of generativity vs self-absorption. The essence of a successful transition is to shift one's life interests and concerns to the development and achievements of the younger generation and to accept and value one's responsibility to care for this next generation of man.

The concept of generativity describes the possible resolution of a mid-life crisis rather than its cause, but I include it here because it seems to me to be closest to the idea that a desire for a sense of personal growth is a deep-seated characteristic of the human organism and that a failure of a sense of growth generates depression and leads to attempts to avoid this stagnation. (It may be that this developmental process is most important for gifted and successful men such as Erikson has studied and may also be of significance for men of early climax stories—for example, Irwin Shaw's *The 80-Yard Run*—where one fears that he never again will do as much or as well in his career.)

Recently Helen Vendler in reviewing Allen Ginsburg's book, *The Fall of America*, describes the despair of Ginsburg's middle age: "Everything is already known, and everything has stopped happening. . . .Friends are now what they will be for good: no one would change. Everything has been encountered: sex, love, friendship, drugs, even fame, even the boundary dimensions of self."

5   Confrontation with Death

Elliott Jaques in his influential paper, "Death and the Mid-Life Crisis," says:

> Family and occupation have become established; parents have grown old, and children are at the threshold of adulthood. Youth and childhood are past and gone, and demand to be mourned. The achievement of mature and independent adulthood presents itself as the main psychological task. The paradox is that of entering the prime of life, the stage of fulfillment, but at the same time the prime and fulfillment are dated. Death lies beyond. . . .I believe, and shall try to demonstrate, that it is this fact of the entry upon the psychological scene of the reality and inevitability of one's own eventual personal death that is the central and crucial feature of the mid-life phase—the feature which precipitates the critical nature of the period. Death—at the conscious level—instead of being a general conception, or an event experienced in terms of the loss of someone else, becomes a personal matter, one's own death, one's own real and actual mortality.

And then, referring to a particular case in his practice, he says, describing the man:

> He began his adjustment to the fact that he would not be able to accomplish in the span of a single lifetime everything

he had desired to do. He could achieve only a finite amount. Much would have to remain unfinished and unrealized. . . .

This perspective on the finitude of life was accompanied by a greater solidity and robustness in his outlook and introduced a new quality of earthly resignation. It reflected a diminishing of his unconscious wish for immortality. Such ideas are commonly lived out in terms of denial of mourning and death, or in terms of ideas of immortality, from notions of reincarnation and life after death, to notions of longevity like those expressed by the successful twenty-eight year old novelist who writes in his diary, "I shall be the most serious of men, and I shall live longer than any man."

Signs to one's self that he is getting old—the hearing, the vision, the hair color, the body functions, the stamina, the teeth, the skin, the rate of healing wounds—are gradual in development and one recognizes that he has stopped growing up, and begun to grow old—that from here on out, everything is downhill. But these indices of aging are nothing compared to the vivid sudden confrontation with the fact of one's own mortality. One of Neugarten's several significant, empirically based observations about the personality change involves time orientation, and a change in mid-life when one stops counting "time since birth" and begins to think of one's life in reference to "time yet to live." Death represents to the middle-aged man the fact that he will not achieve what he thought he was going to achieve. He will not see those places he had planned to see, he will not explore those ideas he had on his future agenda.

One looks on with some pathos, and occasionally with a sense of tragedy, when the attempted mid-life solution to mortality is to intensify efforts and to engage in complicated attempts to master the use of time. It seems to me, as it must to you, that this is a clear expression of the actual or incipient confrontation with death in its fullest sense. Neugarten has suggested in relation here that the central task for middle age relates to the use of time and the essential polarities are between time mastery and capitulation; but this seems to me to pose the question or task somewhat superficially. We can say that one of the major psychological tasks for middle age is resignation to death and a permutation, a reordering, of life priorities. As Jaques shows in his many clinical cases, successful resolution liberates energy and leads on to self-acceptance.

6   Relationships within the Family

As Anne Boedecker writes, "In the family, middle age is generally the time when a man's children are leaving the home for work and families of their own, his wife is readjusting to the role of housewife without children and perhaps entering or reentering the job market, and his parents may be aging to the point of becoming dependent on him." Some writers see this as a period of high tension and conflict within the family system and a period of high risk for the postparental couple. On the other hand, there is a good bit of solid research reporting that couples rate the postparental period as one of the best in their marriage, and have significant role changes only when family continuity is low. Lowenthal and colleagues are studying this empty-nest period as transition period, and we shall know more later as a result.

In any event, two unusual points are noteworthy: Levinson and his colleagues point out that a man during his children's adolescence must inevitably compare a fantasy, his belief in his own power and influence to mold his child into some ideal being, with what is now becoming a reality, and accept the limited nature of his own influence. This reconciliation of aspirations to reality likely is taking place at the same time that his occupational aspiration-achievement gap is being worked through. We do not seem to have many facts about the expression of aspirations for children by parents at this older age level, although the work on earlier childhood aspirations with reference to certain character traits (for example, Kohn) has been charted. The subtleties of the transference of the father's aspirations upon the children has been described, but not counted. *

*Since blue-collar and white-collar workers "top out" at different ages, it might mean that the interaction with the adolescent would be different because the sons might differ in age as much as ten years. On the other hand, since blue-collar workers marry earlier and have children earlier, the age gap may not be as large. The actual facts here bear looking into because the problem may be more acute for the white-collar worker with the older son.

As for husband-wife relations, I want to note the suggestion that comes from Dr. Neugarten and the Committee on Human Development group, and specifically from David Gutmann's cross-cultural work: It is that there are some concurrent age changes in the psychological stances of both men and women that bear on the male mid-life crisis. In essence, the older men are more diffusely sensual, more sensitive to the incidental pleasures and pains, less aggressive, more affiliative, more interested in love than conquest or power, more present than future oriented. At the same time women are aging in the reverse direction, becoming more aggressive, less sentimental, and more domineering. While in the earlier years the husband tends to be dominant, during the aging process he comes to be more dependent. Apparently this comprehensive developmental event of middle and later life acts to reverse or at least equalize the domestic status of the partners, and tends to redistribute the so-called masculine and feminine traits among them, so that through these various sex-role changes there is ushered in the "normal unisex of later life."

What needs to be attended to here in regard to mid-life males—and Lowenthal and colleagues have made an excellent start—is that mid-life female personality changes and trajectories are outward, away from dependency on the husband, away from providing nurturance and support to him, so this source of his recognition, affection, and sense of value becomes precarious, threatens to disappear.

7   Social Status and Role Changes

With this concept we move on to consider simply external events in the male mid-life, where the theories of causation emphasize changes in position in social organization. It is the predictable sequence of changes in status and role through the life span that receives attention from Lowenthal and her colleagues. Specifically, their forthcoming volume reports on four populations facing imminent role-loss transitions of adult life: high-school seniors before starting full-time work; newly-weds before the birth of the first child; parents whose youngest child will leave home within the year; and pre-retirement couples, leaving employment within a year or two. Now Lowenthal, as noted, does not believe that such changes necessarily bring crises; but rather are transitions in personality, are occasions for both incremental and decremental changes, in which one stage is left behind, a phase of life over, but with new growth and development ahead.

Neugarten also has considered the influence of status changes on mid-life personality and, although asserting personality change, she says: "It is an inaccurate view that middle age constitutes a crisis period in the life cycle any more than any other period of life. For most persons middle age brings with it the anticipated changes in family and work and health. Some of these changes are not necessarily interpreted as losses by the people who experience them. Whether perceived as losses or gains, the life events of middle age may produce new stresses for the individual, but they also bring occasions to demonstrate an enriched sense of self and new capacities for coping with complexity."

She says that since we have been socialized into a developmental view, the predictable on-time events when they arrive are not unsettling, "that the events are anticipated and rehearsed, the grief work completed, the reconciliation accomplished without shattering this sense of continuity of the life cycle." But, then she uses her concept of "on-time—off-time" in a new hypothesis about status changes causing mid-life crises: "It is the unanticipated, not the anticipated, which is likely to represent the traumatic event. Major stresses are caused by events that upset the sequence and rhythm of the expected life cycle, as when death of a parent comes in adolescence rather than in middle age; when the birth of a child is too early or too late; when occupational achievement is delayed; when the empty nest, grandparenthood, retirement, major illness, or widowhood occur off-time." *

---

*We should note that there is another class of unexpected traumatic events that must be viewed as stress events inducing crises that are not necessarily related to chronological age or to passage through the social structure. Instead these are cohort experiences, such as wars, depressions—and historically, plagues and holocausts. We do not find any major sociological analysis of the impact of these stress events on adult males in the United States, since the work on the Great Depression of the 1930s, for example, Bakke on unemployment, and more recently Studs Terkel's *Hard Times*.

By way of comment on these seven "causes," we see at the one extreme physiological theories of personality change that might stress the importance of hormonal shifts, while the other anchoring point is a strict sociological perspective that views the life cycle as a succession of social roles with personality change viewed as a product of life-long socialization experiences. Arrayed somewhere in between are the other propositions briefly reviewed above: for example, the mid-life confrontation with death seems virtually unavoidable simply as one gets older, while the crunch of aspiration-achievement discrepancies, or the surfacing of the set-aside "Dream," lack the same inexorability, for both are partly dependent on external happenings.

It seems to me, in conclusion, that the most valid male mid-life description today is that any man can change, in any way, at any time. His personality changes may have one or more of several causes; his transitions should be seen as working through one or another adaptive requirements, moving from one comparatively steady state to the next.

These events need not occur in sequence; some are early, some late, depending on the individual case. The challenges may be stretched out over the 40-60-year-old period. Some men are uneasy about achievement but not yet consciously confronting death; other men are sharply disappointed in their children's personalities but not yet concerned about time left to live. These causes cannot be, I conclude, linked in stages in the sophisticated structural sense, nor are they tied to chronological age; there is no lock-step or assembly-line human development here.

And yet, with all of this, it is certain that some men have crises at some time in their mid-life period, and it seems this must be when men get hit with multiple demands for fundamental personality change in the same year, or month, or week. As one person summed it up: "The hormone production levels are dropping, the head is balding, the sexual vigor is diminishing, the stress is unending, the children are leaving, the parents are dying, the job horizons are narrowing, the friends are having their first heart attacks; the past floats by in a fog of hopes not realized, opportunities not grasped, women not bedded, potentials not fulfilled, and the future is a confrontation with one's own mortality."

References

Bergler, Edmund. *The Revolt of the Middle-Aged Man.* New York: Grosset and Dunlap, 1967.

Bissell, Richard. *Still Circling Moose Jaw.* Boston: Little, Brown.

Boedecker, Anne. "The Impact of Career Success or Failure on the Male Mid-Life Crisis: A Proposal for Research on Adult Development." Unpublished.

Chinoy, E. *Automobile Workers and the American Dream.* New York: Doubleday, 1955.

Clausen, John. "The Life Course of Individuals." In *Aging and Society.* Edited by M.W. Riley, M. Johnson, and A. Foner. New York: Russell Sage Foundation, 1972.

Coleman, R., and Neugarten, Bernice L. *Social Status in the City.* San Francisco: Jossey-Bass, 1971.

Erikson, Erik. "Generativity and Ego Integrity." *Childhood and Society.* New York: Norton, 1950.

Frank, Jerome. *Persuasion and Healing.* New York: Schocken Books, 1963.

Gutmann, David. "The Country of Old Men: Cross-Cultural Studies in the Psychology of Later Life." *Occasional Papers in Gerontology.* Ann Arbor, Michigan: Institute of Gerontology. University of Michigan-Wayne State University, 1969.

Hamburg, David A., and Hamburg, Beatrix. "Occupational Stress, Endocrine Changes, and Coping Behavior in the Middle Years of Adult Life." Unpublished paper, 1974.

Havighurst, Munnichs, Neugarten, and Thomae. *Adjustment to Retirement: A Cross-National Study.* Assen, Netherlands: Van Gorcum, 1969.

Hills, L. Rust. *How to Retire at 41.* New York: Doubleday, 1973.

Jaques, Elliott. "Death and the Mid-Life Crisis." *International Journal of Psychoanalysis* 4, part 4 (October 1965): 502-514.

Kohlberg, Lawrence. "Stages and Aging in Moral Development—Some Speculations." *The Gerontologist* 13, no. 4 (Winter 1973).

Kohn, Melvin L. *Class and Conformity: A Study in Values.* Homewood, Illinois: Dorsey Press, 1969.

Kramer, Morton, and Redick, Richard W. "Epidemiological Indices in the Middle Years." Unpublished paper.

Kuhlen, Raymond G. "Developmental Changes in Motivation during the Adult Years." In *Relations of Development and Aging.* Edited by James E. Birren, ch. 13. Springfield, Illinois: Charles C. Thomas, 1964.

Lear, M.W. "Is There a Male Menopause?" *New York Times Magazine,* 28 January 1973.

Leggett, John. *The Gloucester Branch*. New York: Harper and Row, 1964.

Levinson, Daniel J., and Associates. "The Psychosocial Development of Men in Early Childhood and the Mid-life Transition." In *Life History Research in Psychopathology: III*. Edited by D. F. Ricks, A. Thomas, and M. Roff. Minneapolis, Minn.: University of Minnesota Press, 1974.

LeShan, Eda. *The Wonderful Crisis of Middle Age*. New York: David McKay, 1973.

Lowenthal, Marjorie Fiske, and Chiriboga, David. "Social Stress and Adaptation: Toward a Life-Course Perspective." In *Psychology of Adult Development and Aging*. Edited by C. Eisdorfer and M.P. Lawton, pp. 281 to 310. Washington, D.C.: American Psychological Association, 1973.

Mann, John. *Changing Human Behavior*. New York: Charles Scribner's Sons, 1965.

Neugarten, Bernice L., and Associates. *Personality in Middle and Late Life*. New York: Atherton Press, 1964.

_____, *Middle Age and Aging: A Reader in Social Psychology*. Chicago: University of Chicago Press, 1968.

_____, and Dowty, N. "The Middle Years." *American Handbook of Psychiatry* 1, part 3 (March 1972).

_____. "Personality Change in Late Life: A Developmental Perspective." In *The Psychology of Adult Development and Aging*. Edited by C. Eisdorfer and M.P. Lawton. Washington, D.C.: American Psychological Association, 1973.

_____, and Datan, Nancy. "Sociological Perspectives on the Life Cycle." *Life-Span Developmental Psychology*. Edited by Paul B. Baltes and K. Warner Schorie, ch. 3. New York and London: Academic Press, 1973.

O'Neill, Nena, and O'Neill, George. *Shifting Gears*. New York: E.M. Evans, 1974.

Social Science Research Council. "Description of Proposed Activities, Committee on Work and Personality in the Middle Years." New York, June 1973.

Soddy, Kenneth. *Men in Middle Life*. New York: Lippincott, 1967.

Stern, Richard. *Other Men's Daughters*. New York: E.P. Dutton, 1973.

Thurnher, Majda. "Goals, Values and the Life Evaluations at the Preretirement Stage." *Journal of Gerontology* 29 (1974): 85-96.

Vendler, Helen. Review of Allen Ginsburg's book, *The Fall of America*, in *New York Times Sunday Book Review*, February 1974.

Vorspan, Albert. *Mazel Tov! You're Middle Aged*. New York: Doubleday, 1974.

9

Middle Age and Aging*

Bernice L. Neugarten

Adaptation and the Life Cycle

A life history can be understood only by considering its historical setting. The life cycle of a man born in 1910 differs from that of a man born in 1950. Any historical, economic, or political event varies in personal significance according to the point in the life cycle at which the event occurs. For example, the effects of the Great Depression or the Vietnam War on a young man just finishing school and entering upon economic adulthood differ greatly from those on a middle-aged man at the height of his occupational career. This chapter is concerned with adaptation through time and with life time as differentiated from calendar or historical time.

The interweaving of historical time and life time occurs in the context of a third dimension, that of socially defined time. Every society is age graded, and every society has a system of

*This work originally appeared in the *Journal of Geriatric Psychiatry* 4, no. 1 (Fall 1970): 71-87. Presented at an Interdisciplinary Meeting of the Boston Society for Gerontologic Psychiatry, 6 December 1969. An earlier version of this paper was presented at a conference on "Adaptation to Change," sponsored by the Foundations Fund for Research in Psychiatry, June 1968.

social expectations regarding age-appropriate behavior. The individual passes through a socially regulated cycle from birth to death as inexorably as he passes through the biological cycle; a succession of socially delineated age statuses, each with its recognized rights, duties, and obligations. There exists a socially prescribed timetable for the ordering of major life events: a time in the life span when men and women are expected to marry, a time to raise children, a time to retire. This normative pattern is adhered to, more or less consistently, by most persons within a given social group—although the actual occurrences of major life events are influenced by various contingencies and although the norms themselves vary somewhat from one socioeconomic, ethnic, or religious group to another. For any social group it can easily be demonstrated that norms and actual occurrences are closely related. Age norms and age expectations operate as a system of social controls, as prods and brakes upon behavior, in some instances hastening an event; in others, delaying it. Men and women are aware not only of the social clocks that operate in various areas of their lives but also of their own timing; and they readily describe themselves as "early," "late," or "on time" with regard to the major life events.

The social change that occurs with the passage of historical time creates alterations in the rhythm and timing of the life cycle, leading in turn to changes in age norms and in expectations regarding age-appropriate behavior. Within the family cycle, there are points at which the individual moves from "child" to "adolescent" to "adult" and where, after physical maturity is reached, social age continues to be marked off by relatively clear-cut biological or social events: marriage, the birth of the first child, the departure of children from the home, and the birth of grandchildren. At each of these points, the individual takes on new roles in the family and his status in relation to other family members is altered.

Changes in timing of the family cycle have been dramatic over the past several decades: age at marriage has dropped; children are born earlier in the marriage; longevity has increased, thereby increasing the duration of marriage. Marriage and parenthood imply adulthood within the family cycle, so it may be said that adulthood is reached earlier than before. The average modern young woman marries in her twentieth year, gives birth to her first child within the first year thereafter, bears all her children in the next five or six years, and sees her last-born child in school by the time she reaches thirty-two. Active parenthood is becoming shorter, for children are leaving home at an earlier age. It follows that grandparenthood also comes at an earlier age now than in preceding generations. At the same time, widowhood tends to occur later.

The historical trend, therefore, has been toward a quickening of events through most of the family cycle, followed by an extended postparental interval (now some fifteen to seventeen years) in which husband and wife are the remaining members of the household.

Marriage, although it defines maturity within the family, is no longer synchronous with the attainment of economic maturity. With the increasing needs of the American economy for technical and professional workers, the length of time devoted to education has increased for young people, but without a concomitant delay in marriage. (In 1966, for example, of all males enrolled in colleges and graduate schools, nearly one out of four were married; of those aged 25 to 29, 72 percent were married.)

Changing sex-role patterns with regard to the timing of economic maturity are reflected in the rising proportion of young married women in the labor force. In 1890, only six percent of married women aged 14 to 24 were working; by 1960 it was 31 percent. While the percentages reflect marriages in which husbands are working, as well as those in which husbands are still in school, they reveal in both instances that young wives are increasingly sharing the economic burdens of new households and that they are doing so at younger and younger ages. Economic maturity is being deferred for men, but not for women.

The new rhythms of social maturity impinge, of course, upon other aspects of family life as well. Parent-child relationships are influenced in many subtle ways by the fact that half of all new fathers are under twenty-three and half of all new mothers under twenty-one. Changes in parental behavior, with fathers reportedly becoming less authoritarian and with both parents sharing more equally in tasks of homemaking and child rearing, may be reflections of this trend. The relative youth of parents and grandparents may also be contributing to the complex patterns of help between generations that are now becoming evident, including the widespread financial help that flows from parents downward to their adult children. Similarly, with more grandparents surviving per child and with an extended family system that encompasses several generations, new patterns of child rearing are emerging in which child-grandparent relations take on new significance.

In a recent study of three-generation families in which various styles of behavior by grandparents were delineated, we found that younger grandparents (those under age sixty-five, as compared with those over sixty-five) more often followed what we called the *fun-seeking* pattern. The fun-seeker is the grandparent whose relation to the child is informal and playful and who joins the child for the specific purpose of having fun, somewhat as if he were the child's playmate. Grandchildren are viewed by these grandparents as a source of leisure activity, as an item of "consumption" rather than "production," and as a source of self-indulgence. The relationship is one in which authority lines are irrelevant and where the emphasis is on mutual satisfaction.

Another new trend among the middle aged is for women to go back to work. The proportion of working women in their early 20s is high; it drops off markedly from age 25 to 35 and then rises again. More than 40 percent of all women aged 35 to 44 are now in the labor force and more than 50 percent of those aged 45 to 54. The young child is likely to have his mother at home but his grandmother out working; the adolescent, to have both mother and grandmother working.

A few generations ago, with children spaced further apart, the last child married and the nest emptied when women were in their mid-50s. Today, this event occurs when women are in their late 40s, at about the same time they experience the menopause and the biological climacterium. This is the same age when the census data show the number of women on the labor market taking its sharpest upturn.

These are but a few examples of the way in which historical time and social change are affecting the course and

rhythm of the life cycle, affecting in turn social expectations
with regard to age-appropriate behavior. *

Although there have been many changes in the life cycle,
there also remain many regularities and continuities. While it
is true that the rapidity of social change is unprecedented and
that the explosion of knowledge occurring in the social,
psychological, physical, and biological sciences may upset
many of our present assumptions about human nature,
people's lives in the next few decades are not likely to be
transformed as drastically as some of our newspaper writers
would lead us to believe. Despite the contraceptive pill and the
increased freedom with regard to the occurrence and timing of
parenthood, despite the organ transplants and the promise of
greater control over death, and despite space travel, the
human life cycle is likely to retain its major features for some
time to come. Biologists seem to believe, for instance, that the
human life span is relatively fixed by genetic factors; and even
as they begin to separate the effects of aging from those of
injury or disease, and as greater proportions of the population
live to the biological limits, it is likely to be a long time before the
life span itself can be lengthened.

New methods of biological engineering may alter the
genetic composition of the human species, yet for the foresee-
able future we are likely to deal with human organisms who
will grow and develop to biological maturity in the first third of
the life span, who will continue to change psychologically and
socially in the second and third parts of the life span, and who
will age and die. Accordingly, men and women will continue to
experience many of the same biological, social, and psychological regularities of the life cycle.

Some of these regularities will continue to arise from the
social controls related to age norms and age-appropriate
behavior. Because individuals live in contact with persons of
all ages, they learn what to anticipate. There is a never-ending
process of socialization by which the child learns what facets
of his childhood behavior he must shed as he moves into
adolescence; the adolescent learns what is expected of him as

*The effects of social change upon the timing of major life events
and the creation of new age norms are described at greater length in
an earlier paper (Neugarten and Moore 1968).

he moves from school to job to marriage to parenthood; and the middle aged learn approved ways of growing old. Thus the social ordering of age statuses and age-appropriate behavior will continue to provide a large measure of predictability.

There are certain other regularities of the life cycle that may be said to arise more from within the individual than from without. To draw a dichotomy between "inner" and "outer" is, of course, merely a heuristic device, given a transactional view of personality. As the result of accumulative adaptations to both biological and social events, there is a continuously changing basis within the individual for perceiving and responding to new events in the outer world. It is in this sense that orderly and predictable changes occur within the personality as well as in the social environment.

People change over time as the result of the accumulation of experience. As events are registered in the organism, human individuals inevitably abstract from their experiences and create more encompassing and more refined categories for interpreting new events. The mental filing system not only grows larger but it is also reorganized over time, with infinitely more cross-references and classifications. Not only do middle-aged parents differ from their adolescent children because they, the parents, were born in a different historical period and were therefore subject to different formative experiences, but they differ also because of the effects of having lived longer, of having therefore a greater apperceptive mass or store of past experiences (or, again, a more complex filing system) by which to evaluate any event.

(It is not being cynical to suggest that young people who are demonstrating on college campuses all over the world are subject to the same imperatives of change that stem from the course of the life cycle. This is not to say that people as they age become more conservative politically, for the evidence on this point is moot, but rather that with increasing age, perspectives inevitably lengthen and, as a consequence, attitudes and behavior change. Only a few hippies have remained hippies into their thirties and forties, not only because the social issues have changed and hippie culture itself has altered, but because there are internal pressures to change that stem from movement through one's own life cycle.)

A few such alterations that occur with age can be illustrated from some of our studies carried out in the Committee on Human Development at the University of Chicago over the past decade, where we have been making studies of personality, of adaptational patterns, of career lines, of age norms and age-appropriate behavior in adults, and of attitudes and values across social class and generational lines. While this set of inquiries has not involved longitudinal research on the same subjects (except for one group of 300 older persons who were followed over a seven-year period), it represents a related set of investigations in which the number of men and women participating now totals well over 2,000. Each study is based upon a relatively large sample of normal people, none of them volunteers, all living in metropolitan communities in the Midwest.

In one set of investigations of persons aged forty to seventy from varied walks of life, based upon both interviews and projective data, we found that different modes of dealing with impulse life become salient with increasing age. In middle age, there is an emphasis upon introspection and stocktaking, upon conscious reappraisal of the self. There is conscious *self-utilization* rather than the self-consciousness of youth. Preoccupation with the inner life seems to become greater; emotional cathexes toward persons and objects in the outer world decreases; the readiness to attribute activity and affect to persons in the environment is reduced; there is movement from outerworld to innerworld orientation. A constriction seems to occur in the sixty- and seventy-year-olds in the ability to integrate wide ranges of stimuli and in the willingness to deal with complicated and challenging situations in the environment. We have referred to this increased saliency of the inner life as increased *interiority* of personality. We regard it as reflecting certain intrinsic as well as responsive processes of change, since it was measurable in well-functioning adults by the mid-forties, well before the social losses of aging occurred and well before there was any measurable change in competency of performance in adult social roles.

In the present context this increased interiority is to be regarded as one of the "inner" psychological regularities of the life cycle. Interiority seems, however, to be relatively independent of adaptation or *purposive* behavior. Our studies suggest that interiority is age related and adaptation is not (Neugarten, et al. 1964). In more general terms, adaptational abilities are to be distinguished from age-related personality changes.

A related finding appeared in a different sample of middle-aged adults. In this instance we interviewed at length 100 highly placed men and women concerning what they regarded as the most salient characteristics of middle adulthood. These persons were university graduates: business, professional, and artistic leaders, some of whom appeared in *American Men of Science* and *Who's Who in America*. Both men and women talked of the difference in the way time is perceived. A particularly conspicuous feature of middle-age is that life is restructured in terms of time left to live rather than time since birth. Not only is there a reversal in directionality but also an awareness that time is finite. Middle-aged people look to their positions within different life contexts—changes in body, career, family—rather than chronological age for their primary cues in clocking themselves. It was at first a surprise, then a commonplace, that middle-aged persons when asked their age could not immediately give their exact age but stopped to think, often saying, "Let's see. . .51? No, 52. Yes, 52 is right."

Yet responses like the following were characteristic: "Before I was thirty-five, the future just stretched forth. There would be time to do and see and carry out all the plans I had. . . .Now I keep thinking, will I have time enough to finish off some of the things I want to do?" Or, "Time is a two-edged sword. In some of my friends, it brings anxiety that there won't be time enough. To others, it adds a certain challenge in seeing how much pleasure can still be obtained. But all of us figure backward from the end. . . and estimate how much time we can expect."

The change in time perspective is intimately related to the personalization of death. Death in middle age becomes a real possibility for the self, no longer the magical or extraordinary occurrence that it appears in youth. In women there is the rehearsal for widowhood that becomes characteristic (one that rarely occurs in men); and in men there is the "sponsoring" issue with regard to young associates as well as with regard to one's children, an issue we called "the creation of social heirs."

Increased interiority, changed time perspective, and personalization of death are only a few of the psychological changes that have emerged from our own studies and that we regard as characteristic of men and women as they move through adulthood.

The fact that regularities of change through the life cycle are demonstrable along biological, social, and psychological dimensions leads to the questions of adaptation and the concept of the "normal, expectable life cycle."

Adults carry around in their heads, whether or not they can easily verbalize it, a set of anticipations of the normal, expectable life cycle. They internalize expectations of the consensually validated sequences of major life events—not only what those events should be but when they should occur. They make plans, set goals, and reassess those goals along a time line shaped by those expectations.

The individual is said to create a sense of self very early in life. Freud, for example, in describing the development of the ego, and George H. Mead, in describing the differentiation between the "I" and the "me," placed the development of self very early in childhood. But it is perhaps not until adulthood that the individual creates a sense of the life cycle, that is, an anticipation and acceptance of the inevitable sequence of events that will occur as people grow up, grow old, and die. Adulthood is when he understands that the course of his own life will be similar to the lives of others and that the turning points are inescapable. This ability to interpret the past and foresee the future, and to create for oneself a sense of the predictable life cycle, presumably differentiates the healthy adult personality from the unhealthy.

From this point of view, the normal, expectable life events do not themselves constitute crises, nor are they trauma producing. The end of formal schooling, leaving the parents' home, marriage, parenthood, occupational achievement, one's own children growing up and leaving, menopause, grandparenthood, retirement—in our society, these are the normal turning points, the markers or the punctuation marks along the life cycle. They call forth changes in self-concept and in sense of identity, they mark the incorporation of new social roles, and accordingly they are the precipitants of new adaptations. But in themselves they are not, for the vast group of normal persons, traumatic events or crises that trigger mental illness or destroy the continuity of the self.

That we often err in construing a normal life event as a crisis can well be illustrated in one of our own recent studies of middle age. Wishing to study patterns of adaptation, we began with a study of women, reasoning that women's lives in the middle years were characterized by two major crises: the biological climacterium evidenced by the menopause and the change in roles that follows upon children leaving home. We felt that these two crises for women in their forties and fifties might have measurable effects upon their psychological well-being.

Accordingly, we selected a population of 100 normal women aged 43 to 53 from working-class and middle-class background, all of whom were in good physical health, all married and living with husbands, all mothers of at least one child, and none of whom had had hysterectomies. Five to six hours of interviewing and projective testing were carried out, and we obtained data on a large number of psychological and social variables, including measures of anxiety, life satisfaction, and self-concept. Because this period of life has been relatively unexplored by psychologists, and because psychiatrists have shown special interest in menopause and in questions of the possible relation to so-called involution depressions, this study warrants relatively full description.

Like puberty and pregnancy, the climacterium is generally regarded as a significant turning point in a woman's psychosexual development—one that reflects profound endocrine and somatic changes and one that presumably involves a variety of psychological and social concomitants. Because it signifies that an important biologic function, woman's reproductive life, has come to an end, the menopause has often been described as one of the most critical events of the middle years—as a potential threat to a woman's feminine identity.

Although there is a large medical and popular literature on the climacterium, there is a conspicuous lack of empirical research with normal, or nonclinical women. While an estimated seventy-five percent of women experience some disturbance or discomfort during the climacterium, only a small proportion receive medical treatment, suggesting that conclusions about the menopause drawn from clinical observations cannot be generalized to the entire population.

In the present study, several approaches were employed in exploring the menopause as a focus of concern. Women were asked about their expectations regarding menopause, what they had heard or read about it, what they had observed in other women. Each woman was also asked whether she regarded herself as premenopausal, menopausal, or post-menopausal; what was the basis of her assessment; and what, if any, were the symptoms and reactions she had experienced.

We first divided the 100 women into three groups: those who reported no changes or irregularities in their menstrual patterns and were evaluated as premenopausal; the meno-pausal; and those who had stopped menstruating for at least two years, the postmenopausal. We discovered at once that menopausal or climacteric status was an insignificant variable: that is, it did not differentiate among these women with regard to any of our other variables.

Moving on, we found that these women as a group tended to minimize the significance of the menopause and to regard it as unlikely to produce much anxiety or stress. For instance, when asked to select those factors that worried them most from a list of possible events or sequelae of middle age, only four women of the 100 regarded menopause as a major source of worry. (More than half indicated that "losing your husband" was the greatest concern; "just getting older" and "fear of cancer" were also frequent responses.) When asked, at another point in the interview, what was disliked most about middle age, only one of the women mentioned the menopause. When questioned further, at still another point in the interview, about the best thing and the worst thing about menopause, only twelve women could not mention anything good about menopause but thirty could not think of anything bad about it.

These women were unusually cooperative and eager to talk about themselves, yet even after considerable time was given to the topic on two different interview occasions, only one-third could think of any way that a woman's physical or emotional health was likely to be adversely affected by the "change of life." Some expressed the view that the menopause served to improve a woman's state of health. A majority maintained that any changes in health or emotional status during the climacteric period were caused by idiosyncratic factors or individual differences in capacity to tolerate stress generally. "It depends on the individual. Personally, I think if women look for trouble, they find it." Similarly, when asked about how the menopause affects sexuality, sixty-five percent maintained there was no effect and that any alteration in a woman's sexual life during climacterium must be a function of her attitudes prior to the menopause. (Of the thirty-five women who thought there was change in sexual activity associated with climacterium, half thought sexual activity becomes less important and half thought sexual relations become more enjoyable because menstruation and fear of pregnancy were removed.)

In a specially devised checklist of attitudes toward menopause (Neugarten, et al. 1963), the overwhelming majority (over eighty percent) attributed little or no change or discontinuity in a woman's life to the menopause. About three-fourths took the view that, except for the underlying biologic changes, women have a relative degree of control over their symptoms and need not have even symptomatic difficulties.

In addition to studying attitudes, we devised a checklist of menopausal symptoms based on a careful review of the medical literature (the twenty-eight most frequently reported somatic, psychosomatic, and psychological symptoms—hot flashes, paresthesia, vertigo, headache, insomnia, irritability, depression, and so on) and asked women to report the frequency and intensity of their symptoms (Neugarten and Kraines 1965). We found that overall these women held relatively favorable views of the menopause and did not regard it as a major loss of feminine identity, irrespective of the severity of their symptoms.

We obtained also from each woman a brief psychosexual history, then assessed the degree to which each reported physical or emotional difficulty regarding the first sex infor-mation, menarche, menstrual periods, first sexual experience, pregnancy, and childbirth. The result was that difficulties with menarche, menstrual periods, and pregnancy were related to severity of menopausal symptoms, with those women who reported the most symptoms and who viewed the menopause as disturbing, unpleasant, and unpredictable being those who expressed more negative affect regarding their earlier psychosexual experiences.

Our general conclusions were, then, that there was little evidence in these data to support a "crisis" view of the climacterium and that the crisis theory in the literature probably reflects basic differences between clinical samples and a community sample.

We then moved further in the analysis. To measure psychological well-being, we used several different measures: a set of ratings of life satisfaction, a self-cathexis scale and a body cathexis scale, the Taylor Manifest Anxiety scale (taken from the M.M.P.I.), the I.P.A.T. Anxiety Questionnaire (from Cattell's sixteen-factor test), and a set of measures based on the T.A.A. The correlations between climacteric status, menopausal symptoms, and attitudes toward menopause, on the one hand, and each of the various measures of psychological well-being on the other, were very low (most ranged from 0.11 to 0.35). We concluded, just as we had from the first part of this study, that the menopause was not a crisis event; for if it were, it should have shown a significant relation to the psychological well-being or mental health of these women.

With regard to our second presumed "crisis," the empty nest, our findings were similar. We divided the women according to family stage: the intact stage, in which none of the children had left home; the transitional stage, in which one or more had left, but one or more remained; and the empty nest, or postparental stage, in which all the children were living outside the home. We looked also at those women who had children under age fourteen at home, as compared with those whose youngest child was fifteen or older. We worked out a set of life-styles or role orientations and separated the sample into those who were primarily home oriented, community oriented, work oriented, or mixed home-community oriented. We studied these women also for change in pattern of role activities, assessing the extent to which each woman had expanded or constricted her activities in family roles (wife, mother, homemaker, grandmother, daughter) and in nonfamily roles (worker, church member, club member, citizen, friend, user of leisure time) over the past five to ten years and grouped the women into "expanders," "shifters," "statics," and "constrictors."

The relationships among these social-role variables and our measures of psychological well-being were all low and showed again that our initial hypothesis was wrong. Rather than being a stressful period for women, the empty-nest or postparental stage in the life cycle was associated with a somewhat *higher* level of life satisfaction than is found among other women. Evidently for women in this sample, coping with children at home was more taxing and stressful than having their children married and launched into adult society. Neither was life satisfaction correlated with *role-change* patterns—although the latter finding may be an artifact of our data. (It was of some interest that in this sample life satisfaction was highest in the home- and community-oriented women, and lowest in the work oriented.)

Now that the study is completed, we wonder that we should ever have formulated such naive hypotheses; yet it seemed tenable enough to predict that women who showed high symptomatology at menopause and whose children had left home would be those women who would have shown lower levels of life satisfaction than the other women in the sample.

That this was not so is evidence for the normal, expectable life cycle. Women in their forties and early fifties expect the menopause to occur and see it, therefore, as a normal and natural event. They may have listened to old wives' tales and may have some mild anxieties, which they project on other women, but they know the climacterium is inevitable; that all women survive; and they take it in stride or, as one of them put it, regard it merely as "a temporary pause that depresses." Many welcome it as relief from menstruation and fear of unwanted pregnancies.

The normal, expectable life event too superficially viewed as a crisis event can be illustrated in the researches of other investigators as well as in our own. For example, to an increasingly large proportion of men, retirement is a normal, expectable event. Yet in much of the literature on the topic, it is conceptualized by the investigator as a crisis, with the result that the findings from different studies are at variance, with some investigators unprepared for their discovery of no significant losses in life satisfaction or increased rates of depression following retirement. The fact is that retirement is becoming a middle-aged phenomenon, with many workers, for instance, now offered the opportunity to withdraw from work at age fifty-five. The latest national survey indicates that a surprisingly large proportion of workers in all industries are choosing to retire earlier and earlier, with the main, if not the single, determining factor being level of income—as soon as a man establishes enough retirement income he chooses to stop working. Even more pertinent is the fact that nearly seventy percent of persons who retired *as planned* were content in their retirement, compared with less than twenty percent of the unexpected retirees—those who retired unexpectedly because of poor health or loss of job (Barfield and Morgan 1970).

Death, too, becomes a normal, expectable event to the old, and there are various studies that describe the relative equanimity with which it is anticipated (Munnichs 1966). The fact that old people do not necessarily fear death comes to the young graduate student as a surprise—evidence of an age-graded perception—but the surprise disappears when he discovers that old people more often than not talk calmly and freely about death once the interviewer himself overcomes his own reluctance to discuss it. Judging from the many interviews with old people that are now in our files at Chicago, the crisis is not death, but for some, *how* one will die, whether in the accustomed home and family environment or elsewhere. Some recent findings (Lieberman and Coplan 1970), are of interest on this point. They studied matched groups of old people (matched for age, health, ethnic background, education), one group living in their homes in the community; the second, persons on a waiting list to be admitted to a home for the aged; the third, a group who had survived relocation and who had been living in the institution for two years or longer. Each group was divided into those who were near death and those who were not—or "death imminent" or "death distant." This determination was made by following the groups over a three-year interval to see who died and who survived and then going back and studying their interviews and test performances. Among the death imminent, it was the second group who showed evidence of fear of death, not the first nor the third group; that is, neither of the groups who were living in familiar and stable surroundings. It would appear that it is the prospect of dying in a nonnormal, unexpected circumstance that creates the crisis.

The situation with regard to widowhood is more equivocal; yet even here, as shown in a study by Parkes (1964), while somatic symptoms increased somewhat for both younger and older widows in the months following bereavement, consultation rates for psychiatric symptoms were very high for women under sixty-five but not in women over sixty-five. Is this because by the time a woman reaches old age, death of a husband—a husband several years her senior, in most cases—moves into the category of the expected? On this same point, Baler and Golde (1964), in reviewing some of the epidemiological data regarding the widowed as a high-risk group in terms of mental illness, physical illness, and mortality, indicate that there is excess risk at younger rather than at older ages for both sexes.

All these findings are not to deny that the expectable life event precipitates crisis reactions in some persons, especially in those who come to the attention of the mental health professional; but this reaction is probably true for the minority, not for the majority. Even for the minority, it is more often the timing of the life event, not its occurrence, that constitutes the salient or problematic issue. This observation is not a denial, however, of the fact that the major life events in middle age and old age are losses to the individuals concerned or that grief is their accompaniment. It is to say, rather, that the events are anticipated and rehearsed, the "grief work" completed, the reconcilation accomplished without shattering the sense of continuity of the life cycle.

In drawing the distinction between illness and health, between the clinical and the normal, the psychology of grief is not synonymous with the psychology of mental illness. The relationships between loss, grief, physical illness and mental illness are complex, although "loss" itself is a multi-dimensional factor. Some of Lowenthal's work (Lowenthal, et al. 1967) seems to support the point being made here; old persons who had experienced retirement or widowhood in the three years prior to being interviewed were not more frequently diagnosed by psychiatrists as mentally ill, nor did they find their way into mental hospitals with any greater frequency than others. Mental illness, on the other hand, was associated with self-blame, with reports of having missed one's opportunities, of having failed to live up to one's potentials; in short, with intrapunitiveness.

In summary then, there are two distinctions worth making: first, that it is the unanticipated life event, not the anticipated—divorce, not widowhood in old age; death of a child, not death of a parent—that is likely to represent the traumatic event. Moreover, major stresses are caused by events that upset the sequence and rhythm of the life cycle—as when death of a parent comes in childhood rather than in middle age; when marriage does not come at its desired or appropriate time; when the birth of a child is too early or too late; when occupational achievement is delayed; when the empty nest, grandparenthood, retirement, major illness, or widowhood occur *off-time*. In this sense, then, a psychology of the life cycle is not a psychology of crisis behavior so much as it is psychology of timing.

References

Baler, L.A., and Golde, P.J. "Conjugal Bereavement: Strategic Area of Research in Preventive Psychiatry." *Working Papers in Community Mental Wealth* 2, no. 1. Boston: Harvard School of Public Health, Department of Public Health Practice, 1964.

Barfield, R.A., and Morgan, J.N. *Early Retirment: The Decision and the Experience.* Ann Arbor, Michigan: Institute of Social Research, University of Michigan, 1970.

Lieberman, M.A., and Coplan, A.S. "Distance from Death as a Variable in the Study of Aging." *Developmental Psychology* 2 (1970): 71-84.

Lowenthal, M. F., et al. *Aging and Mental Disorder in San Francisco: A Social-Psychiatric Study.* San Francisco: Jossey-Bass, 1967.

Munnichs, J.M.A. *Old Age and Finitude: A Contribution to Psycho-gerontology.* Basel: Karger, 1966.

Neugarten, B.L., et al. *Personality in Middle and Late Life.* New York: Atherton Press, 1964.

————, and Kraines, R.J. "Menopausal Symptoms in Women of Various Ages." *Psychosomatic Medicine* 27 (1965): 266-73.

————, and Moore, J.W. "The Changing Age-Status System." In *Middle Age and Aging.* Edited by B.L. Neugarten. Chicago: University of Chicago Press, 1968.

————; Wood, V.; Kraines, R.J.; and Loomis, B. "Women's Attitudes toward the Menopause." *Vita Humana* 6 (1963): 140-51.

Parkes, C.M. "Effects of Bereavement on Physical and Mental Health: A Study of the Medical Records of Widows." *British Medical Journal* 2 (1964): 274-79.

10

Grief and Bereavement[*]

David Hendin

"Blessed are those who mourn; for they shall be comforted."
Matthew 5:4

Just as each person must at some time face his own death, so too must he be exposed to the death of a loved one. Whether the loved one is parent, sibling, spouse, or child, the closest surviving relatives face perhaps the most trying emotional experiences in their lives. The bereaved encounter a host of emotions, many of which are bewildering. In their sorrow the bereaved are suitable targets for money-making schemes that revolve around the recent loss. One outstanding example of this in our society is the funeral and its commercial aspects. As Jessica Mitford has so ably described in the *American Way of Death*, the funeral trade is geared to extract far too much money from the bereaved. Expensive caskets, burial plots, memorials, embalming, clothing, and cosmetics for the deceased may cost a survivor a thousand or more dollars— which in a time of exaggerated emotion he gladly spends, even if he cannot afford it.

[*]This work originally appeared as chapter 7 in *Death as a Fact of Life*, by David Hendin, published by W.W. Norton and Company, ©1973 by David Hendin. Reprinted by permission of the publisher; abridged from the original.

Some sort of funeral is an important rite of passage, and in every culture people surrounded burial with ritual. Archaeologist Chester Chard has noted that, "The reason we know so much more about Neanderthaloid Man himself as compared with earlier forms is that he was the first (as far as we know) to dispose of his dead, perhaps the most striking evidence of his increasing humanity." The evolution of man has been measured in part by the way in which he disposes of his dead.

The funeral is thought to serve three general purposes: disposal of the body, aid to the survivors in reorienting themselves after the shock of a loved one's death, and a public acknowledgment of the death.

Culture and religious beliefs dictate to a large degree the mode in which disposal of the dead will be accomplished. The primary purpose of many of the traditional funeral rites—from ancient times to the present—has consistently been to offer solace and a period of healing to survivors. Modern psychiatry and psychology have acknowledged the therapeutic value of these ritual funerary ceremonies.

In Judaism, for example, the activities of the mourner follow a prescribed pattern. Since the bereaved must not weep too long or too severely for the dead, the Talmud—the body of Jewish law—limits mourning to three days for weeping, seven for lamenting, and thirty for abstaining from haircuts and the wearing of pressed clothes.

Jewish ritual also provides for companionship for the bereaved. According to one ancient tradition, mourners are forbidden to eat of their own bread on the funeral day. This necessitated that others visit the home to bring food; presumably they also offered comfort and compassion.

The sitting of shivah lasts for seven days, during which the mourner sits on a low stool and receives consolation from friends and relatives. For eleven months following the death of a parent the bereaved recites a special prayer, the Kaddish, daily. After the first eleven months, however, Kaddish is recited only on the anniversary of the death. Again, this custom prescribes significant mourning (that is, at least a daily prayer) for a set length of time, and prohibits excessive grief (at least in this way) thereafter. Interestingly, although the Kaddish is known as the prayer of the dead, it does not once mention the dead or death. Rather it is a prayer summoning all to acknowledge God as the creator and rule of the world and expressing hope that during the lifetimes of those listening, the Kingdom of God will be established on earth. The *Kaddish*, states Rabbi Simon Greenberg of the Jewish Theological Seminary, in New York, "is a humble and faithful acceptance of God's decree."

In a study by Robert Fulton and Gilbert Geis it was found that American rabbis, whether Orthodox, Conservative, or Reform, tend to see the "purpose of the funeral ceremony in much the same light. For them, the funeral is basically a religious service which not only serves to honor God, but which pays tribute to the deceased. It is a ceremony which assuages the grief of the survivors and is a comfort to them in their loss. The funeral also is seen to be educational, i.e., to arouse thought about a better life."

Another traditional funeral custom is the wake. Literally, the word means *to watch a corpse*. The custom is of unknown origin, although according to sociologist Jerome Salomone, "waking the dead almost certainly was invented before the advent of civilization and is found all over the world."

Formerly waking was an uninterrupted watch of the dead body from the time of death until burial. Most familiar, of course, is the Irish wake, where family and friends gathered to view the corpse and to engage in eating and drinking. The custom of the wake still exists in many societies today, as a specific period when the dead person is exposed for public viewing before burial.

John J. Kane, professor of sociology at Notre Dame University, explains the functions of the wake in this way: "The various preparations required for a wake undoubtedly kept the bereaved busy. And while they were certainly sad, the visitation by large numbers of friends and relatives, who were paying their last respects to the deceased, did offer some comfort. . . .Despite its aspects of merriment, even excessive drinking and brawling, the wake was still intended to be a reverent matter."

One widow, discussing her husband's wake, said it helped her because, "I saw him at home and in the hospital, suffering and in pain. When I saw him in the funeral home it made me feel much better because he was fixed up so nice and he looked so good."

Calling hours and visitations hold similar significance. It is during these times that each religion prescribes that individuals pay their respects, not only to the dead but also to the living.

The modern shift toward funerals in which much of the ceremony is dispensed with in favor of a more personal service can be considered an extension of some of the most profound traditions. Participants in such funerals explain that they seem to be more concerned with humanity than show.

Although arrangements for burial and the funeral itself may be a profound emotional experience for the bereaved, the most difficult period of adjustment takes place in the weeks and months that follow. Few individuals are aware of the deep, often conflicting feelings they may expect to experience, or the psychological and physiological symptoms that are likely to accompany grief.

[. . .]

The evidence that more widowers than widows die during bereavement may be attributable to the amount of emotional stress that is built up in the individual. While women are expected to, and do, freely express their emotions, men are often expected to suppress them. "Men don't cry," they are encouraged to keep a "stiff upper lip."

[. . .]

A survey of the psychiatric literature pertaining to grief shows a fairly general consensus that normal mourning is made up of three phases. First is a short period of shock, second a period of intense grief, and finally a period of recovery and the resumption of normal social life.

In older persons the grief reaction is sometimes far less intense than in younger individuals. It is speculated that this may be due to the fact that older persons have primed themselves for a particular loss, or perhaps have suffered so many previous losses that they become almost immune to the final loss. Their children have left home, they have retired, their parents and peers have died; all of these are losses.

Older persons often expect the death of the spouse or their peers, just as younger persons often anticipate death in their older relatives. "Grief reactions," says Dr. Samuel Lehrman, "are actually much more normal when death occurs in an aged person and has been expected. Under such circumstances, the work of mourning is done quickly, because a certain amount of this work. . . has already preceded the event of death."

This is called *anticipatory* or *preparatory grief*, a situation in which an individual may actually begin to grieve the loss of a loved one before he has died. This may occur when a person learns a loved one is terminally ill, or entering the final phase of a long illness. When anticipatory grief has occurred, the shock phase of grief is often eliminated because preparations have already been made, sympathies expressed, and grief experienced before death. It is gradually replaced by acceptance of the situation. Although sharp grief was already experienced when the outcome became obvious, an acute stage of grief still comes at the time of death.

In counseling the bereaved, Mrs. Delia Battin, chief social worker of Montefiore Hospital's bereavement project, explains, "We try to encourage them to talk about all kinds of details from their lives starting with courtship, marriage, family events to cover the entire relationship through life with the departed." The good as well as the bad must be discussed, for guilt is a common problem with the bereaved. It may be guilt stemming from a recent argument with the deceased, or a long-standing feud. The survivor may be tormented with thoughts of what might have been done for the departed during his final days. "I should have called the doctor two days earlier," is a typical response. A spouse or parent may also feel guilt ridden for no other reason than that he has survived.

Guilt may also be a result of anger toward the deceased. "I knew she couldn't control the fact that she was dying," one young husband said, "but sometimes I was mad at her for leaving me and our daughter." Anger is another universal component of grief. A person may be angry at the world for going on as usual after his loved one has died. He may be angry at the deceased for having left him alone, or at the doctor for "killing" the loved one, or not doing all that was medically possible. One family, upset at the death of an elderly aunt, vented anger at their physician for "not keeping her alive until she got to be one hundred." God or the clergyman may also be targets for anger since they "allowed this to happen."

Those dealing with bereaved persons should be prepared for such anger reactions, and understand their significance. The verbal target is not the actual target of wrath, and emotional outbursts of anger or accusation on the part of the bereaved only reflect a tremendous frustration because of their own inability to prevent the death.

Although such situations may prove difficult, the anger should not be suppressed, but encouraged and discussed. The bereaved may be patiently and gently assured that he, and the doctors did everything they could in caring for the deceased. This may help absolve the person of some of his self-inflicted guilt.

In addition to anger, the bereaved experiences fears of loneliness and abandonment. Loneliness can be terribly frightening, especially to one who has lived with a person for many years and then loses him. Relatives should be encouraged to be available as often as possible—not only for the customary first few days or weeks after the death, but for many months. Loneliness can be allayed to a great degree by helping the bereaved person to feel needed. A young woman, for example, who has lost her father and asks her mother to do something as simple as baby sitting, can offer her a meaningful and therapeutic experience.

As has already been noted, the grieving person finds it difficult to ask for help. Therefore friends and relatives who say, "Call if you need me," or "I'll do anything, just let me know," aren't really offering assistance. Concrete suggestions—an invitation to dinner or an outing—or small gifts of food or other things the bereaved is known to like would certainly be welcome. Help in these more tangible forms is not likely to be refused, and graphically expresses the sympathy and care of the giver. Ideally, special consideration of the bereaved should continue over a period of months. Many bereaved individuals need this extra help and support after a loved one has died.

Unfortunately it is not uncommon for friends and relatives of bereaved individuals to withdraw from them, just as they may have from the dying person. Friends or relatives feel uncomfortable with the anxiety, pain, and sadness of grief, and do not know how to handle their own anxieties. Embarrassed about what to say, they resort to excuses such as, "We don't want to talk about it because we'll upset Auntie."

Excuses or not, according to Dr. Weiner, "That's a lot of baloney. The best thing you can do for a bereaved person is to talk about the dead person." The bereaved can then review the experiences shared with the deceased. Talking out the situation helps the individual experience his loss. Friends and relatives often fear that the bereaved will cry or become visibly upset. In fact, this is exactly what is needed, because it is only by turning grief outward that a person can once again resume normal living. At the same time, it is possible for a friend or relative to encourage too much discussion. The bereaved may indicate that there has been enough talk for a time. If this happens, an understanding person should recognize that what the bereaved may really need is simply the comforting presence of someone who cares.

Varieties of the
Aging Experience

Introduction

In this part of the book is explored the varieties of the aging experience, especially the different settings in which the aged live out their last years. When attempting to organize the chapters included here, it became obvious that I would have to divide the material in such a way as to distinguish types of outcomes. Recognizing that adaptation and coping characterize most human behavior, and wishing to avoid simplistic value judgments, I nonetheless wanted to suggest that some environments may be more conducive to well-being and feelings of self-worth than others. The division of chapters into one section called "Like It Is" and another subtitled "As It Could Be" does represent a judgment on my part, but one that I feel is unavoidable to anyone who reads these selections. As for the third unit on "Extended Families," both the problem-producing and problem-solving aspects are intermingled; clearly, these structures arise from a variety of conditions, and are often responses to necessity, while others are a matter of personal choice.

The first section begins with survey of problem-producing conditions and environments—widowhood, nursing homes, single-room-occupancy (SRO) hotels, and public institutions—even though, with the exception of widowhood, only a small proportion of old people are at risk (less than five percent in any type of institution; I would guess a smaller percentage in SROs). Nonetheless, if conditions of the aged could be conceptualized along a continuum representing involvement in mundane social networks (workmates, friends, family), an examination of the extreme cases of isolation may reveal social forces only latent in less deprived situations. In this sense, then, the chapters in the second section deal with a spectrum of settings and relationships that could be roughly characterized as problem-reducing.

Directly, or indirectly, most of the essays in this part deal with a recurring issue in social gerontology: The balance between activity and disengagement. There is evidence that old age is characterized by a progressive, sometimes mutual (but often unilateral) disengagement of self and society.* Physical decline, lowered incomes, death of spouse and friends must all circumscribe one's range of movement and involvement. The question is whether or not such withdrawal is initiated by the old person as a means of conserving psychic and physical energy, and is thus positively related to adjustment in old age. On the other side are those people who argue that maintaining high levels of interest, activity, and interpersonal involvement are predictive of successful aging, and that unutilized capacities will atrophy and bring on a premature withering away. It is safe to say that some persons will find disengagement adaptive and that others will stagnate; certainly, the older the organism the more likely it is to be disengaged. Nonetheless, extremes of solitude, however helpful as a preparation for death, are associated with a variety of undesirable outcomes in this world. As is often the case with opposing theses, a synthesis embodying the most valid elements of each thesis emerges—in this case, the

*This thesis was first enunciated by Elaine Cumming and William E. Henry in Growing Old (New York: Basic Books, 1961), which set off a lively debate between the disengagement theorists and the activity theorists. For relevant findings, see M.W. Riley and A. Foner, eds., Aging and Society (New York: Russell Sage Foundation, 1968), vol. 1: 353-56.

concept of "selective disengagement" proposed by Streib and Schneider is pertinent, whereby individuals, in accord with their past history and present resources, selectively withdraw from roles, at varying rates. There are principles of social psychology that could predict which roles are given up under what circumstances, for example, rules of interpersonal costs and rewards, and maximization of profit.

The first chapter in Part IV consists of three excerpts from Helena Znaniecki Lopata's impressive, detailed study of widowhood in an American city. One of the problems of widowhood is precisely that the evaluation of women in our society has resulted in an almost total neglect of serious sociological, and societal, attention to a status that the majority of American women will occupy if they survive to age sixty-five. Lopata's book is a model of sociological analysis, and should be read in its entirety; but I have chosen three fairly self-contained selections of interest to readers of this collection. The first section is a succinct survey of the role of the widow in a number of societies; the second offering records interview responses to questions on the major problems faced by respondents; and the third section summarizes Lopata's important findings and her suggestions for ameliorative action. But the social invisibility of so large a number of persons is not easily rectified; it seems as if the world of adults was fashioned for couples only, so that widows (and widowers) make for awkward social arrangements. Also involved, probably as a function of the pervasive tendency to deny death, is a clear lack of institutionalization of the role of the widow—in true, rugged-individualist style, we have left each to work out her own destiny (under increasingly adverse conditions).

The single-room-occupancy hotels of our central cities are both the most impoverished noninstitutional setting for the aged and, paradoxically, the consummate expression of the great American values: To remain independent, self-sufficient, responsible for one's own fate, however unpleasant. That this task is more difficult for women than for

*In Gordon F. Streib and Clement J. Schneider, *Retirement in American Society* (Ithaca, New York: Cornell University Press, 1971).

men should no longer surprise us; that they can do it at all is testimony to human tenacity. Joyce Stephens's fieldwork, interviews, and observations of a limited sample provide a more personalized slice of life than does Lopata's larger, more formalized, and structured analysis of widowhood. Each technique has its advantages and limitations. It is difficult to generalize on the basis of small, highly selective samples, but, on the other hand, one misses the authentic texture and flavor of life when material is reduced to tables and statistics. Both types of data are required, and frequently complement each other; in this instance, the problems of finances and loneliness inherent in the status of widowhood reach ultimate expression in the condition of Stephens's bewigged isolates.

Although at any given time fewer than five percent of our aged are institutionalized, over the course of an individual's old age the risks of being institutionalized are far higher. Even so, these settings have received the lion's share of social science investigation. Perhaps it is easiest to study captive populations, and to get funding for such enterprises. Also, most research is published in journals for other professionals, many of whom practice in these settings. Brody's paper from *The Gerontologist* serves as a case in point, while also providing an excellent overview of research to date on chronic-care facilities and their inmates. It is important to bear in mind that for all the horrors of institutionalization presented in several of the following chapters, many old people do require this type of care, that many more ought to be able to utilize such services, and that the *real* issue is how to provide sufficient and decent care to individuals. One of the surprise findings of the researchers for volume one of *Aging and Society* (Riley and Foner) was that the step to nursing homes and public facilities was very much a last choice for the families of old people, and taken only after other living arrangements were tried and found wanting. An incontinent or ill old person can strain the resources of even the most loving relatives, while the position of total dependence can be equally as stressful for the aged individual. While it can be argued that no total institution can avoid the "Procrustean Bed" problem, it is possible to envisage a more humane, personalized type of treatment facility than those described in the chapters that follow. As Brody notes, the research has been done; we know what ought to be; what is lacking is societal support for doing it.

We would be less than candid if we did not also admit some morbid curiosity among sociologists and psychologists in exotic and extreme forms of human behavior. The study of extreme conditions and manifestations, however, often illuminates processes that are not easily perceived when things are as we expect them to be; we often cannot be sure just why or how ordinary behavior proceeds until it breaks down and the mainsprings of action are exposed. Furthermore we can learn about the society and its members from observing how its marginal individuals are treated and how they react. Does our treatment of the aged infirm and insane simply carry to a logical conclusion attitudes and behaviors implicit in our whole approach to aging and old people?

With respect to nursing-home care as part of a general program of health insurance for the elderly, the United States, among modern industrial societies, has been a late, reluctant, and still imperfect purveyor of services. Medicare was enacted over the protests, political influence, and well-financed publicity campaign of the American Medical Association. The specter of "socialized medicine" still traumatizes the public and its legislators, so that federal and state enforcement of the minimal standards of financial and medical oversight written into the nursing-home provisions of Medicare have been even less than minimal, apparently nonexistent in some states.* The legislation was intended to encourage private entrepreneurs to build and administer nursing homes, in the grand tradition of free enterprise, to compete in the provision of quality services to the aged, at a profit. And it has been most profitable for some; indeed, the chief beneficiaries of Medicare seem to be the physicians and hospitals that fought it so fiercely. If fraud and misrepresent-

*As amply documented by the Special Committee on Aging, United States Senate, Report No. 94-50, A Summary of Developments in Aging: 1974-75, pp. 46-62. In fact, the subcommittee's special report on nursing-home care bears the subtitle, "Failure in Public Policy," and contains supporting papers entitled, "A Litany of Nursing-Home Abuses," and "Doctors in Nursing Homes: The Shunned Responsibility," among others.

ation have plagued the program, it has not been on the part of patients. There is something so infinitely tawdry about all this that it is difficult for researchers to keep their professional "cool," for what has occurred in our proprietary nursing homes exemplifies the worst of both private enterprise (sheer greed) and welfarism (bureaucratic corruption and ineffectuality).*

What, then, of the approximately one million recipients of nursing-home care? Behind the statistics, the newspaper exposés, the public hearings, and the grand jury indictments, are the homes themselves: Social systems involving patients, physicians, nurses, aides, administrators, and the families of patients, each group playing out a complex of roles vis-à-vis the others, constrained by the requirements of the institution to certain attitudes and behaviors. The most subtle and moving insights into what Goffman calls "the underside of total institutions" are often provided by participant observers, and given the high turnover of staff, it has not been difficult for young women to gain entry into nursing homes as aides,** or, in the case of Sharon Curtin, as a private nurse. In her book, Nobody Ever Died of Old Age: In Praise of Old People, Ms. Curtin, a registered nurse, describes a personal odyssey

---

*Mary Adelaide Mendelsohn, Tender, Loving Greed (New York: Alfred A. Knopf, 1974). See also, Richard Titmus, "The Gift of Blood," Transaction/Society 8, no. 3 (January 1971), for a depth analysis of the interplay between social values and social welfare, as exemplified in the system of blood donations characteristic of different societies. In the United States, for example, blood donation is highly commercialized (you can find donation centers near every skid row), full of danger to the recipient because of the low health status of commercial donors, and also subject to periodic shortages. In Britain and other social-welfare oriented societies voluntary donors provide a more stable and less risky supply.

**Claire Townsend, et al., Old Age: The Last Segregation (New York: Grossman Publishers, 1971). Ms. Townsend and her pupils at Miss Porter's School, as part of a Ralph Nader study group, engaged in participant-observation in a number of private nursing homes. This book is primarily taken from the young women's daily logs; the cumulative effect is not unlike exposure to the fabled Chinese water torture: One drop of humiliation after another.

among the aged of America in all the settings I have noted in this section: Retirement villages, SROs, mental hospitals, and, in the excerpt here, the relatively posh Montcliffe Convalescent Hospital, where she attends to the very old and ill mathematics teacher, Miss Larson. Curtin writes in sorrow and in anger, a young woman outraged at the loneliness of the aged; she admits a muckraker's bias, yet also possesses the artist's eye for the telling moment.

In "A Hiding Place to Die" Elizabeth Markson analyzes the state mental hospital as way station to a lonely death, reserved for those already deprived of any claim to dignity. Here, indeed, we reach the nadir of indifference, which Markson places in the context of our culture's denial of death. True, only a small fraction of old people are affected, and yet. . . .

While it may be a facile truism to say that to be black and to be old in America is a double yoke of oppression, the precise ways in which race and age interact to influence one's treatment at the hands of functionaries (and well-meaning sociologists), the allocation of scarce resources, or access to opportunities for self-fulfillment are very subtle indeed. The articles reprinted here appeared in a recent issue (published as this book was being assembled) of the Urban League News, and may well be a response to the call for action that appears in the third section in the chapter by Jacquelyne J. Jackson. I shall have more to say about the condition of America's black aged in this later section, but certainly the conditions described in the Urban League articles belong in the subsection called "Like It Is."

While the indignities and deprivations of old age described in section A could become our lot, too, and are a reproach to a society with pretensions to moral leadership among nations, there is much evidence that our aged are not without great reservoirs of mind and spirit, of tenacity and innovation in utilizing whatever resources are available in order to construct adaptive systems. Most old people wish to remain independent and in the community, and they manage to do so, even the SRO "ladies." Others, like Delores Garcia, in "Una Anciana" grow in dimensions other than years. Another such person is Mary Louise Williams, who describes her experiences in a church-sponsored retirement center in, "One of the Best. . . ." The ideal inputs for personal comfort and development are, as she notes, very expensive and difficult to provide. Although church groups have been very active and innovative in this area (their tax-exempt status is a great advantage), the range of social, recreational, and health services required to meet the needs of a very individualized clientele are costly enough that this option is not yet widely available. And where it is possible, a great deal of goodwill and willingness to participate are required of the resident who seeks to continue to grow and learn.

For the more affluent there are private retirement communities and, of course, opportunities for travel and for migration to areas with high concentrations of other retirees (Florida and Arizona seem to be most favored). A recent study of retired teachers and college personnel,* who retired with median *monthly* incomes of $1,072 for men and $597 for women, indicates that retirement homes were an infrequent choice even for those who could reasonably afford them. In fact, retirement homes were the least common form of residence for all but those seventy-eight and over, and then among the single, widowed, and female, especially.

Arlie Russell Hochschild finds in a most unexpected place that most enduring of human impulses, the quest for community.** Gemeinschaft typically emerges from the daily relationships of family, friends, and workplace, precisely those contacts from which the elderly are cut off. The unintentional community of the residents of Merrill Court is no less functional than the intentional ones of the young or religious orders, and perhaps far less constricting of individuality; necessity may make communards of us all. The story of Merrill Court is a striking example of both the need to generate supportive social structures and of the adaptive capacities of these elderly individuals.

As unconventional as the idea of old-age communes is, this is but one of the intriguing possibilities that Rose

*1972-73 Survey of Retired TIAA-CREF Annuitants, prepared by M. Mulanaphy, TIAA-CREF Educational Research Division, New York.

**Irving Rosow, in a personal communication, rightly contends that this should not have been an "unexpected" finding for sociologists; indeed, quite the contrary.

Somerville has collected from both the professional literature and contemporary fiction. Whether one believes that truth is stranger than fiction or that art mirrors life is beside the point when we find both leading us in the same direction. How applicable to other age groups are the alternative life-styles evolving from the youth culture? We have seen how communes meet a need for Gemeinschaft at any age; and certainly serial monogamy is already part of the middle-age scene. One reads of the aged retirees who prefer to live together "without benefit of clergy" in order not to lose one of their Social Security checks. If we assume that family systems emerge from such mundane considerations as sex ratio, then polygyny for the aged is a perfectly logical development. These are all alternatives that still carry a negative evaluation for many in our society, but the needs for affiliation, for sexual outlet, for interpersonal support stay with us though spouses and friends depart. It is likely, then, that a number of alternatives will become increasingly legitimized for the elderly, just as they have been for younger age groups.*

Poverty, Hochschild notes, is not evenly distributed across society; old people are more likely to have low incomes than are younger adults. This is especially true for the whites of Appalachia and the blacks of any region. We would expect the aged of the hollows and the ghettos to be in the most extreme state of deprivation, but here, too, we find supportive systems operating, based moreover on intergenerational obligations, that is, vertical relationships as opposed to the horizontal network of Merrill Court.

Lozier and Althouse use the concept of "social claims or credits" to describe the resouces of the aged in Appalachia. Lacking power, prestige, and property—the traditional bases of parental control and support—these elders have accrued rights to deference and care from their juniors through a

---

*My own guess is that none of the "alternative life-styles" will attract a sizable number of adherents, at any age, with the possible exception of cohabitation for young unmarrieds. What is of primary significance, I think, is that there are choices: nonmarriage, group marriage, homosexual marriage, communal living, cohabitation, childless marriages, and marriageless children, and one wonders what next.

lifetime of performance on behalf of the collectivity. Such claims are generally recognized by others in the community, and enforced by informal sanctions. This thesis raises a number of questions: Are claims on reciprocal care the basic, if not always the last, resource of the aged of any social class? Cannot this responsibility become a public rather than a private one, in order to minimize the risks of personal antagonisms and whimsy, or will some profoundly important dimension of human caring be lost? Is this an equitable quid pro quo—to release juniors from material bondage (for example, the elders' control over property, jobs, and so forth) in return for an abstract obligation to care? The key here seems to be what the authors refer to as "a social audience attentive to such performances" of caring behavior, an audience socialized to these values and able to exert sanctions. But what if such audiences do not exist?—if the local community is broken up, or radically changed through economic and political forces? Lozier and Althouse, perhaps because they are dealing with small, closely knit groups, emphasize the system-level variables of intergenerational exchange and the effects of others in the environment in determining outcomes for the aged. This is all good, pure sociology, which we often overlook when dealing with relatively isolated individuals; the trick is to find analogous processes in the more fluid, less cohesive groups in other settings.

Conditions of poverty take their toll in many ways. Health status, life expectancy, employment, income, and marital status are all adversely affected by the social and psychological consequences of being born poor—and especially so if one is also a member of a low-status minority group. Much has been written of the presumed pathology of the black family in particular, emphasizing the absence of males from the nuclear family. Rather than continue to blame the victim, recent analyses have stressed the limited opportunities for fulfilling the valued breadwinner role and the way in which welfare regulations penalize families of marginal wage earners in order to account for father absence among the inner-city poor. From this perspective the matrifocal, extended family unit of grandmother, mother, and dependent children is an adaptation to the conditions of existence that serves the functions of primary socialization and emotional support. Of special importance is the pivotal position of the black grandmother; it is she who holds the unit together while her daughters work, and she who attempts to insulate the children from the life of the streets. One of the few empirical studies of the black grandmother is that of Jacquelyn J. Jackson reprinted here, along with Jackson's agenda for a national organization of researchers and activists on behalf of aged blacks. Her study of grandparent-grandchild relationships in one Southern community shows both the enduring strengths of the grandmother and the strains that separate generations in a modern society. For a more personalized glimpse of what "Gran" means to a young black male growing up in the urban North, Curt Davis's memoir of his grandmother, Ms. Eleanor Hackett, says it all.*

Extended familism, typically associated with agricultural societies, as Winch and Blumberg have demonstrated,** may also be found in industrial societies among those groups in which the economic contribution of males is minimal or problematic, thus reducing their authority within nuclear families. In the case of Appalachian whites, the aged males invoke the rule of reciprocity; in the case of blacks, the aged females are still able to perform important functions for family members. Paradoxically, it is precisely where social change most differentiates the generations—among immigrants, blacks, and technologically displaced natives—that extended familism provides the glue that holds kinfolk together, and to some degree preserves the place of the aged within the family system (if not in the larger society).

On the other hand, not all extended familism is a matter of adaptation to deprivation, or a product of immigrant sub-cultures. Among the seven percent of males and fifteen percent of females listed by the Census Bureau as "living with other relatives," there must be many Ida Lynns who have, with

*See also, Ulf Hannarz, "Roots of Black Manhood," Transaction/ Society 6, no. 11 (October 1969).

**Robert F. Winch, and Rae Lesser Blumberg, "Societal Complexity and Familial Organization," in Selected Studies in Marriage and the Family, R.F. Winch and L.W. Goodman, eds., 3d edition (New York: Holt 1968).

some trepidation, chosen to accept an invitation to "move in" with a son or daughter, and for whom the outcome was successful. Ms. Lynn candidly discusses the drawbacks and difficulties of three-generation living, describes her own socialization to the less inhibited world of her daughter, and concludes that, with an appropriate set of rules regarding privacy and finances, such arrangements can be mutually beneficial to all three generations. Why is this not a more typical pattern? Again, the pressures for independence in our society, and the level of geographic and social mobility between generations, are heavily implicated. And, as we noted in an earlier context, intergenerational hostilities engendered during the Oedipal period, especially in a small, child-centered, isolated nuclear family, may never have been so thoroughly resolved (on either side) as to permit the easy comingling of parent and child even decades later. Here, too, the problem of role reversal may enter in: If the older parent now becomes the dependent of his or her own child, another psychological dimension is tapped with unforeseen consequences. For whatever cause, the voluntary three-generation household is an increasingly rare outcome in our society, which, one suspects, may entail losses for all three generations.

"Like It Is"

11

Excerpts from *Widowhood in an American City**

Helena Znaniecki Lopata

The Disorganization of Life with the Death of the Husband

The social roles that widows enter after reaching this position and their life-styles in the cluster of these roles vary greatly from society to society, and even within a single social group. The cross-cultural survey of situations of those widowed throws some light on alternative life-styles and provides a list of factors that contribute to the ascription or choice of any one of these by different widows.

A woman who has been established in a set of social roles usually experiences a disorganization of this pattern immediately after her husband's death. Subsequent to this disorganization, certain changes take place, changes that depend upon the opportunities available for new involvement and life-styles. The degree of change between her life before and after widowhood can be located on a continuum, made up of the actual situations of women all over the world. At one end of

*This work originally appeared as the Introduction, the chapter "Widowhood As the Last Stage in the Role of Wife," and the Conclusion in *Widowhood in an American City* by Helena Znaniecki Lopata, published by Schenkman Publishing Company. Reprinted by permission of the publisher; abridged from the original.

such an analysis continuum we can locate a woman whose life does not become highly disorganized when her husband dies; at the other end, one for whom all roles and relations must be modified. Historical and current data of world societies indicates that the two extremes of the continuum would be *suttee* and either *widow inheritance* or *levirate*. *Suttee*, the self-immolation of a widow on the funeral pyre of her husband, can be judged as the most disorganizing, for every one of her sets of relations experiences total disruption and no reengagement takes place. The least disorganizing situation is *widow inheritance*, the rapid replacement of the husband by another man of the same kin group. A widow who is "inherited" by a close agnate of her deceased husband continues in the same relations with the rest of his kin, particularly if she is assigned the same position in his home as she held in that of the deceased. A similar situation exists in the case of *levirate*, since the late husband remains the social father of her children, while the man who "raises up his seed" often carries out many other duties as a husband. However, the situation of the widow may still be less firm than in remarriage, for she has fewer official rights over the *levir* than over a husband. The degree of life changes in reengagement may be especially low, if the widow is allowed to remain in her own home and to carry on her roles of mother and housewife in a style similar to the one she experienced prior to the death of her husband.

Between the two extremes, but very close to suttee, is the *status role* of widow, which was enforced in traditional India, but is currently decreasing. In this social context a widow, particularly if she was a child bride, had to relate to everyone in such a manner as to maintain the constant status distinctions that cut her off from the normal flow of life. The status role of widow had as its main function the isolation of the woman, reinforced by physical characteristics, such as a shaven head and special clothing guaranteeing distinctive and unattractive appearance.

Most societies with extended family systems have incorporated their widows into the social structure with few problems, either by allowing them to return to (or to remain within) the family of orientation or by finding a new place for them in the late husband's family. In such family structures, widows with grown children usually remain with married sons or daughters, depending on the lineage orientation of the society and the assumption of basic links. The older Chinese or Indian widow with a grown son who inherited the male headship of the family was often able to retain a flow of life similar to that before the death of her husband, because she stayed in her own house. In urban areas of America and even India, widows who break up their housekeeping and move into the homes of married offspring lose many role functions and some social status. In patriarchal and partilineal families, widows are considered outsiders, and their lives become disorganized when the deceased husband's kin insist that the children of that marriage remain with them, while the widow is encouraged to leave. Returning to the family of orientation disrupts not only the in-law relations but also the role of mother.

The kind of life that is available to, or selected by, a widow is determined by many factors, including: the alternative styles developed by her society, her location in the social structure, and her personal characteristics. A major influence is what Paul J. Bohannan calls the set of rights the man and his family gains over the wife through the marriage contract. In its strongest form, the contract gives the husband the right to live with the wife in a domicile judged his, with a division of labor required to maintain the family unit; the right to any property she possesses or obtains during marriage; sexual rights; and *in genetricem* rights, which require her to bear the children who become filiated to his family. Such an arrangement usually ties the woman to her husband's kin even after his death, since she cannot take her children away, and it often means that the kin group inherits many, if not all, of the above listed rights. Thus widow inheritance, levirate, or at least male guardianship may restrict the widow's choice of social roles in societies institutionalizing extensive rights over women by their husbands and in-laws.

Functions Assigned to Widows

The type and content of the social roles available to a widow in any society are dependent upon the hierarchy of functions that she is expected or able to fulfill by her actions or her presence in the group. Various patterns of interaction have been built around these functions by the societies of the world as "solutions" to widowhood. Most of them are dependent upon the fact that women have traditionally been placed, whether by choice or by predetermined division of labor, into the roles of wife and mother. The removal of one of these basic roles is often assumed to free the woman for other tasks or to make other contributions to the group. This is particularly true if she has not yet entered the role of mother or if that set of relations has receded in importance because of the decreasing needs of her offspring.

One of the basic contributions a widow can make to a social group is to continue the role of wife. Two forms of such continuity have been developed: one insists that certain duties of the wife continue to be performed after the death of her husband. In various societies these duties may require the maintenance of his social existence in this life or after-life. For example, widows of the Kganda of Africa are specifically required to "tend the grave" of their dead husband, while remaining socially married to him. The second means by which a widow can maintain the role of wife is by remarriage, either to a man selected for her because of his relation to the deceased or to someone of her own choice. American society tends to encourage the remarriage of young widows, while not being equally concerned with insuring the remarriage of older women who have already spent years in the role of wife.

A function that has often been assigned to widows in linearly oriented societies of either line of descent is that of reproduction. Many groups are very concerned with having their women continue to reproduce as long as biologically possible, and several techniques have been devised for meeting these needs, including the already mentioned levirate and widow inheritance. More often than not the biological father is expected to be the social father, due to assumptions of line "purity," although some groups allow the widow full partner choice. Others insist on combining the role of wife with those of mother and of kin member by insuring that all young widows marry again or at least provide new offspring by selected procedures.

Some social groups define the function of social mother-hood as the most important one for a widow to perform. The procedures for insuring such a role depend on several aspects of the relation of the mother to a child and of the offspring to other members of the community. The social functions of mothering usually involve physical, affective, and socialization care of the new member. Most societies, such as that of the United States, assign this function primarily to the biological mother, minimizing obligations of line continuity and placing most responsibility for child rearing on this woman. In order to do this, she is given the right of control over the means for the child's rearing, such as inherited financial objects, societal support, and the right to make decisions regarding the child's welfare. Special circumstances may limit the rights of women assigned the function of social motherhood. Trusts, guardianship, restriction of facilities, and similar circumstances may severely hamper widows from carrying out the duties of the role. Many European countries allow the biological mother of upper-class children to rear them in the absence of the father, but only under the supervision of a male guardian. The function of child rearing may be connected with the duty of filiation, of guaranteeing that the young grow up as present or future members of the kin line. Whether matrilineal or patrilineal, the system demands that the widow who is allowed to rear her young must insure their identification with the proper group. She is often directly assisted in this process, in a more controlling manner than guardianship, by a male of the line, her brother in the case of a matriarchal group, or her husband's brother in case of a patriarchy.

Another function often assigned to widows is contributing to a work group. Societies with an institutionalized high "bride price" may demand that even an aged woman remain after the death of her husband with the group that had pooled its resources to obtain her. Such a pattern was prevalent in South and Southeastern China, as well as in other societies in which each member of a family is regarded as indispensable to its economic welfare. After a woman is widowed she may be required to continue managing a household work group, to perform economic tasks outside of the home, or to change her schedule to such peripheral tasks as baby sitting, geese walking, or cow tending. Her main contribution may be to free other family members to perform more effectively their economically productive social roles than they could without her help or than she could do. Widows may also be assigned to noneconomic roles outside of the family institution. They may become religious functionaries, tending temples or insuring the proper sequence of necessary ceremonials; they may be educators of the young, contributing to recreational activities; or they may even be politically regulative officials.

Finally, widows may simply be assigned only the responsibility for self-maintenance, with the primary object of saving others the task of caring for them. Part of this function may involve the obligation of serving as models of selected forms of behavior. Older widows may serve as models of aging, reinforcing the concept of human dignity, while young widows may prove the virtue of celibacy, much as a priest does.

Whatever the functions generally assigned to or made available for widows, each social group must develop more than one style, because it has more than one subgroup of widows. Older women cannot be assigned the reproductive function, and the whole class structure may prevent upper-class widows from behaving in a manner inappropriate to the current or the traditional status role to which their fathers and husbands have bound them.

In general, the greatest control over the life of a widow is maintained in patriarchal, patrilocal, and patrilineal extended-family systems where there is a bride price and a strong concern with line continuity. The least control exists in societies with neolocal family groups, self-selective partner choice, relatively high status of women in the nuclear unit, weak kin connections, and strong rights of property inheritance on the part of the wife. The latter configuration is typical of American society, in which the husband and wife select each other, set up their own housekeeping, build up an economic unit that is relatively self-sufficient, and develop companionate relations. However, this type of family structure, which tends to emerge in urban areas, usually reduces the woman to the relatively functionless position of self-maintenance, once the role of mother is diminished through the independence existence of children and the role of wife is diminished through the death of her husband. There are, of course, many other roles available to the American adult reaching into all but the physically incapacitated years, and these could be used to build flexible life-careers and relational cycles.

[...]

Problems of Widowhood

Before examining the various life-styles of women phasing out of the social role of wife, it is necessary to study in greater detail the problems and compensations of widowhood as defined by those who are experiencing them. The respondents were asked: "In thinking over all your experiences since you have become widowed, what do you think is the most important problem of widowhood?" After the answer to this question had been fully probed by the interviewer, the following was asked: "What is the next most important problem of widowhood?" The coding of the answers utilized a set of categories developed out of the exploratory studies and included: loneliness, financial difficulties, problems in rearing children, and the like. Early in the analysis of the answers it became apparent that the simple category of "loneliness" was insufficient, because of the great range of forms this sentiment took in the experiences of different women. It finally became necessary to examine the content of the statements in greater detail. Some respondents were talking of missing their husbands as total persons with whom they had shared a very close and intimate relationship, while others were concerned with the absence of a partner in an activity or even of just a depersonalized presence around whom work could be organized. Whenever possible, the various forms of loneliness expressed by the respondents were listed separately. Unfortunately, since realization of the complexity of this sentiment was derived only inductively from the answers, sufficient probing of its meaning had often not been made in the field, so that many statements proved difficult to code.

Loneliness involves a dissatisfaction with the present level of social interaction, a definition of social relations as inadequate in quality or quantity. *Situational* loneliness tends to be experienced most strongly by people who had been involved in more intensive relations in the past, but who have not been able to retain or reproduce that level nor to modify their expectations of such interaction. In some cases no adjustment is possible, because of barriers in personality or circumstances that prevent the transformation of casual interaction into the desired closer relation, or because of an unwillingness to substitute partners. Most people in modern American society experience situational loneliness. Of course, people can be lonely because they are not involved in an imagined or expected level of interaction that they have never experienced. The outsider, the person fearing a stigmatic position, and the isolate who has not developed the ability of bringing people close to him can be *chronically* lonely. A woman, lonely in marriage, who believes Cumming and Henry when they say that there is a gay society of widows waiting for her after the death of her husband is likely to find only continued loneliness. The young, the old, and the socially unskilled may in the highly integrated years of life dream of social interaction at a level or of a type that makes the available love and friendship seem unsatisfactory.

These facts of human loneliness exist in spite of a culture that still portrays the lonely as the deviant and the maladjusted, while "normal" people are supposed to be permanently enmeshed in fully satisfying relations with others. The result of this belief system is a lack of societally developed techniques to ease the periods of situational loneliness and to reverse chronic loneliness.

Widows who are situationally lonely report one or a combination of the following forms of missing a previously experienced level of social interaction. They are lonely for the husband as: (1) a total individual, a unique person; (2) an object of love; (3) the person making them an object of love; (4) a partner or companion in activities; (5) an escort in couple-companionate interaction; (6) "someone" with whom to talk; (7) a partner in a division of labor within the home or tying her to the economic or social world; (8) "someone" around whom work and time are organized; and (9) "someone" around the house. In addition, many widows feel lonely for a whole life-style previously enjoyed or because they are unable to establish a new type of relationship or retain the level of one previously shared with friends. The interpersonal and very private loneliness that misses the husband for himself as a unique human being, not for what he contributed to the wife, is expressed very strongly by the more articulate respondents. Some women specified the fact that they wanted someone to love, or that they missed the man who treated them as something special and who loved them in a way children and friends do not. A widow whose husband had been ill for a long time misses his love prior to these last years: "Here I am so big and fat, and sometimes I'd be reading and would look up and he'd be sitting there looking at me. And I'd say 'What are you thinking about?' and he would say, 'Oh, I was just thinking how pretty you are.' " On the other hand, many widows miss having an escort and a companion in activities away from home. They do not like going out alone or with other women, since many public places in America cater to couples or to men, but frown upon unescorted females. Whatever the policy, the woman accustomed to being accompanied feels unhappy in situations that seem to her to demand an escort who is no longer available. Single women develop methods of obtaining escorts or of handling themselves efficiently without companions, but the widow has habits and feelings developed in marriage that make both solutions difficult.

Living alone, with no one with whom to discuss daily events, is dificult on many persons accustomed to frequent conversational interaction. Interestingly, a rather large number of women miss having a person around whom they can organize their work. "I miss my husband, I am lonesome," states one respondent, who upon prodding adds, "I'm alone all the time ... even when he was alive, we didn't go anywhere or do too much, but at least he was there to cook for, take care of . . . . Now there is just me." Dinner-time becomes particularly difficult for widows, since wives organize their work in anticipation of the scheduled arrival of husbands. The right to have someone within the home to help in the tasks of its maintenance, which forms another side of the duties of the role of wife, is disrupted by the death of the husband. Not only does widowhood deprive a woman of an object for her duties of cooking and cleaning, but it removes the individual with whom the rights to reciprocal action had already been established. While she cleaned, he repaired, solved electrical problems, and mowed the lawn. The woman is left either with having to take over her late husband's duties or with finding someone else who will carry them out. Since other people in her social circles have already established their social relations with a component balance of rights and duties, the sudden demand that they undertake new duties for the widow may cause role strain. The person asked to do something for the widow has to change his work rhythm and may get into difficulties with people whom he or she served before. A daughter-in-law may resent her husband's sudden assumption of his father's duties to his mother in the home maintenance sphere. An additional factor that makes the removal of the work associate difficult for the survivor is the reluctance of many women to ask for help from others. A marriage is, in some ways, a bargained balance between duties and rights. Widows often have little to offer other people to attract them into a new relation meeting their needs. The needs of a married son or daughter or a friend are already met through arrangements similar to those she has just lost. Financial limitations may restrict the widow's ability to hire people to carry on the work previously done by the late husband. All these problems are summarized as "loneliness."

Also, the division of labor in traditional homes often resulted in passive dependence on the part of the wives. "Lonesomeness, for the kind of life you've had ... your husband made all the decisions and took care of all the financial things, and (now) you have to take care of your own checks and banking and bills, and this is a problem, when you've never done this." This form of loneliness is very different from the one experienced by the "fat" lady quoted before, but it is very real to some women. Finally, the Chicago-area widows, just like those studied by the Harvard Medical School Team and by Peter Marris, miss having "someone around," a presence in the house; someone moving around and available in case of emergencies. This is literally the fear of being alone.

The most lonely and frustrated respondents are the ones who expect someone to take over the relational or task duties previously performed by the husband, and who are without such help. The least desolate are those who have automatic immersion in a primary group, such as a kinship web, or who have satisfactory relations created newly in widowhood. The latter either redistribute the rights, duties, and sentiments focused on the husband among new subjects, or they create new relations that are more than substitutes for the past life-styles. The type of woman able to build a new life is usually the more educated, middle-class or upper-class widow with a breadth of perspective and an initiating manner of role involvement permits her to change her life to meet new needs.

Almost half of the widows list loneliness as their most serious difficulty, and a third name it as the second. Since each form of loneliness was coded separately, more than one reference may come from the same woman who can, for example, miss her husband as an escort to couple-companionate events and as a person. Widows are particularly lonely if they had to lower their self-image by taking a job inferior to a previous one, if she feels other forms of status loss, and if they wish for more male companionship. A satisfactory marriage relation seems to result in feelings of loneliness, but not necessarily in a rejection of remarriage. The concern is with being able to find as good a second husband.

The forms of loneliness that were most often mentioned by the respondents specify missing the husband as a person and as a partner in activities. In spite of the inadequacy of coding clues, patterns of emphasis emerge when the forms are run against background characteristics (see Table 1).

The most heterogenous group is the one that is subsumed under the "person" category, because the typical comment, "I miss Jim," is an all-encompassing statement meaning different things to different people. Those using such a personal description of loneliness are apt to be widows of college graduates or respondents who are themselves service workers. The explanations themselves vary by depth and degree of articulateness, since this category became a catchall.

Those who miss having a partner in activities form a more homogeneous group. They had been dependent upon their husbands as companions in social interaction outside of the home and now do not have the skills, money, or self-confidence to undertake multidimensional activities on their own. Interestingly, women who are concerned with this aspect of loneliness are apt to have also lost a father or a sibling since becoming widowed and to have come from large families.

Table 1: Forms of Loneliness Listed as a Problem of Widowhood

Lonely for:	First Mention Number	Percent	Second Mention Number	Percent
Person of husband	58	26	22	18
Partner in activities	63	28	35	29
Someone around	23	10	21	18
Talking to someone	14	6	5	4
Someone to care for	15	7	9	8
Someone to do things for	6	3	1	1
Other people shun me	29	13	19	16
General loneliness	13	6	8	7
No answer	1*		9*	
Not appropriate (not mention loneliness)	79*		172*	
Percent Base =	221		120	

*Not counted in percent base

Their constricted social-life space is attributed to the absence of the husband not only as an activity companion, but also as its leader.

Those missing having "someone around" the house tend to be overrepresented by black widows in the age decade of the forties and by those with only one to four years of formal education. They do not interact regularly with neighbors, are dependent on accidental contacts, believe that they "seldom" received help from their in-laws since the husband's last illness, and that remarriage is not good because "men cannot be trusted." They want a "live body" in the house, rather than active interaction, but list independence as a major compensation of widowhood.

Those who miss having someone around with whom they can talk are expressing a more active desire for interaction. They are disproportionately represented by high-school drop-outs, whose husbands had the same amount of formal training. Only a "couple" of their friends are also widows, and they fear living with married children because they do not trust themselves to avoid criticizing or overreacting emotionally to the behavior of the other generations. These seem to be women experiencing status decrystallization, in that they fit into more than one social class in different aspects of their lives, who wish for an associate with whom situational strains can be "talked out." Finally, mention should be made of widows who find loneliness a major problem because of missing someone around whom their work can be organized. They are most likely to be white, in their forties, with several living siblings seen only occasionally and without interaction with their neighbors. The overall image is of rather lower-class, quiet, and noninitiating women, who are basically task oriented and have problems in taking on new social relations or roles.

Other problems besides loneliness are listed by the Chicago-area widows. These include financial difficulties, child rearing, decision making, shortage of time, and self-pity. Black respondents are twice as apt as their white counterparts to find widowhood entirely lacking in problems (thirteen percent compared to six percent). The younger women and the blacks of most ages find money a problem, and the latter category of respondent is worried less about loneliness than is the white. One reason may be that these women were less emotionally dependent on the husband, as evidenced by their report of more strains in marriage. Money was listed as the major difficulty by one-fifth of the respondents and as the second problem by another third. The most likely of all categories of population to list this as a problem of first magnitude are the blacks in their sixties, women with five to seven grades of completed education, those who worked most of the time during marriage, widows who changed their working pattern during their husband's last illness, and respondents who went to work after widowhood at the same level of job they held before this event. These women took specific actions to alleviate the financial problems, which were acute. The proportion of respondents worried about finances goes down as the late husband's education achievement goes up. None of the wives of Jewish men expressed a concern about money as the major problem of widowhood, while one-quarter of the widows of Protestants, and a similar proportion of widows of men of any religion who considered their affiliation "very important" focused on this problem. Not surprisingly, women who had to care for their husband at home, who had no money on hand upon his death, and who define themselves now as financially "rather short" or "really restricted" find money to

be a major problem of widowhood. Only a few of the
respondents who define their current finances as "comfortable" mention money in answer to the problems of the
widowhood question. This distribution is consistent with that
of the reported highest income. There is a steady decrease of
the proportion of women listing money as a problem of
widowhood as the amount of the highest past income increases. One-fourth of those who did not know anything about their
finances at the time of the husband's death and of those who
led sex-segregated lives in marriage stress economic problems. In summary, this concern is prevalent among women
who never had much money, who experienced a drop of
income, and who led traditional and restricted lives in the
past. Inadequately trained, they found the maintenance of the
family without its main breadwinner a heavy burden of
widowhood.

The most likely to judge raising a family as a major
problem of widowhood are women whose husbands died
suddenly in accidents or when the wife was in her forties and
the children were young; these women did not experience
anticipatory socialization for widowhood. Only nine percent of
the total group of respondents mention this problem, but they
are disproportionately women with a high level of education
whose husbands obtained a professional or other graduate
degree. The same women are likely to see the postfuneral
changes in themselves as increased activity and independence.
The distributions are not surprising. They were widowed
during the full-house plateau stage of the role of housewife.
Their high educational achievement and socioeconomic status
made them very aware of the difficulty of rearing and socializ-
ing children without the help of the father. After widows pass
this stage of life, they find their existence easier and look upon
the past with a realization that their concern with motherhood
has left them little time to feel lonely.

The few respondents who state that widowhood brought
no problems are distributed unevenly among the various
subcategories of Chicago-area women. Blacks now in their
eighties in age, for example, are disproportionately represented in this group. They expected to be widowed, because of
the high male-death rate in their community, and found no
unanticipated difficulties in dealing with this change in their

life circumstances. Women who believe that they have learned
to take advantage of the freedom of life afforded by widowhood
are also apt to define this marital situation as relatively
problem free. Service workers and respondents with no formal
education are disproportionately represented in the category
of those who answered "none" to the questions about first
problems of widowhood. The picture is generally one of
lower-class women who had been working most of their adult
lives, who had not developed strong companionate relations
with their husbands, who belong to societal subgroups with a
high hostility between the sexes, and who had anticipated
widowhood.

Definitions of a second problem of widowhood were given
by only forty percent of the respondents, but they also reflect
differences in background. In comparison to first problems,
these tend to stress money and the lack of a provider, someone
to earn for the unit, with less frequent reference to loneliness.
As mentioned before, the two sets of answers are not mutually
exclusive. The forms of loneliness that are mentioned as a
second problem are different from those mentioned first and
are given with less prodding. Widows who first listed
loneliness for the husband, in any of its forms, then shifted into
other problems, while widows who originally selected a
different area of difficulty were also less personal in their
second answers. The respondents who listed loneliness as a
problem of second magnitude are represented disproportionately by those who completed only five to seven grades of
schooling and by over half of those who finished only between
one and four grades. These widows have several living
children who seem not to be able to fill the loneliness gap and
lack helpful in-laws. Interestingly enough, although they do not
live with their married children, they are more apt than other
categories of women to see no problems in such an arrangement. Not even their telephone calls offset these feelings, since
the highest proportion mentioning loneliness as a second
problem talks with someone at least four times a day. There is
a possibility that the phone calls, because they are with people
still married, do not alleviate loneliness. One indication of this
is the fact that an unusually large proportion of those listing
loneliness as a second problem have no friends who are also
widows. The whole profile of those who refer to loneliness as a

second problem of widowhood points to women who lack a satisfactory level of contact with people in a similar stage of life. Regardless of whether they miss their husbands as persons or find other problems uppermost, these women are lonely now for human contact. They seem to hold mixed sentiments: wishing remarriage, yet feeling it can cause nothing but trouble; being lonely for people, yet listing "peace of mind" as the most important compensation of widowhood.

Respondents who complain about the lack of a breadwinner as a second problem in widowhood are, strangely enough, likely to have worked themselves most of their married life. Isolation seems less of a problem to them because most of their current friends are widows. As a compensation of widowhood they mention "less work," indicating that the problem of not having someone work for you is partly compensated for by having less work oneself.

The few women who list raising children as a second major problem of widowhood are likely to be very frequent telephone users, talking to someone at least six times a day. They do not know their neighbors and are not sure if they want to remarry. Their best job was as craftsman. In general, this picture suggests the top segment of the blue-collar group, which is family oriented.

Money is a problem of secondary importance to one-third of the 120 women who list more than one source of difficulty. It is of particular significance to women eighty years of age or above, those who dropped out of high school, those who married men with an equal amount of schooling, and those who identify as Jewish. (No Jewish women had listed it in the first place.) The husbands of financially concerned respondents had been working at other than their usual jobs just before death. The widows expect trouble in living with married children because of their own anxiety over noise and commotion. Accustomed to active participation, they define their current social life as quieter than before because of financial restriction and fear of going out alone. As is true of those who listed money as the first major problem, those listing it as a second problem feel financially restricted, or at least "rather short."

[...]

Summary and Conclusions

This work is a result of research focused upon the roles and life-styles of a very specific group of people: American urban widows fifty years of age or older. These women form only a segment of at most two generations of one society; they present a historical instance of people born and brought up under conditions that are not likely to be duplicated in future generations of human beings. However, exploratory investigations of family literature and other sources of sociological data indicate the relevance of this type of study for understanding the broad trends of world change. Not only the United States but many other countries as well are undergoing dramatic modifications in the degrees and forms of urbanization, industrialization, and social complexity. Purposely introduced or repercussive changes are affecting the very foundations of the lives of their members, particularly in their relations to each other and to the larger social structure. The whole process involves people unsystematically, without any institutionalized steps assisting role and relational shifts. The general facts about life changes accompanying these social trends are known. This study hopes to clarify the actual effects of these changes upon the lives of a specific category of societal members, a category that is deeply affected by, and inadequately prepared for, them. By holding constant age over fifty years, sex, marital status, and metropolitan residence, we are able to follow in greater depth the way in which modern life affects social relations than would be possible if all categories of societal participants were covered.

The basic conclusion of this study is that the way in which different types of women reengage in society following the death of the husband reflects their location in the modern social system. The overall trends in social structure are toward increasingly voluntaristic engagement in achieved, functionally oriented social roles that are performed in large groups and contain secondary social relations. The cultural background of many societal members, however, is such as to prevent the utilization of most of the resources of the complex urban world, restricting them to a small social-life space, with almost automatically ascribed social relations. The societies from which most Americans came purposely taught their members to value only long-lasting social relations, to suspect strangers, large groups, and the broader world outside. People were socialized and educated for established social roles, built into packages around the status roles of nobleman, peasant, woman, eldest offspring, and the like. They were discouraged from experimentation in actions deemed inappropriate to such status roles. The basis of traditional societies, many aspects of whose culture survive in modern life—particularly in the family institution—lay in passive stances from all but the elite, that is, acceptance of established modern norms, leadership figures, and personality models for given roles. Each person was dependent upon formalized need suppliers. He was socialized only in his own set of roles, without full understanding of the components of complementary roles. In such a society, wives were able to function only if they had husbands or husband substitutes in the form of kin members who received the rights and provided the necessary tools and cooperative actions. The relatively self-sufficient unit of the farm, the village, the small town, or the ethnic community surrounded each individual from birth to death with familiar faces, behaviors, and demands within a constricted social-life space.

Urbanization, industrialization, and increasing complexity of the social structures have removed the foundations of traditional roles without introducing relevant reeducation or necessary modification in the socialization of existing members. Nor have the societies developed adequate means for preserving the self-identity and dignity of those members who are made obsolete by the changes. People quite capable of living in the society in which they were born and socialized are often unable to function in the society in which they are now located. Extremes of success in matching society and person are clearly visible among urban residents. The modern society is sometimes matched by the "modern" man or woman, who is socialized into a multidimensional problem-solving personality. Such an individual is able to examine the social environment, to determine objectively future goals in many levels of involvement, to think out the possible consequences of alternative solutions for reaching these goals, and to put into action complex but flexible plans. Given seventy-plus years, this kind of person is able to change his social relations, to enter and to exit from social roles as he reaches the different stages of life or redefines his situation, and to constrict or expand his social-life space by self-initiated action rather than reaction to external events.

In the case of widows, such a self-initiating woman, though experiencing strong life disorganization at her husband's death, is nonetheless able to withdraw from, modify, or enter social relations in terms of her own reexamination of life-styles and goals. After the period of temporary passivity experienced in grief, this kind of woman selects certain aspects of the role of wife to be continued after her husband's death and does not try to hang onto aspects impossible to maintain. She relates to adult children in a free flow of interaction, recognizing the self-defined needs of both sides of the relation. She moves away from friendships that were based only on couple-companionate leisure-time activities to ones providing greater or different personal intimacy. She enters or retains roles in the greater community and the society and builds a life-style suited to her individual needs and developed potentials. She remains flexible, assuming that solutions found to be satisfactory at one stage of life may not be so at a later date. Realizing that the presence of her late husband resulted in a role and personality specialization that makes widowhood difficult, she develops substitutes for his contributions by taking over certain of his functions, assigning some to others, or dropping a duty or right entirely. The complexity of the change in her life is likely to be great, but her consciousness of the need to make constant behavioral and relational adjustments is much more developed than that of other widows. Thus, she is not apt to state that she and her life have not changed as a result of the death of the husband. Rather, she spends the time following this event in reexamining the resources of the complex society to see how she can match them with her present and future life goals.

A different type of urbanite is able to retain or duplicate the village type of life for which the traditional socialization prepared her. Ethnic communities still survive in which the residents have lived for decades and in which life may be limited to a particular group of houses, streets, and shops. The rest of the city or the society simply do not exist in the minds or identities of these residents. In the case of a woman, such a situation may prevent any dramatic change from following the death of her husband. Being immersed in kin relations, a very close peer group, or a network of neighbors, such a woman may continue many of her involvements with little modification after becoming a widow. This is particularly true of the lower-class urbanite. A similar lack of change may apply in the case of a suburbanite who had never developed multifaceted relations with the husband, but lived in a sex-segregated world.

A third type of urban widow is the social isolate, either because of her lack of ability to engage in modern society, or because of downward mobility. The widow socialized into passive stances vis-à-vis the world gradually becomes isolated, since the extended kin group or neighborhood are no longer available for contact. Never highly engaged in the broader society, such a widow is unable to retain prior involvements for a variety of reasons, including mobility, poor finances, or health. Friends die or move away and she cannot replace them. She lacks the ability to reengage in new social roles as old ones fall away or to convert relations of greater social distance into closer ones. Such a widow sees the world as inhabited either by old-time contacts with whom she used to be close, or by privacy-invading strangers. For such societal members, each role loss or break in a social relation constricts the social-life space long before the time approved by the social disengagement theory.

The downwardly mobile Chicago-area widow who becomes isolated, though not yet frequent among the older population, will probably increase in proportion with the years to come. She can no longer maintain a prior active and voluntaristic middle-class pattern of social interaction, primarily because she cannot afford to. The loss of her husband and other life changes results in a serious drop in her social status; she cannot maintain contact with former friends or engage in the activities she enjoyed in the past and she rejects presently available relations and activities.

The presence of socially isolated widows in the Chicago-area sample bears further examination, particularly in view of the social disengagement theory that posits a voluntary withdrawal of people and society from each other as age increases. However, those who are socially isolated are not happy with the world. At least, they hold many negative attitudes toward people in general and toward their former intimates. The widows who are socially isolated believe that people take advantage of women in their position, that old friends cannot be replaced, and that it is all right for widows to move soon after the death of the husband. They also think that women in their marital status are sexually propositioned, even by husbands of friends. They do not want more male companionship; while wishing for more friends, they have trouble being nice to past associates whom they define as unhelpful. They feel that their life is easier now than prior to widowhood, in spite of a constriction of income that makes old contacts impossible to retain. Their rejective attitude is reflected by their wish to be left alone. This passive and hostile package of attitudes is reflected by a negative association and significant relation between the social-isolation scale and scores in the roles of wife, mother, and neighbor. This means that the socially isolated achieves her lack of interaction from being low in all three of those roles.

At the other end of the social engagement continuum, widows who have a high frequency of social contact disagree with most of the restrictive statements. These woman reject the belief that children pester them for favors, that widows are sexually propositioned, that other women are jealous of them, that relatives are the only people with whom primary relations are developed, and that people are out to take advantage of them. Their income is not so resricted as to prevent retention of old relationships, and even brothers and sisters have become close to them. Their contact score, added to the positive attitudes, builds up high scores in all the major social roles. Certainly, these two types of women, the socially isolated and the very active, are opposites.

A very basic difference between the strongly engaged women and the social isolates is education. The woman who is passive and uninvolved is apt to have received little education. Skills in building social relations are learned or encouraged in the formal school system and those women who never become involved in this societal structure or who spend few years within it are not apt to engage strongly in other areas of community life during adult and old age. The same characteristics of social class and consequent personality that keep them from school or that result in their dropping out at an early age are the ones that operate throughout life. They led them to a marriage with a man of the same low level of schooling or with one whose accomplishments the widow does not even know. The family income of such people was minimal when the husband was alive, and the widow is financially very restricted at the present time. After the death of a husband with whom she led a sex-segregated life, the woman may be left alone or with small children. Her isolation is made easy by the fact that she was always marginal to the social system and that she was not socialized into any skills for expanded reengagement into society. Fearful and lacking self-confidence, her social involvement is dependent upon chance and the action of others. Having had a hard life in the past, she is often willing just to sit out the rest of her years, without the work or irritation produced by sharing a home or maintaining too close contact with anyone, even her offspring. This same difficulty of life makes her apt not to have living siblings or children; friendship or satisfactory relations at work were never part of her social life.

Other societies protect, provide for, and insure the social involvement of the widow. Decreases in the functionality and availability of the extended family, independence of women, social and geographical mobility, and increasing societal voluntarism have made the case of the isolated widow an increasingly frequent phenomonon.

The generations or types of widows who had been socialized into traditional immersion in ascribed social roles, but who are living in a voluntaristic system of secondary relations or achieved primary ones, face social isolation, loneliness, and restriced social-life space. The widow socialized into a voluntaristic engagement in achieved social roles but no longer having the facilities to retain social involvement faces a similar problem. The best position is that of the widow who was socialized into the modern social system and has enough financial and health resources to participate. Her social relations may be changed as a result of widowhood, but they tend to be multidimensional in a relatively broad social-life space, both in marriage and after recovery from the death of her husband.

Recommendations for Meeting the Needs of Urban Widows

The final question to which a study of widowhood in an American city must address itself is how the acquired knowledge can be applied in practice to help widows. The answer obviously depends upon the needs of each particular widow, her relations to her helpers, and her stage of widowhood. The helpers can be classified, in order of decreasing intimacy to the widow, as: relatives, friends, voluntary associations, the community, and the society. The needs depend upon the unique combination of personality and life circumstances.

The short-range needs of widows, regardless of typology or life circumstances, can be summarized as fivefold:

1. "grief work"
2. companionship
3. solution of immediate problems
4. building of competence and self-confidence
5. help in reengagement.

Grief Work

Psychiatrists working with people who have recently suffered bereavement agree with Eric Lindemann that the most important need at this stage of widowhood is the process of "grief work." The grieving person must be allowed to express his or her emotions, sorrow, guilt, loneliness, and the whole gamut of sentiments activated by the death of a significant other. The American culture performs a disservice to the grieving person by downplaying emotion and deinstitutionalizing mourning rituals. Social scientists in general recommend that the widow be encouraged to cry if she wishes, to talk of her late husband, and of how badly she feels. Family members, friends, and especially trained counselors ought to be available to allow the griever a personal rhythm of working out emotions and of gradually redefining life. All the phases of grief, from shock to final acceptance and willingness to rebuild life, must be worked out, according to Lindemann, Parkes, Maddison, and the other Harvard Medical School psychiatrists and sociologists dealing with this problem.

Companionship

Chicago-area widows explain the help they most appreciated from people right after the death of their husbands in
terms of rather passive companionship, "just being here," or
active sharing of activities. The stress upon "just being here"
indicates a grief-work need, but it also points up a very
realistic problem of widowhood among older people. The death
of a wife or husband at an age after children have left home
often reduces the household to only one person. The widow
must learn to live alone for the first time of her life. Since this
process is complicated by grief and all of its manifestations,
psychologists and the majority of widows advise companionship during the year following the husband's death. The widow
is longing for her husband as a particular individual, for
another person in the house, for someone around to organize
time and work, for a contributor to the maintenance of the
home, and for a partner in a variety of activities. Television
watching and eating, to say nothing of the activities outside of
the house, can be lonely. The widow is not used to going out by
herself evenings, feels like a fifth wheel if she accompanies
couples, fears taking public transportation and going out at
night, and is hesitant about entering public places or functions
without a male escort. Anything friends and relatives can do to
alleviate these problems is a major help. Any program
developed among unmarried or no longer married friends of
the new widow to engage her during mealtimes and weekends
could make an important contribution to meeting her companionship needs.

The need for companionship that begins with grief but
continues into later years is not easily met by former social
intimates. Both the widows and their friends complain about
each other, holding negative attitudes. The friends complain
that the widow makes impossible demands, has a chip on her
shoulder, or is not pleased with their attempts to help. The
widow lives in fear of being dropped by her friends and
ignored by her relatives, partly because the subculture
contains many tales of such desertions and partly because she
does not really feel that she is worth much as an individual.
The latter sentiment is reinforced by the low status of a widow
in American society and by her prior dependent identity as a
wife accompanying a particular husband. There is sometimes

an almost paranoic anxiety about social relations, which results in behavior dysfunctional to continuing satisfactory interaction. Widows refuse invitations that they feel are extended as an act of charity rather than as a result of a desire for their company, yet they are hurt when they hear of a party to which they have not been invited. The set of attitudes that forms the tightest cluster in the relations-restrictive attitude scale reflects the frustration that many widows feel in their interaction with friends, because of the form of help that is or is not offered when they are in grief or even later. Some complain that they are never asked what help they actually desire, but are given only the kind that others wish to offer. They think friends and relatives hold many beliefs and attitudes about widows that are unrealistic and even irrelevant to their needs. "They just don't understand" is their frequently voiced complaint.

Basically, the best recommendation this study can offer to intimates of a widow is to try to understand the emotionally ambivalent nature of her psychological state and consistently give her what *she defines* as her relational needs, without taking offense at slights or even withdrawals. This period is difficult for both parties, but it is the widow, not the friend, who has the strongest cause for irrational and highly demanding behavior. The friends can also examine their own motives, making sure that the withdrawal or diminishing of contact is not due to avoidance of problem situations, only rationalized as "good for the widow." There is a very strong possibility that some truth may be behind the widow's assertion that she is being shunned because of distaste for the whole topic of death or because of jealousy. Realization of the relatively short duration of the grief period should encourage friends and relatives to be really helpful on the widow's own terms.

Advice: Solution of Problems and Competence Building

A very important cause of strain in the relations between a widow and her significant others during the period immediately after her husband's death is too much of the wrong kind of advice. Unfortunately, everyone around her is full of advice, and the bits she receives are often contradictory and irrelevant or unbeneficial from her point of view. Psychiatrists and

lawyers recommend that the widow avoid making any important decisions during the first year of widowhood, because the
possibility of mistakes is great and because her life and outlook
will change after she completes grief work. She may deeply
resent having decided something during this period at the
insistence of a well-meaning friend or relative. Experts also
recommend that people close to the widow not offer her too
much dependency-producing advice. They should simply help
her meet the immediate crises and contribute to her own
decision-making ability by providing the necessary knowledge
and by training her to be an increasingly competent person.
No one should make decisions for her, unless absolutely
necessary to avoid a serious disaster. There are several
reasons for these recommendations. In the first place relatives
are usually ill-informed as to the alternative solutions to many
of the widow's problems. If they feel obliged to interfere in
her life, they should obtain the professional advice of experts,
without assuming that they themselves know what is best for
the widow. Second, a major problem of widowhood is this very
attitude of significant others—that they, not she, know all the
answers to her situation. This attitude diminishes her self-confidence in her own abilities. She depended upon a husband in
the past, but she now must develop the competence and
self-confidence to make her own decisions. The significant
others must help her by showing trust in her resources.
Advice-giving is dysfunctional, if it robs her of self-confidence.
The third disadvantage to advice is that it was worked out
from others' vantage points. It was based on what relatives
and friends think the widow "should" need, or "should" want,
or "should" do, rather than on her own definition of her
situation, needs, and goals. It ignores her personality. Finally,
advice is often contradictory, since it comes from different
sources.

Thus, the most frequent expert recommendation of short-
range help for new widows is to provide opportunity for grief
work, to guarantee quiet companionship as well as partnership in activities, to help directly in solving immediate
problems (such as funeral arrangements, temporary financial
difficulties, and so on), and to refrain from giving advice as to
major changes in life-style. Close associates should make
available the services of experts: ministers, doctors, lawyers,

bankers, and specialists in mental health. Simultaneously, any action that they can undertake to increase her knowledge and skills in problem solving is of immense importance.

Community Help to Widows

The community within which the widow lives can contribute to both her short-range and long-range adjustment. The widow-to-widow program instituted in Boston and New York as a result of research conducted by the Harvard Medical School is an excellent example of societally provided help for such crisis situations. Women who have already gone through the stages of grief contact new widows and offer several different services. In the first place, they make her feel that at least one other person "understands" how she feels. The matching of the caller and the "client" by socioeconomic background is important here, because of the class differences in response to widowhood. In addition, the caller, if adequately trained, can provide specific knowledge about relevant sources of help in meeting new problems. She can come equipped with legal information or at least with an approved list of lawyers. The caller can be informed of work, training, voluntary associations, and other resources available to widows who are unfamiliar with them because of past life-style. Finally, she can keep in continuous touch and be available for future information or comfort. Organizations such as NAIM, the Catholic group for the widowed, or senior women's clubs can serve as an organizing center for such widow-to-widow personal contact and for subsequent group integration. The point is, of course, that an organized and continuing social group is needed to train the callers, to serve as a clearing house of information, and to expand the contact beyond the one-to-one interaction. A group whose whole activity is oriented toward problems of widowhood or one catering to older people would be a natural, not only for carrying out the suggested type of help, but for experimenting with different means of assisting widows.

The widow who has been socially isolated for some time presents a different kind of problem to the community. She is difficult to discover, because of her very isolation, and she needs greater understanding and more intensive attention.

She lacks skills in social relations, and her complex of problems is barrier creating. It took years for her to develop her marginal position vis-à-vis society, and such barriers cannot be broken down in one contact situation. She is not likely to join NAIM (which is, even at its best, limited to Catholic women), a Newcomer's group, or even a club within a church, where she could be individually approached in social interaction. She is the long-term nonmember or drop-out from community life. Welcome Wagons seldom seek her out, because of her poverty, and even when they do, the contact is impersonal.

One of the recommendations of the researchers involved in the study of aging in small towns of Missouri (Philblad and Rosencranz) was that the local churches involve the older person by insuring transportation and programs designed to meet their interests. All voluntary associations in metropolitan centers should be encouraged to help decrease the social isolation and minimal involvement of residents. The first step would be to find the isolated and break down their attitudinal barriers; then the lonely must be reengaged. This is a complex task and should not be undertaken haphazardly as in the past. There should be specific groups within each parent organization who would have the primary function of finding the isolated and the lonely, sending "callers" to them, building trust, and gradually increasing involvement. Steps should include:

1. Canvassing social areas and/or past membership lists to locate inactive members and socially isolated persons;

2. Gathering sufficient background information on the person to facilitate interaction rituals;

3. Selection of a person to initiate the contact who has particular empathy for each type of "client";

4. Training the caller in procedures for initiating contact, developing rapport, and encouraging client involvement in the community;

5. Providing the caller with relevant data about:
   a. the client,

b. resources for the solution of some of the client's problems (Medicare, employment, housing, and so on); steps facilitating entrance into new social roles, especially jobs (how to apply, be interviewed, and so on);

6. Securing facilities for the client's increased participation in the activities of that association or of any other group, for that matter. For instance, transportation, wardrobe expansion (special day for older people at rummage sales), detailed information about events, and particularly company in going to and returning from such events;

7. Making sure that the client is working into the group in such a way that she makes a visible contribution to its functioning.

Several members of NAIM with whom the author spoke during the exploratory stage of this research explained that a "hard case" of widowhood was helped by "putting her to work," referring to voluntary tasks that facilitated the actual functioning of the group. Widows who lack self-confidence and the ability to communicate with others are nevertheless given tasks requiring some social interaction, but they are not expected to blossom suddenly into "social butterflies."

The community and the society at large could set up official agencies supplementing the activities of voluntary associations. Financial advice is badly needed by widows, who often do not take full advantage of existing societal resources because they simply do not know of them. They get help only if they become welfare cases, and even in such situations complete information is not guaranteed. To the middle-class urban dweller, the great ignorance of some of the older widows concerning the law, Social Security, medical care, pensions, and so on, is staggering. Many widows are not aware that buses in Chicago have special rates for the elderly, nor have they ever been to the "loop" or the center of the city. In addition, they do not trust their informants, having discovered from past experience that people around them are also ignorant.

Many of the problems of widows could be solved by just a few hours of undivided and expert attention involving precontact and voluntaristic follow-up. One of the existing governmental offices could set up a limited number of centers to which the widowed could go for specific advice as to the best methods of reengagement in society. Such centers could contain a lawyer, a social worker, a physician, an accountant, and related personnel. Consultants might be available for special cases. In addition, the city, state, or federal government could set up series of lectures, perhaps conducted in such centers or in public housing complexes, which would teach people the simple procedures for developing social interaction. The widows need to learn how to get a job, join an organization, build friendship, look well, and the like. Beauticians, fashion coordinators, and others who train people how to be socially acceptable ought to provide this information to the widows who never learned to be publicly presentable, or who have been out of social circulation so long as to have rusty or out-moded resources. This knowledge is vital in our modern voluntaristic society. It is provided for the young, but the older persons who are very apt to need it do not receive it. There are some programs in "hard core" inner-city areas that teach women to cook, sew, and so on, but these adult-education programs must be expanded to include interactional training of older people.

One of the discoveries of the exploratory period of research on widowhood is the pervasiveness of the "disengagement theory." Many people working with the elderly believe that social isolation is a result of the natural process of withdrawal of the person and the society from each other. This study indicates that factors other than choice are frequently operating to isolate the person. Basically, those who are isolated or lonely are those who lack the skills, money, health, and transportation for engaging or reengaging in society. Widows are either unhappy over their restricted social-life space or "adjusted." Unfortunately, adjustment can refer to the passive decision that life cannot be changed but rather must be waited out. Such widows live in a society that assumes the perfect engagement of all those members who wish to be engaged, in the directions and levels that meet their needs. This study of widowhood indicates that the assumption is false for at least some widows and that much can still be done to reengage people who have for some reason or another suffered breaks in their life patterns or who have always been marginal to the present social system. If such people are to be helped, a fresh view of the relation between the urban, industrial, and complex modern world and its residents is required, and new action programs must be creatively developed.

12

Romance in the SRO[*]

Joyce Stephens

Relationships of Elderly Men and Women in a Slum Hotel

Little is known of the sociological correlates of SRO (single-room-occupancy) hotels and their occupants. Even less is known of the elderly permanent tenants who constitute an increasing proportion of the SRO population. The present research represents an attempt to fill in some of the gaps in our knowledge, through an investigation of the patterns of interaction characteristically established between aged men and women living in the "Guinevere" Hotel, a deteriorating SRO hotel situated in the central core of a large Midwestern city. The data are part of a larger study (Stephens 1973).

Men and Women

The world of the Guinevere aged (ninety-two men and eleven women) is a society composed largely of men, which is typical of SRO hotel populations. Elderly women are considerably less likely to wind up in slum hotels; they tend to be living with family members or in their own homes or apartments. Not

*This work originally appeared in *The Gerontologist* 14 (August 1974): 279-82. This article is to be included, in a more extended form, in the forthcoming *Loners, Losers, and Lovers: A Sociological Study of the Aged Tenants of a Slum Hotel* to be published by the University of Washington Press.

only are there many fewer women in the Guinevere, but they are also in significant ways differentiated from the men. The dominant values of the SRO society come into conflict with the values supporting sex-role identities of the elderly women. Particularly, the all-important value of independence becomes subverted in the case of these women. For them, the consequences include reduced capacity to cope, a greater vulnerability, and an even more extreme isolation and loneliness than the men endure. The subversion of this major value is recognized and often remarked on by tenants.*

The theme of "trying to get something out of them" runs through the relationships established between the elderly men and women. The men are wary and suspicious; the women bitter and resentful. Each predicates the other of trying to use and exploit him (or her).

The probability of these aged men and women working out sustained relationships with each other is attenuated not only by the normative pattern of avoidance of intimacy and binding relationships that constitutes both a basal common meaning in their society and a major coping strategem, but also by conflicting expectancies and demands generated by sex-role prescriptions prevalent in the larger society. In the sex-role differences of this group of elderly people are played out the culmination of the conventional culture's sex-role identity assignments.

For the elderly male tenant in the SRO hotel, the taken-for-granted meanings of this society are capable of being synchronized with life-long male-role definitions; how-

---

*"It don't matter how old a woman gets. They're always clingy, just hopin' to depend on some man."

"They want others to cater to them, to fawn on them. They try to be more dependent, but the men won't put up with it. So, they're more helpless and foolish and lonelier, too, desperately lonely."

"The men are in better shape mentally. I mean, because they're independent and have practicality. But these women are looking for someone to lean on. The men get by, they manage, like, take the carnies. They get out and around. They don't stay in the hotel, they hustle. But the women aren't like the men—levelheaded, and practical. Why, they're just like old housewives who can't stick to the point, who expect others to do things for them while they set (sic) home. And the men won't have anything to do with them. They know they're just trying to get something out of them."

ever, for the elderly female tenant, sex-role patterns of a lifetime are at odds with the assumptions of SRO life. Therefore, the men experience less role discontinuity, since the dominant values of the SRO environment, for example, decision making, independence, behaviors emphasizing instrumentality—are compatible with the sex-role identities and demands that they have lived with more or less all their adult lives. On the other hand, for these elderly women, there is a severe break from traditionally defined sex-role behaviors, such as nurturing, and homemaking, behaviors emphasizing expressiveness that are characterized by their complementary status to the male role.

The elderly women in the Guinevere hotel have not always lived in slum hotels; they have not always been alone. They, more than the men, are likely to have been married, to have raised children, to have been linked up to the conventional life presented by the larger society. Roles of a lifetime, especially those that play such a crucial part in buttressing selfhood, do not die easily; thus, the elderly women are prone to attempt to retain these role definitions and behaviors and associated values regarding self and others and act in terms of them. Such inappropriate behaviors (inappropriate to the SRO society) are countered by sharp rebuffs. The men are wary and determined not to be drawn into relationships that they cannot afford and, to this end, define these elderly women as foolish, boring, and a burden if one is silly enough to give them an opening. The men avoid the women and, in so doing, contribute to a deepening sex-related isolation.

The women appear more vulnerable, less successful at coping, unreconciled to their present status. A favorite and familiar story of these aged women is of the solicitous care still available to them from their families. They will tell you that all they have to do is pick up the telephone and make a call and the son, daughter, grandchild, whoever, will come for them, take them home, care for them. There is no viable basis for these daydreams; children are gone or dead, grandchildren are uninvolved and in some cases have actively avoided and refused to have anything to do with these women. Nevertheless, it is a favorite story, even if no one believes it.

The women are less in tune with things; they are not aware of current events, political issues. They more than the men, try to live in the past, or their reconstructions of imagined pasts—in which they are lovingly and tenderly surrounded by families, an imagined past in which they are "somebody." The adjustment of the women to the world of the SRO is more fragile, more tenuous than that of the men. Ironically, their inappropriate need to revive ways of relating that would allow of intimacy is looked upon in the society of SRO tenants as a cover-up for an exploitative ruse, another hustle.

Prostitution and the Elderly Man

The avoidance that characterizes relationships between the sexes does not mean that there is no intersex mingling. For the elderly men, there is an occasional seeking out of female company. Typically, this means the services of a prostitute. Next to sports, the horses, and alcohol, sex is the most popular subject of conversation among the men. The hotel is worked by prostitutes from the area and a few part-timers who live in the hotel itself. When the Social Security checks arrive on the first of the month, the "prossies" arrive, also, all ages, often on narcotics, and attended by the ever watchful eye of their "sponsor" (pimp), they pour into the hotel bar to work the old men.* Additionally, there are a few middle-aged and elderly women living in the hotel who "trick" now and then to pay their rent.

The arrangement usually takes place in the bar, with the pimp working out the price. Sexual contacts take place in the tenant's room, the whore's "work-bench" (room), or in one of the vacant cars in the hotel parking lot. Most often, they will go to the tenant's room while the girl's pimp waits in the bar. The leniency of the hotel management is an encouragement to the trade, since the prossies have little to fear in the way of reprisals. There is even some deference shown to the prossies and their pimps. There is no contempt for a pimp for, after all,

*Interviews with several police officers and plainclothes detectives assigned to the area confirmed the fieldworker's observations that little is being done to discourage the trade in bodies. The officers said that they used to pick the girls up for suspicion of being a disorderly person but the courts ruled that they could not be held for suspicion of a misdemeanor. Therefore, "their hands are tied."

he has a good hustle. The "chippie," on the other hand, who spends all her trick money on dope and new clothes for her pimp is believed to be a real fool, who has a good hustle that she's throwing away for someone else to "make it" on. The dislike expressed for the chippie is related to the greater likelihood of these elderly men having been victimized by them and their pimps. It is not uncommon for a young, inexperienced prostitute to get the old man drunk and then let her pimp in, who beats up and robs the old man.*

Most of the sexual contacts involve "first-of-the-monthers," that is, on the first of the month the Social Security checks arrive and the elderly men can afford to buy a prostitute's services. The going rate is $10, although some have been known to pay considerably more. "Baldy," a sixty-seven-year-old ex-fighter, for example, paid $60 for a "blow job." He was, of course, drunk. In terms of actual sexual activity, the following accounts by men in the Guinevere and two prostitutes who work in the area are illuminating:

> All hotels have prossies; some hotels have hotel prossies and the manager gets a share. They rent a "workbench" and work right there. They like the old men, well, it's easy money and easy work for them. You have to realize, it's mostly talk. Oh, they'll brag to one another. You can go into the bar and you'll hear them, but that's mostly talk. All this sex talk you hear is just mostly talk.
>
> It's disgusting. A bunch of "d.g.'s" [sex deviates] here. I keep sex in the corner. I don't mess around with the prossies. I masturbate, it's just a matter of release.
>
> The professionals know their business, but them young chippies with their pimps and hooked on dope, and they haven't got the brains of a louse.
>
> It's true all talk winds up about sex. But, they're really just voyeurs, and the talk is part of that. They pay to look, if you understand me. They pay to look at a young girl, and it's no work for her.

---

*It is when several such beatings occur and the manager begins to anticipate delay in getting his rent money from the victims that he initiates a "clean-up" and bans the prossies from the hotel. However, since management's overall policy is to ignore the practice, the clean-up is ineffective and within a few days the situation reverts to normal.

They don't want much and the money's the same. They like to look and maybe touch, but they don't do much more [a twenty-two-year-old black prostitute].

It gives 'em something to feel good about. I had a woman, that kinda stuff, and they can tell the others in the bar. Shit, they're just talking, anyway, they're not doin' [a thirty-four-year-old white prostitute].

At any rate, despite the gap between action and talk, the elderly men at the Guinevere appear relatively willing to allow the prossies to skim off the tops of their checks. However, it is usually a one-shot affair, since these men have neither the finances nor the desire to maintain women on any permanent basis.

Romances between the elderly tenants are rare—sixty-year-old men do not want sixty-year-old women. When romances do develop, they are short-lived and not bragged about. The men will not bring a lady-friend into the bar to show her off but rather are reticent about it. In the words of one seventy-three-year-old women, "romances here are torrid and end abruptly, usually over trivia." Long-term relationships between these elderly men and women are precluded by the conflicting demands and expectations referred to earlier. The women attempt to use the relationship as a vehicle to establish a quasi-family situation—the man will be asked to do things for her, to accompany her downtown, to have dinner with her. The man will view such expectations as exploitative and possessive on her part. At this point, the relationship will usually end. Several of the men reported prior relationships that they had formed with elderly female tenants, only to have to break them off because the women became too "possessive," "jealous," and "demanding." Since the men define the women as seeking a relationship that they cannot afford and do not want, they prefer the pay-as-you-go services of the prostitute.

For their part, the elderly women define the men as only interested in sex and avoid them (they are correct; the liaison with the prostitute constitutes a casual, sharply delimited transaction in which ongoing demands are not made of the relationship). Involvement with a man is a source of unrelenting gossip and friendships between the sexes are always assumed to be fronts for the fact that they are sleeping with each other. The strict proscription agaist "getting too friendly" applies to male-female interaction particularly. Both men and women are inclined to interpret overtures on the part of the other as attempts to exploit and take advantage.

Relationships among the Elderly Women

The institutionalization of mutual suspicion and avoidance that characterizes contacts between the elderly men and women has more severe consequences for the women. This is due to the overall decreased sociability pool from which the women are able to draw. They do not work and, therefore, do not form work relationships; they do not usually frequent the hotel bar and do not have drinking cronies. Furthermore, the women, cut off from the company of men, do not relate well to each other either. The attitudes of the women toward each other revolve around the axes of hostility and jealousy. They are in a permanent kind of competition with each other.*

Interaction among the women takes the form of one-upmanship, with the goal being to establish that one's family and background are definitely superior to the other. This behavior ought not to be viewed as a feminine counterpart to the "conning" behavior of the hustlers who are attempting to demonstrate superior abilities over rivals in their occupation. The competition of the hustlers serves as a socially binding force in that it defines their common interests, skills, and experience. For the women, however, this competitive arena intensifies their bitterness over a life that they cannot leave and cannot live and drives deep barriers between them.

---

*We see here in sharp relief, one of the products of culturally engendered sex-role identities. Women in our society define themselves in terms of their men; when they have not got a man they must look upon all other women as rivals for the man they must somehow get to validate their status. These elderly women who, in all probability, are not going to get men, nevertheless, continue to play out their cultural mandate. They continue to define other women as their competitors and are, as are most women in our society, crippled in their capacity to relate to each other independently of the male-female configuration.

One informant spoke knowingly of the fragility of relationships between the women:

> Friendships between them (women) never last more than a few days. Then they fall out over some paltry matter. Usually over gossip. Some of the feuds and vendettas are years old. Friendships between the men are more permanent because they are hardheaded and practical. They need each other for their work. ____ [a carny boss], now how could he take care of all that by himself? No, he's got to have someone he will know for sure is going to be there; he's got to have his workers. He makes a lot of contacts and holds on to them. But, the women, they're so out of touch with the mainstream. The men don't have anything to do with them. Well, because they can see that they're just interested in using them. Do this for me; oh won't you drive me there? And, of course, the women are quite boring; they live in the past. Not like the men, who have to keep up with the times. But to get back to the women, no, I don't know any of them who have stayed friends. Friends? They're too jealous and suspicious of one another, always gossiping and backbiting on each other. And sooner or later, it gets back, and there you are, they're not speaking anymore.

All-in-all, one cannot but be struck by the poignant appearance of these taciturn and suspicious ladies, with their wigs that do not fit and their veiled hats that, like banners, put forth a brave front. Their loneliness, their isolation are tangible. Their adoption of an exaggerated unapproachability underscores what is a poorer mastery of the coping strategies needed to "make it" in the world of the SRO.

The elderly women living in the Guinevere have had to sacrifice more in the way of role identity in order to survive in the SRO world. The giving up of culturally acquired sex-role identities has not been a facile accomplishment, and, indeed, their somewhat exaggerated enactment of some of the dominant themes of SRO life—suspicion, avoidance, privacy—are attempts to deal with residual meanings and values—dependency, intimacy (values supportive of expressive role playing) —that were appropriate to a sex-role identity that they no longer can dare or hope to hold on to. Above all, they are faced with the continual necessity to develop effective coping behaviors.

That there is even less solidarity among these aged women in a group of people distinctive for its impoverishment of social ties is understandable when viewed in the context of the utilitarian and instrumental thrust of relationships established by the SRO tenants. The residual values of a lifetime that served to support personal and social identity are not appropriate in the world of the Guinevere and must be sloughed off. The fracturing of identity that results is the heavy price that these elderly women must pay in order to continue to maintain themselves as SRO tenants. They have little choice: They, no less than the men, are locked into their situation, by age, poverty, ill health, and their own desire to maintain their independency.

References

Joyce Stephens. "Loners, losers, and lovers." Ph.D. dissertation, Wayne State University, 1973.

13

A Million Procrustean Beds*

Elaine M. Brody

Procrustes was "a legendary highwayman of Attica who tied his victims upon an iron bed, and stretched or cut off their legs to adapt them to its length" (Webster). From the Greek, then, derives the adjective *Procrustean*: Tending to produce uniformity by violent methods" (Oxford Dictionary).

According to the 1970 census, a million people 65 or over, about 5 percent of the total elderly population, reside in institutions of various types. That figure grossly underestimates the number of Procrustean beds.

First of all, Kastenbaum and Candy's recent study, "The 4 Percent Fallacy," suggests that there is at least a 20 percent chance of any aged individual entering a nursing home. The misleading 4 percent or 5 percent figure widely used was derived from cross-sectional rather than longitudinal population data.

*This work originally appeared in *The Gerontologist* 13 (Winter 1973): 430-35. This is a revised version of an invited paper prepared for National Conference of Jewish Communal Service, Philadelphia, 29 May 1973.

Second, various estimates indicate that there may be as many as two million community dwellers whose demographic and health characteristics are comparable to those of the institutionalized. Many of them, because they lack viable options, live in substandard boarding homes characterized as "Human Warehouses" (Roberts), in their own residences without services needed to maintain a decent level of health and well-being, or with families under severe economic, physical, and emotional stress.

It has become fashionable of late to denigrate institutional care in favor of community arrangements called *alternatives*, as though the two were in competition rather than different points along a continuum and as though alternatives exist. Estimates are made that various proportions of older people could be discharged from institutions. However, hard information has not been developed that details the nature, number, and costs of services required and that evaluates how such elderly individuals fare. A comprehensive network of community services surely could reduce the need for institutional care somewhat and enable many community dwellers to live at a better level of health and well-being. But the number of long-term beds needed still would be offset by increased availability of institutions to those formerly shut out and by the simple statistical facts of life.

For example, many who require decent institutional care cannot obtain it. Hobart Jackson and Jacquelyne Jackson point out that for the black aged, the problem is not how to keep them out of institutions, but rather how to get them into institutions willing to accept them. The problem is acute also for other groups such as the poor and the hard-to-care-for patient.

Further, between 1960 and 1970, the number of people 75 and over grew three times as fast as the 65-74 group (Brotman), and the trend will continue. It is that group—the very old old—whose age-related impairments and losses exert pressure for needed institutional care. Clearly, the tasks ahead are to improve the quality of institutions, as well as to develop community services.

Current Social Policy

However, the current social policy scene, the context in which long-term care is being shaped, offers a series of contradictions.

The 1972 Social Security amendments provide for expanded review procedures (to monitor medical services delivery whether by hospitals, nursing homes, or home health agencies) to reduce "inappropriate institutional care." Policy activities such as inspections of nursing homes to ensure standards do not improve the quality of psychosocial care. Emphasis on improving the "quality of life" in institutions is nullified also by PL 92-603's regressive position that "the Secretary shall not require as a condition of participation that medical social services be furnished in any institution."

Where do the elderly go when substandard nursing homes are closed? "Alternatives" are being promoted, but no monies are made available for the required services and in fact are reduced both under Medicare and by the 90/10 provisions under Title I. The verbal pursuit of alternatives is additionally contradicted by the HUD freeze on construction of subsidized housing and cutbacks in training funds.

Changes in Medicare provide for advance authorization for payments for posthospital and ECF benefits and for 100 percent (rather than 80 percent) reimbursement of home services (Part B). But neither provision speaks to the real need of older people—that is, for long-term sustained input of care.

The Revenue Sharing Act (PL 92-512) with its $2.5 billion ceiling allotted to states on a population basis permits the states to spend what they wish for the elderly—all or nothing. Experience tells us that when priorities are allocated, the old are invariably at the bottom of the list.

We are in the midst of a second wave of a massive assault on the most vulnerable segment of society—sick old people who cannot raise their voices in their own behalf. The large-scale discharges of a few years ago from mental hospitals to other institutions is being replayed. This time the exodus will be from nursing homes and homes for the aged that might provide quality care, into bootleg nursing homes and no-care boarding homes, or to families already too sick, too old, too crowded, or too burdened.

Some view these developments as hopeful. One gerontologist states that:

> For the long pull, . . . [the] review structure can be used to unplug the obstacle which led to inappropriate use of institutions for persons who could benefit from other types of help but for whom no financial base exists. If social welfare personnel is involved in this new review mechanism, a new platform can become available everywhere to press for the creation of a personal care, home care network. . . . (Morris)

That is a big "if." Such an attitude recommends making the problem worse so we can press for a solution. The "long pull" has already been too long. No further documentation of the problem is needed. The real way to reduce inappropriate institutional care is to develop community care. *When options are real, those who do not need institutions will not choose them.*

Though at present the picture is discouraging, *because that is so,* it is well to view these matters in perspective and to reassess the goals of long-term care.

Perspectives

The past few years have witnessed a significant upsurge of interest in aging and the aged. If the number of professional publications, stories in the media, and conferences are a gauge, if the task forces on aging established by the major professional organizations and the steady tilling of legislative soil by the Senate Committee on Aging are signs, if the growth of organizations of older people themselves is an indicator, if the leap to high fashion of death and dying is a clue—attention to the older population is an idea whose time must come.

Further, the standards and expectations of the current generation of older people were calibrated by oppression and poverty in the countries from which they came, by their struggle as immigrants, and by the hardships of the Great Depression. But every five years there is a turnover of one-third in the elderly population. The elderly of the future, with higher expectations and greater sophistication will not accept the current conditions passively. The climate is different for disadvantaged groups. Awareness is always the first step to remedies, whether it be awareness of racism, male chauvinism, or agism.

If goals are to be formulated to determine the shape of long-term care, it is useful to look back in history as well as to examine its status at this point in time; to speculate on how the curious assumption developed that institutional care per se is "bad" while community care per se is "good."

It may be that it is convenient to study the deficits of institutional populations in their neat envelopes of bricks and mortar.

It may be that groups of people sheltered together are more visible than those dispersed in invisible misery.

It may be the hope (as yet to be demonstrated) that a sick old person can be maintained more cheaply in the community.

Certainly, among the factors that color popular perceptions of institutional care are the vestiges from an earlier day of attitudes toward several different types of institutions and their residents.

Pauper-Status

In the fourth century, hospitals existed for the care of lepers, cripples, the blind, and the sick poor. By the twelfth century, medical care was practiced in home or office, with only hopeless and homeless cases finding their way to hospitals. The evolution of the hospital as the place for temporary care of acute disease appears to have occurred in the eighteenth and nineteenth centuries.

In the United States, earliest long-term care was tied to concern for "paupers"—the undeserving and the abandoned. The public assumed responsbility for the disabled, handicapped, aged, widows with children, orphans, the feebleminded, the decayed, and the unemployed (Cohen). Attitudes toward such people could be measured by the harshness of the almshouse or poorhouse that was a matter of policy. The 1875 report of New York State stated:

Care has been taken not to diminish the terrors of. . . [the] "almshouse" because it has been deemed better that a few should test the minimum rate at which existence can be preserved than that many should find the almshouse so comfortable a home that they would brave the shame of pauperism to gain admission to it.

The twentieth century witnessed developments such as a specialization of various types of institutions, segregation of different groups of residents and patients, the rise of private philanthropy, the utilization of hospitals for the well-to-do as well as for the indigent, and the beginning of the home for the aged and nursing home as we know them.

The use of nursing homes and homes for the aged for those who were not paupers came somewhat later than the parallel development in hospital care. But deep historical roots are tenacious. The concept of charity with the expectation that the recipient of care be grateful and submissive is still very much alive in both hospital and nursing-home care. Else why would the American Hospital Association recently find it necessary to issue a document called *Statement on a Patient's Bill of Rights?* The first of the twelve rights is "to considerate and respectful care" and the summary statement speaks to recognition of the patient's "dignity as a human being." Elderly institutional residents, it is submitted, are still assigned *pauper status* as were residents of the early county homes, almshouses, and hospitals.

Agism

Another contributor to negative attitudes toward institutions is agism (Butler; Neugarten). Agism is directed at older people individually and collectively, is conscious and unconscious, direct and indirect. Its manifestations are manifold: The phrase "old man" or "old lady" has assumed a pejorative or condescending quality; professionals prefer to work with younger people and are unduly pessimistic about the potential of the old; professional schools ignore or give only token representation to the aging phase of life; older people receive far less than their proportionate share of health and social services and are discriminated against in the job market; ambulance drivers sound their sirens less urgently and drive more slowly when the patient is an older person (Sudnow); advertising glorifies youth, and the attributes of the young are the criteria of beauty.

The agism that pervades attitudes toward all the elderly is intensified with respect to those in institutions. Because so many are mentally impaired, they also bear the stigmata attached to patients in the institutions called *insane asylums* that antedated modern psychiatric hospitals. Because many are frail, dependent, and confused, they are objects of a particularly subtle form of agism that has been perpetrated by incorrect psychodynamic formulations such as "generational role reversal" and "second childhood." The care given by an adult child to his elderly parent cannot be equated with psychological relationship. Psychologically, no matter how old the adult child, he remains child, not parent, to his parent. The behavior of a brain-damaged old person may appear childlike, but he is not a child; half a century or more of adulthood cannot be wiped out.

On Being in an Institution

Much knowledge has been assembled that is basic to the determination of the kinds of programs and atmosphere institutionalized old people require. Directions are indicated by their characteristics and experiences, by the trauma of admission itself, and by the nature of institutional care.

Older people in institutions are characterized by advanced old age (half are over eighty), poverty, impaired mental and physical functioning, multiple chronic disabilities, lack or loss of family, and by having experienced a series of severe personal and social stresses (Gottesman and Brody, for detailed information about the characteristics of the institutionalized).

Though they share these collective characteristics, they are also heterogenous. They include the "young" old as well as the "old" old, the economically well-off as well as the indigent, those who are severely disabled and those who function comparatively well, those who are rich in family ties as well as those who have none, members of minority groups as well as whites. Some have experienced lifelong deprivations or disturbances; for others, problems are age related. Some have been institutionalized most of their adult lives; others were admitted in old age and will live out their lives as long-term care residents; still others are under care for relatively brief periods for convalescence or for terminal illness. They vary widely in personality, life experience, life-style, qualitative interpersonal relationships, and in religious, educational, cultural, and social backgrounds. They share many needs but each individual has his own unique constellation.

A second set of indicators derives from the experiences involved with becoming institutionalized. At the least, the individuals concerned are involved in making a major transition in their way of life. They may face separation from family, home and possessions, and community. Some are deprived abruptly of the cherished traditions and customs of the ethnic context in which they have lived.* Many are afforded insufficient opportunity to participate in the decision-making processes. Some are placed inappropriately. They often are anxious, fearful, and feel abandoned or rejected. Family members may suffer from feelings of grief and guilt. Psychologically, for older people, placement has overtones of death. Some suffer from the phenomenon known as "relocation effect."

The third set of indicators is intrinsic in the nature of institutional life as it exists at present. Some sense of power— some degree of control over one's destiny is critical to the integrity of the human personality. The new resident, by virtue of age status, pauper status, patient status, and his losses and impairments, already has experienced an erosion of his sense of autonomy or self-direction. The institution actively participates in reducing the resident to total lack of power. The fact that most often it is the place of last resort, in itself gives power to institutional management and staff. After all, where will the old person go if he does not like institutional life?

Admission is accompanied by a series of procedures that transfer the individual's power over his own life to the personnel of the institution. The new resident of a nursing home or home for the aged or his family members may sign a medical "permission to treat" form that will be in effect

---

*In this connection, it is interesting to note that in the context of the phenomenal overall growth of long-term beds, the proportion of beds under voluntary auspices, many of which are under religious auspices, remained fairly stable at twenty-four percent (Gottesman and Brody). The major shift was from governmental facilities to proprietaries.

sometimes for many years. Often, medications formerly self-administered are removed. Alcoholic beverages, cigarettes, and certain foods may be prohibited. There are few options about such basic activities as rising and bedtime, mealtimes and menus. Parenthetically, families are often placed in a "double bind" by the mixed messages they receive. On the one hand, they are castigated for having "abandoned" the old person; on the other, their expressions of concern are treated as "interference" or "complaining."

The major streams of research have yielded the well-known litany of what might be called the *iatrogenic diseases* of institutional life: dependency; depersonalization; low self-esteem; lack of occupation or fruitful use of time; geographic and social distance from family and friends, and cultural milieu; inflexibility of routines and menus; loneliness, lack of privacy, identity, own clothing, possessions and furniture; lack of freedom; desexualization and infantilization; crowded conditions; and negative, disrespectful, or belittling staff attitudes.

The unhappiness, submissiveness, anxiety, negative self-image, and other indicators of poor adjustment that have been so thoroughly documented may flow from many different sources. Whatever the cause(s), these older people most often cannot act on their own behalf to remedy their condition but require professional intervention in their interest.

In response to the growing awareness of the needs of the institutionalized, a host of formal psychosocial programs have been developed, such as milieu treatment, individualized treatment, therapeutic communities, group occupational and recreation activities programs, sheltered workshops, behavior modifications, token economies, reality orientation, and re-socialization. Another stream of research is aimed at identifying the effects of different types of institutions and administrators. Certainly, research must proceed in partnership with practice to move us further toward effective care.

But the time for stocktaking is long overdue. It is known that treatment programs effect positive change as do respectful, positive staff attitudes, high degrees of personal autonomy, affection and concern, social interaction, access to outer community, and maximizing independence. Of particular interest is research that tells us of the importance to adjustment of the extent to which institutions can accommodate the individual's personality, modes of adaptation, and life-style. Evidence of the continuity, increased salience, and significance of the value system to favorable adaptation indicates that values are important determinants of the kinds of programs older people will accept. Effective programs, then, must be attuned to those values (Brody and contributors, for review).

Data and clinical observations often complement and support each other. Another of many possible illustrations of the implications of knowledge for practice is recent information on the relocation effect. The literature has indicated that those who are physically ill, confused, and disoriented, or involuntarily located are particularly vulnerable. Practitioners have pointed out that inadequate note has been taken of methods of preventing or mitigating negative effects of moving, such as participation of the older person in the decision-making process, opportunities for choice, and careful preparation for moving via counseling and orientation.

One recent study cites evidence that when older people move to institutions, the environments to which they move rather than their health or other characteristics determine how they fare. Subjects rated as "improved" after moving tended to be found in facilities similar to or better than the one from which they moved (Marlowe). In another investigation, elderly people who were to be moved from one institution to another were carefully prepared for the change. Within a year the mortality rate for one group, which was taken on four anticipatory visits to the place to which they would move, was half that of a control group that made only one such visit (Preparation for Relocation).

In short, research and practice experience have told us beyond question that attending to the psychosocial needs is critical to the well-being—even survival—of the institutionalized elderly.

Each program tested reports "success"; effective treatments have been documented time and time again. But of the million old people in institutions, how many are recipients of such service? How many programs continue and proliferate? How many are firmly embedded in ongoing care?

Patient Status

A strong counterforce that nullifies knowledge about the needed emphasis on psychosocial care is subtle because its motivation is benign.

With the welcome trend toward medical programming in long-term care came badly needed medical, nursing, and paramedical services. These services are delivered by personnel trained in acute general hospitals and psychiatric hospitals and who, therefore, are oriented to the primacy of medical procedures to which all other needs and routines are subordinate. As the number and sophistication of health personnel has risen, there has been a parallel increase in the extent to which their familiar and fixed routines set the overall atmosphere and pattern.

It is interesting to look at the ways in which nursing-home residents spend their time. There is clear evidence from Gottesman's study that in many nursing homes more than half (fifty-five percent) of the residents' waking hours is spent doing absolutely nothing at all; about one-fifth of their time is occupied with basic activities of daily living, such as bathing, dressing, eating, or grooming, and another fifth in other activities (watching TV, reading, socialization, and the like). Only 2.1 percent of their time is occupied by medical or nursing activity of any kind. The amount of time spent in direct doctor-to-patient contact was so slight that it did not merit differentiating for purposes of coding the data (Barney).

Obviously, the amount of time spent does not mean that medical or nursing care is unimportant. But such facts do point up the absence of synchronism between the patterns of care and the needs of people. Institutional residents are assigned *patient-status roles* as full-time professional patients.

Toward a New Model

The critical question is whether places where older people, even impaired older people, live should continue with their borrowed identities. Should the institutional "personality" continue to rely for its developmental direction on the personalities of institutions such as medical and psychiatric hospitals and county homes? Should it not evolve as a new model with its own identity, rather than as a patchwork of borrowed patterns?

It is ironic that despite universal emphasis on the value of older people living in their own homes, *the only social institution that has not contributed significantly to the shape of long-term care is the individuals' own home*. Perhaps a new model should be created that takes as its starting points the people who will live there and the social institution known as "home." Perhaps it is necessary to scrape away the encrusted layers of pauperism, patient status, and agism and begin afresh with people and their needs in the light of available knowledge.

Most institutionalized older people live there for long periods of time. In nursing homes, almost half stay more than two years and seventy percent more than one year; more than forty percent of elderly mental-hospital patients are residents there ten or more years (Gottesman). A person living in a home is a very different concept than a "patient" being treated or given "custodial" care in an institution or a hospital.

Suppose there were studies of the actual living patterns, the normal rhythms of sleep and waking time, eating, social and recreational activities, movements, and health needs of the people institutions serve while they live outside institutions? Suppose the findings provide baseline information for patterning a totally new place for them to live when congregate care is needed? For assembling the mosaic of services in a new way? Suppose the accustomed routines of all disciplines flexed and were reshaped to form a new social matrix? Suppose options, choices, respect were built-in, themselves were institutionalized, rather than constructed as a flimsy superstructure on the firmly frozen basic pattern? Suppose the new places were staffed by new types of personnel whose services and activities were organized as an outgrowth of what was needed, rather than from traditional job descriptions? Suppose the physical environment of the new place were freed from tradition so that bricks and mortar were shaped by the residents' needs rather than those of staff and architect?

Suppose, in fact, the Procrustean beds were discarded in favor of adjustable beds that followed the contours of real people?

Progress toward that goal depends in part on the integration of practice and research, on the modification of attitudes, and on the education and training of those directing and delivering care services. It depends also on social policy that fosters, rather than hampers, the implementation of knowledge.

References

American Hospital Association. *Statement on a Patient's Bill of Rights*. Chicago: AHA, November 1972.

Barney, J. L. "Community Presence as a Key to Quality of Life in Nursing Homes." Paper presented at the 100th annual meeting of the American Public Health Association, Atlantic City, 15 November 1972.

Brody, E. M., and Contributors. *A Guide for Social Work in Long-term Care Facilities*. Washington, D.C.: USGPO, 1973.

Brotman, H. B. "The Older Population Revisited." *Facts and Figures on Older Americans*, No. 2. Washington, D.C.: AOA, SRS, HEW, 1971.

Butler, R.N. "Agism: Another Form of Bigotry." *Gerontologist* 9, no. 4, pt. 1 (1969).

Cohen, E. "An Overview of Long-term Care Facilities." In *A Guide for Social Work in Long-term Care Facilities*. E. M. Brody and Contributors. Washington, D.C.: USGPS, 1973.

Gottesman, L. G. "Aged Patients and Nursing-Home Services." Report to Philadelphia Geriatric Center, 1973.

—, and Brody, E. M. "Psychosocial Intervention Programs within the Institutional Setting." In *Long-term Care: A Review and Analysis*. Edited by S. Sherwood. Manuscript, 1973.

Jackson, H. "Planning for the Specially Disadvantaged." In *Alternatives to Institutional Care for Older Americans: Practice and Planning*. Edited by E. Pfeiffer. Durham, North Carolina: Center for the Study of Aging and Human Development, Duke University, 1973.

Jackson, J. "Really, There Are Existing Alternatives to Institutionalization for Aged Blacks." In *Alternatives to Institutional Care for Older Americans: Practice and Planning*. Edited by E. Pfeiffer. Durham, North Carolina: Center for the Study of Aging and Human Development, Duke University, 1973.

Kastenbaum, R., and Candy, S. "The Four Percent Fallacy: A Methodological and Empirical Critique of Extended Care Facility Program Statistics." *Aging and Human Development* 4 (1973): 15-21.

Marlowe, R. A. "For Relocation of Geriatric Mental Hospital Patients." Paper presented at the twenty-fifth annual meeting of the Gerontological Society, Puerto Rico, December 1972, as reported in *Geriatric Focus* 12, no. 31 (1973): 1,6,7.

Morris, R. "Community Care, Categories and Institutions, More Choice or Less for the Aged and Handicapped?" In *Washington Bulletin*, Social Legislation Information Service, no. 23 (1973).

Neugarten, B. L. "Grow Old Along with Me, the Best Is Yet To Be." *Psychology Today*, December 1971.

Oxford Dictionary of English Etymology. C. T. Onions, ed. Oxford: Clarendon Press, 1967.

Preparation for Relocation. Relocation Report No. 3. Ann Arbor, Michigan: Institute of Gerontology, University of Michigan-Wayne State University, 1973.

Roberts, P. R. *Human Warehouses, A Boarding Home Study.* Pittsburgh: Allegheny County Health Department, (mimeo), 1972. Reproduced in *Congressional Record*, 11 April 1972 (E 3515-3518).

Sudnow, D. "Dead on Arrival." *Transaction/Society* 9, no. 1/2 (November-December 1971): 36-43.

Webster's Collegiate Dictionary. 5th ed. Springfield, Massachusetts: G. Merriam Co., 1947.

14

Except from *Nobody Ever Died of Old Age: In Praise of Old People**

Sharon R. Curtin

The doctor informed the nursing staff and the hospital social worker that Miss Larson was to be transferred to an "extended-care facility." He recommended several places in the vicinity, and the social worker came to talk to Miss Larson.

"Social worker." A strange title and an even stranger woman. Her job at this particular hospital consisted in finding places to send people who were no longer in need of intensive nursing care, who could not be helped by all the technology gathered in a modern hospital, who were, in short, no longer medically interesting or likely to improve drastically. The job was more like that of a travel agent, and the woman had even absorbed some of the impersonal, smiling manner of those thousands of clerks one encounters when trying to buy airline tickets. Miss Larson was convinced this woman was only selling one-way tickets, and was hostile and withdrawn.

*This work originally appeared in *Nobody Ever Died of Old Age: In Praise of Old People* by Sharon R. Curtin, published by Little, Brown and Co., ©1972 by Sharon R. Curtin. Reprinted by permission of Little, Brown and Co. in association with The Atlantic Monthly Press.

"You're very lucky, Emily, my, you don't look ninety-six years old, we've found a perfectly lovely place just down the block from here, a new place run by perfectly lovely competent people recommended by your doctor. Everything will be taken care of before you leave here, I just need a few answers to some simple questions and you can be moved immediately, and doctor says you are to have a nurse with you for a few days until you get used to the change. Now, let me see, I can't get over your being so . . . spry.   This is a lovely new convalescent hospital, with a recreation worker, and a professional staff, and your doctor can see you there. Now, Emily, if you will just tell me your social security number . . . is she listening to me?"

"I think she turned off her hearing aid when you called her by her first name. She regards that as impertinent; she doesn't want to go to this place, and I don't blame her for being uncooperative," I answered. "If you need any information, it should be on her admission forms here. I think Miss Larson understands that she is being moved on orders from her doctor, and there isn't much we can do. But she doesn't feel any need to be polite."

"Doctor says. . . ." The woman was only doing her job. I did not want to be rude, but she showed no understanding of the crushing blow Miss Larson had received. For years, she had managed to avoid a nursing home, and now, through the benevolence of Medicare, she was eligible for, and forced to accept, institutionalization. There was no way the social worker could sugarcoat the pill, no family she could smile at and be helpful to, no gratitude from the withdrawn old lady in the bed.

This was a very determined social worker, however. She explained the process to me: Medicare provided for one hundred days of benefits in an extended-care facility when a patient had spent at least three days in a hospital prior to admission, and was in need of skilled nursing treatment and rehabilitation for the same illness for which admission to a hospital had been necessary. In 1966, when Medicare benefits became available, few extended-care facilities were available. Minimal federal standards of quality were expected—proper dietary supervision, twenty-four hours of personalized nursing service, a clean and safe physical plant geared to rehabilitation and comfort—but most nursing homes could not meet these standards. Federal funds were available, however, for enterprising builders to construct new facilities. The home to which Miss Larson was to be transported had been built as one of a chain on such guaranteed loans. A miracle of social welfare; someone receives money to build special places to take care of people no one knows what to do with; is guaranteed payment from the government for at least part of the care, the first one hundred days anyway; and after that the patient could be readmitted to a general hospital for three days, and back to the extended-care facility; the whole thing more profitable than running a hotel because you charge more whenever "medical" enters the picture, and the overhead is not so much more . . . very enterprising. Small wonder that large motel and hotel chains were the first to move into the new business.

First impressions of Montcliffe Convalescent Hospital were favorable. It was small, just thirty-six patients, and fairly new. The design and decoration of the building was modern California motel; long and low, with large expanses of glass covered by serviceable beige drapes. Every floor was carpeted and walls were newly painted beige. Large and fantastically colored sprays of plastic flowers dominated every flat surface and each room had sliding glass doors opening onto a narrow walk surrounding the building. The place was unimaginative, impersonal, tasteless, but not anything really objectionable. It was simply ugly. Everything was covered in plastic; even the lampshades and chairs shone with pristine plastic newness, untouched by human hands. All in all, it looked like the sort of motel, moderately priced, favored by salesmen because they all look alike and thus come to be homey. A place for transients.

Miss Larson and I were directed to a four-bed room; no, they did not have space available in a two-bed room; yes, they knew it was requested and as soon as space was available. . . please just fill out these forms, sign this release, list all valuables, you know how it is when you are old, you forget what you had. Yes, that is your bed, honey, right by the door, and you can keep your things in the stand right there, nothing on top, please, it looks so messy when one clutters up the tops of things. Just tuck it all away, that's right. Now, dearie, you just rest and the nurse and I shall take care of everything. . . .

The woman in charge of the Montcliffe Convalescent Hospital was a registered nurse. She was required by law, a fixture like firedoors or ramps; new to her job, frightened of old people, and with a tendency to avoid looking you in the eye. She bustled, chirped, patted, pulled, and quickly disappeared. All of the actual patient care was done by the "aides" or "attendants." They are not trained to do their jobs, and they learn by watching other attendants. Their skill and interest depend a good deal on whom they work with the first days. Some are good, some terrible. All are underpaid. It is a job, a job for the unskilled, for women with children to support and no hope in their future; for women whose legs are already swollen and tired from thankless day labor in a million other jobs like this one; they must work, and it is a job.

The room was not unpleasant but very uncomfortable. Four beds, precision lined against one wall, faced a blank beige wall on the other side. Four nightstands, flush against the beds. One chair in the corner. A vague smell, like urine and green soap mixed and used to wash the floors. No color, only beige walls, beige drapes, beige floor, white covers on the beds. Three beds were occupied, two by silent unmoving figures, looking as if a child had placed pillows under the sheets to fool his parents, and the bed nearest Miss Larson's (I already thought of it as "her" spot; she simply sat in the wheelchair, head down, hearing aid off, hands moving restlessly in her lap) was completely filled by an extremely obese—grayly fat, no pink skin, just mounds of bulging, unfeeling flesh— woman, who moved constantly, her lips pulling in and out like a baby waiting to be fed.

It was nearly four o'clock, time for me to be leaving. I wanted out of that place very badly. It was all so clean, so neat, but underneath it felt just like the "Old Folks Home" in Douglas. The smell, the ambience were alike; only the surface was different. We have certainly improved care of the aged in all those highly visible ways like clean linen, modern buildings, professional staff, even fire regulations. The package has been sanitized, wrapped in plastic, and labeled fit for public funding. But it felt the same, and I did not want to leave Miss Larson in that place. However, I smiled a very professional nurse-y smile, efficiently tucked her in bed without letting myself feel compassion, and thought that the doctor must know best, after all, he is the doctor, and refused to meet Miss Larson's miserable, half-uttered pleas that I not leave her alone. I went home, and by morning convinced myself the place was not so bad, that I was simply against institutions without really giving any particular place a chance to be different, and resolved that I would do my best to make Miss Larson's stay comfortable, easy, and as short as possible.

The first morning began with a lecture by the charge nurse. I must help Miss Larson adjust to being in Montcliffe and help her understand that she was not different, that it was very unusual for people to have private nurses in the home, and that a certain routine must be observed in order to encourage independence and rehabilitation. As she talked, I could see the aides pushing patients in wheelchairs out of their rooms and into the hall. Under thin cotton bath blankets, the old people were naked. Some were confused, pulling the cloth off their wrinkled flesh, mouths and hands constantly working, sometimes uttering small wordless cries. Others sat miserably hunched in their chairs and held the thin blankets tightly around bent shoulders. Someone had pulled Miss Larson out of bed and she was sitting in the line, looking around wildly, her neck rigid with indignation. "No, no, I have a nurse, no, no. . .," I could hear her protest.

"Oh, it's bath time for those on the north hall," said the charge nurse. "We give baths twice a week, showers, actually, so much more refreshing, don't you think? And we change the linen, all the linen, at the same time. Old people sometimes don't like to bathe, you know, so we keep them on a very clean schedule. Why, some of them never even move from bed except on bath days."

I could hear Miss Larson. "No, no, I can bath myself, just let me alone, I can do it." Some of the other patients were looking at her, without interest and without pity. We all have to do it, they seemed to be saying. Don't fight it. No distinctions. What makes you think you're so different. Men, women, confused, coherent, all the same. To the showers!

Two aides, one on each side, would pick up the old carcasses, place them in the molded plastic shower chair, deftly remove the blanket, push them under the shower and rather haphazardly soap them down. A few minutes for rinsing, a quick rubdown with an already damp towel, back under the blanket and ready for the next. The aides were quick, efficient, not at all brutal; they kept up a running conversation between themselves about food prices, the new shoes one had bought, California divorce laws. They might have been two sisters doing dishes. Lift, scrub, rinse, dry, put away. Lift, scrub, rinse, dry, put away. And did you hear the one about...

I gave Miss Larson a bath in her room that morning, over the strenuous objections of the charge nurse, who felt I was encouraging separation and dependence. I felt guilty, and my hands were unnecessarily rough as I turned and bathed Miss Larson. It was as if I blamed her for placing me in a position where I had to be miserable, observe misery. How could she do it to me?

The resentment I felt so strongly that first morning seems endemic in places where the aged live. The custodians, whether medically trained or administrative, always seem to have some anger, some residual hatred or fear of their charges. Sometimes I felt it was fear of one's own aging process, or just anger at having to do a very difficult job. Sometimes I saw it as a sort of natural turning away from another's misery, the way one will ignore the open trousers of an old man on the subway. But even if it was a sense of delicacy, of not wanting to intrude on the last years these old people had on earth, it soon progressed to another level. Because the attendants had to physically care for, handle the aging bodies of these old people, they began to treat them as if they were infants, unhearing, uncaring, unable to speak or communicate in any way. The patients were uniformly called honey or dearie or sweetie—or sometimes naughty girl if they soiled their beds—just as one tends to call children by pet names. At that level, the attendants expected gratitude or at least silent acquiescence from the old people and their families. The bodies were kept clean, fed, powdered, combed, and clothed. They were as infants, without modesty or sex or privacy.

The next level involved treating the patients as inanimate objects rather than as any kind of human being, adult or infant. This attitude was most frequent in older staff members and is understandably defensive. "Ahhh, she's just an old lady," they would say. "She's just an old lady." And that seemed to justify all manner of things, including the way blind patients were fed or not fed, according to whim; or how soon an old man was cleaned and his linen changed after he soiled his bed.

And Montcliffe Convalescent Hospital is a *good* hospital. It is expensive, and the bills are occasionally padded. For example, a patient who required linen changes more than twice a week was charged extra; most of these old people lost control of their bowels or bladder frequently, if only because the attendants were not particularly prompt to answer bells. Patients who could not feed themselves were charged a dollar per meal for the service. Drugs were ordered from a local pharmacy, and the pharmacist told me he paid a regular fee for the privilege of providing medication to this particular chain of extended-care facilities. Doctors charged the patients for regular visits, even if the visit consisted of a two-minute how-do from the doorway.

These are all frequent infractions in these types of facilities; you read about them every day. The passage of the Medicare Act does provide better care for some old people; it also lines the pockets and provides better retirement plans for others.

Besides the nursing-care program (baths twice a week, enemas when required, tranquilizers and sleeping pills as directed, part of each day spent out of bed, and so forth) Montcliffe also boasted a part-time recreation therapist. She had not been trained for her job, but she had the disposition and character. Nothing depressed her and she seemed oblivious to the depression around her. Surrounded by "her girls," who were all nodding and fidgeting in wheelchairs and who had not uttered a sound, she would chirp, "Oh, this is such fun, isn't it girls? We must do this [watch television, play bingo, clap hands, whatever] more often!"

Miss Smiles loved programs. If you ever wonder what happens to all the kids you knew in junior high school who played the accordion, or did acrobatic dancing, or recited illuminating poetry; if you ever wonder what an earnest but amateur photographer does with all his colored slides of the Holy Land, the pyramids, the Changing of the Guard; if you wonder where ladies go to do good works these days; let me tell you: they impose themselves on the aged. During the first week at the Montcliffe facility, we had two lectures, with slides, given by local ministers, one lady (in costume) who played the dulcimer and sang songs in an uncertain soprano, and a demonstration of flower arranging. The contrast between the formal, mannered Japanese flower arrangements and the riotous obscenities of the plastic sprays around the room was fairly hilarious. Unfortunately, the lady giving the demonstration had no sense of humor or any other kind of sense; to show arrangements of funeral sprays in a house of the dying shows little sensitivity.

These programs took place in what Miss Larson and I began calling "the parking lot." This was a large room, beige brightened by a touch of bright orange, designated the recreation room by Miss Smiles. Most of the day it was filled with old people—pushed in wheelchairs and left to doze in long lines against the wall, or pulled by the hand of an impatient aide, tottering in to sit in one of the low, plastic chairs. The chairs seemed expressly designed for the discomfort of old bones; they were too low for the aged to move in and out of without help; they were covered with slick plastic, which meant they were cold to the touch in winter and sticky in the summer; and they were hard. Miss Larson refused to patronize the "parking lot"; she said the sight of that many old bodies lined up waiting for the undertaker depressed her. No communication ever seemed to take place between patients; no conversation ever took place in the parking lot. The only people who spoke were those whose job it was to entertain. When no program was scheduled, a large color television set was turned on. The patients were not to touch the set, and it was frequently out of focus. Evidently one old man had, during the last baseball season, become so angry at the television set or his team's bad performance, or the refusal of an aide to change the station, that he had kicked the set. Now there was a small polite sign asking that no one touch the set. The old man, it seemed, was no longer with us, and the television set still refused to work.

I often wondered why there was barely any conversation among the patients. They were not all senile; Montcliffe had a policy against admitting "vegetable cases." Some even seemed anxious to talk, but spoke only to the aides or an occasional visitor. They simply did not talk among themselves and even avoided looking at each other. Those who were not bedridden ate in a common dining room, yet meals were silent, hurried affairs, filled only with the scraping of spoons and the occasional click of slipping dentures. It was true the aides rushed the meals, because they ate after the tables were cleared and everyone was back in the parking lot. But I do not think anyone ever said as much as "pass the salt" or "lovely day today." Among themselves they remained almost mute.

Why? I had thought that one pleasure left to the aged was the time to chat, to share experiences, to tell and retell favorite stories. This was not true at Montcliffe. Why? The reasons were curious and subtle and cruel. For one thing, the staff assumed that any and all remarks were addressed to them, since these old people could not possibly have anything to say. If Mrs. X said, "Lovely day today," to her roommate, Mrs. Y, to give one example, Aide Johnson would answer, "Is the sun in your eyes, dearie? Do you want the curtains closed?" And effectively, slowly, Mrs. X would learn that only the aides had the power of speech.

I think the staff regarded conversation between patients as silly and meaningless, because they believed the patients incapable of thought. But something else was going on: It was as if two patients talking would be a dangerous thing. I saw, on more than one occasion, patients arbitrarily separated in the middle of a quiet chat. I observed two old women, moved, perhaps, by a dim memory of time spent with friends long ago, begin to talk as they waited to have their hair done. One of them was suddenly told she would have to wait until next week and wheeled, still in midsentence, to her room. There was no apparent malice in the aide's action; she seemed to be enforcing some unwritten rule, responding to an institutional credo that said patients must not chat.

Miss Larson entered Montcliffe the last week in October. The air was cool and fresh and in the sun it was quite warm, so we spent a good part of the day outside. I was becoming increasingly impatient with her; her condition was deteriorating in spite of all my efforts. No matter what I did she simply refused to get better. I blamed her for imposing her weakness on me; but whenever she became too demanding, I would just walk away and have a cigarette in the dining room. Shortly after her admission, I arrived at 7 a.m. to find the night nurse indignant and angry. Miss Larson had climbed over the side rails during the night, and had been found in the bathroom.

"She didn't ring or call out," said the nurse. "Her room is right opposite the desk, and I would have heard her. Why, she might have been hurt, and she is so confused. I want the doctor to order more sedation. We can't have her carrying on, and disturbing all the other patients. Finally, we had to put her in restraints and I repeated her sleeping pill. But she kept yelling all the same."

I walked in the room and Miss Larson was indeed in restraints; the look on her face was so angry, it seemed to me someone had tied her up in order to prevent murder. "Get me out of these!" she ordered. "How dare they try to stop me from getting out of bed. I always have to relieve myself at night; and they never answer my bell. Usually they come and hide the cord so I can't even find it. So I crawl over the edge; I've been doing it ever since I came to this place. Now you get me out of these, and tell the doctor I want to see him!"

Miss Larson was not confused; but in a place where all the patients are so sedated that they scarcely move a muscle during the night, she was counted a nuisance. I did not want them to increase her sedation; barbiturates frequently make old people confused and disoriented. Even if she was a pain in the neck, I liked her better awake and making some sense. The problem was she had no rights. She was old, sick, feeble. Therefore she must shut up, lie still, take what little was offered and be grateful. And if she did that, she would be a "good girl."

There she was, ninety-six years old and did not even know she was dependent on society. She thought her thirty years of teaching, her careful hoarding of the little she inherited from her family, and the benevolence of the Social Security Act, with amendments, would guarantee humane treatment in her old age. "You get what you pay for," she told me, "and I want a nurse here, at least during the day, until I'm strong enough to manage on my own. I don't want to depend on those"—with a scornful jerk of her head—"people for anything. I'll pay for your services, but I'm asking as a friend. Don't leave me alone with them. They just want to keep everyone in the parking lot until it's over."

I did not want to leave her alone, and certainly understood her fears. The place was driving me crazy. I would catch myself sitting and staring at the wall with a vacant smile, my hands folded in my lap, just like one of the old people in the parking lot. I found myself ignoring the calls for help that came from rooms other than Miss Larson's because the aides had become so hostile to my "interference." The charge nurse gave me daily lectures on my letting Miss Larson become too dependent, how bad it was for her to get everything she wanted, how demanding she was to the other nurses, poor things. From the outside, Montcliffe Convalescent Hospital looked less like a modern motel and more like a bunker, a concrete dwelling hunching close to the ground, hiding secrets inside. The very air seemed menacing, full of deodorant sprays and powders and soaps and lint from the clothes dryer in the back hall; but underneath that smell, the smell of hidden decay, or urine and dying flesh, still was there, still assaulting the nose every morning at seven o'clock.

She was my friend and I wanted her well, healthy, back at the bridge table. But I could not stay with her forever. I became impatient, even angry, sometimes rough. I could feel a great distance between us—I was young, she was old—that had never existed on the outside. The hostility of them, the others, those people who worked in the hospital, was beginning to permeate the relationship we had. I began to really dislike Miss Larson. And we had been friends.

Miss Larson understood the stakes long before I did. It was a battle for her soul, a fight for her mind, with her weakened physical condition the trump card. Either she could give up, and wheel into the parking lot, or she could keep fighting and have everybody hate her, receive extra sedation to keep her mouth shut, be placed on mind-fogging tranquilizers to stop her demands. She had finally been moved to a two-bed room, out of the "nursery," as she called that original four-bed room, and her roommate was a quiet and rather sweet old lady. Miss Larson, unfortunately, had displaced a woman who had been in that bed for three years and who had been sent to the "nursery" over thin, weak little protests by both women. So Mrs. Gladstone retreated miserably into a shell, apparently determined never to get close to another human being for fear of losing them. Mrs. Lewis could be heard crying just two hundred feet away, but neither woman made any effort to move. Friendships were dangerous, hurtful things in Mont-cliffe. It was not death that hurt so much; it was unexpected, arbitrary deprivation. The staff had such incredible power over the minds and bodies of the old people in their care.

15

A Hiding Place to Die*

Elizabeth Markson

Francis Bacon said, "Men fear death as children fear to go in the dark; and as that natural fear in children is increased with tales, so is the other." Much of this fear of death is valuable for survival, but it has also tended to obscure the actual conditions under which people die. Death has either been romanticized, the Victorian solution, or minimized, as in the United States today. The elaborate American funeral rituals described in Evelyn Waugh's *The Loved One* and Jessica Mitford's *The American Way of Death* are not contradictory evidence on this point, for the actual *act of dying* is shunned and much of the ceremony seems designed to deny that death has really occurred.

Few tales of death have been told by anyone, including social scientists, but the recent work of Barney G. Glaser and Anselm L. Strauss in *Awareness of Dying* and *Time for Dying* and other studies marks the opening of this area of inquiry. The study reported on here supports the idea, first suggested

*This work originally appeared in *Transaction/Society* 9, no. 1/2 (November-December 1971): 48-54.

by Glaser and Strauss, that the anathema of dying is not only a problem for lay people, but also for health professionals, and describes one way in which professionals attempt to avoid the dying. Their success in doing so, it appears, depends on the relative status of the dying person.

There is a norm, subscribed to by at least some professionals, that old people should be allowed to die at home, but in fact most people die in hospitals or other institutions. It is suggested here that though it is desirable to die at home, for it is more comfortable, such comfortable deaths are a privilege accorded only to higher status people. Put another way, the lower the status of the dying person, the less likely are those around him to want to participate in his death.

It is well known that older patients who enter state mental hospitals have an excessive death rate. It has been suggested that this is because they are already dying when they are sent there, the early signs of impending death having been mistaken for insanity. Data gathered in New York State reveal, moreover, that older people tend to have higher death rates in both the state mental hospitals and county infirmaries than they do in any other kind of psychiatric treatment facility. Even those older people who are being treated in general hospital emergency rooms are less likely to die within six months of treatment than are those entering state and county hospitals.

These findings tend to confirm the idea put forward by a number of students of death that the old are sent to lower-status institutions, particularly mental hospitals, to die. The following study of deaths of the aged at a state mental hospital will postulate the processes by which both the laity and professionals make the decision to send patients to mental hospitals when they are not mentally ill, but are simply taking too long to die.

This study of whether those who send geriatric patients to state mental hospitals know of the excessive risk of death is founded on an examination of the medical records of 174 elderly patients who were admitted to Fairview State Hospital during an eight-month period in 1967. The hospital serves two boroughs of New York City and their suburbs and is located near a suburban community. During the period studied, the hospital admitted all patients who applied. The medical and nursing staff supported this open-door policy on the grounds that denial of admission to any geriatric patient would be a disservice to both the patient and the community.

The physical illnesses of the 174 patients detected at the postadmission physical examination (Table 1) make it clear that elderly people with a multiplicity of serious physical illnesses, primarily heart and circulatory diseases, either alone or in combination with other disorders, were being sent to the hospital. Indeed, 44 of the 174 (25 percent) died within 30 days of admission. Those patients with one or more severe physical illnesses included proportionately more of those who died within one month than of those who survived, and this difference is statistically significant.

The old people in this study were not only physically ill, but also grossly impaired. Less than half the group were able to walk without assistance. One quarter were described as "feeble," 11 percent were in wheelchairs and 19 percent were on stretchers, including 6 percent who were comatose. Those patients who were mobile were strikingly less likely to die than those who were feeble or worse at admission. Of the mobile group, only 9.1 percent had died within a month of admission: the figure for the incapacitated group was 38.9 percent.

While it seems evident that moribund patients were being sent to this hospital for the mentally ill, it is possible that these patients were referred to psychiatric care because their behavior mimicked mental illness, as suggested earlier. It might be expected that the dying would resemble at least a portion of those who have an organic brain syndrome but do not die, for both have symptoms of organic origin. To test this hypothesis, the reasons for referral recorded by Fairview's admitting psychiatrists were examined. Virtually all the complaints made about these patients by their families or others interested in having them committed concerned either senile behavior alone or in combination with such major psychiatric symptoms as delusions, hallucinations, or depression, but this was equally true of those who died within a month and those who survived with one exception: the ten comatose patients who could not be examined by the psychiatrist. Six of the eight men and one of the two women in this group died shortly after admission.

TABLE 1 PHYSICAL DISEASES AND DEATHS

Diseases	All Ad- mitted	All Dying Within Month	Dying of Detected Disease
Cancer, all types	7	4	3
alone	2	1	0
with heart and/or circulatory diseases	3	3	3
with digestive and/or genitourinary diseases	2	0	0
with respiratory diseases	0	0	0
Heart and circulatory diseases, all types	85	24	17
alone	58	13	7
with respiratory diseases	8	6	6
with digestive and/or genitourinary diseases	13	2	1
with respiratory and digestive or genitourinary diseases	6	3	3
Respiratory diseases	5	1	1
alone	4	1	1
with digestive and/or genitourinary diseases	1	0	0
Digestive and/or genito- urinary diseases alone	15	6	0
None of the above	62	9	0

The two major causes of death listed on death certificates were heart and circulatory disease and respiratory diseases. There is general agreement that such illnesses are often related.

The totals given for each broad disease type, with the exception of cancer, do not include everyone with that disease, since combinations are given. Thus, the table shows 88 patients with heart disease, 85 in that category plus 3 who also have cancer.

TABLE 2   PHYSICAL IMPAIRMENT AND DEATHS

Impairment	All Admitted	All Dying Within Months	
		N	%
None, walked without help	77	7	9.1
Feeble	43	12	27.9
In wheel chair	19	10	52.6
On stretcher	33	15	45.5
Not ascertained	2	0	—
All patients	174	44	25.3

The difference in death rates between patients on stretchers and those in wheelchairs is not statistically significant. It is possible that some patients who might otherwise have been on stretchers were propped up in wheelchairs for convenience in moving them.

TABLE 3   PRESSURE FOR ADMISSION AND DEATHS

Agents referring patients for admission	All Admitted	All Dying Within Month	
		N	%
Male	69	24	34.8
Formal agents only	19	5	26.3
Informal agents	34	16	47.1
Family only	28	13	46.4
Family and/or community agents	6	3	50.0
Formal and informal agents	11	2	18.2
Agents unknown	5	1	20.0
Female	105	20	19.1
Formal agents only	18	4	22.2
Informal agents	70	13	18.6
Family only	58	10	17.2
Family and/or community agents	12	3	25.0
Formal and informal agents	17	3	17.7
Agents unknown	0	0	—
All patients	174	44	25.3

In sum, it appears that no premonitory or prodromal signs of death that could be distinguished from psychiatric symptoms were detected among this group of old people even in psychiatric examination. This is particularly interesting in view of Morton Lieberman's finding that specific personality changes occur among old people several months prior to death. Lieberman was studying a nursing-home population, however, which may have differed considerably from the group of elderly mental-hospital patients studied here. Further, since our data are drawn from case reports, personality differences associated with either dying or psychosis may have been obscured by inadequate descriptions.

Psychiatric diagnosis at the hospital was apparently routine and cursory. Organic brain syndrome with psychosis was the designation given 114 patients in our study. In more than 88 percent of the cases, the diagnosis differed in either degree or kind from that made by the referring hospital. Follow-up data on patients who survived more than a month showed that more than one third of those diagnosed at admission as suffering organic brain syndrome with psychosis were found to have had no symptoms whatsoever, or to have been only apathetic, with no impairment of memory or confusion. Thus, it might be said that prodromal signs of death were missed in these cursory examinations, perhaps because the examining psychiatrists were aware that psychiatric treatment for the aged was less important than providing a place to die. Granting these reservations, however, the present data suggest that most patients were known or thought to be dying when referred to Fairview.

What seems crucial is that little effort was made to distinguish between symptoms reflecting an acute physical condition as opposed to chronic disorders of aging.

Some psychiatric hospitals have geriatric treatment programs aimed at helping patients get the most out of life, but Fairview's programs were marked by a fatalism that suggests that old people are expected to do nothing more than die. No physical examinations prior to admission were required, although elsewhere in the state such examinations have been shown to reduce inappropriate admissions. In fact, at the time of the study, deaths of those admitted *as well as those refused admission* at a sister hospital with a stringent screening program were only half as great as those at Fairview. This suggests that those responsible for referring the elderly for psychiatric care had learned where to send their dying patients.

Death As a Career

The Fairview program structured the patient's career as one of dying rather than of active physical or psychiatric treatment. While the postadmission physical examination is routinely performed, almost all geriatric patients are classified as being of "failing status because of age and general debility." This designation seems to be applied almost automatically. It certainly is not associated with the presence of physical illness, ability to walk, or chronological age. The role of the physician on Fairview's geriatric wards appeared to be to regularize the patients' deaths by tacitly legitimating the actions of the referring hospital. Thus, the high death rate among old people admitted to the hospital is made to seem part of the "natural" process of dying.

The physical disabilities of those who died within a month of admission are so similar to those of the survivors that the mental disability of *most* of the old people admitted may reflect physical problems. In other words, the admission of *most* of the elderly people to Fairview was probably inappropriate; instead they should have been receiving medical treatment or terminal care for their physical disorders in a general hospital ward.

As for the argument that a sick, confused person is easily mistaken for a mentally ill person, it is significant that young patients are never sent to state hospitals in the moribund condition described above. Patients aged thirty-five, on stretchers, in comas or with intravenous tubes running are unlikely to be found applying for admission to Fairview. Yet such patients exist and often display toxic confusions similar to those of the older patients. The older patient is selected for transfer to the state mental hospital because he is considered in hopeless condition by family and physicians, because of the extreme pressure for hospital beds and because he has compounded the low status of old age with illness, and often poverty. The evidence for these conclusions is reported below.

The pressure that ends with an elderly person being sent to a state mental hospital seems to be begun by the family. Old people coming to Fairview were usually first defined as physically or mentally ill by their families or other community members, usually after a specific health crisis. The patient was either sent directly to the state hospital, or taken first to a medical hospital or nursing home for treatment, depending on available facilities and the attitudes of those in close contact with him.

Among the elderly sent to Fairview, the dying men are somewhat younger than women. The median age for men at death was 74.5; for women it was 78.7. This was not particularly surprising, given the greater life expectancy of women in general. What is surprising, however, is that men whose families have pressed for their admission are more likely to die within a month than men referred only by formal agents such as a nursing home or those referred both by their families and such formal agents. For elderly women, however, this does not seem to be true. There are two factors that may explain this difference. First, there is some reason to believe, from other work I have been doing, that elderly men consistently overrate their health and independence, while elderly women tend to underrate themselves—perhaps a last holding on to the remnants of an instrumental "fit," able-bodied role by the men; women, having greater expressive latitude, can legitimately complain more. Following this line of reasoning, elderly men would perhaps try to compensate and conceal their illness until it became very serious; women, on the other hand, would complain earlier. As soon as complaints become frequent, the family responds by sending the patient to a hospital; men, complaining later, would be in more risk of dying than the female early complainers.

A second factor is differences in family structure. Only 36 percent of the men in the study were still married, but 54 percent of the men who died were married. Women in the study were most likely to be widowed (61.9 percent), and of those who died, 55 percent were widows. Put differently, dying men are most likely to be admitted to Fairview when they become ill and are a burden to their wives who have themselves limited physical (or emotional) strength to deal with an old sick husband who requires nursing care or constant attention. Women, on the other hand, generally outlive their husbands and are most likely to be sent to mental hospitals when they present any kind of management problem, not just terminal illness, to children, other relatives, or to an institution.

Where Are the Children?

It has been observed that having one or more children tends to insulate old people against illness and relatively early death. It might also be expected that parenthood might protect the aged from commitment to a mental hospital for terminal care. This did not prove to be the case at Fairview. While 40 percent of the men and 30 percent of the women admitted had no living children, the likelihood of death within one month was the same for this group as for the group having one or more living children. Nor did the number of children living change the odds. This may mean that once a family has decided to send the patient to the hospital, their contact with him is reduced by distance. Or, the decision to send him to the hospital may result from previous difficulty in getting along with the patient, unusual family relationships or other situations reducing the basis for close ties with the old person. At any rate, in such situations the power the children might have had to postpone their aging parent's death is dissipated. The patient is already socially dead. Only his physical death is lacking.

Most patients did not arrive at Fairview from their own homes, however. Five of six came there from other institutions, most often hospitals. A hospital that is being fully utilized is always in the process of an informal review of patients, seeking out those who can be sent home or referred elsewhere. Combined with this pressure is a feeling, shared by the general public, that general hospital beds are expensive while mental hospital beds are cheap. Whatever the source of this reasoning, it does not apply to these patients. They are suffering serious, often terminal, illnesses; the care they need will cost the same in any setting that shares the same labor market.

Of the patients sent to Fairview from other hospitals, about half were referred by receiving hospitals, that is, general hospitals with psychiatric service designated as reception centers for the mentally ill. Receiving hospitals in

New York City have been the traditional route into state
mental hospitals. They are overcrowded and there is considerable pressure to make a quick disposition of patients without
concern for the refinements of the individual patient's situation. This may be particularly true for the elderly, whose
physical condition is often ignored when a disposition is made.
For example, one elderly male patient in the study had been
taken to a receiving hospital in the city by his daughter, who
stated that he urinated in the hallway and that she "could no
longer care for his needs." He was sent to Fairview on a
stretcher from the receiving hospital, which had neither
admitted nor even examined him. According to the admitting
psychiatrist's report, the patient had bedsores, indicating that
his problems were long-standing. The psychiatrist observed:

> He did not indulge in any spontaneous acts . . . .The eyes
> were open and vision was intact as he blinked when fingers
> were brought close to his eyes. He showed fixed gazing and
> his eyes did not follow any moving object . . . .Patient
> showed no response to demands and showed no withdrawal
> from pain. . . .He retained food in his mouth and wet and
> soiled. He was mute and only made sounds in his throat.

Seventeen days after admission to Fairview, this patient
died of bronchopneumonia. This not atypical case illustrates
that many old people are sent away without adequate social
and medical histories from receiving hospitals and in such
impaired physical condition that it is difficult to determine
whether or not they are mentally ill.

The remainder of the patients admitted to Fairview from
hospitals have been in the medical wards of general hospitals.
Like those from receiving hospitals, they often appear to have
been sent to Fairview because they failed to respond to treatment or failed to die within a short period after being put on
terminal care. For example, a seventy-four-year-old man with
an indwelling catheter was transferred from a medical ward
to Fairview on a stretcher. The admitting psychiatrist reported:

> He was transferred from . . . General Hospital on a health
> officer's certificate because of increasing obtundation [dull-

ness]. The patient was noted to be . . . breathing heavily and in some distress . . . . He was able to respond only to pain and contact with the patient was impossible.

This patient's physical examination after admission indicated merely that he was dehydrated. Five days after admission, he died of congestive heart failure and bronchopneumonia.

Geriatric patients with their numerous medical complaints and limited future are not the favored patients of general hospital personnel, as has been shown by Glaser and Strauss and others. There are, however, institutions like nursing homes specializing in the care of terminal patients. Only five women and five men in the group studied had been sent to Fairview from nursing homes. The cause, ordinarily, was some kind of disruptive behavior. One elderly man who died within a month of arriving at Fairview was admitted from a nursing home with lung cancer and malignant lesions of the brain and bones. While the nursing home had had no difficulty in giving him minimal physical care and controlling his pain, they became upset and turned to Fairview when he threatened to commit suicide. (Upon checking with an internal medical specialist, I was assured that this patient was undermedicated for pain—dosage limited to prevent addiction in a dying patient! Motive for suicide?)

Unlike the general hospital, the nursing home does not seem to be concerned with freeing beds occupied by old people. Nor does the threat of death seem to concern them, but rather deviance. They do not like any threat to orderly and routine dying. For example, nursing-home patients who survived more than a month of Fairview often had been sent for similar reasons: One female paraplegic cancer patient had been referred because she had tried to set her bed on fire.

It seems obvious that this state hospital functions as a geriatric house of death to which the elderly are relegated because of the despair of their families and the pressure on general hospital beds. There seem to be three elements that establish the pattern of withdrawal of interest and abandonment of the aged to a state mental hospital. One of these is old

age itself. The old are already socially dying through relin-
quishment of roles; as they have little future before them, their
lives are considered to have little social worth. But being old in
itself is not enough; most old people do not die in state mental
hospitals.

The second element is the high probability of dying,
though this alone does not automatically lead to Fairview.
Young patients who have terminal illnesses are more likely to
be sent home for short periods of time and to return to die in
the hospital.

The third element is low social status and lack of power.
It has often been shown that the poor and powerless of any age
are generally considered to have less moral worth than those
with more money or those with access to the ear of those with
money. The patients in this study were not only seriously ill
and old, they were also from mostly working-class and lower-
class backgrounds. Only five had had professional occupations
and only twenty-nine had a tenth-grade or better education.
When old age and relatively low socioeconomic status are
merged, the person is doubly worthless for he is neither
productive nor does he have the reputation for past productivity. A combination of great age, powerlessness, and terminal
illness makes one despised by medical and lay people alike
and, unless death comes on schedule, suggests transfer to a
state mental hospital. Here the old are hidden away, or taken
away, from all that is familiar to them and left to await death.
Death here, as Rilke observed, is "factorylike, of course.
Where production is so enormous, an individual death is not
so nicely carried out, but then that doesn't matter. It is
quantity that counts."

Death Rights

The general lack of concern for the way old, sick people
die is clearly a disavowal of any right to a death in stable and
comfortable surroundings where opportunities for physical,
psychological, and spiritual comfort are protected. To some
extent this is changing. All mental hospitals in New York State,
for instance, have recently introduced geriatric screening
programs designed specifically to exclude those patients who
are dying or whose physical condition is the prime reason for

their referral. These screening programs have already enabled some geriatric services to become active psychiatric treatment centers rather than houses of death. But where the old, sick, powerless people who might have died at Fairview will die now remains unresolved.

16

Excerpts on Black Aged from the *Urban League News* *

Older Black Workers Vulnerable in Labor Force

Alphonso Anderson

Our national goal of full employment assumes new dimensions as adjustments are made for changes in retirement practices, technological innovations, and age shifts of the population. The middle-aged and older workers are receiving more attention as their special problems of long-term unemployment, involuntary retirement, and inadequate income are recognized.

These mature workers, generally those aged forty-five and above, find that advancing age influences their ability to remain employed and, when displaced, their ability to find new employment.

There is a continuum of age-related employment and income problems that begin around age 40 and become greater after age 45. Statistics on poverty in 1970 indicate that the number of elderly persons—over age 65—in the poverty category is increasing. Furthermore, employment data suggest

*These works originally appeared in a special issue of the *Urban League News* that dealt with black aged and their problems (1975). Reprinted by permission of each author and the Urban League.

that persons over age 55 represent a potential future poverty group.

The size of retirement income is related to the level of income and the time dimension, including the continuity of employment. To have adequate retirement income, middle-aged persons must have employment opportunities; thus, the years after age forty-five are crucial.

The Middle-Aged and Older Black Workers

One million four hundred thousand blacks, 65 years and older, and thousands aged 45 through 64, have spent their prime years contributing to the growth and greatness of America. However, just as their forefathers were kept in physical slavery, they have been psychologically and economically enslaved all their lives.

The National Caucus on the Black Aged, Inc., reports: "Older blacks are more than twice as likely to be poor as elderly whites—50 percent of the black men and four-fifths of the black women between ages 54-64 had a total 1969 income of less than $4,000. For the 55-64 age group and the 65 and above, white males are receiving about twice as much income as black males. Over half of the total black population resides in the South—three-fifths for the elderly of both sexes. Above age 55, whites are three times as likely as blacks to be living in suburbs, or in the ring surrounding the central cities of metropolitan areas. Fifty-six percent of all blacks are in central-city areas."

Poverty, racism, and institutional rigidity have created a physical environment where blacks have been systematically deprived of adequate jobs, income, and housing, and have provided a psychological milieu where frustrations and repressed agressions become manifest in greater incidence of stroke, heart disease, mental disability, and hypertension than is found in the white population. In jeopardy from the cradle to the grave, the black American finds himself with a higher morbidity and mortality rates at every stage of life, except in a very advanced age group—seventy-five years and above.

It is quite apparent that the middle-aged and black older workers are suffering no temporary aberration, but are experiencing the continuing effects of poverty and racism. These casualties of technology, automation, and cybernetics are not accidents. Advanced mechanization, while adding to the gross national product, is substituting machines for men with increasing frequency. The result is movement out of skilled occupations and semiskilled positions, underemployment, unemployment, and early retirement. These trends strike directly at the most vulnerable segment of the labor force—the middle-aged and older black worker.

Thus, the black middle-aged and older workers find themselves shackled with the legacies of the past, inspiried by the rhetoric of yesterday, yet facing the realities of today.

Future Prospects

When President Nixon signed the Comprehensive Employment and Training Act (C.E.T.A.) on the last day of 1973, provision of specialized services for middle-aged and older workers was specifically authorized by federal statute for the first time.

Title III of CETA deals with federal responsibilities and special manpower target groups. Funds available under this title are to be used by the Secretary of Labor "to provide additional manpower services as authorized under Title I and Title II to segments of the population that are in particular need of such services, including 'chronically unemployed poor, and middle-aged and older men and women.' "

CETA mentions middle-aged and older workers specifically more often than any previous manpower legislation. Moreover, the law affords ample opportunity for pioneering in behalf of black middle-aged and older workers. CETA will expire in mid-1977. Therefore, no time can be lost if this statute is to be used to advance the status of middle-aged and older workers.

Social Factors Affect Mental Health of Aged

Robert N. Butler

President Gerald Ford gave needy Americans a Christmas present in 1974 announcing his plan to cut back food stamps. As a result of his executive order, at least one million older Americans (and up to two million of all low-income citizens) may be unable to receive the benefits of the program. They will be forced to eat even less. Nutrition will suffer. Resistance to infections will decrease and hospitalizations will increase. Such is the wisdom of federal budgetary cost cutting. Stagflation is fought at the expense of poor people, including older people.

Emotional Suffering

Personal and emotional suffering in the later years is already extraordinary among older people. Losses and grief are the frequent accompaniments of the older years. Crises and stresses, occurring rapidly and in multiples, are more common in old age than at any other period of life. Anxiety is common. Depression rises with age. Suicide peaks. Twenty-five percent of all suicides in this nation are committed by people sixty-five years of age and over. Brain diseases, such as those due to "hardening of the arteries" (arteriosclerosis), emerge in old age.

Nonetheless, estimates (for example, by the American Psychological Association) suggest that some three million of the nearly twenty-one million older citizens have unmet needs of mental health services. State mental hospitals curb admissions, claiming that older people's problems are "social" not "mental." Older and chronic mental patients who are already in mental hospitals are pushed out by programs that sound good—"return the patient to the community." The "community," however, comprises all-too-many unsafe and inhospitable nursing homes, welfare hotels, and other facilities where there are minimal standards and services.

Negative Social Conditions

Both the strengths and the problems of old age are complex and are determined by a range of forces—personal, social, physiological (including medical). Old age requires a complex appraisal involving a variety of specialties and disciplines working in concert. Mental health workers, social workers, physicians, home health workers, and others need to join forces to bring assistance to older people buffeted so severely by adverse forces. Whatever problems older people have brought along with them into their later years, they can be overwhelmed with the negative social conditions under which the majority of them live.

If social factors can be so devastating to the mental health of older people in general in the United States, what about minority groups? It comes as no surprise that black, Spanish-speaking, and Asian older Americans fare much worse than white older Americans on all points—income, health, housing, transportation, and so on. Anxiety, dread, despair, and depression are common and understandable human responses to social adversity.

Notable is the remarkable endurance of the human spirit and its capacity for survival.

Agism

If you are elderly you are apt to be subject to the special prejudice and stereotyping of agism. You are an "old fogie," "boring," "useless." Agism refers to discrimination against older people because they are old just as racism and sexism accomplish this with skin color and gender. Agism on top of racism provides a double assault; with sexism, a triple assault. As a group there are no more impoverished people in American society than older black women.

Agism plays an important role in the generally negative opinion about mental health care in old age. Mental health specialists avoid the diagnostic evaluation, care, and treatment of older patients. Mental health training programs rarely focus on older patients. The government-supported National Institute of Mental Health applies less than three percent of its budget to research in this important area. Thus, service, training, and research are all neglected.

Older people have a great need to be listened to. They review their lives in order to make sense of their past and come to terms with death. They need and desire emotional closeness to offset painful loneliness. They want to feel useful. These deep-felt personal concerns cannot be met only by families. Indeed, some twenty-five percent of older people do not have any surviving family members. Social agencies, senior centers, churches, counseling programs, neighborhoods, and the like, must compose viable social networks for communication and personal support.

Senility

One of the problems older people face is the misunderstanding of "senility" by the public and many doctors. There are many causes of confusion, forgetfulness, and so forth, that characterize what is loosely called *senility*. These conditions include drugs, depression, malnutrition, malignancy, febrile conditions, and heart and lung diseases. Unless these underlying conditions are recognized and treated, the mental symptoms may become fixed and irreversible. This is the common fate of many older people of various racial minorities since they do not receive prompt diagnosis and therapy.

Stress Relevance

There is obviously a great need to give national visibility to the mental health needs of the elderly, especially the members of minorities. The relevance of social and economic factors must be strongly stressed.

Racism in the Psychiatric Care of Older Blacks

James H. Carter

The pervasive myths about black people continue to prevail in all areas of health care and is especially acute in the psychiatric care of aged minorities.

Regrettably, the administrators who determine the quality and quantity of psychiatric services to minorities are often not equipped by reasons of training and experience to address themselves to the mental health needs of minorities, for example, elderly blacks. It often comes as a surprise to learn that even today there are mental health programs without any blacks in "policy-making" positions that could assist in eradicating racist practices.

Heterogeneous Group

I contend that the black elderly is a heterogeneous group with their own value systems. I admit that while blacks of all ages share many concerns with the larger community, it is also true that in many respects blacks constitute a unique culture. Therefore, good psychiatric care must reflect these differences. There should be some sensitivity to the attitudes of blacks concerning illness, dietary patterns, feelings about drugs, hospitals, and of being sick.

There is sufficient evidence to support the arguments that aging is experienced differently from culture to culture. Growing old and being black is clearly a condition where the expression "only the strong survive" can unequivocally be applied.

Given the harsh realities of racism, only admiration and respect can be given to those few blacks who are fortunate enough to reach their "golden" years. The conditions of life for blacks stemming from such factors as unemployment, inadequate housing, and poor health care have a direct relationship to life expectancy. Cross-cultural anthropological and sociological studies have called attention to the differences in value judgment, sexual morals, and the social mobility of various cultures. Clinically, however, mental health professionals are usually faced with the behavioral manifestations of attempts on the part of the black elderly to reestablish themselves as being independent with a sense of their own identity.

It is appalling to learn that blacks are systematically excluded from treatment programs because they fail to meet certain "acceptable criteria."

Psychiatrists Administer Medication

The role played by many psychiatrists in public clinics and mental hospitals that treat the black aged and the severely mentally disturbed patients is usually one of administering medications. In the majority of these public facilities, the physician sees large numbers of patients and may never know their names. The patient may be seen briefly where the physician writes prescriptions for two or three weeks and sometimes for several months. This is not to say that medication has no place in the management of the elderly, for the judicious use of medication can be a valuable asset in the treatment of mental or emotional illness regardless of age. Yet to medicate the patient to the point where psychological and social forms of treatment cannot be accomplished is to be frowned upon.

With regard to nursing homes and particularly private institutions, racism has prevented the admission of elderly blacks to those facilities that meet acceptable standards. It is a fact that elderly black men have always been denied admission to homes that have a significant number of white females. As would be expected, the nursing staff often becomes quite upset in interracial settings where black male patients express sexual feelings. In passing, black men of all ages must contend with the old stereotype of being supersexed. One sure way of being denied admission to integrated private facilities is for the black male to exhibit aggressive destructive behavior coupled with sexual misconduct.

There remains much to be done with regard to research. The obvious needs are clear. The solution to the complex problems faced by blacks are elusive. These problems call for more research based upon more adequate interprofessional communication. This is particularly true of treatment methods. It is obvious that research must focus on those aspects of society that seem so directly related to mental illness in blacks, such as slums, segregation, educational deprivation, to mention only a few. Prejudice, ignorance, and lack of empathy accounts for our lack of knowledge about the causes of mental illness among blacks.

Another area where my experience has differed from my colleagues is that of retirement adjustments. Gerontologists consistently point to the fact that the loss of a job or retirement can upset a "delicate balance." It has been my experience that retirement may be faced with a great deal of ambivalence by blacks. For example, blacks who have been the victims of irregular or demeaning jobs may look to retirement with great anticipation. Premature retirement can be seen in any job where blatant racism exists.

Loud Voice of Advocacy

There has been little use made of the information at hand about the black elderly to influence social policies and medical care. We must develop a loud voice that would advocate the necessary changes. Organizations around the country and especially in black communities must join with black mental health professionals in pressing institutions that serve black people in demanding a greater responsiveness to the needs of minorities.

Community Organizations and Minority Aged

E. Percil Stanford

During the last decade and a half, more older blacks have become involved in community organizations and community organizing. The process commonly referred to as *community organization* is usually thought of in three phases: planning, involvement, and implementation. The emphasis placed on each of these elements vary with need, planning style, sophistication of the lay community, and competence of the professionals involved.

Impact of the community organizations on the black elderly depends, in part, on the basic planning that goes into the effort. However, the styles of planning quite often do not fit the philosophy(ies) of the community in question.

The common differences among the styles result from differing starting points (for example, general versus specific problems) and from differing kinds, levels, and blends of citizen and professional involvement.

Citizen Participation

Among the styles, the component most neglected has been citizen participation. Citizen participation has been described to mean the involvement of citizens in determining their own destiny in society from a planning-policy point of view. It is in this area that the older black citizens have not heretofore had adequate opportunity to be effective.

The common reasons given are that older blacks do not know what they want and that many cannot articulate what their needs are, if they do think they know what they want. This has been a political and social cop-out for much too long. What this really means is that black older people have not expressed themselves in the same way as many middle-class professionals. The fact that many community organizers and planners do not take time to really listen to what is being said means that too often the agendas are already set, and there is little chance for meaningful exchange.

The Anglo Perspective

The fact that many minority-ethnic groups have a particular normative structure that they relate to means that community organizers and planners must be cognizant of the basic norms of the community. Traditionally, most planners have not taken these norms into consideration, but have looked at minority communities from the Anglo perspective. It is up to the planners to work with social scientists and the community to understand the nature of the variety of ethnic collectivities that comprise the American society and to grasp the effect of "ethnicity" on behavior when age is the primary variable.

Organizations and agencies designed to support minority older people do not automatically appear in any community. There is a basic need for such agencies or organizations. Many evolve because of formal planning and others because of informal relationships.

Elderly Initiate Programs

In the field of aging, there have been several attempts to organize minority older people into various types of groupings that have not fully considered their needs and wants. Therefore, the organizers of formal organizations and agencies have found that their success rate is not as good as they would like it to be. On the other hand, it has been my observation that many minority ethnic older people have been able to develop support systems of their own based on need. They have not had to depend on formal planning bodies or professional organizers to determine needs or direction for them. The greatest impact of organizations on minority older people has come through those groups that are oriented toward older peoples' needs, for and by the older people, and through organizations that are oriented toward particular ethnic needs.

Examples include such groups as black federations, aging coalitions, Indian tribal councils, and a variety of ethnic caucuses.

Minority Elderly Live Everywhere

Many community organizations developed within the last five years have not adequately served minority aged persons. The primary fault has been not providing services and outreach relevant to existing basic needs. It is time to fully realize that, like anyone else, minority older people reside in a variety of community settings. They find themselves in urban, suburban, and rural settings.

Many of the efforts to work with older minorities have not addressed this difference. It is assumed that because one is a black or other minority older person, they can relate to the modes that are effective in an urban or suburban setting if they live in a rural environment. The basic intent or concept may be sound, but in order to implement the goals of the organization, severe modifications must be made to deal with the older person where he or she is.

Higher Education Institutions

Most major communities have access to institutions of higher education. However, too often the community leadership fails to take full advantage of those institutions, either because of inaccessibility or the lack of knowledge about what the institute has to offer.

I am suggesting that organizations that have minority constituents become familiar with available resources. For example, there are minority persons within many of the institutions of higher education who can provide support by way of identifying other types of resources and also by contributing their own time. There should be an obligation to work with community organizations and agencies that are developing services for minority ethnic groups. Since many of the efforts to work with minority older people are relatively new, there is undoubtedly a tremendous need for assistance. More conscientious efforts should be put forth, on the part of educational institutions, to make known areas of competence that might have an impact on the community. Generally, most institutions have persons who keep up with the most important and significant social changes; therefore, they are apt to be aware of resources that many people who are just beginning to organize do not.

In addition to using the educational institution as a resource, ongoing efforts should be made to involve minority-ethnic older people into the programs of the university. Involvement may be in the form of serving on various committees, boards, and the like, or taking advantage of some of the educational opportunities that are offered (either fee or nonfee).

Isolated Approach

It is difficult to fairly assess the impact of community on black older persons because, in a large sense, communities are only at an "awareness" level in attempting to relate to the needs of this population.

Agencies have heretofore taken an isolated approach to solving problems and addressing the needs of the black elderly. The development of coalitions is an attempt to bridge the gaps between agencies and to encourage the growth of a unified approach.

As a result of federal government programs, local communities are no longer viewed as autonomous, independent entities capable of maintaining themselves. Therefore, community organization is more and more becoming influenced by outside pressures and initiative.

With the proliferation of organizations and agencies designed to guarantee the rights of older people, there is no conclusive evidence that organizations in our communities are having a positive impact on the bulk of the minority older people. The impact will be greatest when meaningful strategies are devised to ensure that the basic needs of the minority older person are met.

As It Could Be

17

One of the Best
Retirement Centers*

Mary Louise Williams

The Isle of Seniliput- or First Impressions

No, not Lilliput. Seniliput. Like Gulliver, I found myself upon
a strange island. Unlike the diminutive inhabitants of Gulliver's
Isle, however, the people here were senile, most of them
seemed to be in their eighties or nineties. Everywhere,
everywhere, old people. People with canes, people with
crutches or walkers, people in wheelchairs. A station wagon
came around on Sunday, the day after I arrived, to pick up
those who wanted to go to church. I decided to go along, but
when I saw with what difficulty most of the passengers
crawled into the wagon, I felt like an imposter.

As a matter of fact, I was quite able-bodied. True, I was
tired after thirty-five years of teaching, but I had retired
considerably younger than most people who retire, primarily
because, like Thoreau, I wanted time to live and to commune
with nature, time to read the many books I had bought and the
magazines to which I subscribed but seldom found time to

*This work originally appeared in The Gerontologist 12 (1972):
38-42.

open. Teaching English, although enjoyable, had necessitated spending long hours of "leisure" time grading papers. I had decided that now was the time to find out about a retirement center—while I was still young enough to know what I was doing.

According to the brochure describing the Center, I could live in a beautiful studio apartment, meet interesting people, participate in numerous creative activities and discussion groups, enjoy the advantages of a nearby university, plus the cultural opportunities of a big city. Groups would be going to symphonies, operas, plays. I could continue to grow socially, intellectually, spiritually. And everyone would be healthy and energetic as well as creative, since a rigid physical examination was required in order to be admitted to the Center.

I was not prepared, therefore, for what I found. It was when I met the elderly people in the station wagon and at Sunday dinner that I was really stunned. I had been on the "Shut-in Committee" in my church back home and I had been sponsor of a Service Club, during my teaching career, which visited the elderly. It is one thing, however, to visit and endeavor to cheer the senile, and quite another suddenly to be classed as one of them. I had a sinking feeling at the dinner. All of those at my table were deaf, and although they wore hearing aids, it seemed to be difficult for them to hear. The chief topics of conversation were their ailments, their grandchildren, and what was wrong with the Center. One man assured me that the Center was a Snake Pit. (He has since left.) The chief activities, I was told, were playing bingo and bridge. (The statement was true for this group and a number of others, but I found there were other activities.)

At night I discovered that the walls of my apartment were apparently made of paper; the sweet, elderly woman on the wall snored! And in the weeks to come, the as-yet unheated, hard, cold, concrete-asphalt floor gave me not only cold feet, but a cold-blooded disposition. When a photographer arrived one morning to take my picture, I refused. When I found he had been sent by the young salesman-minister-director of the Center I was furious. Had he never heard of Martin Buber's "I, Thou" relationship? I asked myself. He wants my picture in the brochure only to help "sell" the Center! He was treating me as a thing for his own selfish purpose! I advised the photographer to take a picture of the very elderly woman limping down the road with the help of her cane. "She will honestly represent this place!" I said, and slammed the door.

I asked one of the younger women (in her seventies, I judged) how she liked the Center. "If I hadn't burned all my bridges behind me," she said, "I would leave tomorrow." Alas, I thought, I had burned all of my bridges behind me. I had paid over $300 just to move my household goods (mostly books). I was now living on a teacher's pension and paying about seventy-five percent of it in rent for my one-room studio apartment. I had said good-bye and accepted farewell gifts. I could not go back and I could not stay. I understood Hamlet's dilemma. "To be, or not to be," I said. I thought of Booth Tarkington's mountain-climbing friend who came to an over-hang and realized that he could not get up and he could not go down. I too had come to an impasse.

It was about this time that I heard of Dr. Joseph Peck's *Let's Rejoin the Human Race*. Since I very much wanted to rejoin, I got the book, and for the first time in many weeks I was able to laugh. What a release—how wonderful—to laugh! I had almost forgotten how. I was glad to learn that Dr. Peck, in his seventies when he wrote the book, had discovered that he was not retired at all; that he had just changed the nature of his work. Instead of practicing medicine, he was writing articles—and books—relative to retirement. "Why not follow Dr. Peck's shining example?" I said. But I was in no mood for writing anything. My contributions to periodicals had been mainly of the educational variety and had appeared in such magazines as *The Michigan Education Journal* and *The English Journal*. I was still at an impasse. Or perhaps I was at Dewey's forked road. Or Robert Frost's two roads:

> Two roads diverged in a wood, and I—
> I took the one less traveled by,
> And that had made all the difference.

Salvation

It was not Dr. Peck's book, however, or even poetry that saved my life. I have always liked poetry, and it was poetry that saved the life of Booth Tarkington's friend; but my salvation has been due primarily to the ravine and to the church sponsoring the retirement center. As I look out my apartment window overlooking the ravine, and watch the chickadees, cardinals, nuthatches, blue jays, and woodpeckers enjoying a feast at my bird feeders on a winter morning; or robins, wrens, and song sparrows building nests or feeding their young on a spring morning, I realize that I am indeed rich. Not many people in a big city, not even people with money, can have the advantages of Thoreau in his hut at Walden Pond. Thoreau went to Walden to have time for living. Poets and philosophers through the ages have found that in order to live fully, one must take time to think and meditate and to appreciate the beauty of nature. This, I recalled, was one of Lew Sarett's roads to salvation. Professor Sarett was my speech teacher at Northwestern University. He lived close to nature for forty years. "The stunted, twisted pine tree at timber line in the Rocky Mountains," he said, "has been beaten and bowed by whistling winds, but it hangs on to the rock and a bushel of dirt at its base. One is deeply moved by the timber pine; one senses its dark beauty." Each of us, like the pine, he believed has "a spirit that can't be broken."

There are many roads into the world of ideas and beauty. The biggest roads for Lew Sarett were teaching and writing. The best road into this world for all of us, he firmly believed, is to maintain the "aesthetic attitude" toward life. One who has this attitude will contemplate all the prose facts of the world with a mind alert to their beauty and implications. "The aesthetic attitude," he declared, "inevitably results in creative work of some kind. It is a philosophy—a way of life."

With this philosophy as a part of my background, I began to find here at the Center not only beauty in nature, but beauty in a number of elderly people. One woman, aged ninety, for example, started a poetry hour. Walk into the lounge any Thursday afternoon at four o'clock, and you will hear the group reading poems of favorite poets such as Longfellow, Whittier, Tennyson, and occasionally poetry by Robert Frost, Carl Sandburg, and other modern poets. At the conclusion of the hour, you will hear hymns played on the Autoharp, perhaps "Day Is Dying in the West" or "Sweet Hour of Prayer." Another ninety-year-old, a missionary in India for twenty-five years, recently wrote an interesting and enlightening article on Kashmir for the paper at the Center. She has given several book reviews at a literary club that I organized. Another resident, a man almost blind, tape records good musical programs, plays, or readings, and invites interested residents to hear them. He seems to have forgotten his handicap.

The best road to my salvation, however, since arriving here, has been the church that sponsors the Center. The senior minister is a man of great intellectual ability and spirituality. Most of the ministers on the staff are outstanding and truly dedicated. To come into contact with goodness, spiritual beauty, and intelligence when one is at an impasse is a healing balm. Aldous Huxley in his *Ends and Means* maintains that the two major virtues are intelligence and love. Certainly one finds these virtues here. Not only are the sermons a great inspiration; so also are the research groups that meet every week and give the "researchers" an opportunity to be with leaders who know more than they. This is of course one of the best ways of learning. It is as if one is continuing university graduate study. Education, most thinking people today agree, is a lifelong experience.

What do we study in our research groups? To date, since I joined the groups, we have read and discussed *The Strong and the Weak* by Paul Tournier, *Modern Man in Search of a Soul* by Carl Jung, *The Shaking of the Foundations* and *Dynamics of Faith* by Paul Tillich, *The Miracle of Dialogue* by Reuel Howe, *Honest to God* and *The New Reformation* by John A. T. Robinson, *Becoming* by Gordon Allport, *The Secular City* by Harvey Cox, and *Human Relationships* by Eleanor Bertine. A few books by Gerald Heard were discussed. All of the books have been interesting and most of them uplifting.

Finding salvation in research groups is due of course not only to the leaders and to the authors of the boks read, but also to the joy of working with people of all ages who are earnestly searching for truth. "We are living at our highest," a great educator once said, "when we are sharing ideas."

The Indian paths to Salvation are those of devotion, of works, and of knowledge. According to the psychological type to which we belong, we usually choose, or put most emphasis upon, one of these paths. My temperament is evidently predominantly cerebrotonic, for I prefer the way of knowledge. It is "fun," to use the vernacular of my students, to keep on learning.

The Ideal Center

Like Gulliver, I have adjusted to the situation. Whether, like Gulliver, I shall depart—or remain at the Center, will depend upon a number of factors. I have stayed so far primarily because I can be close to nature, I can continue graduate study at the church, and I can be of service.

If there is ever to be an ideal retirement center, the leadership, the people, and the program would of course need to be ideal. The leadership in the church that sponsors the five million dollar retirement project, now in its third year, as already indicated, is outstanding. Whether the vision, the goodness, and the greatness of the church leaders can carry over to the Center will depend to a great extent upon the kind of people here and the type of program provided.

As a child I believed that as people grew older they became more and more spiritual until they eventually reached perfection. Although by the time I arrived at the Center, I had met many older people who were far from perfect, and although I was exceedingly far from the goal myself, I still somehow expected to find most of the people radiating spiritual beauty. I found, of course, all kinds of people here as elsewhere. There were a few "status seekers" (the kind Dr. Joseph deplores), and a few who love the limelight and would like, perhaps, to run the Center. There are the very aged and ill who are content to have a place that is warm and someone to take care of them. There are a few cliques. The great majority of people, however, are good, likable, friendly, democratic, quite well educated—people whom one would like very much to have known earlier in life. Younger people are now coming to the Center but due to the fact that at the beginning of the project many elderly semiinvalids were admitted in order to get the Center started, the majority of the residents are still over seventy-five. I have found, however, that it is not age so much as personality and similar interests that determine friendships. It is these factors, too, and of course health, that determine whether residents will want to be participants and contributors or merely spectators.

As a teacher it was always my contention that students should have every opportunity to participate in plays, panel discussions, and all activities in which they were interested. Believing that older people, too, should take part in activities in which they are interested, I more or less, soon after I arrived, appointed myself director of literary activities and started a literary club for all residents who would like to join. The purpose of the club was to read and discuss good stories, plays, novels, poetry, and nonfiction. At our first meeting we discussed Hawthorne's "Dr. Heidegger's Experiment." When my students in American literature class had discussed this story, they invariable came to the conclusion that if they wanted to be good and wise when they were old, instead of miserable like Dr. Heidegger's guests, they would have to start while they were young; they would need to study and use their time well. Discussing the story with a group of eighty- and ninety-year-olds was a different proposition. I asked them, if they could have the opportunity, how many would like to live life over again just as they had lived it. None would. They agreed that if they could profit from their present knowledge and experience they probably would. Some feared, however, that unless they had excellent guidance and more education they might be as foolish as they were before. In other words, both the young and the elderly groups agreed on the necessity of knowing what was right and good, and of having will power if they were ever to achieve perfection.

Our next venture was to read a play at Thanksgiving time. All of the participants agreed that it was good fun and probably therapeutic. The audience enjoyed the reading and asked for more plays. With the assistance of a few young people from the church, we presented Thornton Wilder's *Our Town* and later his *The Happy Journey to Trenton and Camden*. Both the participants and the audience liked these plays immensely. *Suppressed Desires* by Susan Glaspell was recently presented and enjoyed.

Many of the club members have given book reviews. Book reviews and plays have been more popular than poetry and nonfiction. Soon after Kennedy's death, however, it was possible to interest a small group in reading and discussing

Profiles of Courage. Recently a few of us discussed *The Comfortable Pew* by Pierre Berton.

Obviously much time as well as insight are needed to plan and direct worthwhile activities in which people participate. There is some conflict among residents as to the type of program the Center should have. At present the general program chairman is a resident who believes that elderly people are "lonely" and want to be entertained. He therefore provides outside talent of all kinds. At the same time, there is some complaint that entertainments are not well attended.

Whether or not one needs to be entertained depends to a great extent of course on one's educational background and philosophy of life. There are people at the Center as elsewhere who spend much of their time listening to TV. Aldous Huxley, whose *Ends and Means* was for a number of years almost my Bible, maintains that reliance on external stimulation is bad for the character: "For a majority of people. . . purposeless reading, purposeless listening in, purposeless looking at films have become addictions, psychological equivalents of alcoholism and morphinism. Things have come to such a pitch that many suffer real distress if they are cut off for a few days or even a few hours from newspapers, radio, or moving pictures."

Our educational system—the home, the school, the church —and of course all communication media must take the responsibility for this situation. People have not been taught how to use leisure time, nor have they been shown how to rely on their own intellectual or spiritual resources. Too often our homes and schools and even our churches have vied with big business in encouraging competition, individual achievement and success, instead of cooperation. Eric Fromm in his *Art of Loving* insists that we must teach young people to be loving, compassionate human beings. This of course has been the philosophy of our greatest educators and religious leaders through the ages. Pestalozzi, the Swiss educational reformer, declared many years ago that the spirit of the classroom must be the spirit of love. This was the philosophy of the Great Teacher. For some inexplicable reason, however, too many supposedly well-educated people today seem to prefer following big business—even, to some extent, here at the Center. There are benevolent capitalists, of course, but I cannot believe that encouraging competition—whether in the form of stars, grades, honor rolls, or other awards—in school or elsewhere—will make people more loving and compassionate. "Good ends," Aldous Huxley insists, "can never be achieved by inappropriate means."

A year ago when five other residents and I were given awards for having contributed most to life at the Center, I was nonplussed. I appreciated being appreciated, but I wanted very much to make a speech denouncing the awards. I wanted to say (1) that they were unfair, since many ill and elderly people were unable to contribute to the Center, (2) that I believe with Emerson that "the reward for a thing well done is to have done it," and (3) that by the time one has reached sixty, one should have acquired a degree of maturity whereby he knows that it is really more blessed to give than to receive. Feeling that such a speech would be unacceptable or misunderstood, however, I merely thanked the director.

Enlightenment is a long, slow process. If we want ideal retirement centers where everyone has achieved maturity and spirituality, we shall all have to be better educated, and people will need to start planning their future—their retirement— while they are very young. We shall need also to change the "image" too many people have of those who are older, and of retirement centers. At present residents seem to be stigmatized. I was amused as well as somewhat perturbed last fall at an incident that occurred at the church camp. I had had a good time boating in the afternoon with two forty-year-olds, and none of us, I am sure, thought of age. When one of them found out that I was living at the retirement center, however, she came up to me the next morning and, patting me on the back, said patronizingly, "How are you, my dear? I hear you live at the Center!" It is going to be necessary, somehow, to convince people under sixty that although those over the line of demarcation may possibly not be so strong physically, most of them are as strong mentally as they ever were, and—one might hope—stronger spiritually.

Whether a retirement center is the answer for everyone who retires is debatable, but I am convinced that the church-sponsored Center that I have come to know, and like, although not perfect, is one of the best.

18

Communal Life-Styles
for the Old*

Arlie Russell Hochschild

The forty-three residents of Merrill Court (a small apartment
building near the shore of San Francisco Bay), thirty-seven of
them women, mainly conservative, fundamentalist widows
from the Midwest and Southwest, do not seem likely candidates for "communal living" and "alternatives to the nuclear
family." Nonetheless, their community has numerous communal aspects. Without their "old-agers commune" these 60-,
70-, and 80-year-olds would more than likely be experiencing
the disengagement from life that most students of aging have
considered biologically based and therefore inevitable.

The aged individual often has fewer and fewer ties to the
outside world, and those which he or she does retain are
characterized by less emotional investment than in younger
years. This case study, however, presents evidence that
disengagement may be situational—that how an individual ages
depends largely on his social milieu—and that socially isolated
older people may disengage, but that older people supported
by a community of appropriate peers do not.

*This work originally appeared in Transaction/Society 10, no. 5
(July-August 1973): 50-57.

Rural Ways in Urban Settings

Merrill Court is a strange mixture of old and new, of a vanishing Oakie culture and a new blue-collar life-style, of rural ways in urban settings, of small-town community in mass society, of people oriented toward the young in an age-separated subculture. These internal immigrants to the working-class neighborhoods of West Coast cities and suburbs perceive their new environment through rural and small-town eyes. One woman who had gone shopping at a department store observed "all those lovely dresses, all stacked like cordwood." A favorite saying when one was about to retire was, "Guess I'll go to bed with the chickens tonight." They would give directions to the new hamburger joint or hobby shop by describing its relationship to a small stream or big tree. What remained of the old custom of a funeral wake took place at a new funeral parlor with neon signs and printed notices.

The communal life that developed in Merrill Court may have had nothing to do with rural ways in an urban setting. Had the widows stayed on the farms and in the small towns they came from, they might have been active in community life there. Those who had been involved in community life before remained active and, with the exception of a few, those who previously had not, became active.

For whatever reason, the widows built themselves an order out of ambiguity, a set of obligations to the outside and to one another where few had existed before. It is possible to relax in old age, to consider one's social debts paid, and to feel that constraints that do not weigh on the far side of the grave should not weigh on the near side either. But in Merrill Court, the watchfulness of social life, the Protestant stress on industry, thrift, and activity added up to an ethos of keeping one's "boots on," not simply as individuals but as a community.

Forming the Community

"There wasn't nothin' before we got the coffee machine, I mean we didn't share nothin' before Mrs. Bitford's daughter brought over the machine and we sort of had our first occasion, you might say."

There were about six people at the first gathering around the coffee machine in the recreation room. As people came downstairs from their apartments to fetch their mail, they looked into the recreation room, found a cluster of people sitting down drinking coffee, and some joined in. A few weeks later the recreation director "joined in" for the morning coffee and, as she tells it, the community had its start at this point.

Half a year later Merrill Court was a beehive of activity: meetings of a service club; bowling; morning workshop; Bible-study classes twice a week; other classes with frequently changing subjects; monthly birthday parties; holiday parties; and visits to four nearby nursing homes. Members donated cakes, pies, and soft drinks to bring to the nursing home, and a five-piece band, including a washtub bass, played for the "old folks" there. The band also entertained at a nearby recreation center for a group of Vietnam veterans. During afternoon band practice, the women sewed and embroidered pillow cases, aprons, and yarn dolls. They made wastebaskets out of discarded paper towel rolls, wove rugs from strips of old Wonder Bread wrappers, and Easter hats out of old Clorox bottles, all to be sold at the annual bazaar. They made placemats to be used at the nursing home, totebags to be donated to "our boys in Vietnam," Christmas cards to be cut out for the Hillcrest Junior Women's Club, rag dolls to be sent to the orphanage, place cards to be written out for the bowling-league banquet, recipes to be written out for the recipe book that was to go on sale next month, and thank you and condolence cards.

Social Patterns

The social arrangements that took root early in the history of Merrill Court later assumed a life of their own. They were designed, as if on purpose, to assure an "ongoing" community. If we were to visually diagram the community, it would look like a social circle on which there are centripedal and centrifugal pressures. The formal role system, centered in the circle, pulled people toward it by giving them work and rewards, and this process went on mainly "downstairs," in the recreation room. At the same time, informal loyalty networks fluctuated toward and away from the circle. They became clear mainly "upstairs," where the apartments were located. Relatives and outsiders pulled the individual away from the circle downstairs and network upstairs, although they were occasionally pulled inside both.

Downstairs

Both work and play were somebody's responsibility to organize. The Merrill Court Service Club, to which most of the residents and a half-dozen nonresidents belonged, set up committees and chairmanships that split the jobs many ways. There was a group of permanent elected officials: the president, vice-president, treasurer, secretary and birthday chairman, in addition to the recreation director. Each activity also had a chairman, and each chairman was in charge of a group of volunteers. Some officers were rotated during the year. Only four club members did not chair some activity between 1965 and 1968; and at any time about a third were in charge of something.

Friendship Networks

Shadowing the formal circle was an informal network of friendships that formed over a cup of coffee in the upstairs apartments. The physical appearance of the apartments told something about the network. Inside, each apartment had a living room, kitchen, bedroom, and porch. The apartments were unfurnished when the women moved in and as one remarked, "We fixed 'em up just the way we wanted. I got this new lamp over to Sears, and my daughter and I bought these new scatter rugs. Felt just like a new bride."

For the most part, the apartments were furnished in a remarkably similar way. Many had American flag stickers outside their doors. Inside, each had a large couch with a floral design, which sometimes doubled as a hide-a-bed where a grandchild might sleep for a weekend. Often a chair, a clock, or a picture came from the old home and provided a material link to the past. Most had large stuffed chairs, bowls of homemade artificial flowers, a Bible, and porcelain knick-knacks neatly arranged on a table. (When the group was invited to my own apartment for tea, one woman suggested sympathetically that we "had not quite moved in yet" because the apartment seemed bare by comparison.) By the window were potted plants, often grown from a neighbor's slip. A plant might be identified as "Abbie's ivy" or "Ernestine's African violet."

Photographs, usually out of date, of pink-cheeked children and grandchildren decorated the walls. Less frequently there was a photo of a deceased husband and less frequently still, a photo of a parent. On the living-room table or nearby there was usually a photograph album containing pictures of relatives and pictures of the woman herself on a recent visit "back East." Many of the photographs in the album were arranged in the same way. Pictures of children came first and, of those, children with the most children appeared first, and childless children at the end.

The refrigerator almost always told a social story. One contained homemade butter made by the cousin of a woman on the second floor; berry jam made by the woman three doors down; corn bought downstairs in the recreation room, brought in by someone's son who worked in a corn-canning factory; homemade Swedish rolls to be given to a daughter when she came to visit; two dozen eggs to be used in cooking, most of which would be given away; as well as bread and fruit, more than enough for one person. Most of the women had once cooked for large families, and Emma, who raised eight children back in Oklahoma, habitually baked about eight times as much corn bread as she could eat. She made the rounds of apartments on her floor distributing the extra bread. The others who also cooked in quantities reciprocated, also gratuitously, with other kinds of food. It was an informal division of labor, although no one thought of it that way.

Most neighbors were also friends, and friendships, as well as information about them, were mainly confined to each floor. All but four had their best friends on the same floor and only a few had a next-best friend on another floor. The more one had friends outside the building, the more one had friends on other floors within the building. The wider one's social radius outside the building, the wider it was inside the building as well.

Neighboring

Apart from the gratification of friendship, neighboring did a number of things for the community. It was a way of relaying information or misinformation about others. Often the information relayed upstairs influenced social arrangements downstairs. For example, according to one widow.

> the Bitfords had a tiff with Irma upstairs here, and a lot of tales went around. They weren't true, not a one, about Irma, but then people didn't come downstairs as much. Mattie used to come down, and Marie and Mr. Ball and they don't so much now, only once and again, because of Irma being there. All on account of that tiff.

Often people seated themselves downstairs as they were situated upstairs, neighbor and friend next to neighbor and friend, and a disagreement upstairs filtered downstairs. For example, when opinion was divided and feelings ran high on the issue of whether to store the club's $900 in a cigar box under the treasurer's bed or in the bank, the gossip, formerly confined to upstairs, invaded the public arena downstairs.

Relaying information this way meant that without directly asking, people knew a lot about one another. It was safe to assume that what you did was known about by at least one network of neighbors and their friends. Even the one social isolate on the third floor, Velma, was known about, and her comings and goings were talked about and judged. Talk about other people was a means of social control and it operated, as it does elsewhere, through parables; what was told of another was a message to one's self.

Not all social control was verbal. Since all apartment living rooms faced out on a common walkway that led to a central elevator, each tenant could be seen coming and going; and by how he or she was dressed, one could accurately guess his or her activities. Since each resident knew the visiting habits of her neighbors, anything unusual was immediately spotted. One day when I was knocking on the door of a resident, her neighbor came out:

> I don't know where she is, it couldn't be the doctor's, she goes to the doctor's on Tuesdays; it couldn't be shopping, she shopped yesterday with her daughter. I don't think she's downstairs, she says she's worked enough today. Maybe she's visiting Abbie. They neighbor a lot. Try the second floor.

Neighboring is also a way to detect sickness or death. As Ernestine related, "This morning I look to see if Judson's curtains were open. That's how we do on this floor when we get up we open our curtains just a bit, so others walking by outside know that everything's all right. And if the curtains aren't drawn by mid-morning, we knock to see." Mattie perpetually refused to open her curtains in the morning and kept them close to the wall by placing potted plants against them so that "a man won't get in." This excluded her from the checking-up system and disconcerted the other residents.

The widows in good health took it upon themselves to care for one or two in poor health. Delia saw after Grandma Goodman who was not well enough to go down and get her mail and shop, and Ernestine helped Little Floyd and Mrs. Blackwell who could not see well enough to cook their own meals. Irma took care of Mr. Cooper and she called his son when Mr. Cooper "took sick." Even those who had not adopted someone to help often looked after a neighbor's potted plants while they were visiting kin, lent kitchen utensils, and took phone messages. One woman wrote letters for those who "wrote a poor hand."

Some of the caretaking was reciprocal, but most was not. Three people helped take care of Little Floyd, but since he was blind he could do little in return. Delia fixed his meals, Ernestine laundered his clothes, and Irma shopped for his food. When Little Floyd died fairly suddenly, he was missed perhaps more than others who died during those three years, especially by his caretakers. Ernestine remarked sadly, "I liked helping out the poor old fella. He would appreciate the tiniest thing. And never a complaint."

Sometimes people paid one another for favors. For example, Freda took in sewing for a small sum. When she was paid for lining a coat, she normally mentioned the purpose for which the money would be spent (for example, bus fare for a visit to relatives in Montana), perhaps to reduce the commercial aspect of the exchange. Delia was paid by the Housing Authority for cleaning and cooking for Grandma Goodman, a disabled woman on her floor; and as she repeatedly mentioned to Grandma Goodman, she spent the money on high-school class rings for her three grandchildren. In one case, the Housing Authority paid a granddaughter for helping her grandmother with housework. In another case, a disabled woman paid for domestic help from her Social Security checks.

The "Poor-Dear" Hierarchy

Within the formal social circle there was a status hierarchy based on the distribution of honor, particularly through holding offices in the service club. Additionally, there was a parallel informal status hierarchy based on the distribution of luck. "Luck" as the residents defined it is not entirely luck. Health and life expectancy, for example, are often considered "luck," but an upper-class person can expect to live ten years longer than a lower-class person. The widows of Merrill Court, however, were drawn from the same social class and they saw the differences among themselves as matters of luck.

She who had good health won honor. She who lost the fewest loved ones through death won honor, and she who was close to her children won honor. Those who fell short of any of these criteria were often referred to as "poor dears."

The "poor-dear" system operated like a set of valves through which a sense of superiority ran in only one direction. Someone who was a "poor dear" in the eyes of another seldom called that other person a "poor dear" in return. Rather, the "poor dear" would turn to someone less fortunate, perhaps to buttress a sense of her own achieved or ascribed superiority. Thus, the hierarchy honored residents at the top and pitied "poor dears" at the bottom, creating a number of informally recognized status distinctions among those who, in the eyes of the outside society, were social equals.

The distinctions made by residents of Merrill Court are only part of a larger old-age status hierarchy based on things other than luck. At the monthly meetings of the countywide Senior Citizens Forum, to which Merrill Court sent two representatives, the term poor dear often arose with reference to old people. It was "we senior citizens who are politically involved versus those "poor dears" who are active in recreation." Those active in recreation, however, did not accept a subordinate position relative to the politically active. On the other hand, they did not refer to the political activists as "poor dears." Within the politically active group there were those who espoused general causes, such as getting out an antipollution bill, and those who espoused causes related only to old age such as raising Social Security benefits or improving medical benefits. Those in politics and recreation referred to the passive card players and newspaper readers as "poor dears." Uninvolved old people in good health referred to those in poor health as "poor dears," and those in poor health but living in independent housing referred to those in nursing homes as "poor dears." Within the nursing home there was a distinction between those who were ambulatory and those who were not. Among those who were not ambulatory, there was a distinction between those who could enjoy food and those who could not. Almost everyone, it seemed, had a "poor dear."

At Merrill Court, the main distinction was between people like themselves and people in nursing homes. Returning from one of the monthly trips to a nearby nursing home, one resident commented:

> There was an old woman in a wheelchair there with a dolly in her arms. I leaned over to look at the dolly. I didn't touch it, well, maybe I just brushed it. She snatched it away, and said, "Don't take my dolly." They're pathetic, some of them, the poor dears.

Even within the building, those who were in poor health, were alienated from their children, or were aging rapidly were considered "poor dears." It was lucky to be young and unlucky to be old. There was more than a twenty-year age span between the youngest and oldest in the community. When one of the younger women, Delia, age 69, was drinking coffee with Grandma Goodman, age 79, they compared ages. Grandma Goodman dwelt on the subject and finished the conversation by citing the case of Mrs. Blackwell, who was 89 and still in reasonably good health. Another remarked about her seventieth birthday:

> I just couldn't imagine myself being 70. Seventy is old! That's what Daisy said, too. She's 80 you know. It was her seventieth that got her. No one likes to be put aside, you know. Laid away. Put on the shelf you might say. No sir.

She had an ailment that prevented her from bowling or lifting her flower pots, but she compared her health to that of Daisy, and found her own health a source of luck.

Old people compare themselves not to the young but to other old people. Often the residents referred to the aged back in Oklahoma, Texas, and Arkansas with pity in their voices:

Back in Oklahoma, why they toss the old people away like old shoes. My old friends was all livin' together in one part of town and they hardly budged the whole day. Just sat out on their porch and chewed the fat. Sometimes they didn't even do that. Mostly they didn't have no nice housing, and nothin' social was goin' on. People here don't know what luck they've fallen into.

They also compared their lot to that of other older people in the area. As one resident said:

Some of my friends live in La Casa [another housing project]. I suppose because they have to, you know. And I tried to get them to come bowling with me, but they wouldn't have a thing to do with it. "Those senior citizens, that's old-folks stuff." Wouldn't have a thing to do with it. I tried to tell them we was pretty spry, but they wouldn't listen. They just go their own way. They don't think we have fun.

On the whole, the widows disassociated themselves from the status of "old person," and accepted its "minority" characteristics. The "poor dears" in the nursing home were often referred to as childlike: "They are easily hurt, you know. They get upset at the slightest thing and they like things to be the way they've always been. Just like kids." Occasionally, a widow would talk about Merrill Court itself in this vein, presumably excluding herself: "We're just like a bunch of kids here sometimes. All the sparring that goes on, even with church folk. And people get so hurt, so touchy. You'd think we were babies sometimes."

If the widows accepted the stereotypes of old age, they did not add the "poor dear" when referring to themselves. But younger outsiders did. To the junior employees in the Recreation and Parks Department, the young doctors who treated them at the county hospital, the middle-aged welfare workers, and the young bank tellers, the residents of Merrill Court, and the old people like them, were "poor dears."

Perhaps in old age there is a premium on finishing life off with the feeling of being a "have." But during old age, one also occupies a low social position. The way old look for luck differences among themselves reflects the pattern found at the bottom of other social, racial, and gender hierarchies. To find oneself lucky within an ill-fated category is to gain the semblance of high status when society withholds it from others in the category. The way old people feel above and condescend to other old people may be linked to the fact that the young feel above and condescend to them. The luck hierarchy does not stop with the old.

The Sibling Bond

There were rivalries and differences in Merrill Court, but neither alienation nor isolation. A club member who stayed up in her apartment during club meetings more often did it out of spite than indifference. More obvious were the many small, quiet favors, keeping an eye out for a friend and sharing a good laugh.

There was something special about this community, not so much because it was an old-age subculture, but because the subculture was founded on a particular kind of relationship— the sibling bond. Most residents of Merrill Court are social siblings. The custom of exchanging cups of coffee, lunches, potted plants, and curtain checking suggest reciprocity. Upstairs, one widow usually visited as much as she was visited. On deciding who visits whom, they often remarked, "Well, I came over last time. You come over this time." They traded, in even measure, slips from house plants, kitchen utensils, and food of all sorts. They watched one another's apartments when someone was away on a visit, and they called and took calls for one another.

There are hints of the parent-child bond in this system, but protectors picked their dependents voluntarily and resented taking care of people they did not volunteer to help. For example, one protector of "Little Floyd" complained about a crippled club member, a nonresident:

It wasn't considerate of Rose to expect us to take care of her. She can't climb in and out of the bus very well and she walks so slow. The rest of us wanted to see the museum. It's not nice to say, but I didn't want to miss the museum waiting for her to walk with us. Why doesn't her son take her on trips?

The widows were not only equals among themselves, they also were remarkably similar. They all wanted more or less the same things and could give more or less the same things. They all wanted to *receive* Mother's Day cards. No one in the building *sent* Mother's Day cards. And what they did was to compare Mother's Day cards. Although there was some division of labor, there was little difference in labor performed. All knew how to bake bread and can peaches, but no one knew how to fix faucets. They all knew about "the old days" but few among them could explain what was going on with youth these days. They all had ailments but no one there could cure them. They all needed rides to the shopping center, but no one among them needed riders.

Their similar functions meant that when they did exchange services, it was usually the same kind of services they themselves could perform. For example, two neighbors might exchange corn bread for jam, but both knew how to make both corn bread and jam. If one neighbor made corn bread for five people in one day, one of the recipients would also make corn bread for the same people two weeks later. Each specialized within a specializaion, and over the long run the widows made and exchanged the same goods.

Hence the "side by sideness," the "in the same boat" quality of their relations. They noticed the same things about the world and their eyes caught the same items in a department store. They noticed the same features in the urban landscape—the pastor's home, the Baptist church, the nursing homes, the funeral parlors, the places that used to be. They did not notice, as an adolescent might, the gas stations and hamburger joints.

As a result, they were good listeners for each other. It was common for someone to walk into the recreation room and launch into the details of the latest episode of a mid-afternoon television drama ("It seems that the baby is not by artificial insemination but really Frank's child, and the doctor is trying to convince her to tell..."). The speaker could safely assume that her listeners also knew the details. Since they shared many experiences, a physical ailment, a death, a description of the past, an "old-age joke" could be explained, understood, and enjoyed. They talked together about their children much as their children, together, talked about them. Each shared with social siblings one side of the prototypical parent-child bond.

This similarity opened up the possibility of comparison and rivalry, as the "poor-dear" hierarchy suggests. Whether the widows cooperated in collecting money for flowers, or competed for prestigious offices in the service club, bowling trophies, or front seats in the bus, their functions were similar, their status roughly equal, and their relations in the best and worst sense, "profane."

Not all groups of old people form this sibling bond. Although we might expect subcultures to arise in nursing homes, certain hospital wards, or convalescent hospitals, the likes of Merrill Court are rare. It is not enough to put fairly healthy, socially similar old people together. There is clearly something different between institutions and public housing apartments. Perhaps what counts is the kind of relationships that institutions foster. The resident of an institution is "a patient." Like a child, he has his meals served to him, his water glass filled, his bed made, his blinds adjusted by the "mother-nurse." He cannot return the service. Although he often shares a room or a floor with "brother" patients, both siblings have a nonreciprocal relationship to attendants or nurses. Even the reserach on the institutionalized focuses on the relation between patient and attendant, not between patient and patient. If there is a strong parent-child bond, it may overwhelm any potential sibling solidarity. If the old in institutions meet as equals, it is not as independent equals. The patient's relation to other patients is like the relation between *real*, young siblings, which may exaggerate rather than forestall narcissistic withdrawal.

The widows of Merrill Court took care of themselves, fixed their own meals, paid their own rent, shopped for their own food, and made their own beds; and they did these things for others. Their sisterhood rests on adult autonomy. This is what people at Merrill Court have and people in institutions do not.

The Sibling Bond and Age Stratification
The sibling bond is delicate and emerges only when conditions are ripe. Rapid currents of social change lead to age stratification, which, in turn, ripens conditions for the

sibling bond. Tied to his fellows by sibling bonds, an individual is cemented side by side into an age stratum with which he shares the same rewards, wants, abilities, and failings.

French sociologist Emile Durkheim, in his book The Division of Labor, describes two forms of social solidarity. In organic solidarity there is a division of labor, complementary dependence, and differences among people. In mechanical solidarity there is no division of labor, self-sufficiency, and similarity among people. Modern American society as a whole is based on organic solidarity, not only in the economic but in the social, emotional, and intellectual spheres as well.

Different age strata within the general society, however, are more bound by mechanical solidarity. This is important both for the individual and the society. Although division of labor, complementary dependence, and differences among people describe society's network of relations as a whole, they do not adequately describe relations among particular individuals. An individual's complementary dependence may be with people he does not know or meet—such as the person who grows and cans the food he eats, or lays the bricks for his house. And in his most intimate relations, an individual may also have complementary relations (either equal or unequal) with his spouse and children. But in between the most and least intimate bonds is a range in which there are many sibling relationships that form the basis of mechanical solidarity.

In fact, many everyday relations are with people similar and equal to oneself. Relations between colleague and colleague, student and student, friend and friend, relations within a wives' group or "the guys at the bar," the teenage gang or army buddies are often forms of the sibling bond. These ties are often back-up relations, social insurance policies for the times when the complementary bonds of parent and child, husband and wife, student and teacher, boyfriend and girlfriend fail, falter, or normally change.

From an individual's viewpoint, some periods of life, such as adolescence and old age, are better for forming sibling bonds than are other periods. Both just before starting a family and after raising one, before entering the economy and after leaving it, an individual is open to and needs these back-up relationships. It is these stages that are problematic, and it is

these stages that, with longer education and earlier retirement, now last longer.

From society's point of view, the sibling bond allows more
flexibility in relations between generations by forging solidarity
within generations and divisions between them. This divides
society into age layers that are relatively independent of one
another, so that changes in one age layer need not be retarded
by conditions in another. The institution that has bound the
generations together—the family—is in this respect on the
decline. As it declines, the sibling bond emerges, filling in and
enhancing social flexibility, especially in those social strata
where social change is most pronounced. The resulting social
flexibility does not guarantee "good" changes and continuity is
partly sacrificed to fads and a cult of newness. But whether
desirable or not, this flexibility is partly due to and partly
causes the growing importance of the sibling bond.

The times are ripe for the sibling bond, and for old-age
communities such as Merrill Court. In the social life of old
people the problem is not the sibling bond versus the
parent-child bond. Rather, the question is how the one bond
complements the other. The sisterhood at Merrill Court is no
substitute for love of children and contact with them; but it
offers a full, meaningful life independent of them.

The Minority Group Almost Everyone Joins

Isolation is not randomly distributed across the class
hierarchy; there is more of it at the bottom. It is commonly said
that old age is a leveler, that it affects the rich in the same way
it affects the poor. It does not. The rich fare better in old age
even as they fared better in youth. The poorer you are, the
shorter your life expectancy, the poorer your health and
health care, the lower your morale generally, the more likely
you are to "feel" old regardless of your actual age, the less
likely you are to join clubs or associations, the less active you
are and the more isolated even from children. Irving Rosow's
study of 1,200 people over 62 living in Cleveland found that
roughly 40 percent of the working class but only 16 percent of
the middle class had fewer than four good friends. Another
study of 6,000 white working-class men and women showed
that of those over 65 with incomes under $3,000, a full third did
not visit with or speak to a friend or neighbor during the

preceding week. The rock-bottom poor are isolated, but they are not the only ones.

The isolation of old people is linked to other problems. The old are poor and poverty itself is a problem. The old are unemployed and unemployment, in this society, is itself a problem. The old lack community and the lack of community is itself a problem. There is some connection between these three elements. Removed from the economy, the old have been cast out of the social networks that revolve around work. Lacking work, they are pushed down the social ladder. Being poor, they have fewer social ties. Poverty reinforces isolation. To eliminate enforced isolation, we have to eliminate poverty, for the two go together. The social life of Merrill Court residents, who had modest but not desperately low incomes, is an exception to the general link between social class and isolation.

Even if every old person were in a Merrill Court, the problem of old age would not be solved. But, allowing every old person the possibility of such an arrangement could be part of the solution. The basic problem far exceeds the limits of tinkering with housing arrangements. It is not enough to try to foster friendships among the old. Even to do that, it is not enough to set up bingo tables in the lobbies of decrepit hotels or to hand out name cards to the sitters on park benches. This would simply put a better face on poverty, a cheerful face on old age as it now is, at not much social cost.

Merrill Court is not set in any island of ideal social conditions; it is essentially an adjustment to bad social conditions. For the lives of old people to change fundamentally, those conditions must change. In the meantime, Merrill Court is a start. It is a good example of what can be done to reduce isolation. I do not know if similar communities would have emerged in larger apartment houses or housing tracts rather than in a small apartment house, with the married rather than the widowed, with rich rather than poor residents, with people having a little in common rather than a lot, with the very old person rather than the younger old person. Only trying will tell.

Merrill Court may be a forecast of what is to come. A survey of 105 University of California students in 1968 suggested that few parents of these students and few of the students themselves expect to be living with their families when they are old. Nearly seven out of ten (69 percent) reported that "under no circumstances" would they want their aged parents to live with them, and only three percent expected to be living with their own children when they are old. A full 28 percent expected to be living with *other* old people, and an additional 12 percent expected to be "living alone or with other old people."

Future communities of old people may be more middle class and more oriented toward leisure. Less than ten percent of the students expected to be working when they passed sixty-five. A great many expected to be "enjoying life," by which they meant studying, meditating, practicing hobbies, playing at sports, and traveling.

But some things about future communities may be the same. As I have suggested throughout this chapter, communal solidarity can renew the social contact the old have with life. For old roles that are gone, new ones are available. If the world watches them less for being old, they watch one another more. Lacking responsibilities to the young, the old take on responsibilities to the young, the old take on responsibilities toward one another. Moreover, in a society that raises an eyebrow at those who do not "act their age," the subculture encourages the old to dance, to sing, to flirt, and to joke. They talk frankly about death in a way less common between the old and young. They show one another how to be, and trade solutions to problems they have not faced before.

Old age is the minority group almost everyone joins. But it is a forgotten minority group from which many old people dissociate themselves. A community such as Merrill Court counters this disaffiliation. In the wake of the declining family, it fosters a "we" feeling, and a nascent "old-age consciousness." In the long run, this may be the most important contribution an old-age community makes.

19

The Future of Family Relationships*

Rose M. Somerville

The decade of the 1970s has begun with a notable degree of interest in the future of marriage and the family. On both popular and professional levels there have been books, articles, and conferences that reflect increasing discontent with present family functioning and a more determined searching for alternatives. Classroom discussions show "the ambivalence of students toward the institution of marriage and the family as they had experienced and observed it" and more frequent favoring of "no marriage, group marriage, no children" (Wiseman).

This questioning of "the conventional mystique of family life" (Skolnick and Skolnick) is sharper at the student level than among the middle aged and the elderly, and reveals a negative evaluation of the marriages of parents, older siblings, and friends. However, people past their youth are not silent

*This work originally appeared in *The Family Coordinator*, October 1972, pp. 487-98, ©1972 by the National Council on Family Relations. Reprinted by permission of the publisher. This is an expanded version of a paper presented at the Groves Conference on Marriage and the Family, San Juan, Puerto Rico, May 1971.

and are beginning to offer their own self-criticism. Otto reports that in "more than sixty conversations with members of the helping professions concerning their marriages and divorces," it became evident that "even those professionals who considered themselves happily married were increasingly inclined to question the contemporary institutions of marriage and the family" (Otto 1970). Fiction writers, always sensitive to failures in human relationships, are beginning to depict some attempts by the middle aged to move away from traditional modes of functioning.

The college student, the fiction writer, and those in the helping professions come mainly from the advantaged segments of the community. Their criticisms reflect on middle-class marriage, long upheld in family textbooks as a model for the lower class. Perhaps the middle-class backgrounds of those most articulate in their demand for new family forms account for the lack of emphasis on the need for economic changes. Few spokesmen for change perceive marriage and the family as dependent variables, with the nature of the economy pivotal in determining the range of possibilities for the work and family lives of men and women. Nor does fiction broaden this perspective. Most writers tend to take the present economic structure as a given and insist that new family wine can be poured into the old bottles of economic relationships.

The following pages, in reviewing the insights offered by modern creative literature as to present and future functioning of families and parafamilies, are almost of necessity limited to a middle-class perspective. The projections offered for the future can be radically upset by major changes in the economy that may be precipitated not only by the technological potential but also by the pressure of those presently underrepresented in the work opportunity structure: women, youth, ethnic minorities, the aging, and the aged.

Even though fiction does not fill the gaps in long-term reckoning of social change, it is usually at the cutting edge of more immediate changes in male-female and intergenerational relationships. It therefore supplements usefully the findings of research studies and paradoxically provides some of the reality lacking in many family and child development textbooks (Rodman; Klapper). The fiction cited here was selected for the clues it provided to new role definitions in a transitional period. There is no claim that it is typical of contemporary fiction.

While the search for family change has been spearheaded by youth in this country, it has important repercussions among men and women who are middle aged and elderly. In a kind of role reversal, the new relationships talked about and sometimes entered into by young people serve as models for their older relatives. Even if there is disapproval, they become aware of alternatives in life-styles and family patterns. Moreover, since roles are defined by reciprocal expectations, to the extent that youth leaves the family home at a younger age than a decade or two ago, it is not possible for middle-aged parents and elderly grandparents to make children the same focus of their lives as they might have anticipated. Even with children in the home, new definitions of filial responsibility and new criticisms of parental functioning may cause men and women in their middle years to take an even sharper glance at marriage and the family than ordinary interaction with adolescents encourages.

Middle and Older Years: Problems of Definition

Who is middle aged? How old are the elderly? Studies in the family field vary in their operative definitions, with men and women in their fifties considered as middle aged in some studies and elderly in others. It is commonly recognized among gerontologists that psychological, physiological, and social measures of aging would be more precise than chronological age. However, such measures are not yet available, and the poor second best of chronology must distinguish the groups to be discussed here.

Stratification studies suggest that increasing the number of categories allows important distinctions to be made among various population groups. The difficulty of justifying cut off points remains, however. One suggested typology could be Early Middle Age, 30 to 45; Advanced Middle Age, 45 to 65; Early Old Age, 65 to 75; and Advanced Old Age, 75 and beyond. The pejorative reference to those over 30 by youth in the 1960s might justify one cut off, while research on housing patterns and on self-perception might justify the cut off at the other end of the age scale. A split between the first older decade and the second is shown in the increase in custodial care after 75 and the definition of the self as "old" less frequently before 75. An alternative typology that may meet objections that 30 is an inappropriate start for middle age and 45 too soon for advanced middle age would be the following: Early Middle Age, 35 to 50; Advanced Middle Age, 50 to 65; Early Old Age, 65 to 75; and Advanced Old Age, 75 and beyond. Either typology would allow for increasing longevity that is likely in the decade or two ahead. At present half of those over 65 are over 72 and almost one person in five is over 80 (U.S. Department of Health, Education, and Welfare). The discussion in these pages will be based on the alternative typology. It will include all men and women in the second half of their life cycle. The use of the age of the individuals rather than the marriage stage is necessary at this time when conceptualization of the middle years of a marriage and the middle years of an individual leave problems of congruence (Rodgers; Duvall). Moreover, an increase in serial monogamy and in remarriage in middle and older years, both likely in the next decade or two, will provide further challenge to the family life-cycle concept, not only in the timing of progressions from one stage to another, but in definitions of developmental tasks as well.

Early and Advanced Middle Age

The connotations of middle age in contemporary American culture are not positive ones. The term suggests decreasing opportunities and status position for middle-aged incumbents. Also, most individuals vary in their perception of middle age according to their own age and that of their family members. For example, in one college class, students reported their parents in their late thirties would resent being called *middle aged.* Graduate students tend to take issue with classmates who would make the dividing line thirty or thirty-five.

Just as the phrase *affluent society* tended to direct attention away from the bulging pockets of poverty in the 1950s, so too the phrase, the *Command Generation,* used by a popular magazine for those in their forties and fifties who are at the peak of power, can direct attention away from the vast majority of Americans in the lower and the lower-middle classes for whom those years represent a decrease in income. For the more affluent, whose work status may be enhanced in middle age, there is little indication that this stage in life is welcomed (Cuber and Haroff).

Ficton writers see middle age as a time of monotony in monogamy, of troublesome relationships with aging parents, and of complexities in maintaining affectional ties with children of former marriages. In a few instances they try to suggest solutions. In Rimmer's novel, *Proposition 31*, David and Nancy had been married fifteen years and Horace and Tanya twelve when they joined their two families of procreation into "corporate marriage," a design enthusiastically espoused by the novelist for Future Families of America. The story dwells on an attempt to introduce group marriage through the California ballot after the foursome had first tried it and found it advantageous over conventional marriage forms. While the novel can be dismissed as a fantasy world of material plenty and sexual competency, it might be shortsighted to do so. For the millions of young men and women who followed Rimmer from *The Harrad Experiment* into this more total commitment of several couples in early middle age, the significance of the novel may lie not in its suggested shallow solutions to large societal problems but in its confirmation of their fears that interaction, both conversationally and sexually, between husbands and wives tends to deteriorate when monogamous marriages last for more than a decade. It also confirms their hopes for simple solutions. By putting two or three bored couples together, the novel seems to promise, a magical new combination will result. Ellis's judgment that, "It is quite difficult to find a group of four or more adults of both sexes who can truly live harmoniously with one another," finds no reflection in the story.

Perhaps more important, since the story is offered at more or less a single point of time, it provides no insights as to what happens as the couples move into advanced-middle or early-old age. Nor does the story reveal in the given time period when the couples are in early-middle age, how any of the men or women relate to their families of origin. What problems do the parents of the couples have, or the brothers and sisters, in relating to grandchildren or nieces and nephews brought up with new norms of total nudity, multiple sexual partners, and cross-spouse pregnancy? While in a sense these adjustments represent perhaps only a difference in degree rather than in kind from the culture shock experienced today by some older relatives in their relationships with youth, each degree would seem to warrant some anticipatory socialization-to-change not revealed by the novel.

It is in another work of fiction that some suggestion is offered of negative outcomes in the maintenance of kin relationships between unconventional children in their early-middle years and parents in early-old age. Joe and Ruth Allston, in Stegner's novel, have already lost their only son, drowned at thirty-seven, but flashbacks show the troubled intergenerational contacts as the son's choices in education, occupation, and mate selection disappoint his conventional parents (Stegner). Since each generation is socialized to different family expectations, lack of value congruence is likely to mar kin relationships in any period of rapidly changing norms. Resentment and hostility are not limited to the older generation. Adams's study found "not a single young male... keeping in close touch with a divorcee-father" (Adams). Moreover, self-blame may be common among the thirty-eight percent of the elderly who are foreign born or who have at least one parent who is foreign born (U.S. H.E.W.). A short story tells of the self-castigation of an elderly immigrant couple who consider the fault theirs alone when a son of early-middle age visits them rarely (Broyard). However, the more common phenomenon of the elderly who are critical of youth and middle-aged kin seeking solutions that were not common in earlier decades tends to predominate in fiction. Updike's recent novel points up the emotional havoc in a weekend visit of a middle-aged son to his aging mother's home. Although her own marriage had been unhappy, the elderly woman assumes a stance of moral superiority in contrasting its continuance with the divorces of her son and of her new daughter-in-law.

The Future for the Middle Aged: Divorce, Delayed Marriage, Consensual Unions

Divorce
     There are a number of divergent trends and influences that can become more pronounced in the decade or two ahead.

Men and women who are in their middle years today were not exposed in their youth to as broad a social acceptance of divorce as a solution to cessation of spousal affection as young people now are. In the 1970s and 1980s as today's youth enter early middle age, there is a likelihood of more divorces. However, their own socialization experiences as children and adolescents may create a contrary trend that could take two forms. In one, a more cautious attitude toward marriage may result in delaying such commitment and forming unlegalized relationships of varying durability. In the other, wariness may take the form of more careful mate selection and more realistic expectations in the relationship. Consensual unions, less valued than formalized marriages in most societies, are widely accepted nonetheless. Although the origins may lie in economic difficulty and the poorer bargaining position of women where gainful employment is not an alternative available to them, the institution of private commitment may be adapted to emotional and ideological considerations.

Recent changes in divorce laws may similarly have two different outcomes. In one, the trend would be for less careful mate selection since the couple see ease of dissolution correcting any errors in judgment. In the other probability, there would be reinforcement of the trend to delayed marriage or to consensual union, since the ease of divorce may blur the distinction between legalized and nonlegalized relationships. The great increase of middle-aged women in the work force coupled with the women's liberation movement impact on the job opportunity structure and pay levels may change the traditional view of marriage as an economic necessity.

In states that retain costly and complex divorce procedures, there may be reinforcement for the trend toward cohabitation until the couple achieve greater certainty as to their feelings for each other. This may be particularly applicable to those divorced men and women who are considering remarriage, but it may enter into the thinking of the never-married also. Reiss mentions "a trend toward quicker remarriage" in comparing the four or five years it took about half the men and women in the 1950s to remarry after a divorce, with the two years for men and three for women the same proportion took in the 1960s. However, the 1970s are likely to see a modification of this trend. Some clue to change is offered in extension courses on divorce or on the stepparent that attract a high enrollment of divorced people. Middle-aged women mention with some indignation and disappointment the experience of dating men who are ready for consensual but not legalized unions. Most of these women are middle class and were socialized some decades ago when consensual union for that socioeconomic level was a rarity. However, the next decade or two may show the effects of women's liberation movements, some of which stress in their consciousness-raising rap groups the desirability of careers and of living arrangements that maximize personal options and flexibility. The weekend marriage is one of the diverse life-styles suggested. Some of these women will reject legal marriages or remarriages. In any case the echoes of their discussions will reverberate in the thinking of many middle-class men and women, and may influence their behaviors. The middle years may become the period of experimentation because they are relatively free of child rearing. It must be recognized, however, that any solutions that require economic independence and self-support of men and women assume a job market that can accommodate both sexes and all ages.

Sexuality

Whatever the form of the relationship sought, increasing recognition is likely of sexual needs in the second half of life. The culture can be expected to continue to be highly eroticized as the economic payoff of providing sexual stimulation through the mass media, advertisements, and commercial establishments motivates private enterprise in this direction. The impact on men and women in middle years is likely to increase with newer scientific knowledge concerning the sexual potential of women and the positive outcomes of a continued sex life for both sexes. The stereotype of lost sexuality for the postmenopausal woman and the male in early-old age has been in the past both a self-fulfilling prophecy for many and a deterrent to emphatic interaction with the middle aged and the elderly on the part of both kinfolk and the helping professions.

A countertrend could be derived from new awareness of women's rights to control their own bodies. Wives may show less willingness to engage in sexual intercourse as a mere connubial obligation. This could create problems in the sexual relationships of men and women in middle and later years as divergent definitions of rights and privileges are developed. Moreover, the women's liberation movements, with their criticism of using women as "sex objects" in male-female relationships and in the selling of products, may deter the eroticization of the culture. However, the model set by these women of frank discussion of sexuality may create an atmosphere in which sexuality in the middle and later years is more accepted. Family life and sex educators have not sufficiently brought into the classroom the research findings of Masters and Johnson, nor has the professional training of nurses prepared them sufficiently concerning sexuality in the second half of life (Masters and Johnson). New realism in the curriculum of high schools, colleges, and professional schools may mark the coming decade (Somerville 1971a) and if so, will undoubtedly affect the level of understanding among professionals and family members, concerning middle-aged and elderly patients, students, clients, and relatives.

Role Definitions
While fiction is often in the forefront of social development, in many instances aware of changes before the public is, the image of the new woman does not yet emerge from the pages of literature, highbrow or lowbrow. Those who will be middle aged in a decade or two will have had little guidance toward new roles from contemporary fiction. However, in children's books the demand by feminists for a more realistic depiction of role options and diversity of family forms may more quickly be heeded by the publishers. Critical reviews of children's books that perpetuate stereotypical sex-role allocations, and watch-dog committees of professionals and housewives, may result in stories that portray man-woman roles and relationships in more varied ways. The educational impact may be felt by parents and grandparents who buy and read this literature.

The Older Years
The foregoing discussion of the future of marriage among the middle aged has obvious implications for family life in early- and advanced-old age. Divorce by a middle-aged son or daughter may deprive the elderly of grandparent roles or may bring child-care responsibilities to an unwelcome degree. The frequency of interaction with grown children may influence the decision of widowed or divorced elderly men and women to

remarry. Similarly the decision making by the elderly significantly affects the options of the middle aged.

Remarriage

There has been less resistance to remarriage for the
middle aged than for men and women over 65. Nonetheless, by
the 1960s, some 35,000 marriages a year involved people in
early- and advanced-old age (Rubin). The coming decades are
likely to see some marked increases as family and community
pressures against such marriages lessen. Marriage or consensual union would seem to be one of the main solutions for the
lack of companionship felt by the elderly who are either
divorced or bereaved. While several studies stress the amount
of contact maintained between grown children and their
parents, this varies when there is a lone parent as survivor.
The sex of the elderly parent and the sex of the middle-aged
child constitute significant variables (Adams).

Visiting and Help Networks

Intergenerational contacts have in the recent past relied
heavily on female initiative, from "Mum" in the East London
slum to married daughters in the United States, as shown in
the Adams and the Komarovsky studies. Sweetser has seen in
the change from agriculture to industry the explanation for
more mother-daughter closeness. As patriarchal family organization declined, overvaluation of the son lessened. Within
the industrial setting, "role convergence," or the joint playing
by females of housekeeping and mother roles, has been seen as
a binding element in the relationship. What will be the impact
in the decade ahead of women's liberation and zero population
movements upon role convergence? Will friends at work
become closer than kin as women reduce their domestic
involvements? Will the effort to build spousal intimacy begin to
define both friend and kin, in some instances at least, as
extraneous (Otto 1970)?

The story, "A Daughter of My Own" (Gerber), suggests
that the traditional assistance of the young woman's mother in
the first weeks after a baby is born, or in some instances of her
mother-in-law, may not always be welcomed by a young couple
eager to make the new experience theirs alone. Not only the
son-in-law but the daughter herself may also view the older
woman's aid as interference. The story suggests that role

congruence is only one factor in mother-daughter closeness. When "keeping in touch" demands writing and telephone calls rather than face-to-face interaction, there may be a toll in intimacy and level of identification among kin. Continued geographical mobility in the coming decade may intensify the emotional distance even if frequency of contact on a more superficial level continues or magnifies.

Moreover, role congruence may be reduced as two trends become more marked: First, decreased valuation of the mother role; and second, increased participation by men in child care, marketing, cooking, and other activities traditionally allocated to females.

The lack of satisfaction in conventional women's roles permeates the short story, "To Room Nineteen." The inability of an educated, middle-class woman in contemporary London to build either a spousal relationship or a career suggests an extreme level of alienation, but finds sympathetic echoes among American women. The feeling expressed in the story may well affect the part in the coming decade or two that women will play in maintaining the kin network. "Children? But children can't be a center of life and a reason for being. They can be a thousand things that are delightful, interesting; satisfying, but they can't be a wellspring to live from" (Lessing).

More open recognition of negative effects of child-rearing roles on spousal ones may act in the future as a preventive to overinvolvement in the parental role. Research on disenchantment among middle-aged couples, combined with counseling insights, indicates that estrangement begins in the early years of marriage when the woman's interests may be tied too exclusively to the children (Blood and Wolfe; Pineo; Peterson). Moreover, it has been found that overvaluation of the parental role can cause difficulties in the menopausal period. "Many women fear that they now have lost their main purpose in life and are no longer desired by their husbands and families. They feel that they are no longer needed, and become seriously depressed. With the depression comes loss of sexual interest and activity" ("Roundtable"). This has a negative effect on the husband's sexual performance, which is already under some strain. "The incidence of sexual inadequacy in the human male takes a sharp upturn after fifty years of age" (Masters and Johnson). While this is reversible, it requires a favorable psychological environment.

The creation of this environment may be aided by women's liberation ideology. The 1970s are likely to see emphasis on the development of the woman as a person, with her own needs and interests, in which children play an important but secondary role. One outcome may be more spousal interaction in the early years of the marriage with positive outcomes in the later years. Another may be a welcoming rather than a depressed attitude toward the menopause, again contributing to spousal unity in the later years. This might augur further breaches in the relationships of elderly people and their grown children as spouses turn to each other rather than to families of origin. It is possible that an increase in leisure time, likely if an ethos critical of consumerism were to become more dominant, would mitigate the rivalry otherwise predictable between spousal intimacy and relationships with extended kin. Kibbutz experience also suggests that parent-child intimacy and devotion need not be impaired by diminution of parentally performed services (or filially performed ones) or by the increased attention of parents to their work roles and to each other as romantic dyads.

Relatedly, the desire of American women for meaningful work outside the home is likely to increase as women become aware of their unrealized potentialities. The availability of middle-aged and older women to care for their grandchildren, even where their services are welcomed, or of younger and middle-aged women to provide care for ailing elderly parents to a degree that would allow both generations to maintain their own residences, will undoubtedly decrease when more women enter gainful employment. These problems will be exacerbated if more of the thirty-one million American women now gainfully employed become full-time workers.

New Services

One outcome may be the professionalization of some services for the elderly in the coming decade as a substitute for help in health care and household management now being provided by a daughter or other female relative living in close proximity. Services by the elderly may also be professionalized. In lower-income groups the realization that community child-care services may threaten their own usefulness to their married children and decrease interaction with children and grandchildren has created some grandmother opposition to new preschool and afterschool programs. It was a step forward for such programs to begin to involve mothers; the coming decade may see the effort extended to grandmothers. The paraprofessional status may create a nonkin basis for services by and for the elderly. Men and women in early-old age have already demonstrated their ability to supplement the work of nurses in institutions for mentally and physically handicapped children.

Institutions

In the coming decade, however, tensions between the middle aged and the elderly are not likely to decrease when decisions are concerned with the use of nursing homes, joint domicile, or even the kind of funeral (Somerville, 1971b). Those beyond the age of sixty-five were socialized in a period when familism tended to outweigh individual goals and feelings. A strong sense of obligation was deliberately inculcated to ensure that married children took responsibility for their aging parents. The present middle-aged generation is caught between norm shifts. Many observed their own parents performing filial duties. They face a different set of realities, however, such as limited urban apartment space, higher spousal intimacy expectations, increased educational support for youth, geographical mobility, and longevity. Even when they act in light of these realities and the newly developing norms, it is often with a strong sense of guilt and regret.

This is in part intensified by the limited alternatives in kinds of nursing homes and institutions for the aged. It is not only a problem of the gross neglect and low standards in many of these facilities, but also the lack of creativity in connection with them. Some changes require more imagination and empathy than money. It is possible that heterosexual rooming will take the place of sex-segregated wings in nursing and old-age institutions. One outcome may be more meaningful interpersonal relationships within these institutions, including in some instances a sexual component. Relatedly, conjugal visits for the hospitalized elderly may become a routine practice. Individuals have varying needs for privacy and closeness in their later years and will require more sensitive nursing and administration than presently available.

Institutionalization of the elderly has not risen rapidly: In 1940 2.5 percent and in 1960 four percent, with the great majority in advanced old age (Riley). The tendency for the elderly to maintain their own homes as long as possible is likely to continue in the next decades. The elderly parent without a partner, more likely to be the mother not only because of higher survival rates (four widows to one widower in 1970) but also because bereaved and divorced men remarry more quickly than do women, lives alone almost as often as she lives with children. Ethnicity is a variable, however (National Urban League).

As middle-aged children become less available to offer custodial care, the nursing home may become a more common resource. As it becomes more common, it may ease the present lack of acceptance on the part of both the middle aged and the elderly. The aged mother in "The Cost Depends on What You Reckon It In" (Gerber), bedridden with paralysis, had lived with her married daughter's family until lifting her required special handling. Sent to a nearby rest home, she is visited by her daughter three times a day. The timing of these visits so as not to alert other family members suggested that disapproval rather than commendation would have been the response. Nor did the people at the rest home approve her conduct. The director warned her: "The others get jealous. They don't like your mother already, you visit her too much. Them, their children never visit. Only once in a while." The daughter's frantic efforts to mitigate the guilt she felt, knowing her mother would prefer to be back with the family, took the form of food offerings. "'Soup. What do I need soup for? To make me live longer?' 'What kind of talk is that,' I said severely.'Don't you want to live?' My mother stared at me, her blue eyes blazing, and then put the question to me, 'This is living?' "

Anderson's I Never Sang for My Father suggests that the old-age-home solution, even when family finances permit large expenditures, is not welcomed by an older generation with little anticipatory socialization for group life and with traditional definitions of kin as more essential for emotional sustenance than nonkin. Guilt and recrimination permeate the intergenerational relationships when the need of the old father to stay in his familiar surroundings after his wife dies begins to clash with the need for the middle-aged son to establish his family in a different region of the country. Even if a geographic change were not involved, the play suggests the problems that can develop with nobody around to play the housewife role. The son, a widower, is planning to marry a doctor who would hardly be prepared to provide companionship for a lonely old man.

Communes

Will communes provide a solution for the couple in advanced-middle age or early-old age in the coming decades? Three-generation living seems even rarer in communes than in traditional family forms. Among the latter, only about eight percent in 1960 had three generations living together (Riley and Foner). Communes are varied and efforts are under way to distinguish among the many types (Sussman 1971). These emerging experimental structures vary from the single household usually found in urban areas to the several households that more often make up the rural commune. In each of them there are variations in the degree of commitment to monogamy, some resembling the kibbutz with all couples sharing work and resources but not their sexual lives, while in others there are rapidly changing heterosexual alliances and joint commitment to all the children. Still others link biological and social parenthood more closely. Some are groupings of a polygynous or polyandrous kind. What they have in common is group living.

The number of communes in existence at the present time can only be estimated. Otto mentions 3,000 urban communes (1971). However, this estimate may include only those that designate themselves as such. Rural communes are more difficult to count. Whatever the present number, if the communal experience persists and attracts greater numbers of men and women in the coming decade, it may provide anticipatory socializaion for the enforced intimacy with nonkin that characterizes institutional arrangements for the aged. Commune members depend on one another for emotional and economic support, although gifts from parents as well as regular contributions seem in some instances to be an important survival resource. The help pattern of the middle class, characterized by more flow from the older generation to the younger, seems to continue when the children are in communes. However, affectional and ceremonial linkages may not include parents and grandparents. In some communes, the birth of a baby is witnessed amid celebration by all members of the parafamily. The family of origin does not share in the occasion (Skolnick and Skolnick).

One observer declares, "There is a rapidly growing number of communes composed of persons in their mid-twenties to upper thirties" (Otto 1971). Where middle-aged men and women are present in communes, it is more likely to be the urban household in which women with demanding professional careers find that the sharing of a large house with several other couples reduces problems of child care and household responsibilities. Income levels are typically high in this group and permit more privacy and material comforts than in student communes or in rural communes where heavy physical labor is a daily necessity. In the latter the occasional middle-aged member is likely to be the original owner of the land and may be tolerated rather than welcomed. A self-deprecating note permeates interviews with them in the few anecdotal materials so far available. "We have lots of ideas and very little energy," a woman in her mid-forties says of herself and the few others of her peers in one commune (Otto 1971). The tendency noted in some communes for mother and father figures to emerge may create a reluctance on the part of the young to encourage older people to join them. And if the younger people wish to avoid the authority structure typical of the traditional and even the transitional family, the older ones seem to have a corresponding wish to avoid the responsibilities associated with usual family forms.

Retirement Villages and Other Age Groupings

The latter possibility is suggested by the deliberate age segregation that has marked housing among men and women in advanced-middle age and early-old age in the past decade. This all-adult grouping has taken a number of different forms. One is the relatively rare establishment of a household by a group of elderly men and women. This may increase in the coming decade, however. The sexual component in these arrangements is not clear. Perhaps informally and consensually they have moved toward the famous suggestion of Polygyny After Sixty (Kassel). Or they may be establishing relationships that are the group counterpart of the practical and relatively unromantic unions found in some marriages of the elderly (McKain). Student reports on life-styles of elderly grandparents, usually widowed but sometimes divorced, offer clues to greater toleration of these groupings on the part of grandchildren than on the part of the middle generation. When these young adults are middle aged, they may be more supportive of their own parents' attempts to solve the problem of companionship and care. If so, the trend to group marriage or consensual union among elderly men and women will become more evident. This may be congruent also with changed working lives for women in which peer-group attachments begin to outweigh kin contacts.

A more frequently encountered trend toward age segregation is found in the retirement villages, apartment houses for adults only, and trailer courts that with the encouragement of commercial interests, federal funds, and churches, have created concentrations of older men and women. This began in earnest in the 1950s but neither research studies nor fiction reveal very much as yet of the impact of age segregation on the relationships of the various generations. One variable is undoubtedly the degree of geographic isolation, although the recreational setting of some more affluent intentional communities may encourage weekend visiting of elderly relatives by middle-aged kin. Another variable may be the age of admission, in middle age or in old age. Where the age range is large, from the fifties to the seventies, what is the effect on the two generations? Do the middle aged move more rapidly toward old age as a result of daily contact with the elderly rather than with youth? Or do they gain from anticipatory socialization to the problems and opportunities of their final decades that may look less threatening through familiarity. And do the elderly in joint residence with the middle aged experience envy of the broader range of activities undertaken? Or do the elderly suffer less from the depression that often accompanies living with their peers and witnessing the more frequent funerals? As a character in Muriel Spark's *Memento Mori* remarks, "Being over seventy is like being engaged in a war. All our friends are going or gone and we survive amongst the dead and dying as on a battlefield." The presence of those in advanced-middle age may ensure more continuity of friendships for the elderly, and these friendships in retirement villages may increasingly replace kin contacts.

The solution tried in other countries has not appreciably been attempted here: separate quarters for the elderly that are either walking distance from or in sight of other age groups, particularly young children, on the assumption that just as younger people need to view and interact with all stages of life in order to grasp the fullness of existence, older people can find comfort in seeing symbols of a life that will go on after they are gone. The symbols may decreasingly need to be one's own offspring.

Summary

Present efforts to change the family or to substitute other groupings for traditional family forms are likely to accelerate in the next decade or two. Significant forces at work are the women's liberation movement, youth's quest for personal closeness and lesser commitment to the Protestant ethic, and individualism that brings familistic values into question.

Middle-aged and elderly family members are already affected as their younger kin begin to define in new ways the obligations between generations and to substitute friends for relatives in their emotional and recreational lives. Moreover, the middle aged and the elderly are themselves involved in new groupings, finding substitutes for remarriage as consensual couples or as part of larger groups. Among the middle aged and elderly, more are seeking to live in all-adult settings. "Intimacy at a distance" with their grown children, however, requires substitute persons for daily interaction. Those who become middle aged and elderly in the next few decades will undoubtedly carry into their new age groups the effects of experimentation with alternatives to the family and can be expected to modify the options men and women consider appropriate to the second half of life. Fiction offers clues to present discontents and new paths opening up but, like research studies of the family life of the middle aged and the elderly, tends to lag behind the swift changes of the present day. The increase in those over 65 to 20 million men and women today and those 45 to 64 to more than twice that number, and the additional millions in the 35 to 45 years, adds up to a population that must compel the attention of social scientists and creative writers in the decades ahead. The interpersonal relationships of these age groups, among themselves and with the younger generation, will help determine the future of the family.

References

Adams, Bert N. *Kinship in an Urban Setting.* Chicago: Markham Publishing Company, 1968.

Anderson, Robert. *I Never Sang for My Father.* New York: Random House, 1968.

Blood, Robert O., and Wolfe, Donald M. *Husbands and Wives: The Dynamics of Married Living.* New York: Macmillan, 1960.

Broyard, Anatole. "Sunday Dinner Brooklyn." In *Avon Book of Modern Writing, No. 2.* Edited by William Phillips and Philip Zahv. New York: Avon Publications, 1954.

Cuber, John P., and Haroff, Peggy B. *The Significant Americans.* New York: Appleton-Century, 1965.

Duvall, Evelyn Millis. *Family Development.* New York: Lippincott, 1962.

Ellis, Albert. "Group Marriage: A Possible Alternative?" In *The Family in Search of a Future.* Edited by Herbert Otto. New York: Appleton-Century-Crofts, 1970.

Gerber, Jean Merill. *Stop Here, My Friend.* Boston: Houghton Mifflin, 1965.

Hoffman, Adeline M. *The Daily Needs and Interests of Older People.* Springfield, Illinois: Charles C. Thomas, 1970.

Jackson, Jacquelyne J. "Social Gerontology and the Negro: A Review." *Gerontologist* 7 (1967): 168-73.

Kassel, Victor. "Polygyny after Sixty." *Geriatrics* 21 (1966). Reprinted in *The Family in Search of a Future.* Edited by Herbert Otto. New York: Appleton-Century-Crofts, 1970.

Klapper, Zelda S. "The Impact of the Women's Liberation Movement on Child Development Books." *American Journal of Orthopsychiatry* 41 (1971): 725-32.

Komarovsky, Mirra. *Blue-Collar Marriage.* New York: Random House, 1964.

Lessing, Doris. "To Room Nineteen." In *A Man and Two Women.* New York: Simon and Schuster, 1963.

Masters, William M., and Johnson, Virginia E. *Human Sexual Response*. Boston: Little, Brown, 1966.

McKain, Walter C. *Retirement Marriage*. Storrs, Connecticut: Storrs Agricultural Experiment Station, University of Connecticut, 1969.

National Urban League. *Double Jeopardy—The Older Negro in America Today*. Washington, D.C.: National Urban League, 1964.

Neugarten, Bernice L., ed. *Middle Age and Aging*. Chicago: University of Chicago Press, 1968.

Otto, Herbert A. "Communes: The Alternative Life-Style." *Saturday Review*, 24 April 1971, pp. 16-21.

_____, ed. *The Family in Search of a Future*. New York: Appleton-Century-Crofts, 1970.

Peterson, James A. *Married Love in the Middle Years*. New York: Association Press, 1968.

Pineo, Peter C. "Disenchantment in the Later Years of Marriage." *Marriage and Family Living* 23 (1961): 3-11.

Reiss, Ira L. *The Family System in America*. New York: Holt, Rinehart, and Winston, 1971.

Riley, Matilda White, and Foner, Anne. *Aging and Society. Volume 1: An Inventory of Research Findings*. New York: Russell Sage, 1968.

Rimmer, Robert H. *Proposition 31*. New York: New American Library, 1968.

Rodgers, Roy M. "Improvement in the Construction and Analysis of Family Life-Cycle Categories." Ph.D. dissertation, Department of Sociology, Western Michigan University, 1962.

Rodman, Hyman. *Teaching about Families*. Cambridge, Massachusetts: Howard A. Doyle, 1970.

Rollins, Boyd C., and Feldman, Harold. "Marital Satisfaction over the Family Life Cycle." *Journal of Marriage and the Family* 32 [1970]: 20-27.

"Roundtable: Sex and the Menopause." *Medical Aspects of Human Sexuality*. November 1970, pp. 64-87.

Rubin, Isadore. *Sexual Life after Sixty*. New York: New American Library, 1965.

Shanas, Ethel, et al. *Old People in Three Industrial Societies*. New York: Atherton, 1968.

Skolnick, Arlene S., and Skolnick, Jerome H., eds. *Family in Transition*. Boston: Little, Brown, 1971.

Somerville, Rose M. "Death Education as Part of Family Life Education: Using Imaginative Literature for Insights into Family Crises." *The Family Coordinator* 20 (1971b): 209-224.

_____. *Family Insights through the Short Story.* New York: Teachers College Press, 1964.

_____. "Family Life and Sex Education in the Turbulent Sixties." *Journal of Marriage and the Family* 33 (1971a): 11-35.

Spark, Muriel. *Memento Mori.* New York: Lippincott, 1959.

Stegner, Wallace. *All the Little Live Things.* New York: Viking, 1969.

Stinnett, Nick, et al. "Marital Need Satisfaction of Older Husbands and Wives." *Journal of Marriage and the Family* 32 (1970): 428-34.

Streib, Gordon F. "Intergenerational Relations: Perspectives of the Two Generations on the Older Parent." *Journal of Marriage and the Family* 27 (1965): 469-70.

Sussman, Marvin B. "The Experimental Creation of Family Environments: Typology of Family Structures." Paper presented at the Groves Conference on Marriage and the Family, San Juan, Puerto Rico, 1971.

_____. "Relationships of Adult Children with their Parents in the United States." In *Social Structure and the Family: Generational Relations.* Edited by Ethel Shana and Gordon Streib. Englewood Cliffs, New Jersey: Prentice-Hall, 1965.

Sweetser, Dorrian Apple. "The Effect of Industrialization on Intergenerational Solidarity." *Rural Sociology* 31 (1966): 156-70.

Townsend, Peter. *The Family Life of Old People.* Glencoe, Illinois: The Free Press, 1957.

Troll, Lillian E. "The Family of Later Life: A Decade Review." In *A Decade of Family Research and Action.* Edited by Carlfred Broderick. Minneapolis, Minnesota: National Council on Family Relations, 1971.

United States Department of Health, Education, and Welfare. *Working with Older People: A Guide to Practice. Volume 2, Biological, Psychological, and Sociolgical Aspects of Aging.* Washington, D.C.: USGPO, 1970.

Updike, John. *Of the Farm.* Greenwich, Connecticut: Fawcett, 1967.

Wiseman, Jacqueline P. *People as Partners: Individual and Family Relationships in Today's World.* San Francisco: Canfield (Harper and Row), 1971.

20   Extended Families

Social Enforcement of Behavior toward Elders in an Appalachian Mountain Settlement*

John Lozier and Ronald Althouse

Successful aging rests upon the capacity and opportunity for individuals to fit into the social framework of their own societies in a way that will insure security and influence. (Simmons)

The image of a picture puzzle appears in much that has been said about the individual and society. Applied to the case of aging individuals, a successful "fit" for the individual seems to depend upon his being of the "proper shape" for the space available in the "social framework." This analogy facilitates the insight that the degree of fit is as dependent upon the shape of the social framework as upon the shape of the individual.

*This work originally appeared in The Gerontologist 14 (February 1974): 69-80. Research was made possible by grants from the Faculty Senate, West Virginia University. The data used here all come from fieldwork by R.A. between 1968 and the present. We gratefully acknowledge the helpful criticism of H. Russell Bernard and John Griffin, and the support and encouragement of Don Martindale, Robert Maxwell, and Pertti J. Pelto and Harry Schwarzweller.

The analysis presented here arises from our study of a number of case histories of aging individuals, all given pseudonyms, in a community we call Laurel Creek. Although based in the examination of individual careers, this analysis is not psychological but "societal," concerned with "how . . . society organizes and behaves with reference to its older people" (Tibbitts).

In general, we propose that the answer to Tibbitts's question is to be found in examination of elder-junior relationships, as they are constructed through interactions over time in a social setting. Our strategy for approaching an answer in these terms is to make a series of observations of how specific sets of individuals (juniors) "organize and behave" toward specific older persons (elders). This analysis leads to the conclusion that social environment is protective of elders to the extent that there are public assessments of the behavior of juniors toward elders, and to the extent that such behavior is enforced by social sanctions.

We attribute to Simmons the credit for observing that success in old age may be based on a continuing capacity on the part of an elder to influence his juniors through direct manipulation of resources such as labor, knowledge, skill, talent, property rights, and so forth. Pursuing this idea, Maxwell and Silverman have used a cross-cultural approach to demonstrate a relationship between the esteem granted elders and the degree of control of useful information by elders. These authors, along with Simmons, have treated whole cultures as data cases, but it seems reasonable to hypothesize that control of useful information would also be related to the esteem granted different elders within a particular society.

An objection to the view that continuing control of resources is the principal determinant of treatment accorded an elder is the implication that an individual who loses control of resources has no other form of protection.* As Maxwell and Silverman acknowledge, observations of care and respect for decrepit and infirm elders violates the generalization that such attentions result from control of useful information. Their

*We find Gamson's discussion of potential and fluid resources relevant for understanding how control may be achieved.

account is that such an elder may control information that is useful "in the *expressive* sense" (italics original), and Maxwell and Silverman name family anecdotes, kinship information, and other information that "lends historical depth to the family and enhances its survival as a unit."

In our view, the concept of usefulness should not be limited to the conventional contrast implicit in the choice of "instrumental" over "expressive" categories of behavior. An object such as a vase may be useful for keeping flowers, but keeping flowers is useful in other ways; quite literally it may be "instrumental" for "expressing" claims for social status or personal style. Just as clearly, an elder may be kept and cared for because the display of behavior toward him has consequences deemed relevant by juniors.

We are more content to regard behavior as "meaningful" or "significant," and to refer to the "consequences" that flow from behavior, regardless of motive or intent. For us, the capacity of an elder to lend historical depth to the family and to enhance its survival may flow not from the elder's power to influence the environment of the collectivity, but rather from the elder's significance to the collectivity as a socially specified object of the mutual attention of the offspring.*

Our proposal is offered as an equivalent, not an alternative, rephrasing of the previous statement by Simmons. We suggest that *successful aging is based on the continuing existence of a social system in which behavior toward elders has social significance and social consequences for juniors.*

The requirement for continuing existence of the social system arises from our assumption that an individual's place in society is determined by a series of interactions over time. In such a system, the behavior of juniors toward elders is sanctioned by society to the extent that persons outside the particular elder-junior relationship (1) observe, interpret, and assess the behavior of juniors toward elders, and (2) act

---

*Concepts of utility, meaning, and significance are the stock in trade of philosophers. We see in Austin a congenial philosophical statement of related matters. In anthropology, the classic debate between Malinowski and Radcliffe-Brown, nicely resolved by Homans, can be seen as turning on the issue of utility versus meaning. We can decline polemic, but our analysis is more closely akin to that of Radcliffe-Brown.

differentially toward juniors depending upon the nature of the public assessment. The former specification identifies social significance, the latter, consequences or sanctions.

Generally, an individual, elder or otherwise, whether helpful, burdensome, or merely useless, may be an object that is attributed significance by others, and this significance can lead to care and attention. It is not necessary to resort to the broad brush of Veblen to argue for the "usefulness of uselessness." In our analysis, it is axiomatic that public assessments of the reliability or creditability of specific persons are based on observations of their performance in specific socially recognized contractual obligations, formal or informal. One such socially recognized contractual relationship is between an elder and a set of juniors. The typical case would involve the socially recognized obligation on the part of offspring to provide security for their elder parents, seen as a reciprocation of parental care received in childhood.

The public behavior of an individual toward his elders becomes evidence that is processed in gossip and other communications to become a part of a "work-up" or public assessment of the behavior of the individual.* This assessment or personal reputation has consequences for an individual when it influences the decisions of others regarding association with him.

To the extent that public assessments of the behavior of juniors lead to consequences for the juniors, it is reasonable to speak of the elder as holding socially enforced claims, privileges, or credit. These terms refer to "resources" that may supply the basis for influence or security. Referring to the accumulation of resources, Simmons writes that,

> property rights have been perhaps the most flexible, impersonal, and effective means of influencing others with a minimum of physical effort. When such rights are firmly fixed in a society, they generally enable the long-lived to

---

*The idea of a public assessment is found extensively in the work of Goffman, and a number of other writers, most influential here being Goodenough's chapter entitled, "Identity and Personal Worth."

accumulate and store up credits against the harder days ahead. With a backlog of such claims, he is in a position to share in affairs and influence others. . . . It is almost a certainty that, wherever these rights are well developed in society, there is a marked difference between growing old with and without property.

[. . .]

Perhaps the simplest and most universal form of property rights shared by the aged has been the exchange of gifts and the receipt of fees for services rendered or in the fulfillment of obligations made. . . .

What Simmons says of property rights we hold to apply also to our concept of social credits or claims. Society enforces the prerogatives of aged property holders through the same process that protects any other individual, since a violation of the legal rights would be a threatening precedent to all. We suggest that the credits and rights of elders that are attributed to them as a result of the public assessment of a lifetime's performance are also enforced for elders as for others. Just as violation of property may lead to legal sanctions, violations of reciprocity in recognized relationships lead to social sanctions, through gossip and the formulation of a negative public assessment, and ultimately through reduction or withdrawal of reciprocity.

Following this reasoning, the means by which an individual maintains influence and security as he grows older is through the conservation of a positive credit balance in socially recognized claims against others. This generalization applies literally to the accumulation and conservation of a positive credit balance in the form of "money in the bank," since money is recognized stored value par excellence. Of course, when "money in the bank" can be used analogically to describe social circumstances like "having trustworthy friends," we can see how appropriate it may be to speak of investing in social exchanges with kin, associates, and friends

who may be relied upon to return the value invested in them.*
We presume that trust is always more than merely a
sentiment.

In what follows, we sketch the social process as it occurs
in a social system that extends out from a center at "Laurel
Creek," West Virginia. The information contained in the
studies of old persons in Laurel Creek is from participant
observation, informants' generalizations, as well as
interviews.

Laurel Creek

Laurel Creek, a community of some 800 inhabitants in 183
households, is located near the Kentucky border in southern
West Virginia. The locality has been continuously occupied
since the earliest Meadowses and Tanners settled there on
land granted them for service in the Revolutionary War. As
other settlers continued to arrive throughout the nineteenth
century, subsistence was based in agriculture, with a modest
amount of trade in corn to markets in the Ohio area. With full
settlement of the hollow, there developed five distinct
neighborhoods, associated with the secondary creeks, each
with its principal families and predominant specialties—
Tanners were carpenters, Meadowses were millers, Spriggs
were smiths, and so forth. The five neighborhoods, historically
associated with separate churches and elementary schools,
are still recognized today, bound together now as then through
common relationship to the "association field" at the main
forks of Laurel, a central location on which social, religious,
economic, and other joint activities occurred in early times
and on which the consolidated school now stands.

From early times, the organization of joint economic
enterprises was an important activity for individuals who took
responsibility for collectivities within the settlement. In
production and marketing, first of farm produce, later of
timber and than coal, a local family head would arrange to

*The acknowledgments for ideas regarding politics and ex-
change are impossible to tease out in detail. Our most proximate
inspiration has been from Bailey, Salisbury, and Whitten in political
anthropology, and from Blau in political sociology.

pool capital and labor and would negotiate on behalf of several family groups or a bloc of the community with middlemen and buyers in outside markets. Such communal transactions declined toward the end of the nineteenth century as land speculation and external influence through railroad development disturbed the stability of reciprocities built in earlier times.

Some mining for coal began in the last decade of the nineteenth century, but the coal boom did not really get under way until the 1920s. With development of large production mines in the 1940s, the numerous small operations, of which Laurel Creek had several, became obsolete, and ceased to operate during the recession of the 1950s. While work in mining has been an important element in the economy of Laurel Creek since the turn of the century, few men have experienced a stable lifelong career in mining, while virtually every male of mature age has spent some part of his work life in mining. Except for the Depression period, farming has grown steadily less significant as a major activity, but has continued as a supplement to other income and a refuge in "hard times."

Like other settlements in the counties of this region, Laurel Creek has contributed heavily to the stream of migrants who make their way to the cities, armed with information and connections through the networks of prior migrants, as a consummation of a ritual "coming of age" in which they fix their sights on "success" outside the protective closure of local groups. As a result of heavy out-migration in the early adult years, the demographic profile of Laurel Creek shows a disproportionately high frequency of children and elderly people. Some 20 to 25 percent of the household heads are permanently disabled or receive Social Security, while at least 40 percent of the remaining family heads receive assistance from one of several welfare programs in the county. The remaining families realize economic stability through some mix of employment and business enterprise, combining public employment (postmen, state and county road crews, teachers, wardens, and the like), employment with private enterprises (ranging from occasional contract work to regular work in mining, timbering, sawmill, and so forth), and direct business enterprises (from short-term labor contracting to diversified business including wholesale, retail, real estate, and other forms).

There is a persistent fiction of strong and reliable family links, and deep confidence in traditional ways in Laurel Creek. The legendary patriarchs of past times are identified as models of the successful career. It is generally asserted that young people would prefer to remain at home if opportunities were available to them.

The strength of family, kin, and community ties may be accepted as a statement of the cultural ideal, but we caution against accepting it as a representation of reality. The complex reality is that individuals and family groups vary widely in actual and potential access to resources, organizational strength, range of options, and so forth. The variable circumstances that may apply to individuals make it inaccurate to speak of "typical" persons, young adult, mature, elder, or any other category. Given the lack of economic opportunity locally, the typical young adult weighs migration against remaining at home and normally chooses to migrate. But any individual decision is based on an assessment of concrete alternatives that vary widely.

Altogether, it appears that many migrants might not return even if jobs were to be available, because they have come to value some of the social and cultural features of the migrant situation. With conditions as they are now, young men in Laurel Creek compete with any mature male for regular employment; the limited skills and aptitudes required convey no great advantage or disadvantage for seniority or for competence. Rather, because success in maintaining employment depends to a large extent on maintaining patron-client or other exchange relationships, the opportunities available to youngsters are highly variable. A certain degree of patronage toward the young is publicly approved, in the interest of keeping some of the young at home; but from the perspective of youth it always appears that secure relationships are held by more senior persons.

In this context, a successful mature career in Laurel Creek may involve the preparation of a social environment in which one's own offspring may be introduced as early as possible into viable exchange relationships. Indeed, our view is that the capacity of mature adults to facilitate the entry of younger persons into advantageous associations with others is a crucial element in the establishment of subsequent junior-elder obligations.

Some Elders in Laurel Creek

To order the case studies, we have first divided them by *locus of career*. Our first six cases represent careers that have been principally located in Laurel Creek throughout their lifetimes. Two further cases deal with individuals whose careers were mainly outside the Laurel Creek settlement, but who have returned to their childhood homes to live out their elder years. Peculiar features of these later cases have led us to dub them *cash-ins*. Of the 53 households classified as old (over 60), 14, or about 25 percent, fall in the cash-in category.

Our second ordering principle is *initial resources*. "Martin Tanner," "Keither McCloud," and "John Meadows" all began life with substantial social and economic resources, while "Moses Tanner," "Denzil Ball," and "Eugene Wiley" each began with modest resources; these are the case studies of careers located in Laurel Creek. Of the two cash-ins, "Fred Madden" began with substantial resources, while "Clyde Stanton" began with modest resources, but each pursued a career that took him outside the local system and ultimately returned him to Laurel Creek.

The idealized conception of the role of the elder male is represented by the example of "Old Preacher Martin" Tanner, who died in 1953, a man remembered in legendary terms as one with boundless energy and strength, whose efforts in religious, social, economic, and political activities profoundly influenced the social environment of others. But "Old Martin" is a legend, and our principal interest here is the social environment of aged individuals in the early 1970s, and the place of those individuals in the social environment of others.

Careers Based on Substantial Initial Resources

Martin Tanner

"Old Preacher Martin" Tanner had a son who bears the same name, but unlike his father, Martin Tanner at age seventy is an insignificant individual. He is viewed by the community as a lazy fellow, but not a "no-count" nor even "down-and-out,"* because he maintained himself throughout his life at a respectable level, first as a dependent of his father, and subsequently through the gradual liquidation of his share of the common inheritance. In his old age, Martin Tanner lives with his wife in the old Tanner home, surrounded by neighbors who have built on parcels of land purchased from him. From older mature neighbors, or from their offspring, Martin and his wife obtain occasional services such as transportation and help about the house, but even these services are secured principally through the enduring legacy of his father, for Old Martin continues to inspire the respect of Martin's neighbors. Services to Martin help to keep the neighborhood in respectable order, and link Martin with the respectability of the family name.

Keither McCloud

The successor to Preacher Martin was Keither McCloud, whose family roots in Laurel Creek are as shallow as Martin Tanner's are deep. Keither McCloud, aged sixty-seven in 1970, came to Laurel Creek as a young man to teach in the local school and subsequently married Sarah Sage, daughter of a main family group in Laurel Creek. From rather prominent family background in the county, McCloud had been sent to college where he obtained a degree even though only normal school was required, and he recalls playing tennis in college with a man who was to become a U.S. Senator from West Virginia.

In early life, McCloud had worked in the mines, but this was for occasional income and not a major career choice. After his marriage, he took over a small store that had been built by his father-in-law, and constructed a major business with gas station, garage, and apartments. In the meantime, he continued to teach and became principal of the elementary school.

McCloud achieved a phenomenal degree of trust with people of the area and he trusted them as well. His son points

*"No-count" and "down-and-out" are cultural labels; the former may be glossed as "not respectable," while the latter is "respectable but ineffectual or out of luck."

out that McCloud lost $70,000 in bad debts with the heavy out-migration of the 1950s, and the fact that he was able to absorb such losses without being ruined is perhaps evidence of the scale of McCloud's financial success.

When McCloud was forty years old, he experienced conversion to the faith and a call to preach; by the following spring he had been baptized, and in less than a year he was working as associate pastor with Old Preacher Martin Tanner, who was the Freewill Baptist pastor. McCloud came to be considered among the best preachers of the area and is credited with organizing many revivals and the construction of three churches. He was designated Revival Preacher for the local Freewill Association and was so successful in his religious associations that he was able to bring the statewide conference of Freewill Baptist to Laurel Creek in the middle 1960s. By this time, the mantle of authority had been smoothly and clearly passed from Old Preacher Martin to Keither McCloud.

McCloud always resisted opportunities to assume political office but remained very influential as an intermediary patron throughout the district. He could organize support or opposition for political candidates, and because of his relationship to religion he was often involved in the mediation of disputes and conflicts in the settlement. People say that when McCloud took interest in a man's plight, "it didn't have to go to law," because Keither could take care of it, and he was regarded as one who would give fair and impartial judgment.

Much of the activity that took place in McCloud's store consisted of Keither's bringing together the needs of people and the services of others he could count on. Individuals with emergency needs could come to McCloud for help, but the most important element of his position was his capacity to be patron or sponsor for individuals who had earned his favorable opinion. The support of Keither McCloud, who could supply information, recommendations, and established channels of communication and entry, could be crucial to an individual's ability to obtain and maintain employment and for the arrangement of private, public, or governmental affairs.

Sarah Sage McCloud is the most notable of the "real ladies" of Laurel Creek and has been influential through personal dealings, in the store, and in church activities. Keither and Sarah had eight children, who received a considerable amount of college education. Except for one daughter, the children have migrated; the daughter who remains is unmarried and living at home, where her care of the house frees the parents for community activity. In her own right, this daughter has contributed notably through participation in the Head-Start program.

The eldest son, Keither Junior, was the only child to complete college, and Junior recently received his doctorate in education. Although his professional career took him out of the area, Junior has increasingly sought to return to the state in recent years. He has been offered a county superintendency of schools, but he feels that with his qualifications he can achieve a position at the state level. Junior McCloud has already invested in land in communities surrounding Laurel Creek and of course will share in the common inheritance of the McCloud estate on Laurel Creek. Although not yet of middle age, Junior McCloud already anticipates returning to the area in his retirement, as a gentleman, where he feels comfortable and where he has retained masterful social relations even though residing out-of-state.

Keither Senior supported his eldest son's career development and in the last years prior to his death by cancer, recognized Junior as the one responsible for maintaining the family as a unit.

Keither McCloud Senior died in 1972. More than 3,000 people attended the viewing of the body, and people estimate that there were more than 1,000 people at the graveside. Letters and telegrams came from clergy and school associates through to the state and beyond. And the family was pleased to see a full column in the county newspaper given over to a discussion of his achievements and his successes and his life work in the county and in his religiouis activities.

In referring to Martin Tanner as an "insignificant" person, we mean to suggest that behavior toward him has few consequences for juniors, because there are few, if any, persons for whom neglect of Martin Tanner would result in a negative public assessment. Martin is one of the old people who may be ignored with impunity; attention toward him is optional.

Keither McCloud is a significant individual in the community in that behavior toward him could have consequences for a great many persons and a disrespect or neglect of McCloud could have negative effects on the public assessment of almost everyone. Of course, it is obvious that as McCloud continued to function actively until his death, he was capable in many ways of enforcing the behavior of juniors toward him through the direct manipulation of resources and information. We nevertheless feel that a view of the significance of behavior of juniors toward elders lends a dimension to the case of Keither McCloud that is essential. This point is most easily demonstrated by reference to McCloud's son, Keither McCloud Junior.

At the point where Junior McCloud had achieved a capacity to succeed independently of his father through the practice of a professional career, the direct sanctions of his behavior toward his father, either from public assessment or from his father's direct influence, might have been rendered ineffective. But Junior McCloud continued to sustain his father, operating in social networks that kept him prominent and relevant to the people of Laurel Creek, visiting with great frequency and making himself accessible to visits from them. As a result, Junior McCloud has obtained for himself a public assessment that already secures for him the option of returning in retirement or sooner. More immediately, however, it is evident that Junior is managing his relations with Laurel Creek not merely with a view toward returning, but also with a view toward achieving prominence on a different social scale, through professional performance on the state level.

In summary, Junior McCloud played out the role of junior in the elder-junior relationship with Keither McCloud, and his performance appears to foreshadow his own full assumption of elder status at the appropriate time. Parenthetically, it is noteworthy that Martin Tanner, although like Keither Junior the namesake of his famous father, never became known as Junior Tanner. In Laurel Creek, the use of Junior in such cases tends to imply that the individual so named is a fully qualified successor to the senior, a condition that clearly did not apply to Martin Tanner. The fact that Keither McCloud Junior is called *Junior* McCloud constitutes authentic evidence of the public assessment of his performance.

John Meadows

Like Martin Tanner, John Meadows is the principal contemporary descendant of the earliest settlers. At seventy-six, Meadows lives with his wife in a modest but well-kept home on the original homestead. John's grandfather and father were both farmers and preachers and they operated a grain mill that was established even earlier.

John's father, in addition to farming, organized timbering operations in the early twentieth century, and his prominence in the community was reflected in leadership participation in the so-called regulators, a hooded constabulary enforcing the morals of the community. In various ways, John Meadows's father was politically important in the community and beyond, and John has maintained these connections throughout his lifetime.

In his young adulthood, Meadows worked as a foreman with a major coal company, a position that made possible the sustained employment of his three brothers in coal mining. He married Virgie Sprigg, a schoolteacher who was the daughter of a prominent businessman and timber-mill operator in a neighboring settlement.

In his adult life, he led the Meadows Gospel Singers, which was widely known through their performances on radio. Following the pattern of father and grandfather, John Meadows became a preacher, and in recent years, along with Keither McCloud, was the only other ordained preacher in the community.

John and Virgie had four children. Like the McCloud children, these were considered well off, and had various advantages, including the opportunity for college. The two eldest, both daughters, completed college and migrated with their husbands to urban situations.

John's sons were regarded as major hell-raisers in their adolescence. John was able to protect them from the consequences of their behavior and provided much support for them to develop careers via college education. Neither stayed in college; Philip, the eldest, left for Columbus to work in a mattress factory, after marrying a girl from a neighboring community in Kentucky; and within a couple of years, Bill, the younger, joined Philip.

With the passage of time, pressure on the sons to return to Laurel Creek began to build, especially after John retired from the mines and discontinued regular preaching. Over and over again, he tried to induce the sons, particularly Philip, with offers of housing and other opportunities. Both sons remained aloof from their father's appeal, until Philip lost his job in 1964. At this point, John offered to find Philip a job at home, and Philip returned. He moved with his wife and family into a house directly across from John and Virgie, next door to some other rental property John owned. John arranged for Philip to go on welfare for several months and went about arranging with the county assessor and the party chairman to get Philip enrolled in a course to train fire wardens. Within a year after his return, Philip was a deputy fire warden in the county.

Philip was content with his work and the community environment, but pressures mounted as demands from his parents interfered with the serenity of his own household. Philip's wife Sarah says that "within a month or two there was no privacy at all, no front door on the house." John insisted on services from Philip at any time, claiming privileges in the elder-junior relationship, even when Philip had other plans. Philip's relationship was seen by the community as one of considerable dependency, and a public assessment began to emerge, regarding Philip as a relatively weak individual who was being used by his father. The public assessment of Philip complements that of John, whose demands were viewed as excessive, and who came to be described as a "contentious old son-of-a-bitch."

The relationship between Sarah and her mother-in-law also became very uncomfortable, and Sarah began to withdraw, as she put it, to "hide out as much as possible." This conflict built to the point that after two years, Sarah began to suffer "crying fits," and a near nervous breakdown, culminating in hospitalization and a hysterectomy.*

*Hysterectomy is not infrequent in this region and is regarded as a treatment for emotional distress.

Philip reports that he might have stayed but for the growing realization that he was being "used and abused" by his father. We view this report as an indication of Philip's awareness of the public assessment of his behavior toward his father, which in this case was seen as dependent and supportive to an extent unrequired by the circumstances. Sarah urged departure from Laurel Creek for the sake of the education of their daughters, and this became a demand when Sarah found on a trip to Huntington that she could find employment herself. Through friends and associates, Philip also found work in Huntington, and thus after seven years in Laurel Creek, the family left again. Subsequent visits became less frequent and this situation persisted in 1970.

Some of the reasons for the failure of John's efforts to keep Philip at home can be seen in the personal styles of the various parties involved, but we do not find in such an approach an adequate societal analysis. We regard John's circumstances as representing a deteriorating power position within Laurel Creek. Having retired from preaching and from the mines, he was already withdrawing from areas in which sponsorship could be maintained; although his word as a retired foreman was often good, he was not on the spot to make the kind of direct negotiations that foremen and bosses are frequently able to carry out. At about this time, his wife's retirement from teaching terminated the assumption that she had some direct influence in the school.

But as important as any decline in his own resources was a sharp increase, in the middle 1960s, of resources in the community from federal welfare and development programs, which effected an inflation rendering his own resources less valuable in exchange. Recognizing these new programs as detrimental to his own relative strength, he found himself in hostile opposition on more than one occasion. He opposed the use of church property for the Head-Start program and justified his position moralistically, although people generally felt that he "just didn't hold to the program." Direct and overt attacks on the deputy sheriff, insinuating that the office was being used for family gain, and other hostile and venomous attacks that occurred even within the church, sustained the public assessment.

In spite of his unpropitious behavior, John Meadows had enough social credit to maintain himself, as well as to place Philip in employment. Beyond this, however, he could not transfer credit to Philip, nor could he assist Philip to achieve a position where he could develop a wider network of exchanges and patronage through his own efforts. Here, Philip's behavior could have made a difference; using his father's limited credit, he might have achieved a career that would be successful within the local system. But Philip had options, and weighed against the above was the possibility of an independent career as a migrant. This is the option he took, and he is assessed in the community now as one who did well and achieved a creditable success.

John Meadows is seen today by the community as a withdrawn old man, of slight significance in the dealings and plans of others in the settlement. It is important to note, however, that his irascibility might have been considered acceptable if he had continued to hold viable resources for exchange. As it was, he held only credit for past exchanges, and in calling up such credit he was expected to assume an elder role that would not make life unduly hard on his juniors. Failure to fulfill this expectation left John's security in old age unenforced by social sanctions.

The situation remains unresolved, however. The community fiction of family solidarity is sorely damaged by the spectacle of an individual approaching death in isolation from family, and it is likely that the community would not continue to tolerate Philip's neglect if John's condition is assessed as terminal. Should John die under such circumstances, Philip's social credit would be liquidated, and he would then have no basis for returning to Laurel Creek, other than the formal legal basis for inheritance. Such a situation would likely lead to liquidation of the estate, and the timbering of the virgin forest that John has been preoccupied with saving. This would be John's ultimate tragedy, and for the community, a lesson in the kinds of outcomes that can be expected to result from the interaction of circumstances, behaviors, and strategies like those that were manifest in this case.

Careers Based on Modern Initial Resources

Moses Tanner

Moses Tanner, aged seventy-five, is a nephew of Old Preacher Martin. The Tanner name conveys respectability, but Moses's father was regarded as an irresponsible individual, incommensurable with his uncle. In 1970, Moses Tanner lives with his wife on a portion of the old homestead, surrounded by the houses of five of his six sons. Here, relatively isolated from the rest of the community, Moses enjoys the care and attention of his own children who have worked in close association with their father throughout their careers.

This situation arose from Moses's steady and reliable performance first working at timber contracts and then as a labor contractor for timbering. He took his sons into a labor group as they matured, and each developed his own career through the various ramifications of the timber industry, built up from employment with the saw mill to which timber was delivered. The family group was able to sustain individuals through difficult times and to facilitate the exploitation of opportunities available to individuals; for example, one of the younger sons left for four months to obtain training as a timber grader. This skill, like the key skills each brother has attempted to acquire, further secures the family's relationship with the local mill operator.

The Moses Tanners do not participate much in the community, and their religious association is with a small sectarian group that supplies a more personal experience for them. All of the sons married wives from outside the settlement, and the public view is that the Tanner family members are seen mostly in transit through the community to job and shopping outside.

Recently, the eldest son has come to take a major role in organizing the activities of the family, but the group is collective and not authoritarian. Moses regards his sons as good, hard-working, reliable, cooperative, skillful; he finds in his situation a satisfying personal version of the patriarchial role that he enjoys describing for the really great old-timers of the past.

Moses Tanner achieved what is viewed locally as a successful career to old age, at a scale that is modest but impressive. However, the occupational specialization that formed a key element in the family strategy probably cannot supply the basis for a continuation of the collective strategy in the generation of the grandchildren. It is expected that these grandchildren will leave like most others, working out their own fates with whatever help they can achieve by negotiating with others. In those negotiations, they are greatly assisted by the favorable public assessment that has been a result of the display of reliability and industry presented by Moses and his sons. In other words, the sons of Moses Tanner have qualified themselves and have qualified their own children as worthy recipients of the kind of sponsorship that might be arranged by persons such as Keither McCloud. The successful organization of the family group around old man Moses and his sons increases the possibility of social mobility in the generation of the grandchildren.

Denzil Ball

Denzil Ball was born in "Doublelick Creek," a small neighborhood physically and socially isolated from the rest of Laurel Creek, and labeled with the pejorative term *no-count*, implying an absence of redeeming social qualities. But Denzil himself has become exempt from the label.

Denzil moved from Doublelick to main Laurel Creek as a young man, and married Jenetty Sage, a girl from a secondary line of one of the most respected families. He earned a favorable reputation in the community through reliable performance as a coal miner.

We omit much important detail regarding Denzil Ball because it constitutes a story in itself, but the relevant essence here is that Denzil became a major organizer of contract labor for occasional and part-time work, initially to supply employment for himself and his sons during the coal recession of the 1950s and later for the benefit of many others. This temporary and occasional work was mainly sought by younger men not yet in a position to arrange steady work, and Denzil's role was publicly viewed as a helping one; his constituency was the set of young folks, perhaps with a new baby or one on the way, who were deserving of a break.

The result of a number of years in such activity is that Denzil came to help a great many individuals, each to a relatively modest but symbolically very significant degree. By the nature of the work, he was freed of the obligation of maintaining individuals in employment; probably consistent resort to employment from Denzil would have had negative consequences for the public assessment both of Denzil, because he would be cutting the publicly justified support for young people in need, and for the one employed, because he would achieve a negative public assessment as one who could not arrange steady work.

Ball is seen as a politically independent individual, whose organizational capacities are not absorbed by any political faction. He remains in viable exchange relationships with his own son and with a son-in-law who are in opposing political camps and even provides resources to each without compromising his independence. The details of how this is accomplished involve a discussion of marriage alliances and of the outcome in which no set of kin-defined juniors relies predominantly or exclusively on resources supplied by Denzil. For present purposes, the result is that Denzil has helped many juniors who are not his kin and has earned a general kind of community credit.

It is not surprising that Denzil Ball presents himself and is viewed as a Christian person in his social role. He is the kind of individual for whom the religious form of reference and address "Brother" is a routine and standard usage. Brother Ball is a principal leader and lay minister in a small offshoot of the Church of God in the area. This church group split from the main church recently as the latter has become identified with a more status-conscious and upwardly mobile pattern of behavior; thus Ball's religious affiliation is a manifestation of an egalitarian image.

Another aspect of Ball's helping role as an elder is his performance as a mediator in family disputes, principally between adolescents and their parents. Since younger people have been extensively associated with him through his labor organizing, he is in a crucial position to enforce settlement of such conflicts. Moreover, at any given time, one is likely to find unrelated adolescents, either male or female, living temporarily with Denzil and Jenetty and the two grandchildren who reside with them. The Balls have the complete trust of the community, and people observe of a youngster who takes refuge with Brother Denzil, "at least he is learning to work."

In local terms, the career of Denzil Ball is a principal example of achieved respectability and success. His case provides a convenient basis for denying that the poverty of Doublelickers and others is due to discrimination. At the same time, his structural association with youth, even into his elder years, affords the maximum opportunity for such a message to be conveyed to the young.

Eugene Wiley

The final example of an individual whose career, such as it is, is located in Laurel Creek, is Eugene Wiley, who at age seventy-one lives with his wife in a small and decrepit shack situated on property he supposedly leases for $10 a year. His subsistence has always been dependent upon various welfare programs. The shacks of two of his sons are on the same plot and the community regards all as "no-counts." A third son is living in Doublelick Creek, where Eugene was born; two other children have migrated, but there is no public knowledge of their whereabouts or conditions, because there is no public interest in them. The Wiley family is outside any of the family networks through which information about children travels, through which most people can learn of the condition of all the community offspring whoever they may be.

The Wiley household illustrates the most despised category of people in the community, people who are publicly assessed as not only lazy and untrustworthy but also morally corrupt. It is said that they and others like them remain on welfare only because they deliver their votes to the political machine and thus they take blame for the corruption of the political process. The Wiley household is dependent upon the lowest form of patronage, public patronage through formal administrative institutions.

It is obvious that Eugene Wiley is isolated from work or social arrangements in the community. Neither he nor his wife attend church. Since his wife has become "sickly," she is occasionally visited by church members who view such visits as their charitable Christian duty; this behavior becomes significant more as a public claim for virtue before the rest of the community than as a transaction with the old woman herself.

Wiley's sons are in their late thirties and early forties now, and a similar career pattern is emerging. They are occasionally involved in work, as Eugene has been in the past, but this is only of the most degrading and menial kind. They might be hired, for example, to do yard work, fence posting, roofing, cleaning a chicken coop, or other odd jobs. Such work among respectable members of the settlement would normally be done on a noncash cooperative basis, as an element of routine reciprocities, if it was not done by contract with a businessman. When the Wileys do such work it is for cash, which tends to trivialize the work and to maintain the low status of the worker, for cash payment entails no implication of future reciprocity.

The public assessment of Eugene Wiley has been so well established and long standing that he has long since lost any chance for generating social credit. Of no help to his own sons in development of their own social credit, Eugene expects and receives no particular care or attention from them. The disadvantage suffered by the offspring of individuals socially classified as "no-count" can now be seen to arise not simply from a deficient socialization but also and importantly from the absence of significant opportunities to display behavior that leads to a favorable public assessment. Care and attention for a father who has been publicly assessed as a worthless bum does not reflect credit on the son, but more likely would be viewed as foolish and absurd.

Cash-ins: Cases with Locus of
Career Outside Laurel Creek

About twenty-five percent of the old people (over age sixty) in Laurel Creek have returned there after adult lifetime careers outside the community. As has been implied in the discussion of Keither McCloud Junior, migrant careers do not necessarily require the severing of social connections with

Laurel Creek, but the physical separation makes the maintenance of reciprocities somewhat problematic.*

The situation of one who returns to Laurel Creek after long absence is that his social credit based on reciprocities is relatively weak, even though his economic situation may be relatively sound. Thus he is obliged to exchange cash for services that others might receive as a display of attention by juniors. For the most part, cash-ins are not isolated strangers but are identified with kin networks and join existing family groups; nevertheless, they are obliged to exchange cash for services because there are no juniors specifically obligated to them as individuals.

The difficulties with typification and generalization apply here as before; however, and in lieu of attempting to resolve them at this time, we present two cases of cash-in careers for illustrative purposes.

Fred Madden and Jane Sage Madden

Jane Sage Madden is the older sister of Sarah Sage McCloud, while Fred Madden was born and raised in a neighboring community. Thus the cash-in return to Laurel Creek was Jane's return, and not Fred's. While in other cases discussed, the perspective of the male has been easiest to use, in the case of Fred and Jane Madden a mixed perspective is helpful.

Fred and Jane married in the early 1920s, after Fred became acquainted with the community through working with John R. Tanner of Laurel Creek. The couple immediately migrated, not to an urban situation but to a coal camp in the southern part of the county, along with Jane's younger brother Henry (who also has returned as a cash-in) and a few other Laurel Creek people who moved out with the coal boom of the 1920s.

Fred was fairly successful in mining, although there were periodic layoffs, but in the 1940s, Fred and Jane moved with their four children to Columbus, where Fred found work in construction, as a bricklayer and carpenter.

---

*See Schwarzweller, Brown, and Mangalam, and Althouse and Lozier for more on migration and return migration in the region.

Both in the coal camp and in Columbus, contact with Laurel Creek was maintained not only through return visiting, but also through service as a kind of half-way house for young persons and families from Laurel Creek. Jane, a very resourceful woman, became a key figure in the migrant network, playing a role of sponsoring "aunt" for Laurel Creek youngsters, including the children of Keither McCloud. It was Fred's involvement in construction that brought Ronny McCloud, the youngest of Keither's children, into the plumbing trade. But the home situation managed by Jane, which could accommodate counseling and psychological support as well as stop-over visits, was perhaps more important than specific job referral.

At the time of Fred's retirement, the option of a return to Laurel Creek began to appear attractive, especially to Jane. Their four children had married and settled in suburban Columbus. Fred and Jane, evaluating the options, saw that they could do very well in Laurel Creek, where they were known and respected, and the urban alternative had no great appeal, since they had never ceased to think of themselves as Laurel Creekers.

Initially, Jane was interested in securing some property and attracting her own children to join them on Laurel Creek. This did not appeal to the children, who were well situated in Columbus. In any case, they had grown up in coal camps and did not have the attachment to Laurel Creek that their mother had, even though they had participated extensively as youngsters in the network of activities associated with the community. Jane and Fred remain content to live on the Left Fork of Laurel, in proximity with Jane's brother and her cousin and in close association with Sarah and Keither McCloud.

The Maddens are elderly now and do not move about much. They depend heavily for services on arrangements made by Keither and Sarah McCloud. They had been away from the community for a long time, and although the service they have performed in the migrant network is publicly acknowledged, the beneficiaries of their help are themselves not present, by reason of the very success of that help.

In view of their capacity to help migrants, Fred and Jane were an important resource for Keither McCloud, because he could help others in Laurel Creek by referring them to Fred and Jane. Thus the basis in reciprocity for their security in Laurel Creek was in their exchange relationship with Keither and Sarah. But because the kinds of services elders may need, such as delivery of groceries, minor home repairs and maintenance, and transportation, are not of a sort that Keither and Sarah would directly supply, Fred and Jane obtain such services mostly for cash. The usual pattern would be that Keither would ask a young person to do services for Fred and Jane, and Jane would be sitting there with her pocketbook and would pay immediately.

Especially Jane, but also Fred, got acquainted with many of the older people in the settlement, and find the environment a pleasant one. Their home is one that was built initially by Preacher Martin Tanner, as a rental unit. In this little cluster of 14 houses, 10 are occupied by couples or individuals over 60 years of age. Of these 10, five are "cash-ins." Here in a relatively recent and new neighborhood, other elders are within walking distance. This is a satisfactory environment for the cash-in life-style, although it is quite different from the situation of many elders whose careers have been within Laurel Creek, who continue to live dispersed about the area each in the location that has been his for a lifetime, with kin of three or more generations as neighbors.

Fred and Jane are naive, or provide an appearance of naivete, about the political activities of the area. Economically independent of others, with pension and savings resources, as well as property from common inheritance, they live almost entirely within a small peer group of elders, except for occasional visits they get from their children. Theirs is a respectable place in the settlement, but they are really quite outside the main structure of economic, social, and political services and processes of the community.

Clyde Stanton

Clyde Stanton's father came to Laurel Creek as a timberman and subsequently worked with the railroad as it extended throughout the county. Clyde grew up on Laurel Creek and in his early adult life worked in timber, on WPA, and intermittently with the state road commission. He was known as a hell-raising, gun-toting, hard-drinking, story-telling character from his youth. He and his wife, also raised in Laurel Creek and the daughter of a notorious individual, had four children.

In the 1940s, Clyde and his family moved to Columbus, where he did factory work until his retirement in 1962. During his period in Columbus, they were not isolated entirely from Laurel Creek, which continued to obtain some news regarding their condition. There is no knowledge of the whereabouts or condition of Clyde's two sons today, but the community has followed the notorious career of his sister, Mary, which has also involved his daughter Fanny.

The background is set with Clyde's move from Laurel Creek to Columbus, at about the same time that his sister Mary and her husband, Jim Lewis, did the same. After Jim's death, Mary operated a boarding house for old men, assisted by Clyde's daughter Fanny. The two women were prosecuted and convicted for cashing checks taken from the mail directed to men living at the boarding house. A further important detail is that Fred Lewis, son of Mary and Jim Lewis, married Clyde's daughter Edith, that is, his own first cousin.

When Clyde and his wife returned to Laurel Creek in 1962, they took up residence in a small house situated in the Left Fork cluster where Martin Tanner, Fred and Jane Madden, and others already mentioned reside. He was a familiar person to the community, not only because his early reputation as a colorful individual was dramatic enough to be remembered, but also because his migration to Columbus had not occurred till he was into his thirties. However, he had no social capital and could not call on anyone in the community for services, except through cash payment.

Clyde's need for services was relatively great as he became sicker, for he suffered from cancer and required care at home, as well as regular transportation for treatments. Perhaps because of these needs, which would not be supplied by the community, Clyde set about bringing his daughter Edith and her husband Fred Lewis to Laurel Creek, about a year after his return.

This solved some of Clyde's problems, but created others because Fred Lewis himself was an abrasive person who alienated many persons in Laurel Creek and through association with Clyde probably diminished Clyde's already modest standing. But Fred does supply the transportation that Clyde needs, while Edith can help about the house and garden.

Perhaps the one thing that has been significant for Clyde since his return has been his conversion to faith. About two years after his return he was baptized and became a professed Christian. This is considered an important and proper event, demonstrating that even a man with some notoriety behind him could make things right. Keither McCloud and others are willing to recognize this conversion and to acknowledge him as a part of the community.

At sixty-five, Clyde is functionally an old man, relatively confined to the neighborhood. He may appear at the store or elsewhere and he may even repeat tales of bravado and of notoriety about his own early life, in a modest way trading in entertainment that such tales can provide to others. But he still must spend cash and pay for everything he gets from others, to maintain their services and their interest, and to compensate for the social disadvantages of his notorious past and the unfavorable assessment of his son-in-law Fred Lewis.

Clyde's is a case very different from that of Fred and Jane Madden. In both cases, however, the time of retirement after a work career with a degree of success opened up options, to either maintain themselves outside Laurel Creek where their careers had been located, or to return to Laurel Creek to "cash-in." In both cases, we think that the homeward move was selected because the economic resources of these old people would go farther in Laurel Creek than they would in an urban setting. The existence of residual ties to the area make a cash-in strategy easier to play, but do not appreciably alter the fact that the individuals are not integral to the local social system. There are examples in Laurel Creek of persons existing in the cash-in style who never lived in Laurel Creek, who simply purchased property there as it became available. Normally such individuals would have some connections with the general region, but it would not be impossible for strangers to enter a place like Laurel Creek and to arrange a satisfactory cash-in situation.

Concluding Discussion

Among the eight case histories of old people in Laurel Creek, West Virginia, the complex variation in conditions precludes a formal analysis of data at this time. However, although the study of cases prevents inappropriate simplifications, this also makes concluding discussion difficult.

Our assumptions regarding human conduct are: that cognitive operations and strategic planning influence behavior, which alters the organism's environment, and that outcomes or consequences become the subject of further cognitive operations. The social process is vastly complicated by the fact of communications among individuals regarding cognitions, behavior, and consequences. From repeated observations of particular individuals, a public definition of careers arises; and from communication of personal assessments of careers, public assessments arise. To the extent that such assessments are harmful or helpful for the individual concerned, these socially produced environmental conditions constitute social sanctions.

In our judgment, Laurel Creekers act according to our assumptions that behavior leads to consequences and that a degree of control over behavior and consequences is possible through strategic planning, limited by the circumstances of a physical and social environment.

Each case is intended ideally to illustrate how the circumstances of an elder can be viewed as the outcome or consequence of a social and historical process that defines the individual's career. The universal assumption that foresight and planning can in some degree influence careers makes it reasonable for us to speak of *strategies for aging*. We caution that this does not imply self-consciousness as we use it, but rather that just as one can and does assess the consequences of "a move" in chess independent of the player's consciousness of them, and thus the strategic implications of "the move," we can assess the consequences of social behavior and thus its strategic implications.

Martin Tanner, for instance, is a relatively insignificant person in his old age because display of care and attention toward him is not obligatory in the socially defined and enforced performances of any junior or set of juniors. About the same is true of Eugene Wiley. The difference between their social careers lies in different degrees of initial resources, coupled with disparate public assessments of the family connections. Tanner is granted polite acceptance largely because he is the son of Old Man Martin and because he acquired the inherited resources to live a respectable lifestyle. Wiley, on the other hand, is rejected because his origins are socially disparaged and because he is living evidence of a disreputable life-style. As elders, neither is strategically significant as an object of the display of care and attention by juniors. The fact that failure by juniors to care for Tanner and Wiley provokes no negative sanctions merely confirms the established public assessment.

By contrast, both Keither McCloud and Denzil Ball possess elder status with considerable social protection because display of care and attention toward each of them is strategically significant for numbers of juniors. While there was some considerable difference between the initial resources of these two elders and in the evaluation of their family origins, both won high public assessment as reliable, trustworthy men and acquired long reputation through steady help for other people as well as the community in general.

Through his educational, business, and religious activities, McCloud achieved an influential assessment for himself and was integrally involved in the process by which the assessments of others were produced. Even the display of care and attention by Keither's eldest son, publicly presumed to have a sentimental basis, has significance, since this display has possible long-range career consequences in terms of the public assessment of Keither Junior.

Denzil Ball's career likewise leads to a position of strategic significance to numbers of juniors. Display of care and attention toward either Keither or Denzil provides opportunity to enhance the social credibility of nearly everyone in Laurel Creek, not only because of normal obligations, but as an affirmation of one's conformity with the public's assessment, as a declaration of loyalty to community dealings.

Whereas McCloud and Ball are properly "upstarts" in the sense that neither one is associated with long-time kin networks, Moses Tanner and John Meadows represent original settler families on the contemporary scene. Both Tanner and Meadows are associated with family traditions in which the image of the distinguished elder patriarch has been a powerful reality and prized myth.

Moses Tanner's career led to elder circumstances that are publicly assessed and privately experienced as a satisfying personal version of the patriarchal role, albeit on a modest local scale. On the other hand, in pursuit of the same kind of a patriarchal image, John Meadows's career has been a frustrating private experience and increasingly assessed publicly as a failure. Together, these cases provide a lesson for Laurel Creekers, and others, showing the importance of moderation in ambition, and caution in expectations. Generally, these careers reveal the kinds of consequences that arise from the interaction of behaviors and environment.

Perhaps the careers of a plurality of those growing older in contemporary urban settings are more closely related to those of the Maddens and of Clyde Stanton. These cases develop from careers predominantly outside Laurel Creek, ending with homecoming to Laurel Creek in order to "cash-in." The cash-in return to the rural community is typologically intermediate between the "traditional" system in which the social environment of elders is constructed by a collective memory forged through a series of public assessments emerging over the span of a normal lifetime and the "rationally" institutionalized system that protects the social environment of the aged, through formal and legal institutions based mainly in economic measures of value, where public assessments are rendered less relevant as mechanical information storage replaces memory. Among the cash-ins the individual is captured in immediate transactions to negotiate an environment for his elder years with a combination of cash and a specialized coin whose exchange value is limited to the local system.

From the outset, we attempted to develop a societal perspective on aging that focuses on the social environment of aging persons as a strategy for understanding the experience of individuals. This implies that we also must view aging persons as a part of the social environment of juniors.

The research approach indicated is an investigation of the extent to which the circumstances of elders are controlled or determined by the strategic behavior of others, especially juniors. We do not suggest that successful aging is simply a product of an individual's astute efforts on his own behalf. We believe that success for an elder is a product of the efforts of members of a collectivity on his behalf.

Conduct leading to successful aging involves the construction of a protective social environment, through the obligating of juniors, within a social system that can be counted upon to enforce the obligations. In such an environment, the elder has a degree of security that frees him from the requirement for immediate control or for constant attention to his resources.

In the more traditional setting, behavior toward elders is publicly observed and assessed, with consequences for the junior individual. To the extent that the anticipation of these consequences influences the behavior of juniors, social sanctions exist. But where individuals are insulated or isolated from the sanctioning influence of a social audience that can give and store credit for the caring behavior displayed by a junior, such behavior loses its significance, or strategic value, whatever its sentimental value may be.

What modern society no longer provides for in its protection of the aged is the opportunity for juniors to display caring behavior toward elders before a social audience attentive to such performances. What it gains for its juniors is a measure of release from the demands of elders, which are costly, sometimes capricious, and even oppressive for the junior's independent careers.

References

Althouse, R., and Lozier, J. "A Case History of Urban Industrial Migrant Relocation to Their Original Mountain Neighborhoods of Southern Appalachia," Department of Sociology and Anthropology, West Virginia University, mimeo.

Austin, J. L. *How To Do Things with Words.* New York: Oxford University Press, 1965.

Bailey, F. G. *Stratagems and Spoils: A Social Anthropology of Politics.* New York: Schocken, 1969.

Blau, P. M. *Exchange and Power in Social Life.* New York: John Wiley and Sons, 1964.

Gamson, W. A. *Power and Discontent.* Homewood, Illinois: Dorsey Press, 1968.

Goffman, E. *The Presentation of Self in Everyday Life.* New York: Doubleday-Anchor, 1959.

—. *Strategic Interaction*. Oxford: Basil Blackwell, 1970.

Goodenough, W. H. "Cultural Anthropology and Linguistics." In *Report of the Seventh Annual Round Table Meeting on Linguistics and Language Study*. Edited by P. L. Garvin. Reprinted in Bobbs-Merrill Reprint Series in Language and Linguistics, no. 29, 1957. *Cooperation in Change: An Anthropological Approach to Community Development*. New York: John Wiley Science Editions, 1966.

Homans, G. C. "Anxiety and Ritual: The Theories of Malinowski and Radcliffe-Brown." *American Anthropologist* 43 (1941): 164-72.

Maxwell, R. J., and Silverman, P. "Information and Esteem: Cultural Considerations in the Treatment of the Aged." *Aging and Human Development* 1 (1970): 361-92.

Miller, G. A.; Galanter, E.; and Pibram, K. *Plans and the Structure of Behavior*. New York: Holt, Rinehart, and Winston, 1960.

Salisbury, R. F. "Politics and Shell-Money Finance in New Britain." In *Political Anthropology*. Edited by M. Swartz; V. Turner; and A. Tuden. Chicago: Aldine, 1966.

Schwarzweller, H. K.; Brown, J. S.; and Mangalam, J. J. *Mountain Families in Transition*. University Park, Pennsylvania: Pennsylvania State University Press, 1971.

Simmons, L. W. "Aging in Preindustrial Culture." In *Aging in Today's Society*. Edited by C. Tibbitts and W. Donahue. Englewood Cliffs, New Jersey: Prentice-Hall, 1960.

Tibbitts, C. "Origin, Scope, and Fields of Gerontology." In *Handbook of Social Gerontology*. Edited by C. Tibbitts. Chicago: University of Chicago Press, 1960.

Veblen, T. *The Theory of the Leisure Class*. New York: New American Library Mentor Edition, 1953 (1899).

Whitten, N. E. "Strategies of Adaptive Mobility in the Colombian-Ecuadorian Littoral." *American Anthropologist* 71 (1969): 228-42.

21

Aged Blacks: A Potpourri in the Direction of the Reduction of Inequities*

Jacquelyne Johnson Jackson

Among the earliest gerontological papers on black aged were probably three first appearing in *Phylon* (3, 5, 20). Since then such papers have multiplied, but this proliferation has failed to produce sufficient interest in improving the objective social conditions (for example, income, housing, and transportation) of black aged, nor has it aided those experiencing involuntary relocation in the onslaught of urban renewal and highway programs. These are serious problems.

This chapter focuses specifically upon (a) grandparental roles in a contemporary urban Southern setting and certain implications of those roles relative to sociocultural conditions of aged blacks; (b) the National Caucus on the Black Aged, a group recently developed to focus attention and action upon significant service, training, and research gaps relative to

*This work originally appeared in *Phylon,* the Atlanta University Review of Race and Culture. This paper was partially supported by the Center for the Study of Aging and Human Development, Duke University Medical Center, Durham, North Carolina, Grant 5 T01 HD00164 of the National Institute of Child Health and Human Development, and by the U.S. Public Health Service Grant #MH 1655402.

black aged; and (c) a specific proposal to reduce the minimum age-eligibility requirements for Old-Age, Survivors, Disability, and Health Insurance (OASDHI) for blacks, so as to reflect the racial disparities in life-expectancy rates. These three facts, interfaced in highlighting racial inequities, are set forth below.

Grandparental Roles among Southern Blacks

Perhaps the most impressive finding about the black grandparental roles is their striking similarity to comparable findings about nonblack grandparent-grandchild patterns. If so, the emphasis often placed upon the "peculiarity" of "black grannies" may be unwarranted or unduly exaggerated. These findings tend to be in general agreement, for example, with those of Shanas, et al. (18), Shanas and Streib (19), Townsend (21), and Young and Willmott (22) in such areas as (a) emphasis upon the unusually vivid presence of grandmothers especially in kinship networks, with an important task being involvement in grandchild rearing; (b) more involvement of grandmothers than grandfathers in activities with grandchildren; (c) closer bonds among grandmothers, daughters, and grandchildren than among grandfathers, sons, and grandchildren; and (d) the presence of extended or three-generational families within urban areas.

Frazier's classic description of "Granny: The Guardian of the Generations" depicted an energetic, courageous, and devoted "granny" whose prestige and importance were great during and after the Civil War. "Granny" continued watching "over the destiny of the Negro families as they have moved in ever-increasing numbers to the cities during the present century," wrote Frazier, with the gradual increase in patriarchal authority in family relations and in female economic subordination, decreasing "granny's" prestige and importance. Frazier made no explicit mention of grandfathers (4). A majority of the grandmother subjects in this study still resemble Frazier's "granny." Grandmothers are still generally more important than grandfathers, but the importance of the latter within black, urban kinship systems is increasing, necessitating a reassessment of black families and a burial of extant myths.

Kahana and Kahana (14) noted that most grandparental studies focused only upon them rather than upon both them and their grandchildren. This section is traditional in focusing upon grandparental perceptions only, but atraditional in focusing upon black grandmothers and grandfathers. Specifically, analytical data about interactional and subjective roles between (a) grandparents residing in predominantly low-income, urban-renewal areas and the grandchildren they see most often, and (b) selected comparisons of the grandparental subgroupings are presented.

The subgroupings of the sampled sixty-eight black grandparents, whose ages, marital statuses, and subgroupings are detailed in Table 1 below, were as follows: (a) by sex, grandmothers and grandfathers; (b) by age, younger (that is, under 50 years) and older (that is, 50+ years); and (c) by household composition, grandparents living alone and grandparents not living alone. No significant age difference characterized the latter subgroup. Using t, both the grandfathers and older grandparents were significantly older than their subgroup counterparts (p < .001). The subjects reported approximately (a few were imprecise) 391 grandchildren, about 5.8 grandchildren per subject. Almost 12 percent had no granddaughters; almost 15 percent no grandsons. Table 2 contains selected background information of these grandchildren.

A modified form of the Adams Kinship Schedule (1) was used to collect data in personal interview settings within the subject's homes. Following Adams, interactional characteristics referred to the frequency of interaction and kinds of or occasions for interaction with grandchildren, including telephone contacts and letter writing, or the non face-to-face means of keeping in touch. His eight "contact types" (that is, home visiting, social activities, voluntary organizations, working together at the same occupation and location, rituals, communication, aid received from a specific relative, and aid given to specific relative) were modified to seven: home visiting, social activities (including reading), church, luxury gifts, communication, aid received from grandchildren, and aid given to grandchildren. The subjective characteristics were affectional closeness, value consensus, identification, and obligation.

TABLE 1

BLACK GRANDPARENTAL SUBGROUPINGS
BY AGE AND SAMPLE SIZE

SUBGROUPING	N	Age (in years)	
		X	s
By sex:			
All grandmothers	54	59.4	13.6
Older, with spouse	6	66.7	7.5
Older, without spouse	33	66.5	7.6
Younger, with spouse	3	45.0	0.0
Younger, without spouse	12	40.0	6.7
Employed	9	49.4	12.4
Nonemployed	45	61.4	13.0
All grandfathers*	14	69.3	7.8
Older, with spouse	5	73.0	4.5
Older, without spouse	9	67.2	8.3
Employed	4	62.5	9.6
Nonemployed	10	72.0	4.8
By living arrangements:			
All grandparents	26	64.2	11.6
Living alone	38	59.7	13.7
Not living alone			
By age:			
Younger grandparents	15	41.0	6.4
Older grandparents	53	67.2	7.7

*No grandfathers were under 50 years of age.

TABLE 2

BACKGROUND DATA ON GRANDCHILDREN BY GRANDPARENTAL SUBGROUPS

CHARACTERISTIC*	GRANDPARENTAL SUBGROUPS					
	Grandmothers (N = 54)* 100.0	Grandfathers (N = 14)* 100.0	Grandparents Living Alone (N = 26)* 100.0	Grandparents Living Not Alone (N = 38)* 100.0	Grandparents Younger 100.0	Grandparents Older 100.0
Percent Base:	Percentage	Percentage	Percentage	Percentage	Percentage	Percentage
Number of grandsons:						
none	14.3	37.5	13.0	16.7	23.1	19.2
one	16.3	0.0	8.7	13.3	30.8	7.7
two	18.4	18.8	30.4	13.3	15.4	19.2
three+	51.0	43.8	47.8	56.7	30.8	53.8
Number of grandaughters:						
none	21.6	31.3	30.4	16.1	15.4	25.9
one	21.6	18.3	30.4	16.1	15.4	22.2
two	9.8	6.3	8.7	12.9	15.4	7.4
three+	47.1	43.8	30.4	54.8	53.8	44.4
Grandchildren's residence:						
in same household as grandparent	30.4	0.0	0.0	34.5	46.2	16.7
in same city as grandparent	37.0	40.0	52.4	27.6	38.5	37.5
in northeastern states	19.6	40.0	38.1	20.7	15.4	14.6
elsewhere	13.0	20.0	9.5	17.2	0.0	31.3
Ages of grandchildren:						
under six years	25.6	14.3	14.3	29.6	58.3	13.3
6-11 years	27.9	42.9	33.3	25.9	25.0	33.3
12-17 years	20.9	28.6	19.0	29.6	8.3	26.7
18+ years	25.6	14.3	33.3	14.8	8.3	26.7
Grandchildren's marital status:						
married	41.2	33.3	62.5	22.2	0.0	44.4

*Percentages were computed upon available responses, so N is sometimes less than given.

Determination of affectional closeness is in answer to the question: "How close would you say you feel to your. . .?" Responses of "quite close" and "extremely close" are combined and designated as strong feelings of closeness. Value consensus is ascertained by the following question: "Do you and your. . .agree in your ideas and opinions about the things you consider really important in life?" Answers of "yes, completely," and "yes, to a great extent" appear to indicate substantial value consensus, as distinct from value divergence. Idealization of or identification with the relative is determined by responses to this question: "Would you like to be the kind of person your. . .is?" Close identification is based upon the responses "yes, completely," and "in most ways." Feelings of obligation are ascertained . . . by asking . . . how important certain reasons for keeping in touch are in relation to a particular relative (1).

Findings

In general, when the data were controlled for grandparents with at least one son with offspring and at least one daughter with offspring, who either both resided elsewhere (that is, not within the same locality as the subject) or within the same location as did the subject, the grandchild seen most often was the daughter's, as opposed to the son's, child, a finding consistent with Young and Willmott's observation that grandchildren usually interact more frequently with their mother's mother than with their father's mother (22). Rare exceptions in this sample were among subjects whose son's offspring resided with them.

Interactional Characteristics

Possible responses for frequency of interaction between a grandparent and grandchild ranged from daily through "never during the past year." Percentage data in Table 3 depict frequency of interaction in five "contact types" for subjects interacting at least "once during the year" with the grandchild.

Grandparental Subgroupings Emerged

Younger grandparents, grandparents living alone, and grandmothers were more likely to report home visiting than were their respective counterparts, true even when the data were controlled to exclude grandparents and grandchildren in the same household. Those living alone and those not living alone differed since the latter reported greater frequency of contact ($p < .05$).

The modal form of interaction in social activities was "shopping, exclusive of grocery shopping," with joint movie attendance especially rare. Reading was largely restricted to interaction with preschool grandchildren. Table 4 contains a rank ordering, in decreasing frequency, of these activities.

The data on church revealed that older grandparents, grandparents living alone, and grandfathers reported less frequent church activities (most often joint attendance at regular Sunday morning worship services) with grandchildren than their counterparts. Younger grandparents were far more likely to be accompanied by or to accompany a grandchild to church than were older grandparents ($p < .05$), attributable partially to greater shared residence among the former. Joint church activity decreased as the ages of the grandparents and grandchildren increased.

Excepting younger grandparents, subjects reported infrequent or no luxury gift-giving to their grandchildren, a finding explicable perhaps by such variables as (a) a greater likelihood of young grandparents being employed; and (b) greater likelihood of grandparents providing younger grandchildren with luxury gifts and older ones with practical gifts.

Nonface-to-face communication patterns investigated were (a) telephoning grandparent-grandchild contacts; and (b) written communications among grandparent-grandchild pairs not residing within the same city. No more than one third of any grandparent subgroup reported writing to a grandchild within the preceding year. More had received correspondence from their grandchildren. Grandfathers, as well as grandparents living with others, were less likely to have had telephonic communication with grandchildren than grandmothers and grandparents living alone, but the differences were insignificant. Older grandparents were significantly more likely than younger grandparents to have such interaction ($p < .05$), an artifact, perhaps of more grandchildren living with younger grandparents. While few subjects reported relatively frequent (that is, monthly or more often) telephone contact, most

TABLE 3

RESPONSES TO INTERACTIONAL ITEMS BY GRANDPARENTAL SUBGROUPS

CHARACTERISTIC*	GRANDPARENTAL SUBGROUPS					
Percent Base:*	Grandmothers 100.0	Grandfathers 100.0	Grandparents Living Alone 100.0	Grandparents Living Not Alone 100.0	Grandparents Younger 100.0	Grandparents Older 100.0
	Percentage	Percentage	Percentage	Percentage	Percentage	Percentage
Frequency of contact with grandchild:						
daily, same household	29.3	0.0	0.0	32.0	50.0	15.9
monthly, or more often	43.9	53.8	60.0	36.0	40.0	47.7
at least once during past year	24.4	30.8	35.0	24.0	10.0	29.5
not at all during past year	2.4	15.4	5.0	8.0	0.0	6.8
Home visiting:						
yes	31.3	27.3	42.1	11.8	60.0	26.3
no	68.8	72.7	57.9	88.2	40.0	73.7
Social activities:						
going to the park	22.0	15.4	10.0	20.0	36.4	16.3
attending the movies	4.8	0.0	0.0	3.8	0.0	4.5
grocery shopping	35.7	15.4	15.0	42.3	54.5	25.0
shopping, other than grocery	45.2	15.4	30.0	46.2	63.6	31.8
local or other trips/vacation	28.6	7.7	15.0	26.9	27.3	22.7
reading	14.3	7.7	5.0	11.5	18.2	11.4
church	45.2	23.1	35.0	42.3	72.7	31.8
Luxury gifts:						
yes	32.4	33.3	15.8	47.4	75.0	23.7
no	67.6	66.7	84.2	52.6	25.0	76.3
Communication:						
S writes out of town grandchild	28.6	25.0	27.3	33.3	0.0	28.6
S written by out of town grandchild	53.3	33.3	58.3	30.0	0.0	47.8
no telephone communication on special occasions or emergencies	42.3	21.4	31.3	38.9	0.0	42.4
telephone communications monthly or more frequently	15.4	28.6	25.0	16.7	14.3	42.4

*All percentages based upon interaction having occurred at least once during the past year.

TABLE 4
RANK ORDER OF THE FREQUENCY OF SOCIAL ACTIVITIES BETWEEN GRANDPARENTS-GRANDCHILDREN

RANK ORDER*

Social Activity	Grandparents Living				Grandparents	
	Grandmothers	Grandfathers	Alone	Not Alone	Younger	Older
Shopping other than grocery shopping	1	2	1	1	1	1
Grocery shopping	2	2	2.5	2	2	2
Going to the park and/or walking	4	2	4	4	3	4
Movies	6	6	6	6	6	6
Trips/vacations	3	4.5	2.5	3	4	3
Reading	5	4.5	5	5	5	5

*1 = greatest frequency of occurrence; 6 = least occurring activity.

reported at least one call (usually an emergency or a "special occasion" day) during the preceding year.

Table 5 contains responses concerning grandparent-grandchild aid patterns. A minority perceived their grandchildren as "not much help at all," a statement verbalized most often by grandfathers (50 percent), and less often by those who were not living alone (37 percent), older (33 percent), living alone (28 percent), grandmothers (25 percent), and younger (20 percent). But inquiry about specific aid revealed that a majority had received assistance from grandchildren during the preceding year. Their modal responses were not instrumentally, but affectively, oriented: disregarding the "not much help at all" response, the modal response for younger grandparents and grandparents living alone was "visits"; for the remaining subgroups, "A feeling of usefulness." Those living alone received more visits from grandchildren than those not living alone (p<.05), while the latter received greater assistance with household and/or yard chores (p<.05) than the former. Younger grandparents also received more chore assistance than older grandparents (p<.05), and more advice from grandchildren as well (p<.05).

The modal form of grandparent-grandchild assistance was child care; almost 44 percent of the grandmothers, 56 percent of grandparents living with others, and 82 percent of the younger grandparents, had grandchildren residing with them. A smaller proportion of the subjects "babysat" with school-age children awaiting parental arrival at residences other than those of the grandparents. Younger, as contrasted with older, grandparents provided more direct financial assistance to a grandchild and/or his parents (p<.01); they were also more involved in patterns of luxury and practical gift-giving to grandchildren (p<.01), child care (p<.001), and housing (p<.05). Grandmothers were more involved as child-care agents than grandfathers (p<.05), as were grandparents not living alone compared with those living alone (p<.001). Among the latter subgrouping, those not living alone tended to engage in greater luxury and necessary gift-giving as well (p<.05).

While impressionistic judgments suggested that the older grandparents had been far more active in grandchild rearing earlier, it was quite clear that grandparental involvement in

TABLE 5

MUTUAL AID PATTERNS BETWEEN GRANDCHILDREN AND GRANDPARENTS

			GRANDPARENTAL SUBGROUPS			
			Grandparents Living		Grandparents	
CHARACTERISTIC*	Grandmothers	Grandfathers	Alone	Not Alone	Younger	Older
	Percentage	Percentage	Percentage	Percentage	Percentage	Percentage
Aid received from grandchildren:						
financial assistance	12.5	0.0	10.5	11.8	20.7	7.9
feeling of usefulness	35.3	36.4	26.3	42.1	57.1	31.6
house or yard chores	27.8	18.2	5.3	35.0	55.6	18.4
visiting	31.3	27.3	42.1	11.8	60.0	26.3
transportation	6.5	0.0	5.3	6.3	0.0	5.3
gifts	18.8	9.1	15.8	23.5	20.0	15.8
advice	12.5	9.1	10.5	11.8	40.0	7.9
writing letters, reading, etc.	3.1	0.0	0.0	5.9	0.0	2.6
"not much help at all"	25.0	50.0	27.8	36.8	20.0	33.3
Aid given to grandchildren:						
indirect financial assistance	15.2	0.0	0.0	17.6	50.0	5.3
direct financial assistance	30.6	18.2	15.8	40.0	75.0	17.9
necessary gifts	33.3	9.1	10.5	89.5	66.7	18.4
housing	36.8	27.3	15.0	42.9	66.7	27.5
assistance with illness	11.8	9.1	0.0	16.7	16.7	10.3
child care	43.6	9.1	5.3	56.5	81.8	23.1
took grandchild on a special trip	6.3	10.0	0.0	5.9	20.0	5.4
advice	52.8	33.3	42.1	42.9	75.0	42.5
keeping after school until parent arrives	8.8	9.1	0.0	15.8	16.7	7.7
other	14.3	0.0	16.7	10.5	0.0	14.8

*All percentages based upon interaction having occurred at least once during the past year.

child rearing is directly related to the grandchild's familial structure: grandparental involvement, as Frazier (4) indicated, increased with the absence of the grandchild's parent.

Subjective characteristics

Qualitative data on affectional closeness, value consensus, identification with grandchild, satisfaction of present contact with grandchild, and the primary initiant of grandparent-grandchild contacts were available for analysis. A majority of the subjects verbalized strong affectional closeness between themselves and their grandchildren. Only grandmothers considered themselves significantly closer to grandchildren than did grandfathers (p<.05), but grandparents living with others and younger grandparents tended to report greater closeness than their counterparts, suggesting probably the importance of considering more closely sex, age, and residential proximity in future grandparent-grandchild studies.

Value divergence was more typical than substantial value consensus, but the greatest congruence of value consensus between grandparents and grandchildren was found among grandfathers, which warrants an investigation of black generational transmission of political socialization and advocates for the aged. Older grandmothers displayed the most distance in grandchild-grandparent value consensus. In addition, less than five percent of the subjects closely identified with grandchildren. Almost twenty percent rejected any close identification (that is, they would not like to resemble the grandchild in any way).

Obligatory kinship ties were apparent. Most subjects, and particularly younger grandparents and grandparents living with others, felt that the obligation of "keeping in touch" was very important. Excepting younger grandparents, all of the subjects placed greater emphasis upon the obligatory than upon the enjoyable aspect of "keeping in touch." Older grandparents and those living alone desired greater grandchild contact. Compared with their respective counterparts, they were significantly less likely to be satisfied with the present contact levels (p<.05). A very small percentage of older grandparents (two percent) and grandparents not living alone (four percent), however, felt that less frequent grandchild contact would be desirable.

Most subjects felt that grandchildren should live near (but not necessarily with) their grandparents, and provided rationalizations categorized as unilateral and bilateral needfits (for example, "Grandchildren can be a lot of help to their grandparents," "Grandparents can help parents with children," and, "Because we need each other") and kinship obligations (for example, "Everyone should be close around their family"). Equally important, almost fifteen percent of the subjects feeling that grandchildren should not live near grandparents cited the necessity of physical generational separation so as to reduce problems for the grandparent (for example, "Do not want to be worried with them") and/or the grandchild (for example, "It tends to spoil the child") and emphasized parental responsibility. Almost twenty-five percent of the subjects stressed the primary responsibility of parents for rearing their own children in neolocal residences. Most were specifically concerned about possible detrimental effects of extremely close grandparent-grandchild residential proximity upon development of independence in a maturing grandchild; and, to a less extent, child-rearing roles constraining grandparents with "other fish to fry," as they develop or maintain new roles as they aged.

In general, grandchildren were not considered the initiants of the grandparent-grandchild contacts. Grandfathers also did not perceive themselves in this role, but considered a parent of the grandchild as the primary contact agent for them. Younger grandparents and grandparents living alone rarely regarded themselves as prime contact agents either, inasmuch as those younger grandparents with spouses felt that the spouses actually initiated the contact most often, and both groups felt that their own children also served as links between themselves and grandchildren. Younger grandparents and grandfathers, however, were more likely to telephone a grandchild than the reverse, whereas grandchildren were more likely to contact grandmothers, older grandparents, and grandparents not living alone. The only significant subgroup distinction occurred in that grandfathers were more frequent initiators of telephone calls with grandchildren than were grandmothers (p<.05).

Discussion

Apparently these grandparents prefer children's children to live near, but not with, them, and younger to older grandchildren (9, 10, 11, 13, 14). Very old grandparents appeared more concerned about proximity in the event grandchildren were needed for instrumental and affective support. Relationships among affectional closeness, value consensus, and identification were unclear, but they are probably related to such preferences as those mentioned above. Any postulation of a "generation gap" per se between black grandparents and their grandchildren is too vague. That is, far greater specificity and empirical data about those gaps which may exist are needed, with particular emphasis upon separation of spurious or superficial gaps (for example, clothing or hairstyles) and substantial ones (for example, divergence upon dominant values). Age is not a sufficient explication of generation gaps in dominant values.

The specific contact types investigated suggested relatively infrequent grandchild-grandparent interaction, due perhaps to an artifact of the study in focusing directly upon those rather than upon other contact types, and/or to such variables as inadequate income, transportation, and awareness of or free and friendly access to available resources. The general findings clearly point up some problem areas, a specific one being public housing.

In this connection, empirical data on relationships between housing and kinship patterns among blacks are clearly warranted. For example, grandparent-grandchild patterns may be affected positively and negatively by public-housing policies for the aged. For blacks at least, alternative forms of housing (for example, age-segregated and age-integrated) within the same locale are desirable. Telephone service should be available. Single blacks dependent upon public housing (and especially when such dependence is fostered through their involuntary relocation as a result of urban renewal and highway programs) should not be forced (as is true in some localities) to accept one-room or efficiency apartments, but should be permitted to occupy at least one-bedroom apartments, if they prefer such an arrangement.

Physical space permitting brief or extended visits from relatives should be available.

These findings about black grandparents and their grandchildren help to debunk myths of the death of the "black grannies"; the "powerful matriarchies" ruled by "black grannies"; and the disintegrating or ephemeral kinship ties between aged and aging blacks. They indicate that many black grandparents serve as a point of anchorage for grandchildren and provide kinds of supports for them unavailable from their own parents. In that sense, the grandparents take on the responsibilities of and function as individual departments of welfare. Many black families, in all probability, adhere to familial norms characteristic of the larger culture. Finally, these data are most significant in helping to delineate the tremendous need for such an organization as that of the National Caucus on the Black Aged, to which I now turn.

The National Caucus on the Black Aged
As already indicated, the National Caucus on the Black Aged (hereafter, NCBA) is particularly concerned about dramatizing and reducing those significant gaps characteristic of services to, training for, and research about black aged (including, of course, the very significant gaps occurring in housing, inasmuch as the vast majority of aged blacks are residing within substandard housing).

NCBA was organized in November 1970, largely through the efforts of Hobart C. Jackson, Chief Administrator, Stephen Smith Geriatric Center (4400 West Girard Street, Philadelphia, Pennsylvania) and Robert A. Kastenbaum, Director, Center of Psychological Studies of Dying, Death, and Lethal Behaviors, Wayne State University (Detroit, Michigan). Its most immediate missions were (a) dramatizing the plight of aged blacks; and (b) having a significant impact upon and input into the 1971 White House Conference on Aging. This Conference had been charged with the major responsibilities of drafting a national policy for the aged in the decade ahead.

In November 1970, NCBA concluded its organizational meeting by forwarding a telegram to President Richard M. Nixon. That communication:

(A) Calls upon President Nixon and Secretary Romney (HUD) "to develop plans by November 1971 for correcting and replacing the deteriorated housing in which seventy-five percent of aged blacks live": and for maintaining home ownership among the black aged.

(B) Calls upon President Nixon and Secretary Richardson (HEW) to develop by November 1971 plans for moderate, liveable income for the aged—an income meeting Bureau of Labor Statistics standards.

(C) Calls upon President Nixon and the administration's Special Assistant on Aging to develop proposals by November 1971 for nondiscriminating programs and services including adequate transportation, and police protection for aged blacks.

(D) Calls upon the President to direct all states of the union to go directly to the black aged for their ideas, recommendations, and preferences as a preparation for the White House Conference on Aging that has been projected for late 1971.

(E) Calls upon the President to see that the black aged are adequately represented at the White House Conference by requiring each state to select at least thirty percent of their delegations from among blacks.

(F) Calls upon the President and Secretary Richardson to increase substantially the number of black-trained professionals and paraprofessionals in the fields of geriatrics and gerontology (16).

Dramatization of the plight of the black aged may proceed in a number of directions. Suggestions include much individual and group support of the above objectives. Programs may be developed within academic institutions, local communities, professional and other organizations, and at whatever levels feasible in garnering support. Perhaps especial emphasis might be placed upon income, health, housing, and transportation inasmuch as these usually rank high among problem areas specified by blacks themselves.

Those planning the 1971 White House Conference on Aging had designated nine "need areas" for concentration for policy recommendations in developing a national policy for aged: (a) income; (b) housing; (c) health; (d) nutrition; (e) education; (f) transportation; (g) retirement roles and activities; (h) spiritual well-being; and (i) employment and retirement. Specialists on aging were involved in the preparation of background or position papers focusing upon the current statuses of these need areas as they related to (a) services, facilities, and programs; (b) planning and evaluation; (c) training; (d) research and demonstration; and (e) government and nongovernment organizations. Technical committees were appointed to examine and act upon these position papers and were mandated to isolate the major issues for discussion by delegates to the Community, State, and National Conferences on Aging. In addition, national organizations throughout the United States were asked to send representatives to the National Organizations' Task Forces to assist in making policy recommendations on these need areas, and during the spring of 1971, a number of local conferences and regional hearings on aging occurred. In most states, the month of May was set aside for the State House Conference on Aging, from which policy recommendations would also be channeled to the National Conference.

For the most part, black representation on these various levels, including those requested to prepare position papers, those invited to participate actively in organizing and planning the various conferences, and so on, has been small. One of the ways in which NCBA envisioned itself as having an impact upon the White House Conference on Aging was through significant representation of blacks on the various levels leading up to and through the National Conference. Thus, as noted in the telegram content referred to earlier, NCBA was very much concerned about each governor in each state including at least thirty percent black representation among the state delegates to the National Conference. Some governors explicitly received specific requests to this effect. Greater assistance in insuring the implementation of this goal was needed in every state. Assistance is yet invaluable in helping to reduce racial inequities confronting black aged in particular and the aged in general.

NCBA certainly recognizes the need for increased development of black aging specialists and is very much concerned about further utilization and expansion of opportunities leading to such specialization. It may also be significant that the federal funding programs underwriting gerontological centers and/or special programs over the past decade have effectively excluded, for whatever reasons, black colleges and universities. Until 1971, no black institution of higher learning provided any training program in aging.* It is also important that increasing numbers of black students, whether students at predominantly white or predominantly black institutions, become aware of the critical needs for personnel in geriatrics and gerontology, fields that can be entered from various disciplines (for example, sociology, psychology, social work, medicine, nursing, dentistry, public administration, demography, nutrition, biology, architecture, urban planning, recreation, economics, and the ministry).

This writer, at least, is seriously concerned about "who plans the planners." Relatively few blacks occupy key positions within federal agencies underwriting the bulk of the major research, training, and service programs for the aging, including those which, on occasion, underwrite such projects involving black subjects. There is a significant need for an enlargement of the pool of black policymakers within the three major branches of the federal government, as well as of policymakers, irrespective of race, who are concerned about the reduction of inequities confronting black and other aged minorities (for example, American Indians, Mexican-Americans). The greater presence of such policymakers may be of significant value in gaining enactment of my proposal to reduce minimum age eligibility for OASDHI so as to reflect the disproportionate racial life expectancies.

Reduction of Minimum Age-Eligibility Requirements, OASDHI

It has elsewhere been noted that inasmuch as blacks tend to die earlier and to perceive of themselves as being old earlier chronologically than do whites, some structural modification in the current system of determining minimum age-eligibility

---

*In July 1971, largely through the efforts of NCBA, Fisk University was awarded a grant of about $92,000 by the Administration on Aging for such a program, leading to a master's degree in sociology.

requirements for Old-Age Survivors, Disability, and Health
Insurance (OASDHI) may be useful in reducing certain specific
racial disparities (8, 12). In 1968, it was specifically proposed
that:

> the minimum age eligibility for retirement benefits should be
> racially differentiated to reflect present racial differences in
> life expectancies. Remaining life expectancies at age forty-
> five may be an appropriate base for computing such differ-
> entials (12).

In December 1970, the following resolution was submitted
to President Richard M. Nixon for consideration:

> Whereas available data (Herman B. Brotman: Useful Facts
> #19, Life Expectancy, National and by State, 1959, 1961,
> Administration on Aging Memorandum, HEW, Washington,
> D.C., April 1967) indicate that nonwhites, on the average,
> can expect to live fewer years than is true of whites (for
> example, for those born in 1900-1902, at birth, nonwhite
> males could expect to live 15.7 years fewer than could white
> males, and nonwhite females could expect to die 16.0 years
> earlier than could white females; and, for those born in
> 1959-1961, nonwhite males, on the average, could expect to
> die 6.1 years earlier than white males, and nonwhite
> females could expect to die 7.7 years earlier than white
> females); and
>
> Whereas the present Social Security legislation fails to
> consider this racial differential in life expectancy in deter-
> mining the minimum-age eligibility required for qualification
> for Social Security benefits earned by workers; and
>
> Whereas nonwhites are therefore discriminated against in
> being denied a proportionate number of years to receive
> such benefits as are eligible whites;
>
> Be It Therefore Resolved That the minimum-age eligibility
> for such retirement benefits should be racially differentiated
> to reflect present racial differences in life expectancies so
> as to reduce the discriminatory gaps in earned benefits
> which now occur; and
>
> Be It Therefore Resolved That the 1971 White House
> Conference on Aging will include this recommendation as
> one of its recommendations forwarded to the Congress of the
> United States and to appropriate federal agencies for action

thereupon to institute legislatively minimum-age requirements reflecting such differences in life expectancy by
race.*

Such a proposal has generated some interest; it has also raised
some issues. In general, the issues raised have focused upon
(a) the historical coverage of black workers under social
insurance and demographic factors related to black aged; (b)
the ethicity and/or feasibility of excluding other significant
minority groups from the initial proposal; (c) the specific fact
that black beneficiaries may tend to receive proportionately
more benefits, as compared with payments, than do white
beneficiaries; and (d) refinement of the specific proposal,
including a more precise specification of the methodology to be
employed in determining racially differentiated, minimum-age
eligibility requirements.

Historical Background of Coverage of Black Workers Under Social Security

As Schiltz has explained quite cogently, old-age insurance
is based "at least loosely on the insurance principle, while
old-age assistance is usually perceived as a public assistance
program." The critical difference between the two programs is
located "either in the criteria for determining the benefit
amount or in the method of financing." Old-age insurance is
social insurance "because the benefit level is related to
previous wage history, and *all participants are entitled to
benefits, whether or not they are in need*," and "because the
costs of the program are borne by employer-employee
contributions." Old-age assistance, on the other hand, is
public assistance in that "the benefit level must be established
by the needs of the individual (a 'means test') and *only those
persons in need are eligible for benefits*," and because it is
"financed out of the general revenues of the State and Federal
governments"(17). The proposal to reduce racial inequities

*Jacquelyne J. Jackson to President Richard M. Nixon, December
1970.

currently encouched within existing OASDHI legislation focuses largely upon social insurance, upon that program to which blacks have contributed their own earned monies, and in which they, themselves, have earned the right to maximum beneficiary participation. In addition, the fact that many black recipients of old-age assistance were denied participation in old-age insurance and are therefore entitled through their earned rights as well to the monies they receive should never be overlooked.

As is well known, the Social Security Act of 1935 effectively excluded a significant proportion of black workers from coverage by excluding especially agricultural and casual laborers and private household domestics. The enactment of the Federal OASI Program (effective 1 January 1940) extended such exclusion by adding to the above categories domestics employed in club, fraternity, and sorority houses on college campuses. Thus, the vast majority of employed blacks were not covered under social insurance, an obvious and highly deliberate form of employment discrimination.

The 1935 Act continued to contribute heavily toward the necessity for a number of aged blacks to rely upon old-age assistance and, thereby, to be victims of the derogatory label of "people on welfare." More significantly, such a procedure helped undoubtedly to contribute toward the disproportionate accumulation of black people on welfare, a fact often forgotten when racial comparisons of old-age assistance recipients are made.

The Social Security Act Amendments of 1946 continued racial segregation by still excluding agricultural laborers, casual laborers, and domestic servants and by maintaining age sixty-five as retirement age, an age at which most blacks who have even contributed to the old-age insurance coffers were themselves dead. It was not until the Acts of 1950 and 1954 that coverage was finally extended to most agricultural laborers and domestic workers (with the 1954 qualifiers including earning a minimum of $50 within a given quarter from a single domestic employer and $100 annually from an employer of agricultural laborers).

Subsequent amendments to the Social Security Act of 1935 have resulted in extended coverage to the vast majority of blacks today, and selected provisions of the coverage to which they are entitled under the Social Security Act and Act Amendments, as of 1969, are available elsewhere (2).

Demographic Factors

Unfortunately, detailed data in developing a national profile of black aged in 1970 are not yet available from the U.S. Bureau of the Census. However, preliminary data indicated that an increasing proportion of black aged were metropolitan dwellers and that one out of every two black aged had annual incomes at or below the poverty level. The median 1969 income for aged black males was $1,491; for females, $1,050. Approximately six percent considered themselves as unemployed members of the labor forces.*

In 1960, nonwhite aged constituted a proportionately larger unit of the nonwhite rural nonfarm (7.4 percent) and rural farm (6.2 percent) population than was true of the urban population of nonwhites (5.7 percent). The median age for those at least 65 years of age was about 71 years. Almost all had received less than an elementary education. Most of the males were married, living with spouse, whereas the majority of females were widowed. A larger proportion were active within the labor force in 1960 than was apparently the case in 1970. If that trend of declining participation within the labor force is valid, then it certainly provides additional rationale for the proposal at hand. There also appeared to be no significant decline in poverty among black aged during the decade.

The Ethicity and/or Feasibility of Excluding
Other Significant Minority Groups

The overriding emphasis in this chapter upon black aged is readily explicable by two dominant factors: (a) the writer is black; and (b) her gerontological concerns have focused sharply and almost solely upon black aged. Black aged also constitute well over ninety percent of all nonwhite aged. Moreover, many gains labored for by blacks accrue to other

*Mimeographed preliminary data compiled by the National Urban League for Inabel Lindsay, 1971.

minority groups as well. However, in terms of political and other strategy, it may be useful to extend such a proposal to incorporate other groups. Certainly American Indians and Mexican-Americans, who have even lower educational levels and life-expectancy rates than do blacks, ought to be included, and there is no objection to that (as well as the inclusion of similar groups). The issue of including women as a categorical grouping, inasmuch as women generally outlive men, may often be used merely as a "red herring," and such an inclusion is rejected. This proposal is geared only toward the reduction of racial inequities, wherein the standard for computing new minimum-age eligibility requirements would be based upon racial differences between black and white males and black and white females.

Too often in recent months especially, black caucuses involved in the very difficult tasks of improving significantly the opportunities and utilization of those opportunities for blacks have been confronted with, "But what about the women?" The concern has not been with black women (a concern, incidentally, which too few black male industrial and educational recruitment agents seem to remember), but with women in general (or at least those involved in women's liberation movements). It is, in a very real sense, perhaps unfair to place the burden of liberation for all minority groups, including the aged, upon blacks, who have limited resources available and limited access to the power system. Therefore, black demands for black aged should be regarded as legitimate demands in their own right.

Racial Comparisons of Proportionate Receipt of Benefits

Much has been made of the fact that black OASDHI bene-ficiaries may tend to receive proportionately more benefits (as compared with actual contributions to the insurance system) than do whites. Orshansky has written that:

> Public programs are administered without respect to race and, though limited in what they pay, are relatively more generous to the aged whose previous earnings were lowest or whose current need is greatest. . . .By and large, racial differences in income are less among aged persons drawing old-age, survivors, and disability insurance benefits than

among those not benefitting from this income-support program (15).

It is, of course, true that those with proportionately lower actual contributions to OASDHI do tend to receive proportionately higher benefits from OASDHI. But it is also true that a significantly larger proportion of blacks entitled to such benefits do not, as already noted, live as long as whites on the average and, therefore, they are denied the equivalent possibility of receiving benefits for a proportionately equal amount of time. A substantial number of low-income whites (who far exceed the number of low-income blacks) also receive proportionately more from OASDHI than do whites with higher lifetime earnings. What is of most importance, however, is the fact that blacks pay proportionately more into OASDHI than do whites. As an illustration, compare Worker Black A and Worker White B, with annual 1970 incomes of $7,800 and $12,000 respectively ($A = .65B$). Both A and B invest $390 (5 percent) of their incomes in OASDHI. That OASDHI investment of $390 = .05$ of A's income and $.0325$ of B's income. Thus, this black worker would have invested 1.75 percent more of his income into the system than did the white worker. Thus, his proposal can be supported on the basis of greater proportionate contributions among blacks and disproportionate receipt of benefits by blacks (with the latter occurring primarily because of their earlier deaths).

Refinement of the Specific Proposal

A number of persons have suggested that the precise method of determining racially equitable benefits should be developed prior to a public presentation of the proposal. As sound as that suggestion may be, federal agencies employ a sufficient number of technicians capable of working out the details of such a proposal and implementing it, should the basic principle be accepted. The base for determining racial differences should be established at birth, inasmuch as racial differences in life expectancies, attributable to many racial differences within the sociocultural environment, begin at or before birth (for example, prenatal nutritional factors); and modifications might be undertaken decennially. Thus, 1910 racial life-expectancy data at birth could be employed as the baseline standard for determining minimum-age eligibility requirements for OASDHI recipients, beginning 1972; 1920 data could be utilized for 1982, and so on. The chief point is that the minimum-age eligibility requirements should be lower for blacks than for whites until such time as there is no longer any difference in their life expectancies at birth; or to put it another way, where racial differences adversely affect blacks, public programs should not operate "colorblind."

Summary

The triple focus of this chapter was upon (a) a description and analysis of Southern urban black grandparental roles, emphasizing certain implications for current policies surrounding black aged; (b) the National Caucus on the Black Aged, stressing its urgent missions of dramatizing the plight of the black aged and having a significant impact upon the 1971 White House Conference on Aging, where policy recommendations for the aged in the decade ahead will be formulated, as well as its general concern for increasing substantially services to, training for, and research about black aged; and (c) a specific proposal to reduce the minimum-age eligibility requirements for recipients of Old-Age, Survivors, Disability, and Health Insurance (OASDHI, a form of Social Security) so as to reduce the racial inequities now extant, wherein blacks are far less likely to receive proportionate benefits as whites, even though they may be very likely to have invested proportionately more of their lifetime earnings into Social Security, inasmuch as they tend to die earlier than do whites.

The interfacing of these foci occurred largely in that the grandparental data point toward the need for improved economic and housing conditions for grandparents, for their children, and for their children's children. The National Caucus on the Black Aged is significantly concerned about improving these adverse conditions and, in this connection, seeks assistance from all relevant resources (including those blacks who are not yet aged). The specific proposal to realize greater racial equity between aged whites and blacks is one response to the need to improve the deplorable income plight of many black aged: in this case, a specific improvement in obtaining benefits that black aged themselves have earned.

There is need for greater attention upon black aged at the three basic levels of research, training, and services (6, 7), and it is hoped that this chapter may play a small part in contributing toward the gradual increase in effective research, adequate training producing increased personnel, and, above all, meaningful services available to aging and aged blacks.

References

1. Adams, Bert N. *Kinship in an Urban Setting.* Chicago: Markham Publishing, 1968.

2. *Annual Statistical Supplement, 1968. Social Security Bulletin.* Washington, D.C.: U.S. Government Printing Office, 1969.

3. Beattie, W. M., Jr. "The Aging Negro: Some Implications for Social Welfare Services." *Phylon* 21 (Winter 1960): 131-35.

4. Frazier, E. Franklin. *The Negro Family in the United States.* Chicago: University of Chicago Press, 1939.

5. Himes, J., and Hamlett, M. "The Assessment of Adjustment of Aged Negro Women in a Southern City." *Phylon* 23 (Summer 1969): 139-47.

6. Jackson, Jacquelyne J. "Social Gerontology and The Negro: A Review." *The Gerontologist* 7 (September 1967): 168-78.

7. Jackson, Jacquelyne J. "Exhibit A. Negro Aged and Social Gerontology: Current Status and Some Emerging Issues." In *Long-Range Program and Research Needs in Aging and Related Fields.* Hearings before the Special Committee on Aging, United States Senate, Part I, Survey, December 5 and 6, 1967. Washington, D.C.: U.S. Government Printing Office, 1967.

8. Jackson, Jacquelyne J. "Letter." In *Economics of Aging: Toward a Full Share in Abundance.* Hearing before the Special Committee on Aging, United States Senate, Part I, Survey Hearing, April 29-30, 1969. Washington, D.C.: U.S. Government Printing Office, 1969.

9. Jackson, Jacquelyne J. "Kinship Relations among Older Negro Americans." Paper read at the Eighth International Congress of Gerontology, Washington, D.C., August 1969.

10. Jackson, Jaquelyne J. "Urban Negro Kinship Relations." Paper read at the Annual Meeting of the American Sociological Association, San Francisco, California, September 1969.

11. Jackson, Jaquelyne J. "Changing Kinship Roles and Patterns among Older Persons in a Black Community." Paper read at the Annual Meeting of the American Psychological Association, Washington, D.C., September 1969.

12. Jackson, Jacquelyne J. "Aged Negroes: Their Cultural Departures from Statistical Stereotypes and Rural-Urban Differences." *The Gerontologist* 10 (Summer 1970): 140-45.

13. Jackson, Jacquelyne J. "Kinship Relations among Urban Blacks." *Journal of Social and Behavioral Sciences* 16 (Winter 1970): 1-13.

14. Kahana, Boas, and Kahana, Eva. "Grandparenthood from the Perspective of the Developing Grandchild." Mimeographed, Washington University, St. Louis, Missouri, 1969.

15. Orshansky, Mollie. "The Aged Negro and His Income." *Social Security Bulletin* 27 (February 1964): 3-13.

16. *Philadelphia Tribune*, 14 November 1970, p. 21.

17. Schlitz, Michael E. *Public Attitudes Toward Social Security, 1935-65.* Research Report No. 33, U.S. Social Security Administration. Washington, D.C.: U.S. Government Printing Office, 1970.

18. Shanas, Ethel, et al. *Old People in Three Industrial Societies.* New York: Atherton, 1968.

19. Shanas, Ethel, and Streib, Gordon. *Social Structure and the Family: Generational Relations.* Englewood Cliffs, New Jersey: Prentice-Hall, 1965.

20. Smith, T. Lynn. "The Changing Number and Distribution of the Aging Negro Population of the United States." *Phylon* 28 (Winter 1957): 339-54.

21. Townsend, Peter. *The Family Life of Old People.* Glencoe, Illinois: The Free Press, 1957.

22. Young, Michael, and Willmott, Peter. *Family and Kinship in East London.* London: Routledge and Kegan Paul, 1957.

22

Memories of My Grandmother *

Curt Davis

Some people need a lifetime to discover their true soul, their Weltanschauung, their perspective. When they find it, it is practically an epiphany. I found mine early in someone else and liked it well enough to keep it. My grandma, short and squat, white haired and fair skinned, with sagging breasts but upraised heart, so defined my self from the days when she would rock me on her knee as we sang, "Jesus Loves Me," to the last words she spoke to me, that it was more a privilege than an off-handed duty to forever incorporate her into myself.

Eleanor Hackett—alternately Gamma, Gam, Grandmother, and Evil Woman—was a woman who always carried herself with dignity, never sloppily. You cannot imagine her slouching in a chair (occasionally when she would sit she would spread her legs a bit wider than protocol allowed, but slouch—never). Even when she knelt in prayer, as she did every evening, she was able to walk about, she did not rest on the bed: She used it as something sacred, as the vehicle driving

*Reprinted by permission of the author.

her to a moment's communion with her Lord. Her children always said she should have been a teacher. She could recite the first verse of "O Tannenbaum!"—in Deutsche—right up to her last Christmas. Maybe her daughters still think she was not a teacher. I know better.

Mama had to work every day making filaments for car headlights and Father was a self-employed Willy Loman, so Gamma—who had raised her own pair of daughters and my brother as well—was mine all day before I went to kindergarten and she was always there whenever I came home from school for lunch or at the end of the day or if I was sick. She had taught me to read before I entered school; so well, in fact, that I was reading on a third-grade level that first year, to the delight of my teacher—another wonderful, grandmotherly woman—and the resentment of some of my peers. But Gams showed me the joy in reading and consequently in learning that would be but one of her legacies. Everybody at school, from principal to teacher to friends I would bring home, loved my Grandma, too, because she was just that way: No airs, but politeness in every glance and word, concern for the other person, and a laugh whose infection was curable only by death, and even then it chimes every so often in my soul.

When I was six years old, Grandma had a heart attack while sitting on the toilet. I vaguely remember police and firemen coming to the house and removing her to the hospital. But, as far as I could see, neither that nor a small cancer on her nose a year or so later really jeopardized her—or us. She was just going away for a bit of rest and maybe a test or two, but she would be back. She would always be back, because I was there and she had to do for me and take care of me and tell me about me. And about God, too, and growing up. And she would have to play Movie Nishuls with me on the front porch in the summertime and inside in the winter. One of us would give the initials of a movie to the other. She would rarely stump me, but sometimes she got my initials more quickly than I thought she would, particularly if I gave her Wallace Beery titles.

Many is the night I remember her sitting in a strong-backed chair in the second-floor bedroom, near the window, all lights out in the room but because I could not sleep she brought her own luminous soul in to see what she could do. She would grab me from the bed, prop me on her round knee, point me toward the window to see the fireflies and moths play catch-me-if-you-can with the street lamps, and sing, "Jesus Loves Me," or, "Open Up Your Heart and Let the Sunshine In," or a hymn or a Christmas carol or something.

Grandma never seemed to have any hobbies. Looking back, I guess she just didn't have the time. Unless you could call God her hobby. She taught Sunday school for forty years—the years I was in her class, I *really* felt like a teacher's pet, and I would answer her questions about the Pentateuch in terms of Charlton Heston in Cecil B. DeMille's epic and she would smile a bit and say, "Yes, Curty." When I was not in her class, the inspiration filtered down Sundays and throughout the week. Once I said something anti-Christ to see what she would do. I had an upset stomach and she gave me some Pepto-Bismol. A catchphrase at the time was, "It (you, he, she) sends me," so I said, "Oh, it sends me—right up to the Lord Jesus Christ." My Gams was aghast, set the bottle and spoon down and said in a tone of hurt and disappointment that made my eyes feel like welts and my heart a bruise: "Don't you ever say that again." I apologized immediately, but I still may not be exorcised of that. By her, yes; by me, no.

Of course there were things over the years that annoyed me about her, like her insistence that I change clothes when I came home from school. And the fact that she knew me better than I knew myself. She knew of my cross-fertilization of sexual identities and acknowledged it a couple of times to my fury and inability to adjust to it at the time. Most of her wisdom was gift wrapped in one-liners and reactions to a story or situation and not in lectures. We rarely discussed a topic in total detail, except for my brother's broken marriage and my mother and aunt's constant bickering. Grandma's eyes may not have been 20-20 but her perception was and some of those soulful looks felt like they could kill me. My *self* was still wet behind the ears—and any other appendage you would care to mention. And Grandma's examples of self-knowledge sometimes felt like that snapped towel that gathers no moisture. It was this introspection that led me to affectionately nickname her "Evil." She understood *all* the implications.

We always knew we loved each other. She, of course, said it more than I, but on holidays and birthdays I always said it. But holidays and birthdays do not go on forever and there would be one November morn when I could not say it to her face. I would have to look into the mirror and say it to myself. She had always said she just wanted to live to see me through high school, so she would know I had the credentials for some kind of job. On one of those knee-nights by the window, she had told me that I could be whatever I wanted to be, in this world, that I was to let no one stop me. She murmured, "But even if you're a garbage collector, be the best garbage collector you can be." Gams saw me graduate from grammar and high schools. From then on it would be icing on the multilayer cake.

My first year at Hamilton College was a difficult one. My first semester I got grades ranging from A to F. I had never got an F and I did not quite know how to handle it, but Gams, when I made that phone call home, admonished me; however she also made me know that the world kept on going and I could climb right back on that horse and turn a fall into a leap over a row of bushes. I did. Whenever I would call home, it was always nice when she would answer the phone to say, "Yes, operator, I'll accept the charges." It meant stability, the old fort, peace among warring nations and warring sisters and it meant belief and trust and an old gray mare who was becoming what she did not used to be. Even then, though, as an undergraduate, I sensed some of my striving was for her as well as for me. I wanted to unveil at least one iced layer before the inevitable wind-down.

Toward the end of my senior year, I started making plans for commencement. I wanted parents, of course, brother and his girlfriend of the moment, aunt and, oh-Lord-yes, grand-mother to come. For a few months she had said I should not be surprised if she did not make it. She was tired. After almost sixty years of housekeeping, the woman was tired. I told her she had to come, even mentioning the fact that this was all extra (that is, post-high school). She knew all of that, but could not promise me. I got fraternity brothers to write to her (she was such a hit with two in particular; one—who was to face the death of both parents over the next four years—who so loved her he had nothing to say to me when I made My Call to him), which she really appreciated but could not acquiesce to. I graduated without her there, but with her there.

That July she was led to the hospital, shaking so that she could barely grasp the fence railing outside the house and I knew this time she would not be back. Two days after she entered the hospital, I had to go to Connecticut for a four-week workshop in drama criticism. I wrote to her often and called home every week. One Sunday I called at one o'clock and my aunt answered, saying my mother was at the hospital. That was before visiting hours, but I did not press. I probably did not want confirmation. Mother called me when she came home to say Grandma was not doing well. I asked if I should come home and she said she had thought about asking me. We all knew I would have to be there if she were dying. I spoke to my advisor at the theater and told him I would have to leave. He understood and drove me to the train station the next day. I arrived at home at 12:45 Monday afternoon and went right to the hospital. There she was, in her semiprivate but still claustrophobic room, bars pulled up on the sides of the bed. Tubes were inserted in the nose, the hands that had steadied me on her knee so often were grasping the bars so they would not flutter like the wings of a mortally wounded butterfly. I gasped silently but did not break stride. She looked up and said, "Oh, Curty." I leaned over to kiss her still soft cheek and kept my lips there for an extra moment. She asked me if I was eating well up there—a Yiddishe mama straight through—and I filled her in on how exciting it all was. I stayed for an hour or so and then could take no more—at one point I turned my head and asked God to take her so she would not have to shake anymore; she could just dance before Him. That evening I returned and she looked better, sitting up against several pillows. She even winked at me as I entered. I fed her some Italian ice as she had done throughout my childhood (we used to bet on the flavor the merchant had that day—raspberry was my favorite, lemon hers, but today the flavor was orange). With ten minutes left for visiting, my aunt said her goodnights and I went to my grandma, bent down to kiss her once again and hugged her deep. I said to this blithe but towering spirit. "You know I love you very much." She patted me and whispered, "You're a good boy, Curty," and I left the room.

She died less than an hour later. At least I had come down from Connecticut, at least I had seen her one more time, at least I was the one to hand her over to the One she had taught me so much about. And at least she knew that I was comfortable in the career I had chosen—and that I was not forgetting to eat. Now the cake was iced.

23

Three-Generation Household in the Middle Class*

Ida Lynn

This is my fourth year of retirement from the California Public School System. Since I entered the System after some years of teaching in England, I knew that my retirement pension would be adequate but limiting and thought of returning to England where my expenses, especially medical, would be lighter. (I have always kept in close contact with my family in England). Naturally I did not like the thought of being so far from my only daughter, her husband, and two children, but also in my mind was the idea that by telling them of my plan I relieved them of any feeling of responsibility for Mama! I shall always remember how good it felt to hear Stephanie say that they wanted me to "stay around," that it was ridiculous of me to think of going "back there" and, as an irresistible argument, that their children needed a grandmother.

Still, I had heard so many of my age group, sisters, friends, colleagues, say with great feeling that they would

*Reprinted by permission of the author.

never "move in" with their children, that only disaster could follow if one gave up one's own place, and so on, that I had accepted the concept that for me and for my daughter's family, living too close would be a bad thing. In particular I thought of Jim, my son-in-law. I like him—always have, and did not think he deserved to have mother-in-law always around.

So, since their home was to be in New Jersey and I was in California, I asked them to look out for an apartment for me while they were house hunting. Stephanie wrote that they found apartments to be too costly and that they had dicovered a house with an area that could be completely self-contained for me; living room, bedroom, private entrance, staircase, bathroom, and a small room that could be a kitchen or study or dining room. I learned later that they had searched all over New Jersey to find such a place that would be within their means to buy. The house is close in to town, old-style three story with octagonal rooms in the front, very large meadowlike area in back, and beautiful.

Stephanie and Jim, Libby who is now thirteen, Jennifer now four, sundry cats, and I have been together for four years now and it really seems to be working. I have my own car and drive myself to shops, the doctor, dentist, and the like, but Stephanie drives if I want to go further afield, for I am not a secure driver in unknown territory! Stephanie and Jim can use my car freely as a second car, and very often invite me along on out-of-town excursions in their station wagon.

My door can be closed if I want privacy or if I feel they need to know they are not overseen or overheard, but the door usually stands open when I am home and children, cats, and adults wander in and out. I have a big color TV, while the family set is smaller and is in the parents' bedroom; naturally this attracts the children especially. We usually decide together which programs to watch, though I know that if necessary I have the final word.

I have my own refrigerator but cook in Stephanie's kitchen. I am available for babysitting and enjoy it since I rarely go out in the evening, but Stephanie does not abuse this circumstance nor do I ever feel that it is *required* of me. We have done a lot of planting in front of and around the house and have shared the work and the cost. We both have indoor plants in profusion and I usually repot and doctor any that need help in all rooms. Neither Stephanie nor I are compulsive house cleaners. We keep our own areas picked up and clean when necessary. Libby does kitchen chores for her family and is paid for doing so. I am in good health and like to be active and from the beginning Stephanie has encouraged me to "go out and do things." I fix meals if she is unable to be home and neither of us is rigid about keeping our food apart, though we do not help ourselves to each other's supplies without asking.

These are practical matters that somehow have worked themselves out very easily. More important, emotional and psychological matters have also worked out. We seem to have either a built-in or a learned flexibility that helps considerably, while Jim's attitude has been another major contribution. He is tolerant of the other person's point of view, is uncritical of appearances and actions of others. He believes that each person is entitled to follow her/his own course, so long as it does not encroach on the rights of others.

Problems have arisen; it would be foolish to pretend otherwise, just as it is foolish to pretend that a marriage continues without problems, but problems are dealt with as soon as and as openly as possible—no silent brooding over grievances. For example, I tended to be too indulgent with the children, to give too lavishly with toys and clothes, to supply candy, cake, and so on (but not between meals!). Stephanie asked me not to do it; that was it; no injured feelings involved. Libby has tried to criticize her parents to me; I have told her I will not discuss them with her and it stopped there. I was overprotective of and fearful for Jenny, who is extremely active and venturesome. Stephanie and Jim let me know that they wanted her to grow up dependent upon herself as far as possible and to take her own risks. I learned to look away and keep quiet, realizing that her *parents* would keep a watchful eye and interfere when necessary.

I was raised in an atmosphere of restriction. Children should be seen but not heard; they should only speak when spoken to. It took many years of adulthood before I broke the bonds of these restrictions for myself. Stephanie discussed with me the truth that children are people with rights; that they should feel free to state their position and defend their cause without fear of the physical superiority of the adult. It is good, and healthy—can be a little noisy, but stimulating and usually ends in agreement and/or laughter. We laugh a lot.

Jenny is a restless child at night. She rarely stays in one bed until morning. Sometimes she will arrive in my room with her pillow and soft toy, carefully shut the door to keep out the cats and climb into bed. As soon as she awakes in the morning, I hear, "I'm hungry, how about a pancake," and we go down to fix breakfast. Another time it might be Stephanie who arrives in the night, having deserted Jim because Jenny is occupying the major part of their bed—all very flexible!

My education is continuing. When I was a teenager, sex was utterly taboo as a subject in my home. No spoken or printed word on sex was allowed in the house. I was married before I knew of homosexuals, lesbians, bisexuals. Stephanie is majoring in sociology on the Livingston campus. I have now read an astonishing list of books on different "sex life-styles," plus many on the cause of liberation for women. They are passed on to me when Stephanie has read them. I type her term papers (with one finger). I have gone as a delegate from N.O.W. to the Lesbian Task Force and to a State meeting of N.O.W. in Clinton Prison. I, whose tongue was incapable, and I mean that literally, such was my inhibition, of pronouncing earthy four-letter words, now read them, type them, say them more naturally than the substitute words I previously used. (When I go to England, as I do quite often, I enter the world of my siblings, and speak my preliberation language.)

We have freely discussed the fact that I shall probably have physical problems as the years pass, and what courses we may follow. I have made my own "final arrangements" as far as possible, so that there is no hush-hush on that topic. In the meantime, I have started a part-time job that I thoroughly enjoy; Stephanie is working hard at college, running her home, catering, laundering, bookkeeping, doctoring; Libby is an A student and extremely active socially at school; Jenny plays more with so-called boy toys, real tools, climbing apparatus, and so on, than she does with dolls and wonders aloud why boys and men have a penis and girls and mothers do not; the cats eat the plants and tear up the furniture; and Jim holds the place together—its Great!

The Uses of Social Gerontology

Introduction

Explicitly or implicitly, all the chapters in this book contain items on an agenda for change on behalf of the aged: in attitudes and values, in the distribution of goods and services, in the allocation of social roles, and in the operation of public institutions, to list the most obvious. It is a fashionable platitude of social science that we must first find the question before moving to the answer, and in a sense this is what social gerontology has been all about: defining and shaping the "problem" of old age in such a way that certain policy recommendations flow logically from the analysis. Students frequently ask why we do social science, and what good is it? And we frequently ask ourselves "social science for whom"— our research subjects, other professionals, policymakers, the state of science?

Many studies of the aged have been undertaken with government and foundation grants in hopes that the data will be useful to policymakers, as well as providing dissertation and publication material for the researchers. Much of this research does become grist for legislative mills, and much is published in professional reports and journals that help practitioners in the actual care and treatment of the elderly (both in institutions and in the community). It might be argued that social gerontologists, social workers, and others involved in services to old people have a vested interest in churning out such studies, and would be out of work if the condition of the aged ceased to be problematic. This cynicism seems unwarranted in the light of the deep strain of moral indignation that is so clear in the essays in this book, and throughout the literature: to study the aged is to become an instant advocate of change. Besides, if we only wanted to get grants and build reputations, we would select more congenial or less depressing topics.

Another way in which social science does do things, that is, to have an effect, is that any new information or insight adds to the armamentarium with which we can shape the conditions of existence; knowledge is at least the power to understand what is going on, to foresee and perhaps forestall unintended consequences (although this action in turn produces other unanticipated effects). In any case, simply being exposed to new information subtly alters the existing state of things; for example, that undergraduates now learn anything at all about aging and the elderly will somehow influence their attitudes and behaviors toward the aged, and possibly their own perceptions of self.

As another example, what the aged and their physicians learn about old age may have immediate effects on the quality of their lives. Although it is one of the most reprinted papers in social gerontology, Isadore Rubin's analysis of the myth of the "sexless older years" remains a classic statement of the extent to which role expectations actually influence behavior. While it would be excessive to claim that Rubin's many writings on this topic were a major factor in the sexual liberation of the elderly, his work nonetheless alerted other professionals to the self-fulfilling nature of erroneous stereotypes. By the time that Masters and Johnson's findings worked their way into the public consciousness, the idea of geriatric sex had lost much of its titilating value. Thus, in 1974, we could witness a television interview with an elderly cohabitating couple whose only negative vibes came from some of their children who felt the relationship was unseemly.

How much effect do we have on the general public? Disillusionment follows closely upon the realization that the reams of research on nursing homes, for instance, has not dented the public consciousness. Perhaps we must wait until someone's hand is found in the till before a groundswell of indignation develops—the exposé of nursing-home operations in the *New York Times* almost daily in January 1974 and December 1975* may accomplish what all our careful research has not. It seems impossible that citizens will not react to the knowledge that inadequate facilities have not been taken to court because the enforcement agencies are short of funds and manpower, while the indicted nursing homes have unlimited legal assistance, all paid for by Medicare! Note, that the understaffing or lack of patient care does not seem to produce as strong a reaction as the rip-off aspects. (So even when corrective action is taken, it may be for less exalted reasons than those which ought to disturb us.)

What can we do? Chip away, wherever and whenever we can. My own chapter on "Stereotypes of the Aged" was written at the request of the editors of the *Journal of Communications*, for a special issue on the aged and the media. Here was an opportunity to reach a new and influential audience, through an objective analysis of commercial mass communications, presenting what we had found out to be the realities of old age and chiding the industry for their role in perpetuating destructive myths.** This may have no greater impact on programming that should be more accurate and helpful to all age groups than did publicity on nursing homes, but we must keep trying to get the message through (as Camus reminds us, the ancients knew that pushing those boulders uphill may be all the meaning there is).

---

*For example, the articles by John Hess on the operations of nursing-home proprietors in New York City and State and extensive reporting of the Hearings of the State Legislature and Senate Committees that followed the exposures by investigative reporters.

**Since the publication of this chapter, a number of television programs on the aged have been aired, some of which have directly attacked these stereotypes. Most notable was the serious broadcast by WNEW Metromedia, produced with the assistance of the National Council on Aging, which presented a spectrum of positive life-styles and experiences of old people. Commercial sponsorship of such programming, however, remains a pious hope.

The fruits of social gerontology are of some value to many besides the toilers in the academic fields, most especially to those engaged in political activity on behalf of the aged. We have already mentioned the rise of interest groups centered on the passage of Medicare in the 1950s, and the emergence in the 1960s of professional organizations devoted to research and publication. Indeed, ever since the Townsend Movement for guaranteed pensions attracted a large following of old people in the 1930s, some form of organization of and for the elderly has carried on the quest for adequate health and income legislation. For the most part, however, these lobbies have had only limited impact on Congress or the federal bureaucracy, unless they were also supported by major nonage-based political allies.

Today, again, we may be witnessing the build up of "age power" through a number of apparently well-financed and well-organized national associations. The National Council on the Aging, representing almost 1,500 social welfare groups, has been funding research and media projects,* as well as acting as a political lobby for the past two decades. The National Council of Senior Citizens, organized around the Medicare struggle, has remained intact to support other interests of the elderly. The National Caucus on the Black Aged, as we have seen, is active on a broad range of issues. A relatively articulate and affluent segment of the elderly, primarily teachers, are represented by the National Retired Teachers Association and the American Association of Retired Persons. These groups are, for the most part, "establishmentarian" in that they seek to influence legislators and laypersons within existing political and socioeconomic structures; their boards of directors are composed of such respectable types as business leaders, university professors, politicians, and clergy.

---

*In addition to funding the TV program noted in the last footnote, NCOA has recently published a most important study, The Myth and Reality of Aging in America, by Louis Harris and Associates, 1975. This Harris Survey polled both aged and younger persons regarding the image and reality of older people, and found the two aspects widely discrepant: That is, the image held by the public in general, including older respondents, was much more negative than the reality reported by older respondents for themselves (another instance of "pluralistic ignorance").

It should be no surprise that the decade 1965-75, which brought us the civil-rights movement, student protest, antiwar activity, and the new feminists, should also have produced a grassroots militant movement among the aged. The function of radical subgroups for any social movement is to hold out a vision of the best that could be accomplished, to remind everyone of ultimate goals, and thus ever to be a political gadfly. Such a group is the Gray Panthers, whose statement of purpose, goals, and methods for achieving these ends are outlined in chapter 26.*

Closing this book is the contribution of Matilda White Riley, sociologist par excellence, who has taken the study of old age as the starting point for a major extension of social theory. In such fashion do our conclusions become beginnings: in this case, the definitive compilation of research findings up to 1970 serves as the springboard for a sociology of age stratification. Riley proposes that conceptualizing society as composed of age strata provides new insights into the operation of the social system, as well as into the lives of individual role players. In chapter 20 Lozier and Althouse spoke of understanding social systems through consideration of the shapes of the pieces and of the places they are supposed to fit. More elegantly, the theory of age stratification does just this, analyzing the number** and characteristic of role players on the one hand, the positions open to them in various

*The Panthers may be unique in combining all the aims of the major movements of the past decade; their platform contains statements against agism, sexism, militarism, and racism, as well as sympathy for such youth-culture goals as amnesty and legalization of marijuana. In a personal letter to me, Maggie Kuhn, national convener and guiding spirit of the Panthers, repeated the remark of one delegate to the 1975 Gray Panther Convention: "We are on a long pilgrimage, and a lark."

**The question of numbers is not as simple as it seems. In earlier chapters we noted how the proportion of the aged fluctuates by birth cohort, which will affect the degree to which the aged are "visible" or perceived of as an important segment of the population, how many claimants there are for resources, and so on. A thorough examination of the many ways in which the number of babies born in a year can have effects throughout the life course on the personal histories of these individuals can be found in Joan Waring's essay, "Social Replenishment and Social Change: The Problem of Disordered Cohort Flow," *American Behavioral Scientist* 19, no. 2 (November-December 1975): 237-56.

subsystems on the other, plus the principles and channels of role allocation that link actor and status. Professor Riley's chapter provides a ready summary of where we have been in social gerontology, and presents challenges for the future in both policy and research.*

It is not always easy to see how developments in social theory or methodology can do much to change the social systems we would like to make more responsive to human needs. Many activist sociologists believe that excessive concerns with intradisciplinary matters is a form of moral masturbation, essentially conservative, establishmentarian, and supportive of the status quo, part of the very problem of the oppressed. But effective action depends upon knowing just what to change, on perceiving the interconnectedness of things, and in anticipating latent consequences. Solid research, grounded theory, and sophisticated methods are in the long run more effective tools for change than rhetoric and good intentions. Verstehen is not instant insight, but the outcome of exploring the myriad forces impinging upon an individual in particular locations in the broader social structure. It is from this knowledge that we can construct a different reality, if we choose.

*An early but impressive fruit of the sociology of age stratification are the two issues of the *Journal of Social Issues* 30, nos. 2-3 (1974), under the editorship of Vern L. Bengston and Robert S. Laufer, collectively titled, "Youth, Generations, and Social Change." And, more recently, the *American Behavioral Scientist* 19, no. 2 (November-December 1975), an issue devoted to "Age in Society," edited by Ann Foner.

24

The "Sexless Older Years": A Socially Harmful Stereotype*

Isadore Rubin

It has been suggested that our culture has programmed marriage only until the child-raising period has been completed (10). If this is true of marital roles in general, it is especially true of sexual roles in the later years. Society has not given genuine recognition to the validity of sexual activity after the child-bearing years, creating a dangerous stereotype about the "sexless older years" and defining as deviant behavior sex interest and activity that may continue vigorously into these older years. Thus, for example, the opprobrious term *lecher* is never coupled with any age group but the old; the young are *lusty* or *virile*.

A Self-Fulfilling Prophecy

This stereotype has until recently placed its unchallenged stamp upon our culture. In the late 1950s, undergraduates at Brandeis University were asked to take a test to assess their attitudes toward old people (23). Those taking the test were requested to complete this sentence: "Sex for most old

*Reprinted by permission of The American Academy of Political and Social Science, 3937 Chestnut Street, Philadelphia, Pennsylvania 19104. This work appeared in *The Annals,* March 1968, pp. 86-95.

people. . . ." Their answers were quite revealing. Almost all of these young men and women, ranging in age from seventeen to twenty-three, considered sex for most old people to be "negligible," "unimportant," or "past." Since sex behavior is not only a function of one's individual attitudes and inter- actions with a partner, but also a reflection of cultural expectations, the widespread belief about the older person being sexless becomes for many a "self-fulfilling prophecy." Our society stands indicted, says psychiatrist Karl M. Bowman, of grave neglect of the emotional needs of aging persons:

> Men and women often refrain from continuing their sexual relations or from seeking remarriage after loss of a spouse, because even they themselves have come to regard sex as a little ridiculous, so much have our social attitudes equated sex with youth. They feel uncertain about their capacities and very self-conscious about their power to please. They shrink from having their pride hurt. They feel lonely, isolated, deprived, unwanted, insecure. Thoughts of euthanasia and suicide bother them. To prevent these feelings, they need to have as active a sex life as possible and to enjoy it without fear (7).

Most of our attitudes toward sex today still constitute— despite the great changes that have taken place in the openness with which sex is treated publicly—what a famous British jurist has called "a legacy of the ascetic ideal, persisting in the modern world after the ideal itself has deceased" (40). Obviously, the ascetic attitude—essentially a philosophy of sex-denial—would have far-reaching effects upon our attitude toward the sexual activity of those persons in our society who have passed the reproductive years. Even so scientific a writer as Robert S. de Ropp, in his usually excellent *Man against Aging*, betrays the unfortunate effects of our ascetic tradition when he says:

> For sexual activity, enjoyable as it may seem in itself, still has as its natural aim the propagation of the species, and this activity belongs to the second not the third act of life's drama (12).

In addition to our tradition of asceticism, there are many other factors that undoubtedly operate to keep alive a strong resistance to the acceptance of sexualilty in older people. These include our general tradition of equating sex, love, and romance solely with youth; the psychological difficulty that children have of accepting the fact of parental intercourse; the tendency to think of aging as a disease rather than a normal process; the focusing of studies upon hospitalized or institutionalized older people rather than upon a more typical sample of persons less beset by health, emotional, or economic problems; and the unfortunate fact that—by and large— physicians have shared the ignorance and prejudices equally with the rest of society (29).

It is significant, however, that centuries of derogation and taboo have not been successful in masking completely the basic reality that sex interest and activity do not disappear in the older years. Elaine Cumming and William E. Henry point out that our jokes at the expense of older people have revealed considerable ambivalence in the view that all old people are asexual (10). The contradictory attitude that people possess about sexuality in the later years is also well illustrated by the history of the famous poem "John Anderson, My Jo," written by Robert Burns almost two centuries ago. In the version known today, the poem is a sentimental tribute to an old couple's calm and resigned old age. The original folk version— too bawdy to find its way into textbooks—was an old wife's grievance about her husband's waning sex interest and ability, which makes very clear that she has no intention of tottering down life's hill in a passionless and sexless old age (8). It is also interesting to note that sexuality in older women was an important part of one of Aristophanes' comedies. In his play *Ecclesiazusae* ("Women in Parliament"), Aristophanes described how the women seized power and established a social utopia (15). One of their first acts was to place sexual relations on a new basis in order to assure all of them ample satisfaction at all times. They decreed that, if any young man was attracted to a girl, he could not possess her until he had satisfied an old woman first. The old women were authorized to seize any youth who refused and to insist upon their sexual rights, also.

The Harmful Influence of the Myth

A British expert in the study of aging has suggested that the myth of sexlessness in the older years does have some social utility for some older women in our society who may no longer have access to a sexual partner (9). However, the widespread denial of sexuality in older persons has a harmful influence that goes far beyond its effect upon an individual's sexual life (35). It makes difficult, and sometimes impossible, correct diagnoses of medical and psychological problems, complicates and distorts interpersonal relations in marriage, disrupts relationships between children and parents thinking of remarriage, perverts the administration of justice to older persons accused of sex offenses, and weakens the whole self-image of the older man or woman.

A corollary of the failure to accept sexuality as a normal aspect of aging has been the tendency to exaggerate the prevalence of psychological deviation in the sexual behavior of older men and to see in most old men potential molesters of young children. Seen through the lenses of prejudice, innocent displays of affection have often loomed ominously as overtures to lascivious fondling or molestation. It is common, too, to think of the exhibitionist as being, typically, a deviation of old age.

Actually, the facts indicate the falsity of both of these stereotypes. As research by Johann W. Mohr and his associates at the Forensic Clinic of the Toronto Psychiatric Hospital showed, "contrary to common assumption, the old-age group is the relatively smallest one" involved in child-molesting (31). The major age groups from whose ranks child-molesters come are adolescence, the middle to late thirties, and the late fifties. The peak of acting out of exhibitionism occurs in the mid-twenties; and, in its true form, exhibitionism is rarely seen after the age of forty.

In relatively simple and static societies, everyone knows pretty much where he stands at each stage of life, particularly the older members of the group. "But in complex and fluid social systems," notes Leo W. Simmons, "with rapid change and recurrent confusion over status and role, no one's position is so well fixed—least of all that of the aging" (37). For many aging persons, there is a crisis of identity in the very sensing of themselves as old, particularly in a culture that places so great a premium upon youth. David P. Ausubel notes that, just as in adolescence, the transition to aging is a period where the individual is in the marginal position of having lost an established and accustomed status without having acquired a new one and, hence, is a period productive of considerable stress (2). Under such conditions of role confusion, aging persons tend to adopt the stereotype that society has molded for them, in sex behavior as in other forms of behavior. But they do so only at a very high psychic cost.

For many older people, continued sexual relations are important not so much for the pleasurable release from sexual tension as for the highly important source of psychological reinforcement that they may provide. Lawrence K. Frank has said:

Sex relations can provide a much-needed and highly effective resource in the later years of life when so often men face the loss of their customary prestige and self-confidence and begin to feel old, sometimes long before they have begun to age significantly. The premature cessation of sexual functioning may accelerate physiological and psychological aging since disuse of any function usually leads to concomitant changes in other capacities. After menopause, women may find that continuation of sexual relations provides a much-needed psychological reinforcement, a feeling of being needed and of being capable of receiving love and affection and renewing the intimacy they earlier found desirable and reassuring (19).

The Growing Body of Research Data

Gathering data about the sexual behavior and attitudes of the aging has not been an easy task. To the generalized taboos about sex research have been added the special resistance and taboos that center around sexuality in older persons. For example, when the New England Age Center decided to administer an inventory to its members, they included only nine questions about sex among the 103 items (1). The nine questions were made deliberately vague, were confined largely to past sexual activities, and were given only to married members. Leaders of the Center felt that if they had asked more direct questions or put them to their unmarried members, those people would not have returned to the Center. In California, a study of the attitudes of a sample of persons over sixty years old in San Francisco during the early 1960s including just one general, open-ended question about sexual attitudes, apparently because of the resistance that many of the researchers had about questioning subjects in the area of sex (16). Psychiatrists reporting on this research before the Gerontological Society noted that the people involved in research in gerontology are being hamstrung by their own attitudes toward sex with regard to the elderly in much the same way in which the rest of society is hamstrung with regard to their attitudes toward the elderly in such matters as jobs, roles, and those things which go into determining where a person fits into the social structure.

Fortunately, although no sample has yet been studied that was sufficiently broad or typical to present us with a body of norms, a sufficient amount of data now exists that leaves no doubt of the reality of sex interests and needs in the latter years. While it is true that there are many men and women who look forward to the ending of sexual relations, particularly those to whom sex has always been a distasteful chore or those who "unconsciously welcome the excuse of advancing years to abandon a function that has frightened them since childhood" (39), sexual activity, interest, and desire are not the exception for couples in their later years. Though the capacity for sexual response does slow down gradually, along with all the other physical capacities, it is usually not until actual senility that there is a marked loss of sexual capacity.

With the research conducted by William H. Masters and Virginia E. Johnson, who observed the anatomy and physiology of sexual response in the laboratory, confirmation has now been obtained that sexual capacity can continue into advanced old age (30). Among the subjects whose orgasmic cycles were studied by these two investigators were 61 menopausal and postmenopausal women (ranging from 40 to 78) and 39 older men (ranging from 51 to 89). Among the women, Masters and Johnson found that the intensity of physiologic reaction and the rapidity of response to sexual stimulation were both reduced with advancing years. But they emphasized that they found "significant sexual capacity and effective sexual performance" in these older women, concluding:

The aging human female is fully capable of sexual performance at orgasmic response levels, particularly if she is
exposed to regularity of effective sexual stimulation. . . .
There seem to be no physiologic reasons why the frequency
of sexual expression found satisfactory for the younger
woman should not be carried over into the postmenopausal
years. . . . In short, there is no time limit drawn by the
advancing years to female sexuality.

When it came to males, Masters and Johnson found that
there was no question but that sexual responsiveness weakens
as the male ages, particularly after the age of sixty. They
added, however:

There is every reason to believe that maintained regularity
of sexual expression coupled with adequate physical well-
being and healthy mental orientation to the aging process
will combine to provide a sexually stimulative climate within
a marriage. This climate will, in turn, improve sexual
tension and provide a capacity for sexual performance that
frequently may extend to and beyond the eighty-year level.

These general findings have been supported by various
types of studies that have been made over the course of the
years. These studies include the investigation by Raymond
Pearl in 1925 into the frequency of marital intercourse of men
who had undergone prostatic surgery, all over the age of 55
(34); Robert L. Dickinson and Lura E. Beam's studies of
marriages and of single women, including a number of older
single women and widows (31); the Kinsey studies of the male
and the female (27, 28); older men studied at outpatient clinics
by urologists at the University of California School of Medicine
at San Francisco (17); extended study by Duke University
psychiatrists of Negroes and whites living in the Piedmont area
of North Carolina (32); Joseph T. Freeman's study of older men
in Philadelphia (20); a study of patients attached to a geriatric
clinic in New York (22); a survey of veterans applying for
pensions (6); a questionnaire survey by Sexology magazine of
men over 65 who were listed in Who's Who in America (36);
and a study of sex attitudes in the elderly at the Langley Porter
Neuropsychiatric Institute in San Francisco (16).

No Automatic Cutoff Date

All of these indicate the continuation of sex needs, interests, and abilities into the later years despite the gradual weakening that may take place. The Kinsey group, quite contrary to general conceptions of the aging process in sex, found that the rate at which males slow up sexually in the last decades of life does not exceed the rate at which they have been slowing up and dropping out of sexual activity in the previous age groups (27). For most males, they found no point at which old age suddenly enters the picture. As far as females were concerned, the Kinsey investigators—like Masters and Johnson later—found little evidence of any aging in their capacities for sexual response (28). "Over the years," they reported, "most females become less inhibited and develop an interest in sexual relations which they then maintain until they are in their fifties and even sixties." In contrast to the average wife, the responses of the husband dropped with age. Thus, many of the younger females reported that they did not desire intercourse as often as their husbands. In the later years of marriage, however, many of the wives expressed the desire for coitus more often than their husbands were then desiring it.

The Duke University survey—reported by Gustave Newman and Claude R. Nichols—found that only those persons who were seventy-five or older showed a significantly lower level of sexual activity (32). This study found that Negro subjects were sexually more active than white subjects; men were more active than women; and persons lower in the social and economic scale were more active than those in the upper-income group. A possible explanation of the greater activity reported by males lies in the fact that men and women of the same age were reporting on different age groups. The wives, on the average, would be reporting on sex activity with a husband who was perhaps four years older.

Despite the fact that masturbation has been usually considered an activity that ends with maturity, for many older persons, this practice apparently continues to serve as a satisfactory form of release from sexual tensions when a partner is, for one reason or another, not available (13, 36).

Several of the studies suggest a correlation between early sex activity and a continuation into the late years. The Kinsey group found that, at age fifty, all of the males who had been sexually active in early adolescence were still sexually active, with a frequency about twenty percent higher than the frequency of the later-maturing males (27). They report:

Nearly forty years maximum activity have not yet worn them out physically, physiologically, or psychologically. On the other hand, some of the males (not many) who were late adolescent and who have had five years less of sexual activity, are beginning to drop completely out of the picture; and the rates of this group are definitely lower in these older-age periods.

They conclude:

The ready assumption which is made in some of the medical literature that impotence is the produce of sexual excess, is not justified by such data as are now available.

Freeman (20) found that the sex urge of persons in advanced years correlated strongly with their comparative sex urge when young, and a similar finding was reported by the Duke University survey (32).

Masters and Johnson report the same finding, with additional emphasis upon regularity of sexual expression as the essential factor in maintaining sexual capacity and effective performance for both males and females (30):

When the male is stimulated to high sexual output during his formative years and a similar tenor of activity is established for the thirty-one-forty-year range, his middle aged and involutional years usually are marked by constantly recurring physiologic evidence of maintained sexuality. Certainly it is true for the male geriatric sample that those men currently interested in relatively high levels of sexual expression report similar activity levels from their formative years. It does not appear to matter what manner of sexual expression has been employed, as long as high levels of activity were maintained.

Factors Responsible for Declining Sex Activity

On the basis of present data, it is not possible to sort out the emotional element from the purely physiologic factors in the decline in sexual activity of the older male. Some animal experiments have shown that changes in the external environment can result in changes in sexual drive. When aging rats had the opportunity for sex activity with a number of partners, for example, the number of copulations increased considerably (5). However, as soon as male rats reached a certain age, they failed to respond to females (26).

Many men also find that, with a new partner, a new stimulus is given to their virility (4). However, often these men return to their old level within comparatively short periods of time (27, 38). Present data lead us to conclude, with the Kinsey investigators:

> The decline in sexual activity of the older male is partly, and perhaps primarily, the result of a general decline in physiologic capacity. It is undoubtedly affected also by psychologic fatigue, a loss of interest in repetition of the same sort of experience, an exhaustion of the possibilities for exploring new techniques, new types of contacts, new situations (27).

Masters and Johnson, on the basis of their clinical work with older males, describe six general groups of factors that they believe to be responsible for much of the loss of sexual responsiveness in the later years: (a) monotony of a repetitious sexual relationship (usually translated into boredom with the partner); (b) preoccupation with career or economic pursuits; (c) mental or physical fatigue; (d) overindulgence in food or drink; (e) physical and mental infirmities of either the individual or his spouse; and (f) fear of performance associated with or resulting from any of the former categories.

The most constant factor in the loss of an aging male's interest is the problem of monotony, described by the Kinsey group as "psychologic fatigue." According to Masters and Johnson, many factors may produce this: failure of the sexual relationship to develop beyond a certain stage; overfamiliarity; lack of sexual interest on the female's part; aging and loss of personal attractiveness of the female.

A major deterrent for many men is preoccupation with the outside world and their careers. Overindulgence in food and drink, particularly the latter, takes a high toll. According to Masters and Johnson, secondary impotence developing in the late forties or early fifties has a higher incidence of direct association with excessive alcohol consumption than with any other single factor.

As each partner ages, the onset of physical or mental infirmities is an ever-increasing factor in reducing sexual capacities. The harmful effect of this is sometimes multiplied by the negative or discouraging attitude of the physician. Once a failure in performance has occurred because of any of the factors, the fear of failure becomes an additional factor in bringing about withdrawal from sexual activity. "Once impotent under any circumstances," remark Masters and Johnson, "many males withdraw voluntarily from any coital activity rather than face the ego-shattering experience of repeated episodes of sexual inadequacy."

The very scanty data concerning the sexual attitudes of older persons suggest a more positive attitude toward sex among men than among women, with women being more "culture bound" and still showing strong evidences of the effects of the Victorian age in which they acquired their attitudes toward sex (16). A study of dreams of residents of a home for the aged and infirm, on the other hand, indicates a contrasting difference in emotional tone of the sexual content of the dreams of men and women: "Whereas in men sexual dreams revealed anxiety, failure, and lack of mastery, in women they usually depicted passive, pleasurable gratification of dependent needs" (3).

The Unmarried Have Sex Needs, Too

It is not only the married who have sexual needs. Aging widows, widowers, and single persons, who make up an increasingly large segment of our population, face even greater problems in respect to sex than do the married. In the survey by Newman and Nichols, only seven of the 101 single, divorced, or widowed subjects reported any sexual activity with partners (32). Apparently, the strength of the sexual drive of most elderly persons is usually not great enough to cause them to seek a sexual partner outside of marriage in the face of social disapproval and the difficulties of such an endeavor. Interestingly, however, thousands of older couples were reportedly living "in sin—or what they think is sin" because marriage would mean loss of social security payments (33).

Dickinson and Beam reported that in their study of widows ranging from sixty to eighty years of age there was evidence of masturbation (13). They reported that when these women underwent pelvic examinations they showed such marked sexual reactions that they found that "it is desirable to relieve the patient's embarrassment by hurting her, lest she have orgasm." Since many older women are quite troubled by their practice of masturbation, marriage counselors have stressed the importance of helping older persons to accept this practice as a valid outlet when they feel the need for it (25).

The Great Need for Information

Persons who have worked with "senior citizens" and "golden age" clubs have reported the great need for knowledge, the confusion, and the eager hunger for information about sex shown by persons in these clubs (16). The many perplexing problems that they raise indicate the extent to which such information is needed to help people solve broader questions of remarriage and interpersonal relationships during their later years. The growing incidence of disease states in these years—each of which may require a difficult readjustment in sexual and other relationships—makes it essential that older people be provided with this information openly and consistently (35).

It should be clear, however, that unless our entire culture recognizes the normality of sex expression in the older years, it will be impossible for older persons to express their sexuality freely and without guilt. Physicians are particularly crucial in this respect; unless they are convinced of the psychological importance of sexual functioning in the later years, they can do irreparable harm to their patients' sexuality (18, 24). Fortunately, at long last, medical schools and medical publications have begun to take steps to correct the glaring lacks in the education of medical students, which have in the past resulted in the creation of a body of medical practitioners who, by and large, shared the general prejudices of our society concerning sexuality in older persons.

References

1. Armstrong, E. B. "The Possibility of Sexual Happiness in Old Age." *Advances in Sex Research*. Edited by H. G. Beigel. New York: Hoebel-Harper, 1963.

2. Ausubel, D. P. *Theory and Problems of Adolescent Development*. New York: Grune and Stratton, 1954.

3. Barad, M.; Altshuler, K. Z.; and Goldfarb, A. I. "A Survey of Dreams in Aged Persons." *Archives of General Psychiatry* 4 [April 1961]: 419-24.

4. Bernard, J. *Remarriage*. New York: Dryden, 1956.

5. Botwinick, J. "Drives, Expectancies, and Emotions." *Handbook of Aging and the Individual*. Edited by J. Birren. Chicago: University of Chicago Press, 1959.

6. Bowers, L. M.; Cross, R. R., Jr.; and Lloyd, F. A. "Sexual Function and Urologic Disease in the Elderly Male." *Journal of the American Geriatrics Society* 11 (July 1963): 647-52.

7. Bowman, K. M. "The Sex Life of the Aging Individual." *Sexual Behavior and Personality Characteristics*. Edited by M. F. Martino. New York: Citadel, 1963.

8. Burns, R. *The Merry Muses of Caledonia*. Edited by J. Barke and S. G. Smith. New York: Putnam, 1964.

9. Comfort, A. Review of *Sexual Life After Sixty* by I. Rubin, *British Medical Journal* (25 March 1967): 750.

10. Cumming, E., and Henry, W. E. *Growing Old*. New York: Basic Books, 1961.

11. Dearborn, L. "Autoeroticism." *The Encyclopedia of Sexual Behavior*. Edited by A. Ellis and A. Abarbanel. New York: Hawthorn, 1961.

12. de Ropp, R. S. *Man against Aging*. New York: Grove Press, 1962.

13. Dickinson, R.L., and Beam, L. E. *A Thousand Marriages*. Baltimore: Williams and Wilkins, 1931.

14. _____. *The Single Woman*. Baltimore: Williams and Wilkins, 1934.

15. Einbinder, H. *The Myth of Brittanica*. New York: Grove Press, 1964.

16. Feigenbaum, E. H.; Lowenthal, M. F.; and Trier, M. L. "Sexual Attitudes in the Elderly." Unpublished paper given before the Gerontological Society, New York, November 1966.

17. Finkle, A. L., et al. "Sexual Function in Aging Males: Frequency of Coitus among Clinic Patients." *Journal of the American Medical Association* 170 (18 July 1959): 1,391-93.

18. _____, and Prian, D. V. "Sexual Potency in Elderly Men before and after Prostatectomy." *Journal of the American Medical Association* 196 (11 April 1966): 139-43.

19. Frank, L. K. *The Conduct of Sex*. New York: Morrow, 1961.

21. Freeman, J. T. "Sexual Capacities in the Aging Male." *Geriatrics* 16 (January 1969): 37-43.

21. Friedfeld, L., et al. "A Geriatric Clinic in a General Hospital." *Journal of the American Geriatrics Society* 7 (October 1959): 769-781.

22. Friedfeld, L. "Geriatrics, Medicine, and Rehabilitation." *Journal of the American Medical Association* 175 (19 February 1961).

23. Golde, P., and Kogan, N. "A Sentence Completion Procedure for Assessing Attitudes Toward Old People." *Journal of Gerontology* 14 (July 1959): 355-63.

24. Golden, J. S. "Management of Sexual Problems by the Physicians." *Obstetrics and Gynecology* 23 (March 1964): 471-77.

25. Hutton, L. *The Single Woman*. London: Barrie and Rockcliff, 1960.

26. Jakubczak, L. F. Report to the American Psychological Association, 31 August 1962.

27. Kinsey, A. C.; Pomeroy, W. B.; and Martin, C. E. *Sexual Behavior in the Human Male*. Philadelphia: W. B. Saunders, 1948.

28. _____, and Gebhard, P. H. *Sexual Behavior in the Human Female*. Philadelphia: W. B. Saunders, 1953.

29. Lief, H. I. "Sex Education of Medical Students and Doctors." *Pacific Medicine and Surgery* 73 (Reburary 1965): 52-58.

30. Masters, W. H., and Johnson, V. E. *Human Sexual Response*. Boston: Little, Brown, 1966; "Geriatric Sexual Response," pp. 223-70.

31. Mohr, J. W.; Turner, R. E.; and Jerry, M. B. *Pedophilia and Exhibitionism*. Toronto: University of Toronto Press, 1964.

32. Newman, G., and Nichols, C. R. "Sexual Activities and Attitudes in Older Persons." *Journal of the American Medical Association* 173 (7 May 1960): 33-35.

33. *New York Times*, 12 January 1965.

34. Pearl, R. *The Biology of Population Growth*. New York: Alfred A. Knopf, 1925.

35. Rubin, I. *Sexual Life after Sixty*. New York: Basic Books, 1965.

36. _____. "Sex over Sixty-five." *Advances in Sex Research*. Edited by H. G. Beigel. New York: Hoeber-Harper, 1963.

37. Simmons, L. W. "Social Participation of the Aged in Different Cultures." *Sourcebook in Marriage and the Family*. Edited by M. Sussman. 2d. ed. Boston: Houghton Mifflin, 1963.

38. Spence, A. W. "Sexual Adjustment at the Climacteric." *Practitioner* 172 (April 1954): 427-30.

39. Stokes, W. R. *Married Love in Today's World*. New York: Citadel, 1962.

40. Williams, G. *The Sanctity of Life and the Criminal Law*. New York: Alfred A. Knopf, 1957.

25

Stereotypes of the Aged*

Beth B. Hess

Old people never did fit
their "image," but the big
story is the emergence of
a truly new breed

My qualifications as an expert on aging come from a three-year total immersion in the social science research literature as a member of the study group assembled at Rutgers—the State Univeristy under the direction of Matilda White Riley. Our first task was to assess the state of knowledge regarding aging and old people, to which end I searched out, read, abstracted, and evaluated the methodological reliability of hundreds of research papers in psychology and sociology dating from roughly 1950 to the present. This information was collated, codified, analyzed, and organized along with demographic, physiological, and medical data into

*This work originally appeared in the *Journal of Communication* 24 (Autumn 1974): 76-85, ©1974 by the Annenberg School of Communications. Reprinted by permission of the publisher.

Volume One of Aging and Society: An Inventory of Research Findings, edited by Matilda White Riley, Anne Foner, and associates.*

Having thus worked our way through thousands of pages of research, and having produced a volume of almost 600 pages of carefully weighed and interpreted "findings," we were nonetheless distressed at how very little one could say for certain about any aspect of aging or the lives of old people today. Most studies were of limited value, the findings contradictory, the methodology faulty, and knowledge gaps abysmal. While the broad demographic data were reliable, comparisons were often more complex than they appeared, while reliance upon cross-sectional studies led to erroneous conclusions. More important, what we did find out about America's elderly frequently contradicted what we thought we knew about old people as a matter of common sense.

For instance, in our earlier, taken-for-granted world, old people were relatively unproductive workers, suffered precipitous declines in intelligence, were emotional and financial drags on their adult children, preferred to and actually did in large numbers live with their children, tended to be removed from active participation in the society, to have lost sexual capacities, to be wracked by despair and anxieties, and ultimately dumped by uncaring kin into public institutions.

In fact:

—Old people remaining in the labor force generally perform at comparable levels to younger workers; often better in tasks requiring experience, though somewhat poorer in those depending upon speed (12).
—Declines in intelligence that are marked in cross-sectional data appear less so in longitudinal studies (12).

*Volume Two, Aging and the Professions, edited by Matilda White Riley, John W. Riley, Jr., and Marilyn E. Johnson, appeared the following year, devoted to essays on applications of the research findings to the several professional fields concerned with old people: social work, nursing, architecture, law, and so forth. In 1972, the third and last volume was published: A Sociology of Age Stratification, edited by Matilda White Riley, Marilyn E. Johnson, Anne Foner, and associates.

—Old people are as likely as not to have given help to adult children, while slightly more than one-third report receiving occasional gifts of money from their children (12).

—Approximately 80 percent of men and women over 65, in 1965, were living as heads of households or as wives of the head. Of the remainder, only 12 percent lived with their children, and only 4 percent in institutions (12). However, of those with living children, over one-fourth did live in the same household, while over 80 percent lived within one-hour's distance from the nearest child (12).

—While frequency of sexual intercourse declines with age (from age 20 on), many old people remain sexually active into their 70s, depending upon the availability of partners and willingness to utilize other outlets (12).

—Voting rates, in 1965, for persons 75+ were *higher* than for those aged 21-24 (12).

—Self-evaluations are positive across a range of traits, including body image (12).

—Institutionalization is typically a *last* resort for the families of the aged, and is usually preceded by a shift in the old person's ability to function or in the capacities of others to care for him or her (12).

Although the condition of the aged *is* indeed more deprived than that of younger cohorts, or even of the elderly themselves at earlier life stages, many negative stereotypes are clearly not supported by the research data.* That such myths (both positive and negative) are frequently shared by old people leads us to examine the process of communication: How and what information or misinformation about old age is conveyed and received by all age groups?

---

*Palmore and Whittington (9) recorded a widening gap between old and young age groups in economic, social, and residential terms. The decline in status and satisfactions of the aged, they note, is a feature of modern, industrial societies. The authors support the definition of the aged as a "minority group," due precisely to the negative stereotypes noted above, residential segregation, discrimination, and the development of a unique subculture.

I shall attempt to specify some of the constraints upon both purveyors and customers of the mass commercial media that might result in the generation and maintenance of mythical representations of the aged

A sociological model of mass communications has already been diagrammed by Riley and Riley (11), which locates both communicators (C) and recipients (R) in their respective networks of reference groups, mutually influencing the messages transmitted, and shows the whole process embedded in an overall social system at a historical moment.* Figure 1 adapts the Riley and Riley paradigm to the set of exchanges we shall be discussing. To specify the elements in the model:

1. *Sender of message* (C), in the commercial media, is influenced (among other groups not specified here) by two major sources of revenue: those who advertise through the medium, and those who purchase the medium (listeners, watchers, buyers, subscribers). Obviously, since age groups vary in consumer power, they will be differentially targeted, and this disparity will be greater to the degree the medium depends upon advertising revenue rather than direct sale.

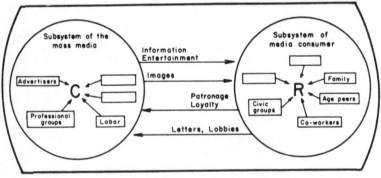

Figure 1:   **Mass communications in society**

2. *Receiver of messages* (R) is a member of number of reference and identity-conferring groups, all of which provide milieux for the processing and interpretation of messages. Age is clearly one of the most relevant of reference group criteria.

*Sociology sometimes seems like playing with Chinese boxes, yet of all social activity, communication is the least amenable to study in a social vacuum; thus, the particular system-based approach of sociology is preeminently suitable. The message is the medium in its institutional setting within the societal context.

3. *Messages* are two-way exchanges, in which information and entertainment are the manifest outputs of the media, in return for audience willingness to consume. However, there is a latent dimension to media messages—in the images one receives about the "self." If we do indeed tend to see ourselves as we perceive others see us, one clue to how others evaluate people with characteristics like ours is the way they are dealt with in the media. Do they, for instance, occupy positions of power; are they the focus of affection; are they heroes or villains?*

4. *In the societal context,* salient features of the contemporary scene, with respect to C, include the economics of mass communication, the dominance of television, and the making of America into a "societal village." On the other side, the R population contains a larger proportion of people over sixty-five than before; couples typically have a decade or more of joint survival after the last child leaves home, and more individuals are retired from work in relatively healthier condition than in the past: In sum, a new stage has been added to the life course of Rs: the postparental or "empty-nest" phase.

Although it is not explicit in the model, we must also take into account the degree to which various segments of R are dependent upon the several media for information and entertainment. A number of studies have shown old people to be high consumers of news programs and newspapers (10, 16); presumably, as other sources of contact are lost or placed beyond their means, those remaining and which require least effort and money to utilize become increasingly important.

*Gecas (3), building upon Laswell's 1948 formulation, notes that a latent, if not manifest, function of the mass media "is that of socialization through presentation of models, the transmission of information and ideas, and the expression of values and attitudes" (p. 680). Although concerned with sex and class categories, these insights are also applicable to age groups: Popular literature, and we would extend this to other media representations, expresses and reinforces the popular expectations of various groups, the differing "definitions of the situation." In depicting these differences, the media also sustain them. "An examination of the imagery presented in this literature, then, is one way to grasp the norms and values of a society and of a historical period" (p. 681).

How, then, have the media served the aged?

With respect to entertainment, television per se, perhaps regardless of content, has been of invaluable service to old people. In an article addressed to retired persons, Peterson (10) notes that television personalities can become substitutes for individuals no longer available to the viewer on a daily face-to-face basis, and that the afternoon soap operas "bring people into their lives." Television permits the old person, especially those who live alone, to maintain the illusion of being in a populated world, and to this extent must reduce feelings of isolation. Radio, similarly, brings the sound of life into an otherwise empty room.*

Regarding the dissemination of information, again, radio and television certainly keep the aged informed on what is happening to everyone else. But it is precisely information about old people themselves that we are concerned with in this paper, and here the track record is spotty. As Schramm (16) pointed out a few years ago (and little seems to have changed since), the media have overlooked the very fact of the emergence of old people as a major segment of the population, with as varied a range of characteristics as any age group. Indeed, the myths and stereotypes fail to capture the reality of old age in America precisely because there is no monolithic "aged" or any one successful way to age. Possibly, as Tuchman (19) notes, that which goes against common sense is simply not perceived as "fact" and the newsperson is loath to purvey it.

However, advertisers are by no means indifferent to those who form a large share of the audience for the early-evening newscasts. Commercials for hair darkeners, laxatives, denture adhesives, and Geritol—products designed to minimize

---

*However, for the downwardly mobile, formerly middle class but currently recipients of Old-Age Assistance, Tissue (17) finds that "television, newspapers, books, hobbies, etc. may serve to pass the time, but they do not appear to provide a sufficient buffer against the combined shock of retirement, downward mobility, and poverty."

the effects of normal aging—are regularly seen with the early-evening newscasts.*

If we now attempt to "explain" media performance in the terms of our conceptual model, clearly the Cs most dependent upon advertising revenues cannot be expected to program for and about old people. The elderly are first of all "poor consumers" because of their low incomes, uncertainty about the future, and unwillingness to invest in products they may not live long enough to enjoy fully.** Second, old people are "poor copy": They remind us of role loss, deprivations, and ultimate demise, none of which is a helpful product association.

It is to the written mass media, more expensive and more difficult to procure, that young and old alike must turn for the kind of knowledge that would correct the stereotypes. News-weeklies, Readers Digest, women's magazines, and the "family-oriented" periodicals are important, if also infrequent, purveyors of up-to-date information on aging, while the New York Times Magazine (2, 5, 6) has had three such articles within the last few months (on sexuality, longevity, and nursing homes). However, to convey a full range of information on a particular segment of the population often requires the production of a specialized periodical, which also serves an isolation-reducing, solidarity-enhancing function (for example, Ebony or Ms.), with emphasis on successful role models. The journal Modern Maturity, for the several million members of the American Association of Retired Persons (primarily teachers) is one such source. The economics of mass distribution of specialized periodicals may effectively inhibit the emergence of a more broad-based, newstand-type publication.

*One notes some ambiguity in the images presented. On the whole, old age is to be minimized, but recent series of Sominex and Alka-Seltzer commercials feature old people as authority figures who attest to the time-proven reliability of the product—which clearly contradicts the "common-sense" belief that old people have outdated knowledge. Other advertisers are beginning to use similar promotions.

**I am reminded of my grandfather, who I am sure is not atypical, who refused to buy a suit for the last decade of his life, feeling that he would not get his money's worth out of it.

In the larger context, Cs operate in a society in which youthfulness is the valued state of being, in which wrinkles, grey hair, lack of zap, and irregularity must be eradicated along with spotty glassware, grimy sinks, and dirty floors. Since we have never accepted gracefully the physical changes of middle age, how can the transition to old age be anything but stressful? And where are role models who could demonstrate avenues of successful aging? This question becomes crucial when we remember that today's old people are the first to survive in large numbers into an old age of retirement from work and family roles, in fair health, and with a good deal of confidence in their capacities for coping. Because this is a "new" stage in life, there are few models to follow, and few institutionalized norms to guide them. Many, too, are inhibited in their enjoyment of leisure by the lingering effects of the work ethic: if productivity is good, nonproductiveness must be somehow sinful.

Turning now to the specific constraints on the old person as receiver of messages, we have already noted (a) the reliance upon, and high consumption of, media output, and (b) the unique characteristics of today's elderly. The salient variable, however, may be the degree of reference group imbeddedness. That is, a crucial condition for the maintenance of mythical representations is the *relative* structural isolation of the elderly. (Note *relative*, since one myth concerns the abandonment of the aged by uncaring children, and another features grandma as a perpetual busybody.) Many exigencies of aging are at work here: death of spouse and friends, retirement and consequent loss of workplace contacts, declining vigor, lowered incomes, and higher probability of chronic illness. Old people are less likely than younger ones, or than themselves at younger ages, to be involved in ongoing webs of primary relationships; consequently they are more likely to receive media messages without the opportunity to test the validity of such inputs through conversation with others. Thus the "social construction of reality," whereby interacting individuals build a world of meaning, that makes sense of their separate experiences and allows a degree of mastery over the environment, becomes more problematical for old people (or, indeed, for any isolated members of the

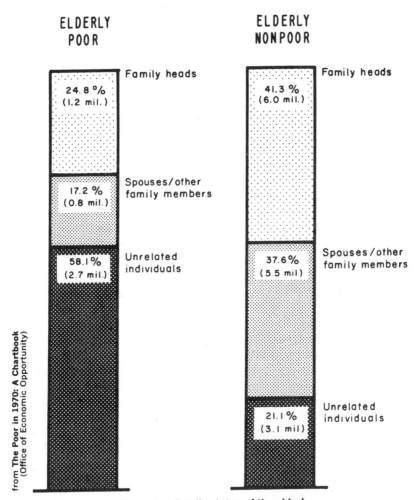

Figure 2:   Family status of the elderly

society) than for those in a number of primary groups. We do know that the old people most cut off from daily intimate relationships are likely to have mental and physical disabilities, low self-esteem, high suicide rates, and so on (1, 7, 12, 17, 18). It is, however, often difficult to disentangle cause and effect: The isolation may be a consequence of impairment; or both isolation and impairment may be the consequence of absolute and relative poverty.*

Nonetheless, the majority of old people are adapting to a denigrating environment, coping with fiscal and health decrements, seeing their children and grandchildren, frequently maintaining friendships, enjoying sexual outlets, and even finding leisure not all that sinful (12, 18).

Clearly, these individuals know they are not like the stereotyped version of an old person, yet how is this cognitive dissonance resolved? Many, of course, do not preceive themselves as "old." It seems plausible, though I know of no conclusive study, that for others the phenomenon of "pluralistic ignorance" is operative, "the pattern in which individual members of a group assume that they are virtually alone in holding the social attitudes and expectations they do, all unknowing that others privately share them. This is a frequently observed condition of a group that is so organized that mutual observability among its members is slight" (8). Pluralistic ignorance, complemented by the process of the self-fulfilling prophecy, suggests that some old people will come to behave in the stereotyped manner, while others believe that everyone else does. Either way, the stereotype remains untested. For example, Isadore Rubin (15) has written extensively on what he sees as the harmful self-fulfilling effect of the general belief that old age brings loss of sexual capacity. In a similar fashion, other myths may be limiting the adaptive capacities of the aged. In the absence of high levels of interpersonal contact, the burden of information dissemination falls upon the media.

Finally, what of the Rs who are not elderly? If old age is as anxiety producing as the attempts to suppress its manifestations indicate, it is doubtful that many younger persons would willingly expose themselves to media presentations of old age

---

*As Hochschild (4) neatly puts it: "Isolation is not randomly distributed across the class hierarchy; there is more of it at the bottom." Again: "The isolation of old people is linked to other problems. The old are poor, and poverty itself is a problem. The old are unemployed and unemployment, in this society, is itself a problem. The old lack community and the lack of community is itself a problem."

even when the tone is upbeat.* We are unlikely to want to find out more about what we refuse even to think of. More crucial, perhaps, is that the relative isolation of the elderly is also the relative isolation of other age groups from the elderly. Not that three-generation households were ever a typical form in the United States (another myth), but it was likely that relatives lived in close proximity and that intergenerational contacts were daily occurrences, even between nonkin. Young persons could hardly avoid learning by observation what lay ahead; anticipatory socialization was built into everyday life.

Without detailing the internecine conflict among sociologists of the family concerning the nature of contemporary intergenerational exchanges, the data show that while parent and grandparent generations are engaged in mutual gift- and service-giving, visit frequently, and feel psychologically close to one another, the overwhelming preference and actual choice of old people is to live alone (12, 18). If one is refuting the thesis of the isolated nuclear-family system, these traits are cited as evidence of a "modified extended family." If, on the other hand, one emphasizes the independence of living units and the voluntary nature of exchanges, the contemporary structure is more accurately called a *modified nuclear-family* system. What is at issue here is more than a semantic quibble, since periodic interaction, however intense, is different from extensive day-to-day exposure to the lives of the aged. Here again, the historical context and societal variables such as residential mobility patterns have an impact on personal life, in this instance the socialization opportunities and experiences of the different generations. And, once again, we must look to media representations to fill in knowledge gaps—if these representations are accurately conveyed by C and willingly sought out by R.

It was the hope of all involved in the *Aging and Society* undertaking that our codification of valid data, and explora-

*This must be a major problem for life insurance companies, as much of their advertising indicates. In a radio commercial I heard recently, a young husband announces that he has bought a policy during lunch-hour; his wife squeals her unwillingness to hear more about it. While reinforcing the stereotype of hysteria and fiscal irresponsiblilty in women, the ad does tap a basic reluctance of young people to think of death.

tion of the implications of these findings, would eventually lead to the inception of meliorative programs based upon accurate assessments of needs, deficits, and strengths of old people. More attention has indeed been paid to the aged in the past several years, but much, much more remains to be done—by federal, state, and local policymakers and, if our analysis here has any validity, by the media. The *Journal of Communication* may provide the momentum required for programming that would present information, role models, and positive images of aging to all age groups. Ironically, the media have thus far missed a truly "big story"—the emergence of a "new breed" of old people, and the ways in which they have demonstrated, once again, the remarkable capacity of human beings to adapt, under extraordinarily trying circumstances, to generate new norms, to devise supportive social structures, and to survive with dignity and grace.

References

1. Bock, E. Wilbur, and Webber, Irving L. "Suicide among the Elderly: Isolating Widowhood and Mitigating Alternatives." *Journal of Marriage and the Family* 34, no. 1 (February 1972): 24-31.

2. Cherry, Rona, and Cherry, Laurence. "Slowly the Clock of Age." *The New York Times Magazine,* 12 May 1974, pp. 20ff.

3. Gecas, Viktor. "Motives and Aggressive Acts in Popular Fiction: Sex and Class Differences." *American Journal of Sociology* 77, no. 4 (Jaunary 1972): 680-95.

4. Hochschild, Arlie Russell. "Communal Life-Styles for the Old." *Transaction/Society* 10, no. 5 (July-August 1973): 50-57.

5. Jacoby, Susan. "Waiting for the Eng: On Nursing Homes." *The New York Times Magazine,* 31 March 1974, pp. 13ff.

6. Lobsenz, Norman M. "Sex and the Senior Citizen." *The New York Times Magazine,* 20 January 1974, pp. 8ff.

7. Lopata, Helena Z. "Loneliness: Forms and Components." *Social Problems* 17, no. 2 (Fall 1969): 248-62.

Merton, Robert K. "Reference Groups and Social Structure." In *Social Theory and Social Structure.* Revised and enlarged edition. Glencoe, Illinois: The Free Press, 1957.

9. Palmore, Erdman, and Whittington, Frank. "Trends in the Relative Status of the Aged." *Social Forces* 50 (September 1971): 84-91.

10. Peterson, James A. "uide to TV Viewing." *Modern Maturity,* April-May 1974, pp. 44-46.

11. Riley, John W., Jr., and Riley, Matilda White. "Mass Communication and the Social System." In *Society Today, Volume Two*. Edited by Robert K. Merton, Leonard Bloom, and Leonard S. Cottrell, Jr. New York: Harper and Row, 1965.

12. Riley, Matilda White, and Foner, Anne. *Aging and Society, Volume One: An Inventory of Research Findings*. New York: Russell Sage Foundation, 1968.

13. Riley, Matilda White; Riley, John W., Jr.; and Johnson, Marilyn E., eds. *Aging and Society, Volume Two: Aging and the Professions*. New York: Russell Sage Foundation, 1969.

14. Riley, Matilda White; Johnson, Marilyn E.; and Foner, Anne; et al. *Aging and Society, Volume Three: A Sociology of Age Stratification*. New York: Russell Sage Foundation, 1972.

15. Rubin, Isadore. "The Sexless Older Years." *The Annals of the American Academy of Political and Social Science* 376 (March 1968): 86-95.

16. Schramm, Wilbur. "Aging and Mass Communication." In *Aging and Society, Volume Two: Aging and the Professions*. Edited by Matilda White Riley, John W. Riley, Jr., and Marilyn E. Johnson. New York: Russell Sage Foundation, 1969.

17. Tissue, Thomas. "Downward Mobility is Old Age." *Social Problems* 18 (Summer 1970;): 67-77.

18. Troll, Lillian E. "The Family of Later Life." *Journal of Marriage and the Family* 33, no. 2 (May 1971): 263-90.

19. Tuchman, Gaye. "Objectivity as Strategic Ritual." *American Journal of Sociology* 77, no. 4 (January 1972): 660-79.

26

Statement of Principles*

The Gray Panthers

Major Concerns
Preamble:

Like racism and sexism, agism is a destructive force that permeates our social institutions. In all our efforts to help solve societal problems, our primary goal will be to attack any manifestation of agism, as well as racism and sexism.

The following priorities are used for guiding us in planning resources, advocacy, and information:

*Advocating participatory democracy and concern for all residents in institutional settings and participants in educational institutions, social service programs, and other social institutions.

*Adequate governmental and private support of mass transportation systems with minimal or no cost to consumers.

*Enactment of a national health-care program, through a public corporation rather than commercial insurance companies; an improved delivery system; and preventive care (includ-

*Reprinted by permission of The Gray Panthers, Ms. Margaret E. Kuhn, National Convener, 3700 Chestnut Street, Philadelphia, Pennsylvania 19104.

ing home care, institutional care, and alternatives to institutional care).

*Abolition of arbitrary and compulsory retirement and age discrimination in employment. Adequate job training and new career possibilities.

*Systematic approach toward the abolition of poverty with such measures as adequate, universal guaranteed income, radical tax reform, guaranteed employment opportunities, and adoption of national compulsory standards for private pension systems and adequate supervision of the standards.

*Renewed effort by the government and industry to encourage and support a national program of housing with a thorough cultural mix of all age groups, income levels, and racial backgrounds.

*Continued efforts to obtain unconditional amnesty for all resisters and deserters in the Southeast Asian war. Redirection of monies now poured into military programs and equipment into efforts to solve problems that concern people in their daily living.

*Reform of our educational system to include programs and opportunities for people of all age groups at minimal or no cost to participants.

Who We Are

We are a group of people—old and young—drawn together by deeply felt common concerns for human liberation and social change. The old and young live outside the mainstream of society. Agism—discrimination against persons on the basis of chronological age—deprives both groups of power and influence.

We believe that the old and the young in our society have much to contribute to make our society more just and human, and that we need to reinforce each other in our goals, our strategy, and our action.

Older persons in this society constitute a great national resource, which has largely gone unrecognized, undervalued, and unused. The experience, wisdom, and competence of older persons are greatly needed in every sector. Creative and innovative ways must be found to enable older people to make their contribution to a new age of liberation. Many older persons have freedom—freedom to think, reflect, and act.

Jobs and families can no longer be jeopardized by radical actions. Older people have demonstrated their ability to cope and survive. Nevertheless, many have been discarded in this technological age and alienated from themselves and society at large. This alienation, if joined with positive self-awareness, can become a liberating social force.

Besides being a movement of older and younger persons, as Gray Panthers we consider ourselves distinctive in the following ways:

*We are against agism that forces any age group to live roles that are defined purely on the basis of age. We view aging as a total life process in which the individual develops from birth to death. Therefore, we are concerned about the needs of all age groups and agism directed at any age group.

*We have a flexible structure as opposed to a bureaucratic organization: A network with multiple leadership and with no formal membership or dues.

*We accept and work with cultural, racial, ethnic, and religious diversity both within the movement and in society. We look for options rather than conformity.

*We have a strong sense of militancy. Our concern is not only for education and services, but for effective nonviolent action with an awareness of timing and urgency.

*We advocate a radical approach to social change by attacking those forces that corrupt our institutions, attitudes, and values, such as maternalism, racism, sexism, paternalism, militarism, and extreme nationalism.

How We Work

We focus on action and consciousness raising, building a network of people and groups in different regions sharing common goals and joint support. At the present time there are emerging networks in most cities in the United States, with a network mailing list of over 7,000 nationwide.

In December 1973 we merged our activities with those of the Retired Professional Action Group, supported by Ralph Nader's Public Citizen, Inc.

We serve as a clearing house for exciting and productive ideas and projects, and as a channel for communication and information. We meet regularly to consider issues and provide mutual empowerment and stimulation. Our newsletter, The Network, functions as a forum and a tie-line.

We are trying on the future for size.

The special input of young people grows from conditions that are frequently parallel of those the old. We complement each other by sharing our different insights and experiences. The energies and enthusiasm of the young, linked with fresh insights and idealism, are powerful forces, too. Powerlessness and pervasive alienation from society affect young as well as old, in ways that can be destructive, but that have great potential for creative action. The ingredient of freedom from overburdening responsibilities and fearful conformity is also present here. The young and the old have such freedom today. Both groups are gaining in self-awareness and corporate strength. The potential of our coalition has barely been glimpsed. We need to reinforce each other in our goals, our strategy, and our action.

What We Want

1. To develop a new and positive self-awareness in our culture that can regard the total life span as a continuing process in maturity and fulfillment.

2. To strive for new options for life-styles for older and younger people that will challenge the present paternalism in our institutions and culture, and to help eliminate the poverty and powerlessness in which most older and younger people are forced to live, and to change society's destructive attitudes about aging.

3. To make responsible use of our freedom to bring about social change, to develop a list of priorities among social issues, and to struggle nonviolently for social change that will bring greater human freedom, justice, dignity, and peace.

4. To build a new power base in our society uniting presently disenfranchised and oppressed groups, realizing the common qualities and concerns of age and youth working in coalition with other movements with similar goals and principles.

5. To reinforce and support each other in our quest for liberation and to celebrate our shared humanity.

27

Social Gerontology and the
Age Stratification of Society*

Matilda White Riley

One decade after "the" White House Conference, and on the
eve of another, all of us involved in research in gerontology
can survey with satisfaction the amount of information
accumulated in these ten years and the impact of this
information upon professional practice, public policy, and
popular attitudes. That much remains to be done is patent to
all gerontologists. We have reached a point where we can pick
and choose among alternative strategies.

*This work originally appeared in The Gerontologist 11, no. 1
(Spring 1971): 79-87. Paper presented at a symposiumn on Research
Goals and Priorities in Gerontology, 23rd Annual Scientific Meeting of
the Gerontological Society, Toronto, 23 October 1970. A more
extensive treatment of this topic is contined in Riley, Johnson, and
Foner, A Sociology of Age Stratification. This is the third volume of a
series on Aging and Society, published by Russell Sage Foundation,
under a grant from the Ford Foundation. In addition to the authors of
the third volume, the following persons have read earlier versions of
this manuscript and made valuable criticisms and suggestions: Beth
Hess, Robert K. Merton, Mary E. Moore, M.D., and John W. Riley, Jr.

What we propose as a high priority for the future is a sociology of age stratification. Gerontologists working in social science fields have amassed a remarkable body of facts on two main topics: being old and growing old.* Our immediate aim is not so much to add to these facts and ideas as to look at them from a fresh perspective. This perspective emphasizes not just old age, but all the age strata in the society as a whole as well; it emphasizes not just aging, but also the societal processes and changes that affect aging and the state of being old.

What do we mean by age *stratification*, which is only now emerging as a new field of sociology? A comparison with the well-established sociology of class stratification is provocative. In that field, two concepts, hueristically stimulating as analogues to our concepts of age strata and aging, have demonstrated their power in explaining diverse social phenomena. These concepts are *social class* (variously defined in terms of inequality of income, prestige, or power) and *social mobility* (consisting of upward or downward movement between lower and higher classes). These concepts of social class and social mobility, which any one of us can grasp intuitively from first-hand experience, have proved scientifically useful in defining and suggesting answers to many important questions. We shall list four sets of these questions briefly, because they may stimulate us to find answers to similar questions in relation to age and aging.

First, how does an individual's location in the class structure channel his attitudes and the way he behaves? Here there is much evidence that, for example, a person's health, his desire to achieve, his sense of mastery over his own fate, or the way he relates to his family and to his job depend to a considerable extent upon his social class.

Second, how do individuals relate to one another within, and between, classes? Within class lines, many friendships are formed, marriages often take place, and feelings of solidarity tend to be widespread. Between classes, relationships, even if

*A team of us at Rutgers required several years to gather, abstract, and organize this impressive body of knowledge before we were able to produce an inventory of research findings, roughly, 600 pages of *selected* social science results, in Riley, Foner, and Associates.

not solidary, are often symbiotic, as people of unlike status live harmoniously in the same society. However, there seems to be greater opportunity between rather than within classes for cleavage or conflict, as exhibited in struggles over economic advantages or clashes in political loyalties.

Third, what difficulties beset the upwardly (or downwardly) mobile individual, and what strains does his mobility impose upon the group (such as his parents of one class) whom he leaves behind and upon the new group (such as his wife's parents of a different class) who must now absorb him?

Fourth, to the extent that answers can be found to these three sets of questions, what is the impact of the observed findings upon the society as a whole? If there are inequalities between classes, for example, what do these portend for the prosperity, the morality, or the stability of the overall structure of classes? What pressures for societal change are generated by differences, conflicts, or mobility between classes?

The literature on these four aspects of class stratification is impressive, pregnant with insights that might be extended to analyses of kindred phenomena. Our concern is to test the utility of the questions it evokes for understanding old age as just one stratum in a society stratified or differentiated, not by class, but by age. Thus we shall start by thinking of society as divided into strata according to the age of its members. *People at varying ages differ in their capacity and willingness to perform social roles* (of student, spouse, worker, or retiree, for example). Moreover, the age strata differ in the social *roles* members are expected to play and in the rights and privileges accorded to them by society. At any given period of time, old people must live as members of such a society, finding their place in relation to the other members who are younger than they, and making choices among whatever opportunities are available to them. Over time, not only old people but also people of different ages are *all* growing older, moving concurrently through a society that itself is undergoing change.

Age Stratification and the Individual

To ask our first question, then: How does an individual's location within the changing age structure of a given society influence his behavior and attitudes? (Mannheim). In the sociological literature generally it has been well established that individuals are conditioned by society. As Robert Merton puts it, "Structure constrains individuals variously situated within it to develop cultural emphases, social behavior patterns, and psychological bents" (Merton). Similarly, it has been well established in the literature of social gerontology that the state of old age reflects the structural context, showing wide variations (as well as some similarities) when primitive and modern societies are contrasted (Simmons), or even when modern, Western nations are compared with one another (Burgess; Havighurst, Munnichs, Neugarten, and Thomae; Shanas and Associates). But how does it come about that, *within* a given society at any given time, individuals located in *different age strata* differ from one another? How are older individuals set off from the middle aged and from the young?

The answer to such a question as this involves two distinct dimensions of time: a life-course dimension and a historical dimension. These two dimensions can be thought of as coordinates for locating the individual in the age structure of society. On the first dimension, individuals at the *same* stage of the *life* course have much in common. They tend to be alike in biological development, in the kinds of roles they have experienced, (such as worker, spouse, parent of dependent child), and in the sheer number of years behind and potential years ahead. People at *different* life-course stages tend to differ in these very respects. The rough index of this life-course dimension is years of chronological age—we say that a person is aged twenty, or in the age category forty-five to sixty. But chronological age is of interest to us, not intrinsically, but only because it can serve as an approximate indicant of personal (that is biological, psychological, and social) experience—and this experience carries with it varying probabilities of behavior and attitudes. This life-course dimension is the familiar one that includes the age-related organic changes affecting physical and mental functioning and that links the biological and the social sciences.

But there is a second time dimension for locating an individual in the age strata that also affects his probability of behaving or thinking in particular ways. This dimension refers to the *period of history* in which he lives. People who were born at the *same* time (referred to as a *cohort*) share a common historical and environmental past, present, and future. For example, when Americans born in 1910 had reached the age of thirty, they had all (in one way or another) experienced World War I and the Great Depression, they were all currently exposed to World War II, and they all confronted the future of the 1940s through the 1970s. People who were born at *different* times (that is different cohorts) have lived through different intervals of history; and even when they encounter the same historical situation, they may, because they differ in age, experience it differently. Thus any one of us—just as we might be ethnocentric—is almost certainly (to add a needed term to our vocabulary) *cohort-centric*. That is, we view old age, or any other stage of life, from the unique point of historical time at which we ourselves are standing. The rough index of this historical (or environmental) dimension is the date, or the calendar year. Here again our concern is not with dates themselves, but with the particular sociocultural and environmental events, conditions, and changes to which the individual is exposed at particular periods.

It comes as no surprise, then, that each of the age strata has its own *distinctive subculture*. By age differences in subculture we mean that a cross-section view of society shows, for myriad characteristics, patterns that are closely related to age. In our own society today, familiar instances of the differing subcultures among young, middle aged, and old include such varied aspects of life as labor-force participation, consumer behavior, leisure-time activities, marital status, religious behavior, education, nativity, fertility and child-bearing practices, or political attitudes—to name only a few. Such age-related patterns differ from time to time and from place to place, as do all the age strata in a society—not the old alone—display differences (or similarities) in behavior and attitudes on the two dimensions of life course and history.

If we want to go beyond a mere description of these age-related subcultures, however, we must examine them further, which leads to our next topic.

Age Stratification and Social Relationships

The second set of questions suggested by the analogy between class stratification and age stratification points to the utility of exploring *relationships* both *between* and *within* age strata. For not only the behavior and attitudes of discrete individuals, but also social relationships—people's positive or negative feelings and actions toward each other—are channeled through the age structure of the particular society. Thus a sociology of age stratification, by investigating these relationships, should help to illuminate the nature of old age.

Many aspects of the cleavages or the bonds between old and young, dramatized by philosophers and poets of the ancient past, are still widely discussed today. Is there an inevitable gap between generations? Do the elderly constitute a disadvantaged minority group, regarded with prejudice by the majority? Or do they control important centers of power, refusing to yield to the young? Are old people likely to form political blocs, seeking to solve their own problems with little regard for the rest of society? And, if many conditions foster intergenerational conflict or exploitation, what other conditions foster relationships of harmony or reciprocity?

As a preliminary to addressing such momentous issues, one small illustration of the sequential relations among generations within the family will point out the interconnectedness of the age strata. If we start with the elderly generation of parents and their adult offspring, a well-known finding from the gerontological literature reports widespread exchanges of material support. This support varies in amount and kind, ranging from financial contributions and care in illness to baby-sitting and help with housework and home repairs. Contrary to previous notions of an upward flow of contributions *to* older people, the flow of support between aged parents and their adult offspring appears to be two-directional, either from parent to child or from child to parent as need and opportunity dictate (Riley, Foner, and Associates). Indeed (in the United States, at least), the proportions of older people who *give* help to their offspring appear to exceed the proportions who *receive* help from their offspring (Shanas and Associates; Streib; Streib and Thompson).

Let us now, however, include in the example still a third generation of the family, for it is our contention that many a commonplace observation about old people can take on new significance through extension to other age strata. Let us move from the flow of material assistance between aged parents and their middle-aged children to the flow between this middle

generation and their young children. The principle can be
illustrated by one small study (Foner) in which parents of
high-school students were asked what they would do with
money unexpectedly received. Only two percent said they
would use it to help their aged parents. But this was not
because they would spend it on themselves or save it for their
retirement; it was rather because, in the main, they would
reserve it to help their children get started in life. Furthermore, the aged generation concurs; they do not expect
repayment. The middle generation, then, does not neglect the
old because of preoccupation with their own needs (in fact,
they are far readier to offer help than are their aged parents to
want or to accept it), but because of their preoccupation with
the needs of their young children. In short, the flow of material
support tends to be, not reciprocal, but sequential—with each
generation (regardless of its means) attempting to aid the next
younger generation.

As such a finding intimates, many middle-aged parents,
by investing their resources in the future of their young
children, are not only restricting any potential help they might
give to the older generation; but they are also restricting the
accumulation of assets for their own later life. In this example,
then, extension of the analysis from the oldest to the youngest
generation in the family helps to clarify one aspect of the
meaning of old age. Any lack of family support for aged
parents now appears, not as willful indifference or neglect,
but as an expression of normative agreement among all the
generations about the direction in which aid should flow.

Many other conditions of the aged might similarly be
better understood against the backdrop of the other strata
with whom old people live and relate. Consider the work force
data on older men as this might be compared with the differing
circumstances of employment of younger people at various
periods of history. In the early days of the Industrial
Revolution in England, the father (or grandfather), as a skilled
workman in his own right, could take his children with him into
the factory, himself training the adult sons and supervising the
little children throughout the long workday (Smelser). Thus his
authority within the family could penetrate into the workplace,
preserving traditional ties among the generations. If such an
arrangement encouraged between-strata solidarity, then the

subsequent changes in conditions of work may have undermined this basis. More recently, in the United States, quite another set of changes have marked the relative positions of older men and boys in the work force. Between 1900 and 1930, while the majority of older men remained economically active, the proportion of boys aged 10 to 15 who were fully employed declined from 25 percent to only 6 percent. Since World War II, as older men have been winnowed from the labor force, boys, too, are being extruded; the Census no longer counts children under 14 in compiling labor-force statistics, and the participation rates of boys from 16 through 19 show slight but consistent declines. Thus older men today live in a society where the situation of both the old and the young must be interpreted in relation to the productivity and economic prestige of men in their middle years (Kalish).

Such examples suggest a general principle: Important increments to gerontological knowledge are obtainable by studying the entire age-differentiated society, not merely the old. The same principle holds when the research focus is on relationships *within* rather than *between* age strata. Here we shall simply allude to the concern of gerontologists with questions of age similarity as a basis for friendship, or age homogeneity as a feature of residential settings for older people (Madge; Riley, Foner, and Associates). It has been shown that, outside of family groups, older people tend (although by no means exclusively) to have friends who are similar to themselves in status characteristics—notably age— that signal mutuality of experiences, tastes, or values. However, as the sociological literature shows (Hess), such choice of age mates is only a special case of the widespread phenomenon of homophily (or similarity among friends in status or in values) (Lazersfeld and Merton).

Age homophily, not only among the old but also at younger age levels, may be especially pronounced in the United States today as a number of factors converge to produce solidarity within age lines. Simply the rapidity of social change, for example, can sharpen the differences among strata and can thereby contribute to a sense of uniqueness among members of each single stratum. The expansion of education has extended the social (and often the physical) segregation of age similars from children in the lower schools to older adolescents and even to young adults in colleges and universities (Parsons and Platt). Today's middle-aged people, too, many of whom have left the city to rear their children in the suburbs, have experienced long years of age-homogeneous neighborhood settings (Starr). And old people because of increasing longevity retain larger numbers of their age peers as associates (Spengler). In many respects, then, we live in an *age-graded* society, with a high potential for strong ties to develop within each age stratum.

However, the possible long-term consequences of such heightened conditions of within-stratum solidarity may be double-edged. On the one hand, homophily may be beneficial to the individuals involved. Age peers have long been recognized as easing the transition from childhood to adulthood (Eisenstadt); and they may perhaps aid adjustment in old age and at other points of transition in the life course as well. On the other hand, if age peers increasingly turn to each other for aid and comfort, detriments to relationships between strata may ensue as ties between generations may become attenuated or the potential for cleavage or conflict may be increased.

Aging and Cohort Flow

It is the third set of questions—those relating to the processes of *mobility* of individuals from one stratum to another—that brings into bold relief certain similarities, but also the essential differences, between class stratification and age stratification.

At points of similarity between the two processes, much can be learned about aging from the rich literature on class mobility. We tend to take aging for granted (much as before the development of physiology as a science, laymen took their bodily functioning for granted). Yet, when aging (social, psychological, and biological) is viewed as mobility through the age strata, it is revealed as a process that entails many of the same tensions and strains as class mobility. Aging individuals must pass through key transition points in the society—from infancy to childhood, for example, from one school grade to the next, from adolescence to adulthood, or from work life to retirement (Clausen). And the degree of strain engendered by such transitions depends upon diverse social conditions—upon the continuity or discontinuity in the role sequences (Benedict); upon how fully institutionalized a particular role may be (Donahue, Orbach, and Pollak); upon the internal consistency of role expectations, facilities, and sanctions,* or upon how effectively people are trained or socialized at every stage of life (Brim; Brim and Wheeler). For example, consider the stress entailed in our society because we crowd formal education almost exclusively into the younger stages of life rather than spreading it over the life course as individuals require it. Since we do not regard students as full-fledged adults, what tensions must be endured by the young person who stays in the role of student beyond adolescence well into adulthood (tensions that are all too evident in universities today)? What difficulties beset the older person if, in order to obtain the further education he needs or desires, he must sacrifice his job? Like social mobility, too, aging places strains not only upon individuals but also upon the groups through which the aging individual passes. Thus a family must regroup itself after the marriage of its youngest child, or a community after the death of an elder statesman. Similarly, group adjustments are necessitated by the advent of new members like the birth of a child into a family, the entry of a new class of children into a school grade, of the move of a widowed old person into the household of her married daughter.

Despite such similarities, however, aging differs from class mobility in certain fundamental respects. Exactly because the analogy breaks down in these respects is age stratification revealed in its full uniqueness and in its intrinsicality to social change. In the first place, mobility across social classes affects only selected individuals, who can move either upward or downward, and who can reverse direction at different stages of life. But mobility through the age strata is, of course, universal, unidirectional, and irreversible. Everybody ages. Everybody changes over his life course as personality develops, experience accumulates, and adjustments are made to new roles. Nobody can ever go back, although individuals may age in different ways and at different rates.

*Back claims ambiguity for retirement that, although socially defined as a right of the individual, offers low rewards and is socially undervalued.

In the second place, knowledgeable as we are about the inevitability of aging, we take much less cognizance of the inexorability of birth and death, and of the endless succession of cohorts (or generations of individuals born at the same time)—for which there is no precise parallel in class mobility. Yet the sociology of age stratification requires examination of the fact that, within a given society, different cohorts can age in different ways. Each cohort is tied through its date of birth to societal history. Thus the aging of each new cohort is affected by the special situation of that cohort's particular era in history—by the changing cultural, social, and material conditions in the society and by events in the external environment. While all the members of one particular cohort move together over their life course through the same period of time, the various cohorts in the society can differ because they start at distinct times. Cohorts can also differ markedly in size and in composition (in the proportions of males and females, for example, or of blacks and whites, or of natives and foreign born).

Consider a few examples of intercohort differences in the way people have aged in our own society in the past. Epidemiologists tell us that, in comparison with women born a century ago, today's women have experienced menarche at earlier ages and menopause at later ages (National Center for Health Statistics; Susser; Tanner). That is, the period of potential fertility has appreciably lengthened. In practice, however, recent cohorts spend fewer years of their lives in childbearing. Women have telescoped the phase of actual reproduction, having fewer and more closely spaced offspring nowadays than did their mothers or grandmothers (Glick and Parke). Moreover, the trauma of reproduction have been drastically reduced, as fewer women die in childbirth and fewer of their infants die.

Most striking of all the cohort differences, perhaps, are those in longevity—in the proportions of cohort members who outlive the ills of infancy, who escape maternal deaths and the other mortality risks of young adulthood, and who thus survive into the higher ages of the life span. The average lifetime (estimated at only two to three decades among cohorts born in ancient Rome or in medieval Europe) has risen in the United States from four decades among cohorts born in the mid-nine-

teenth century to an estimated seven decades among those
born in the mid-twentieth—a situation apparently unparalleled in human history.* The profound implications of such
cohort differences in longevity can be intimated by just one of
the many associated changes, the one called the *revolution in
family structure* (Glick and Parke; Shanas, 1969).** The single
nuclear household of a century ago (parents and their
children, sometimes including a grandparent) has been replaced, because of increased joint survival, by several
generations of related nuclear households: the young couple
with their dependent children, the middle-aged parents, the
aged generation of grandparents, and the great-grandparent
who also often survives.

What do such differences between earlier and later
cohorts presage for the people who will become old in the
future? Speculation about many of these differences can prove
fruitful of hypotheses. We might speculate, for example, about
the extended period of husband-wife relationships in the
middle years: The more recent couples have had more time to
accumulate assets, or to learn independence from their
offspring, or to prepare themselves for retirement. But not all
predictions about future implications of cohort differences are
entirely speculative, since everybody who will reach sixty-five
during this century or during the early decades of the
twenty-first century is already alive. Much information is
already in hand about the size of existing cohorts, for example,
or about their place of birth or their educational level. Thus,
apart from unforeseeable changes (such as through wars,

---

*To be sure, infant deaths weigh heavily in these averages.
Moreover, the data are based on hypothetical, rather than true,
cohorts. *See* Riley, Foner, and Associates.

**Among couples born a century ago, the last child in the family
was married, on the average, at about the same time as the death of
one of the parents. But among recent cohorts, husbands and wives
typically survive together as two-person families for a good many
years after the last child has married and left home. Changes in
family structure are associated with changes, not only in longevity,
but also in childbearing and in household-living arrangements; *see*
Riley, Foner, and Associates.

depressions, or major shifts in migration or in values), fair estimates can be made about numerous characteristics of old people at particular dates in the future. The size of the aged stratum at the turn of the century will reflect the small numbers of babies in the Depression cohorts; but the size of the aged stratum will predictably increase again in the early decades of the coming century with the influx of the "baby boom" cohorts born after World War II (Spengler). In respect to nativity, the much-studied cohort who had passed age sixty-five or more by 1960 had contained a sizable proportion of early immigrants who were largely illiterate and unskilled, whereas the more recent cohorts who will reach old age in subsequent decades contain fewer and better educated immigrants. Or in respect to formal education, we know that over seventy percent of the cohort aged 75 or more in 1960 had had less than 9 years of school, contrasted with only seventeen percent of the cohort aged 25 to 29, who will not reach age 75 before the year 2005 (Riley, Foner, and Associates). We are aware, also, of many changing societal or environmental conditions, not all of them salutary, that may influence in special ways the future life course of existing cohorts—such as, for example, the spread of pollution might have the greatest effect on young cohorts subject to a full lifetime of exposure, or as the increase of smoking among women might bring female death rates more nearly into line with the currently higher male rates. We cannot overestimate the importance of charting such cohort differences for an understanding of old age.

Age and Social Change

We have been discussing the dual processes affecting individuals (or cohorts of individuals) in a society: aging as a social, psychological, and biological process; and the succession of cohorts that do not all age in exactly the same ways. We shall now ask how these processes relate to the macrocosm of the changing society (Ryder) of which the old people who concern us are one integral part.

Mannheim once proposed a tantalizing mental experiment. Imagine, he said, a society in which one generation lived on forever, and none followed to replace it. Let us, as social scientists, policymakers, and professional groups, make such an experiment! If everybody grows old together, what distinctions might remain between old and young? A few moments' thought are enough to suggest the ineluctable connections among the succession of cohorts, aging, and age stratification. For in contrast to Mannheim's imaginary society, our own consists of successive cohorts, each with its own unique life-course pattern. It is clear that these cohorts fit together at any given time to form the age structure of young, middle-aged, and aged strata. And over time, as the particular individuals composing the particular strata are continually moving on and being replaced, the society itself is changing.

Certain connections now become apparent between the flow of cohorts and the age-related societal patterns and changes in individual behaviors, attitudes, and relationships (noted in the first sections of the chapter). In the simplest case, because successive cohorts often age in different ways, some of these societal patterns and changes can be viewed as direct reflections of the differing cohorts that comprise the age strata at particular periods. Education is a noteworthy example of the significance of cohort flow for cross-sectional differences among age strata (Riley, Foner, and Associates). The rapid pace of educational advance over the century, leaving its mark on successive cohorts of young people now sets the age strata clearly apart from one another. And these strata differences in education have incalculable importance for many aspects of behavior and attitude—for prejudice, feelings of powerlessness, narrow ranges of interests and friendships, and the like. Of course, such strata differences do not remain fixed. Not only do new cohorts come along, but society itself can change in its related institutions and practices as well. The age pattern of education today is a reversal of that in earlier societies where the old were honored for their greater knowledge. If one looks ahead from today's knowledge explosion, the information gap between the very young and even the not-so-young is deepening, creating pressures to change the entire structure of education if people beyond the earliest years are to maintain competitive quality.*

*If such a change is not effected, we may expect increasing convergence of age and class stratification as education achieves preeminence among the distinguishing criteria of social class.

In another example, the cross-section age patterns for drinking or smoking have shown a general decline from younger to older strata; and these differences among strata are in part reflections of the past tendency for each new cohort to espouse these practices to an increasing degree (Riley, Foner, and Associates). Today's younger cohorts, however, may be introducing new habits that could, over the next decades, drastically change the cross-section age pattern. A recent campus interview elicited the student comment, for example,that "upperclassmen still prefer beer, but a large majority of underclassmen prefer pot. Pot is big in the high schools, and it is very popular with freshmen who just came out of that environment. The trend is definitely away from beer" (Cicetti).

Are these newcomers to the college likely to set the pace for the cohorts that follow?

In such instances, changes in societal age strata can be interpreted as the shifting composite of cohorts who, themselves affected by differing historical backgrounds, have aged in differing ways. In other instances, life-course differences among cohorts in one social sphere appear to stimulate further changes in other spheres. For example, far-reaching shifts in the relations between men and women at various ages—the decreasing differentiation between the sexes or the greater freedom of sexual behavior—might be traced in part to a reversal in cohort patterns of female participation in the labor force (Riley, Foner, and Associates). Many cohorts of women born during the late nineteenth century showed steadily declining rates of participation over the life course. Following World War II, a new pattern began to emerge as many married women entered the labor force during their middle years, although work-force participation of young women in the child-rearing ages remained low. The conjunction of these cohort trends meant that, for a considerable period, it was only the young mothers with little children whose labor-force participation was low. This situation may have prompted a classic observation (foreshadowing the full force of the women's liberation movement) that "for the first time in the history of any known society, motherhood has become a full-time occupation for adult women" (Rossi). Women at other times and places shared motherhood with demanding labor in the fields, the factory, or the household.

Can we expect that full-time motherhood is now institutionalized and will persist into the future? If so, we may be victims of our own "cohort centrism"—one more proof that our understandings of society are influenced by our particular historical background. For this full-time preoccupation of American mothers with their young children seems already to be eroding as recent cohorts have developed a rather different pattern. Not only have the proportions of married women in the labor force during their middle years more than doubled, but there have been pronounced increases also among young married women, even those with little children (Manpower Report of the President). Thus it may appear to historians of the future that full-time motherhood was a peculiar phenomenon, existing in American society only for a few decades of the twentieth century. Whatever the future may actually hold, the example begins to suggest how the confluence of cohorts with differing life-course patterns in one respect (economic activity of women) can change society in other respects as well. Think, for example, of the mature women who no longer "retire" from major social roles many years before their husbands retire from work. Or think of the young husbands and wives who now share the work of homemaking and infant care. May such changing work habits result in entirely new modes of relationship in the family and—if only because of the widespread unavailability of working wives for daytime activities at home or in the community—in other social institutions?

In addition to the impress of cohort succession upon the history of society, it can sometimes happen that innovations emanating from a single cohort ramify rather quickly through the other age strata, without awaiting the lag over a long series of cohorts. Thus the excessive size of the "baby boom" cohort born after World War II has required drastic adjustments throughout a society unprepared to absorb it—from the initial requirements for obstetrical facilities through the successive pressures on housing, schools, the job market, the marriage market, and so on into the future. Among the many other widely discussed instances are the increased financial burden borne (through transfer payments) by the remainder of society because so many retired old people have inadequate incomes (Bernstein; McConnell); or the potential changes in the ethos surrounding work and leisure as large numbers of old and young no longer participate in the work force (Donahue, Orbach, and Pollak; Riley, Foner, Hess, and Toby). It has even been suggested that a completely revolutionary "consciousness," now informing the values and behaviors of many young people, may affect the entire society (Reich).

To return to the immediate topic of this essay, we offer a special challenge to the oncoming cohorts of social gerontologists—not merely to continue looking for new materials, but also to reexamine and fit together the existing materials in a new way. We suggest a review of old age as one ingredient in the societal macrocosm, inseparable from and interdependent with the other age strata. We suggest a review of aging and of the succession of births and deaths as integral parts of societal process and change that follow their own rhythm and that in themselves constitute immanent strains and pressures toward innovation. Such a sociological review can, we submit, help to explain old age and aging and can at the same time suggest potential solutions to some of the problems of great immediate concern.

In sum, the forces of social change, whether through deliberate intervention* or as an indirect consequence of existing trends, are not only constantly affecting the aging process, but are also bringing new influences to bear on the situation, on the characteristics of persons who are old, and on the younger age strata with whom old people are interdependent. Discovery and evaluation of the implications for old age of these forces for change constitutes a whole new field of opportunity for social scientists, professional groups, and policymakers in gerontology.

---

*Many possibilities for intervention in the several professional fields are discussed in the series of essays in Riley, Riley, and Johnson, in which experts discuss the implications of social science knowledge for public policy and professional practice affecting older people.

References

Back, K. W. "The Ambiguity of Retirement." In *Behavior and Adaptation in Late Life*. Edited by E. W. Busse and E. Pfeiffer. Boston: Little, Brown, 1969.

Benedict, R. "Continuities and Discontinuities in Cultural Conditioning." *Psychiatry* 1 (1938): 161-67.

Bernstein, M. C. "Aging and the Law." In *Aging and Society, Volume Two: Aging and the Professions*. Edited by M. W. Riley, J. W. Riley, Jr., and M. E. Johnson. New York; Russell Sage Foundation, 1969.

Brim, O. G., Jr. "Adult Socialization." In *Socialization and Society*. Edited by J. A. Clausen. Boston: Little, Brown, 1968.

_____, and Wheeler, S. *Socialization after Childhood: Two Essays*. New York: John Wiley and Sons, 1966.

Burgess, E. W., ed. *Aging in Western Societies*. Chicago: University of Chicago Press, 1960.

Cicetti, F. "Campuses Revisited: New Trends at Seton Hall." *Newark Evening News*, 30 September 1970.

Clausen, J. A. "The Life Course of Individuals." In *Aging and Society, Volume Three: A Sociology of Age Stratification*. Edited by M. W. Riley, M. E. Johnson, and A. Foner. New York: Russell Sage Foundation, 1971.

Donahue, W.; Orbach, M. L.; and Pollak, O. "Retirement: The Emerging Social Pattern." In *Handbook of Social Gerontology*. Edited by C. Tibbitts. Chicago: University of Chicago Press, 1960.

Eisenstadt, S. N. *From Generation to Generation: Age Groups and Social Structure*. Glencoe, Illinois: The Free Press, 1956.

Foner, A. "The Middle Years: Prelude to Retirement?" Ph.D. dissertation, New York University, 1969.

Glick, P. C., and Parke, R., Jr. "New Approaches in Studying the Life Cycle of the Family." *Demography* 2 (1965): 187-202.

Havinghurst, R. J.; Munnichs, J. M. A.; Neugarten, B. L.; and Thomae, N., eds. *Adjustment to Retirement: A Cross-National Study*. Assen, The Netherlands: Koninklijke van Gorcum, 1969.

Hess, B. "Friendship." In *Aging and Society, Volume Three: A Sociology of Age Stratification*. Edited by M. W. Riley, M. E. Johnson, and A. Foner. New York: Russell Sage Foundation, 1971.

Kalish, R. A. "The Old and the New as Generation Gap Allies." *Gerontologist* 9 (1969): 83-89.

Lazarsfeld, P. F., and Merton, R. K. "Friendship as Social Process: A Substantive and Methodological Analysis." In *Freedom and Control in Modern Society*. Edited by M. Berger, T. Abel, and C. M. Page. New York: D. Van Nostrand, 1954.

McConnell, J. W. "Aging and the Economy." In *Handbook of Social Gerontology*. Edited by C. Tibbitts. Chicago: University of Chicago Press, 1960.

Madge, J. "Aging and the Fields of Architecture and Planning." In *Aging and Society, Volume Two: Aging and the Professions*. Edited by M. W. Riley, J. W. Riley, Jr., and M. E. Johnson. New York: Russell Sage Foundation, 1969.

Mannheim, K. "The Problem of Generations." In *Essays on the Sociology of Knowledge*. Edited and translated by P. Kecskemeti. London: Routledge and Kegan Paul (1928), 1952.

Manpower Report of the President, March 1970. Washington, D.C.: USGPO, 1970.

Merton, R. K. *Social Theory and Social Structure*. Rev. ed. Glencoe, Illinois: The Free Press, 1957.

National Center for Health Statistics. "Age and Menopause, United States 1960-62." *Vital and Health Statistics, 1966*. PMS Pub. no. 1000-Series 11, no. 19. Washington, D.C.: USGPO, 1966.

Parsons, T., and Platt, G. M. "Higher Education and Changing Socialization." In *Aging and Society, Volume Three: A Sociology of Age Stratification*. Edited by M. W. Riley, M. E. Johnson, and A. Foner. New York: Russell Sage Foundation, 1971.

Reich, C. "Reflections: The Greening of America." *New Yorker*, 26 September 1970, pp. 42ff.

Riley, M. W.; Foner, A.; and Associates. *Aging and Society, Volume One: An Inventory of Research Findings*. New York: Russell Sage Foundation, 1968.

Riley, M. W.; Riley, J. W., Jr.; and Johnson, M. E., eds. *Aging and Society, Volume Two: Aging and the Professions*. New York: Russell Sage Foundation, 1969.

Riley, M. W.; Johnson, M. E.; and Foner, A., eds. *Aging and Society, Volume Three: A Sociology of Age Stratification*. New York: Russell Sage Foundation, 1971.

Riley, M. W.; Foner, A.; Hess, B.; and Toby, M. L. "Socialization for the Middle and Later Years." In *Handbook of Socialization Theory and Research*. Edited by D. A. Goslin. Chicago: Rand McNally, 1969.

Rossi, A. S. "Equality between the Sexes: An Immodest Proposal." *Daedalus*, Spring 1964, pp. 607-652.

Ryder, N. B. "The Cohort as a Concept in the Study of Social Change." *American Sociological Review* 30 (1965): 843-61.

Shanas, E., and Associates. "Family Help Patterns and Social Class in Three Countries." Paper presented at the meetings of the American Sociological Association, Miami, 1966.

Shanas, E. *Old People in Three Industrial Societies*. New York: Atherton Press, 1968.

_____. "Living Arrangements and Housing of Old People." In *Behavior and Adaptation in Late Life*. Edited by E. W. Busse and E. Pfeiffer. Boston: Little, Brown, 1969.

Simmons, L. W. "Aging in Preindustrial Societies." In *Handbook of Social Gerontology*. Edited by C. Tibbitts. Chicago: University of Chicago Press, 1960.

Smelser, N. J. "Sociological History: The Industrial Revolution and the British Working-Class Family." *Essays in Sociological Explanation*. Englewood Cliffs, New Jersey: Prentice-Hall, 1968.

Spengler, J. J. "The Aged and Public Policy." In *Behavior and Adaptation in Late Life*. Edited by E. W. Busse and E. Pfeiffer. Boston: Little, Brown, 1969.

Starr, B. C. "The Community." In *Aging and Society, Volume Three: A Sociology of Age Stratification*. Edited by M. W. Riley, M. E. Johnson, and A. Foner. New York: Russell Sage Foundation, 1971.

Streib, G. F. "Intergenerational Relations: Perspectives of the Two Generations on the Older Parent." *Journal of Marriage and the Family* 27 (1965): 469-76.

_____, and Thompson, W. E. "The Older Person in a Family Context." In *Handbook of Social Gerontology*. Edited by C. Tibbitts. Chicago: University of Chicago Press, 1960.

Susser, M. "Aging and the Field of Public Health." In *Aging and Society, Volume Two: Aging and the Professions*. Edited by M. W. Riley, J. W. Riley, Jr., and M. E. Johnson. New York: Russell Sage Foundation, 1969.

Tanner, J. M. *Growth at Adolescence*. 2d ed. Oxford: Blackwell, Davis, 1961.

Contributors

Ronald Althouse is associate professor of sociology at West Virginia University, where he continues his research on the elderly of Appalachia.

Alphonso Anderson is New York City Regional Representative for the National Council on Aging, and an authority on problems of minority participation in the labor force.

Inge Powell Bell is professor of sociology at Pitzer College in the Claremont Colleges. Her major interest is social movements, best represented by her book, *CORE and the Strategy of Nonviolence*.

Orville G. Brim, Jr. is president of the Foundation for Child Development, New York City. His interests in adult socialization remains undiminished, especially with respect to the male at mid-life.

Elaine M. Brody is director of the Department of Social Work, Philadelphia Geriatric Center, and author of a number of papers on geriatric social work and long-term institutional care, a collection of which is to be published soon.

Harley L. Browning is associate professor of sociology at the University of Texas at Austin and director of the Population Research Center.

Robert N. Butler, M.D., is a gerontologist and psychiatrist in Washington, D.C., where he also serves on the faculties of the Washington School of Psychiatry, Howard University, and at George Washington University. His recent book, *Why Survive: Being Old In America*, is a powerful brief for change in our treatment of the elderly.

James H. Carter, a graduate of Howard University, is assistant professor of psychiatry at the Duke University Medical Center.

Robert C. Coles, research psychiatrist at Harvard University, is also a renowned field researcher and observer, best represented by his collection, *Children of Crisis: A Study of Courage and Fear*.

Sharon R. Curtin, R.N., is a native of Wyoming and 1971 winner of an Atlantic Grant, which permitted her to make the travels recorded in *Nobody Ever Died of Old Age: In Praise of Old People*, part of which also appeared in *Atlantic Magazine*.

Curt Davis, a 1971 graduate of Hamilton College, has been a reporter for *People* and *In-the-Know* magazines, and is currently an associate editor of *Encore, American and Worldwide News*, a biweekly newsmagazine published in York City.

David Gutmann is professor of psychology at the University of Michigan. He has utilized the methods of clinical psychology in comparative, cross-cultural studies of aging personality at sites in the Southwest, Mexico, and the Middle East.

David Hendin, a journalist, is science editor of Newspaper Enterprise Association, and a participant in the Task Force on Death and Dying of the Institute of Society, Ethics, and Life Sciences. Mr. Hendin's reportage earned a citation from the National Society of Medical Researchers in 1972.

Beth B. Hess, associate professor of social science, County College of Morris, Dover, New Jersey, is also an associate of the Russell Sage Foundation Program on Aging.

Arlie Russell Hochschild is an associate professor of sociology at the University of California, Berkeley, and the author of a book about the communal life of old people, *The Unexpected Community*. She continues her work in aging with an article in the *American Sociological Review*, "Disengagement Theory: A Critique and Proposal."

Jacquelyne Johnson Jackson teaches at the Duke Univerisity Medical Center, publishes frequently on the black aged, and continues her efforts on their behalf through the National Caucus of Black Aged.

Helena Znaniecki Lopata is professor of sociology at Loyola University, Chicago, where she directs the Center for the Comparative Study of Social Roles. Among her many research interests are those of special concern to aging women, and, most recently, the life histories of immigrant women.

John Lozier is professor of sociology at West Virginia University, where he continues his research on the elderly of Appalachia.

Ida Lynn leaves her three-generation household almost every weekday to work at the Morris County, New Jersey, A.V.A.

Commission Film Library; and, when she has saved enough, to take cruises to such exotic places as North Africa and the Greek Isles.

Elizabeth Markson, is director of Research and Evaluation, Massachusetts Department of Mental Health, and adjunct professor of sociology at The State University of New York at Albany. Her forthcoming book, *Trends in Mental Health Evaluation* (edited with David Allen, M.D.), reflects her interest in improved institutional and community care throughout the life cycle.

Bernice Neugarten, professor of human development at the University of Chicago, has published extensively for over a decade on many aspects of social gerontology. Among her most recent contributions is the volume, *Middle Age and Aging*.

Matilda White Riley, for many years a professor of sociology at Rutgers—the State University of New Jersey, is now chairing the department of sociology and anthropology at Bowdoin College, Brunswick, Maine. She also directs the Russell Sage Foundation Program on Aging.

Irving Rosow is professor of medical sociology at Langley Porter Institute, University of California, San Francisco. He is an authority in both social gerontology and adult socialization theory, as exemplified in his major books, *Social Integration of the Aged* and *Socialization to Old Age*.

Isadore Rubin, before his recent death, was editor of *Sexology* magazine, and a leading figure in the field of sex education and marriage counseling. His publications include works on sexuality for adolescents as well as the aged.

Rose Somerville is professor of sociology at San Diego State University, author of numerous articles on family life, and prolific book reviewer for the *Journal of Marriage and the Family*. Her most recent book, *Intimate Relationships*, exemplifies her blending of life and literature, and her concern with a life-course approach to the sociology of family.

E. Percil Stanford is director of the Center on Aging at California State University, San Diego.

Joyce Stephens is currently teaching and doing research at the University of Queensland, department of sociology and anthropology, Brisbane, Australia. A collection of her essays on the occupants of single-room residences will be published this year by the University of Washington Press.

Mary Louise Williams remains an active member of her retirement center in Columbus, Ohio. She is especially delighted with the attention and requests for reprints generated by her article on the center.

Michael Zimmerman is a graduate student in sociology at Rutgers—the State University, New Brunswick, New Jersey. He is planning to continue his research in the history of old-age poverty in America for his doctoral dissertation.

Index